SURVIVING SPANISH CONQUEST

CARIBBEAN ARCHAEOLOGY AND ETHNOHISTORY

L. Antonio Curet, Series Editor

SURVIVING SPANISH CONQUEST

INDIAN FIGHT, FLIGHT, AND CULTURAL TRANSFORMATION IN HISPANIOLA AND PUERTO RICO

KAREN F. ANDERSON-CÓRDOVA

The University of Alabama Press
Tuscaloosa

The University of Alabama Press
Tuscaloosa, Alabama 35487-0380
uapress.ua.edu

Hardcover edition published 2017.
Paperback edition published 2022.
eBook edition published 2017.

Typeface: Baskerville

Cover image: Columbus landing on Hispaniola, December 6, 1492, greeted by Arawak Indians. Engraving by Theodor de Bry, c. 1594; Library of Congress, LC-USZ62-59702
Cover design: Michele Myatt Quinn

Paperback ISBN: 978-0-8173-6058-0

A previous edition of this book has been cataloged by the Library of Congress.
ISBN: 978-0-8173-1946-5 (cloth)
E-ISBN: 978-0-8173-9090-7

To my husband, Mark, my son, Roberto Pablo,
and the memory of my parents, Blanca and Bob

Contents

List of Illustrations ix
Acknowledgments xi
List of Abbreviations xiii
Introduction: Cultures in Contact 1
1. The Inhabitants of the Caribbean at the Time of Columbus 15
2. The Spanish Conquest and Colonization of Hispaniola and Puerto Rico 29
3. Cultural Transformations: Indian Response to Contact 54
4. Aboriginal Demography in the Antilles 73
5. The Voluntary and Forced Movement of Indians among the Islands and the Mainland 120
6. Spain's First New World Frontier and "Taínoness" Today 150
Appendix 1: Historical Evidence for Interisland Movement of Indians, from Columbus's Diary of the First Voyage 167
Appendix 2: Chronology of the Indian Slave Trade: Legislation and Other Pertinent Documentary Evidence 171
Notes 185
Bibliographic Essay 211
References Cited 217
Index 253

Illustrations

Figures

1.1. Taíno chiefdoms of Hispaniola 22

2.1. Hispaniola: Late-fifteenth-century geography 30

2.2. Hispaniola: Spanish settlements under Ovando 37

2.3. Puerto Rico: Early-sixteenth-century geography 44

5.1. The Antillean Islands 122

5.2. Early Spanish explorations of Tierra Firme 129

5.3. Geography of the Indian slave trade 135

Tables

4.1. Aboriginal Population of Hispaniola based on Sixteenth-Century Sources 79

4.2. Contact Aboriginal Population of Hispaniola, Later Estimates 81

4.3. Population Densities in Hispaniola versus Selected Polynesian Chiefdoms 85

4.4. 1514 Repartimiento: Total Number of Indians Allotted by Categories and Town 88

4.5. Percentage of Service *Encomienda* Indians and *Naborías* per Town and Average Number of Indians per Community 91

4.6. Percentages of Service Indians by Town and Relationship with Community Averages 92

4.7. Relationship between Service Indians and Service Indian *Allegados*, and between *Naborías* and *Naborías Allegados* by Town 93

4.8. Indian Population Displacement by Town 94

4.9. Displacement of Service Indians by Town 95

4.10. Estimated Indian Population of Towns before the 1514 Repartimiento 96

4.11. Estimated Service Indian Population of Towns and Community Averages before the 1514 Repartimiento 96

4.12. Total Number of Allotments by Type of *Encomienda*, Number of *Encomenderos*, and Town 98

4.13. Relationship between Number of *Caciques* Allotted and Number of *Encomenderos* Receiving Service *Encomiendas* by Town 100

4.14. Aboriginal Population of Puerto Rico, Historical Estimates 107

4.15. Total Number of Black Slaves, Indian Slaves, and Free Indians, 1530 Census of Puerto Rico 108

4.16. Details of the 33 Individuals Reporting Free Indians in San Juan, 1530 Census of Puerto Rico 110

4.17. Details of the 24 Individuals Reporting Free Indians in San Germán, 1530 Census of Puerto Rico 112

4.18. Legal, Marital, and Professional Status of Slave Owners, in San Juan, 1530 Census of Puerto Rico 114

4.19. Legal, Marital, and Professional Status of the 33 Individuals Reporting Free Indians in San Juan, 1530 Census of Puerto Rico 115

4.20. Summary of Legal, Marital, and Professional Status of Individuals in San Germán Who Reported Owning Slaves, 1530 Census of Puerto Rico 116

4.21. Legal, Marital, and Professional Status of the 24 Individuals Reporting Free Indians in San Germán, 1530 Census of Puerto Rico 116

4.22. Summary of Legal, Marital, and Professional Status of Slave Owners Reporting Indian Slaves and/or Free Indians for the Island of Puerto Rico, 1530 Census 117

Acknowledgments

This book is the culmination of many years of research and interest into what happened during the early years of Spanish colonization in the Caribbean, specifically the contact between the European colonizers and the Caribbean islands' indigenous inhabitants. It is my attempt to synthesize historical, ethnohistorical, and archaeological sources to provide a narrative of the early formative years of the colonial Caribbean that focuses on what happened to their indigenous populations and how they coped with the new reality of exploitation into which they were unwittingly thrust.

Research material for this volume was gathered originally at the University of Florida Libraries Latin American collection in Gainesville and, more recently, at the Georgia State University Library, Atlanta, especially its interlibrary loan office. Other institutions that I have consulted in my research throughout the years include the Puerto Rican collection at the University of Puerto Rico Main Library, Río Piedras; the University of Puerto Rico's History Department, Faculty of the Humanities, Río Piedras; the Institute of Puerto Rican Culture, the Center for Advanced Studies of Puerto Rico and the Caribbean in Old San Juan; and the State Historic Preservation Office, Office of the Governor, San Juan.

I am intellectually indebted to Caribbean historians Jalil Sued Badillo and Francisco Moscoso of the University of Puerto Rico for igniting my interest in the topic, and to Frank Moya Pons of the Academia Dominicana de la Historia for his support and interest in my research. I wish to especially mention the influence and generosity of my doctoral mentor, the late archaeologist Benjamin Irving Rouse. I also acknowledge the assistance of staff at the Puerto Rico State Historic Preservation office for their invaluable help in tracking down references and for providing access to their digital archaeological site files—Diana López, Berenice

Sueiro, Miguel Bonini, Lillian M. Lara Fonseca, Agustín Graterole, and José Marull.

I also want to thank the University of Alabama Press's anonymous peer reviewers and Kathleen Deagan for their constructive comments on a previous draft of this document. I trust that the final version reflects their positive input, and I acknowledge that any errors or omissions are my own. Another heartfelt thanks goes to Antonio Curet for his words of encouragement about my work and the viability of this volume and for providing references and PDFs of various articles. Thanks as well to Caribbean scholars Roberto Valcárcel Rojas, Jorge Ulloa Hung, and Lynne Guitar, who generously shared their research with me. Thanks also to Wendi Schnaufer, my editor at University of Alabama Press, for her guidance throughout and for arranging for the production of the figures that are included in this volume. These are based on the original figures drafted by archaeologist Jesús Vega. Special mention also to copy editor Penelope Cray and managing editor Jonathan Berry for their expertise. I also thank my sister Blanca Anderson for proofreading my English translations of original Spanish language sources, and historians Frank Moya Pons and Joe Sánchez for their suggestions in translating Spanish judicial and administrative terms into English.

A very special thanks to my husband, Mark R. Barnes, for his steady, constant encouragement as I worked on this project. He read and commented on the numerous drafts of this volume and helped me track down sources and bibliographic references. This book would not have been written without his unwavering support. I cannot thank him enough.

List of Abbreviations

AGI Archivo General de Indias (General Archives of the Indies)

BAGN *Boletín del Archivo General de la Nación* (*Bulletin of the General Archives of the Nation* [Venezuela])

BHPR *Biblioteca Histórica de Puerto Rico* (*Historical Library of Puerto Rico*)

CC *Cedulario cubano* (*Cuban Royal Decrees*)

CMEIC *Cedulario de la monarquía española relativos a la isla Cubagua* (*Spanish Monarchy Decrees Regarding the Island of Cubagua*)

CMEPV *Cedulario de la monarquía española relativos a la provincia de Venezuela* (*Spanish Monarchy Decrees regarding the Province of Venezuela*)

CP *Cedulario puertorriqueño* (*Puerto Rican Royal Decrees*)

CRV *Cédulas reales relativas a Venezuela* (*Royal Decrees regarding Venezuela*)

CDIHE *Colección de documentos inéditos para la historia de España* (*Collection of Original Documents for the History of Spain*)

CODOIN *Colección de documentos inéditos relativos al descubrimiento, conquista y organización de las antiguas posesiones españolas de América y Oceanía.* Series I (42 vols.) and Series II (25 vols.) (*Collection of Original Documents regarding the Discovery, Conquest, and Organization of the Former Spanish Possessions in America and Oceania*)

CDHFSHA *Colección de documentos para la historia de la formación social de Hispanoamérica* (*Collection of Documents for the Social History of Hispanic America*)

DRHPR *Documentos de la Real Hacienda de Puerto Rico* (*Puerto Rico Treasury Documents*)

DIHM *Documentos inéditos del siglo XVI historia Mexicana* (*Original Documents of Sixteenth-Century Mexican History*)

ENE *Epistolario de Nueva España* (*Collected Letters of New Spain*)

HDPR *Historia documental de Puerto Rico* (*Documentary History of Puerto Rico*)

ICDHH *Inventario colección documentos históricos Herrera procedentes del*

Archivo General de Indias (*Inventory of the Herrera Collection of Historical Documents from the General Archives of the Indies*)

PRDJBM *Puerto Rico en los documentos de Don Juan Bautista Muñoz* (*Puerto Rico in the Documents of Don Juan Bautista Muñoz*)

RC *Real Cédula* (*Royal Decree*)

RCCGSD *Reales cédulas y correspondencia de gobernadores de Santo Domingo desde la regencia del Cardenal Cisneros en adelante* (*Royal Decrees and Correspondence of the Governors of Santo Domingo from the Regency of Cardinal Cisneros Onward*)

RP *Real Provisión* (*Royal Provision*)

SDDJBM *Santo Domingo en los documentos de Don Juan Bautista Muñoz* (*Santo Domingo in the Documents of Don Juan Bautista Muñoz*)

Introduction

Cultures in Contact

The early contact period in the Caribbean marked the beginning of the modern world, a time when Europe and the Americas first collided and when the kaleidoscope of peoples who were immersed in the encounter interacted and inevitably transformed their landscape and themselves. New cultures, ethnicities, and sociopolitical systems emerged and developed and forever changed both the Old and New Worlds. Within this vast scope, this volume focuses on the Indian aspects of the Spanish-Indian contact, primarily in the islands of Hispaniola and Puerto Rico, from 1492, the year of "discovery," to 1550, which marks the end of most, although as we shall see, not all, historical references to the presence of Indians on these islands.

This focus on how the native inhabitants of these islands responded to and were transformed by their interactions with the Spanish complements historical and archaeological research on the Spanish side of contact and adaptation to the Caribbean islands (Lyon 1981; Marrinan 1982; McEwan 1983, 1986; Cusick 1987; Deagan 1985b, 1988, 1990; Ewen 1987, 1991; Reitz 1986; Williams 1986; Willis 1980, 1984; Ortega 1982; Ortega and Fondeur 1978a; Deagan and Cruxent 1993; Bray 1993).

Hispaniola and Puerto Rico were the first two Caribbean islands of the Greater Antilles to be conquered and colonized by the Spanish. Historic documents reflect in detail the first conflicts between Western civilization and indigenous cultures in the New World. The processes of change and their outcomes can therefore be studied at their most vivid and conflictive tones on these two islands. Generally, Hispaniola and Puerto Rico are also the islands for which historical and archaeological documentation is more readily available.

However, because of Cuba's and Jamaica's kinship to these islands, and their relevance to the study of Spanish-Indian interaction in the Caribbean, information from historical and archaeological research on

Cuba, and, to a lesser extent, Jamaica, is included for purposes of comparison (Domínguez 1978, 1983; Knight 2006; García Castañeda 1949; Ibarra 1976; Morales Patiño 1947; Pichardo Moya 1945; Rivero de la Calle 1978, 1983; Romero Estèbanez 1981; Zerquera y Fernández de Lara 1977; Valcárcel Rojas and Martinón Torres 2013; Mira Caballos 1997, 2000a; Valcárcel Rojas et al. 2010; Valcárcel Rojas 1997, 2012, 2016; Morales Padrón 2003).

Indian Heterogeneity and Spanish-Indian Contact in the Early Caribbean

One aspect of the Indian response to contact emphasized here is the issue of Indian heterogeneity. By this I mean the presence in these islands of more than one Indian ethnic group. I am aware of the scholarly quicksand involved in assigning ethnic affiliation to past cultures based on historical and archaeological data (Barth 1969; Allaire 1977; Rouse 1986; Curet 2014). However, it is clear from the evidence for movement of Indians into and out of the islands that various ethnicities coalesced at this time, and this fact has implications for the study of early inter- and intraethnic interactions and their possible outcomes.

This volume's main focus is the Indian aspect of the Spanish-Indian contact in early sixteenth-century Hispaniola and Puerto Rico within the context of two related processes: Indian out-migration from these islands and Indian in-migration into these islands. These two processes, the former one voluntary in the sense it was exercised by the Indians to avoid contact with the Spanish, the other forced upon the Indians as a deliberate Spanish policy to enslave them, acted to further alter the ethnic and cultural milieu of contact. The nature of the "cultures in contact" had thus transformed since the beginning of the colonization period, further complicating the study of the historic Indian populations of the islands.[1]

These processes, which were occurring simultaneously during the first 50 years of contact, are significant in understanding the culture-contact scenario in these islands. First, they demonstrate the ethnic diversity of the native Caribbean populations involved and the different ways in which they interacted among themselves and with the Spanish; and second, they provide important clues to support the argument that Indian survival during this period included a significant number of "foreign" Indians and not just the native Indians of Hispaniola and Puerto Rico. The heterogeneity of ethnic groups implied by this movement in and out of the islands has significant implications for the study of culture contact during this period and, when combined with the historical evidence for rapid Indian demographic decline, suggests this as another factor contributing to the disintegration of native island communities. In addition, these processes have obvious implications for the interpretation of the early historical archaeological record. These have been considered by some historical archaeologists studying the Caribbean (see, for example, Deagan 1985a:293; García Arévalo 1978a), and more recently by Valcárcel Rojas (2012, 2016), who documents the presence of foreign Indians in the contact-period cemetery of the Chorro de Maíta site in Holguín province, Cuba.

Approaches to Contact Studies

Historically, anthropologists have utilized different theoretical concepts to study the changes that occur when different peoples and cultures interact. One of the earliest concepts employed was that of acculturation. This term was coined by American anthropologists in the beginning decades of the twentieth century to categorize a series of studies focusing on changes that occur when different cultures come into contact. In most early definitions of acculturation, contact refers to actual physical encounters between members of different cultures that are sustained enough to produce change. Acculturation assumes the changes that can be observed and analyzed come about as a result of contact between *two or more* cultures.

Theoretically, the concept of acculturation applies to all the cultures in contact and does not distinguish between dominant and subordinate cultures (see Herskovits 1938), but in practice anthropologists generally concentrated on changes occurring in the subordinate culture (Redfield, Linton, and Herskovits 1936; Linton 1940; Spicer 1961b; Colombres 1977; Aguirre Beltrán 1970; Fitzhugh 1985). As pointed out by Cusick (1998:128), the underlying assumptions were that native (in the sense of non-Western) cultures would inevitably become westernized and that anthropologists' role was to document how and under what conditions this occurred. An exception to this was Foster's (1960) pioneering work on the Spanish side of contact situations and his concept of conquest culture, a concept that has been applied by archaeologists working in early-historic-period sites (Willis 1976).

In the Memorandum for the Study of Acculturation, prepared by the Social Science Research Council in 1936 (Redfield, Linton, and Herskovits 1936), acculturation is defined as follows: "Acculturation comprehends those phenomena which result when groups of individuals having different cultures come into continuous first-hand contact, with subsequent changes in the original patterns of either or both groups" (Bohannon and Plog 1967:182).

Linton follows the same definition but emphasizes that acculturation is a particular type of culture change whose stimulus derives from the condition of "continuous first hand contact" (1940:500–501). He also classifies the different processes in which cultural elements are transferred and incorporated into the receiving culture, and establishes the fundamental distinction between contact situations of directed versus undirected change (Linton 1940:501; see also Spicer 1961a:519–520).

This distinction is particularly important in the context of Spanish-Indian interactions in the Caribbean, where directed change was the norm, and is also useful when comparing these interactions with the undirected change characteristic of the sixteenth- and seventeenth-century interactions among the English, Dutch, and French, and the Indians of the Lesser Antilles. More recent criticisms of acculturation studies have also pointed out the continued relevance of this distinction (Cusick 1998:137).

The 1953 Social Science Research Council Summer Seminar of Acculturation (Broom et al. 1954) defined acculturation as follows:

> Culture change that is initiated by the conjunction of two or more autonomous cultural systems. Acculturative change may be the consequence of direct cultural transmission; it may be derived from non-cultural causes, such as ecological or demographic modifications induced by an impinging culture; it may be delayed, as with internal adjustments following upon the acceptance of alien traits or patterns; or it may be reactive adaptation of traditional modes of life. Its dynamics can be seen as the selective adaptation of value systems, the processes of integration and differentiation, the generation of developmental sequences, and the operation of role determinants and personality factors [Bohannon and Plog 1967:256–257].

This definition is similar to the one previously cited in the sense of emphasizing acculturation as a particular type of culture change occurring under certain conditions and of clearly placing the unit of study or level of abstraction (Bee 1974:24–25, 112–113) as that of cultures, as opposed to individuals or societies. However, it differs by introducing the term "autonomous cultural system," which it defines as "one which is self-sustaining—that is, it does not need to be maintained by a complementary, reciprocal, subordinate, or other indispensable connection with a second system" (Bohannon and Plog 1967:257). These authors equate this term with what anthropologists usually call "culture" and clarify the need to delimit the acculturation field to studies that focus on changes occurring to groups of individuals of different cultural traditions (hence the historic dimension) that come into contact (Bohannon and Plog 1967). Nevertheless, it is important to point out that autonomous cultural systems that come into contact may, as a result, quickly cease to be autonomous and yet still be subject to change. This was certainly the case in the Caribbean, where native Indian chiefdoms quickly disintegrated as a result of direct, sustained contact with the Spanish colonizers.

There is an important distinction between North American scholars of acculturation studies, who focus on the "cultural dimension," and Latin American scholars, who insist that acculturation, by definition, involves a situation of interdependency between two distinct cultures created by the contact conditions themselves (Aguirre Beltrán 1970:39), wherein the indigenous culture is subordinate to and in conflict with the dominant culture (Colombres 1977:25). These authors also stress the importance of considering the processes by which previously autonomous cultural systems (interethnic systems, according to Colombres 1977:25) are integrated into the society in which they operate. Therefore, acculturation studies need to assess both the social and cultural aspects of contact, including the power relations that ensue during contact. This is critical in the study of enslaved Indian or African groups in the Caribbean islands.[2]

Another important aspect included in the above-cited definition of acculturation is the consideration of noncultural causes of change. The importance of noncultural causes is amply demonstrated by ethnohistoric and archaeological studies on the effects of European-introduced diseases upon large areas of North America preceding actual physical contact between Indian and European peoples (Dobyns 1983; Ramenofsky 1987; Smith 1984). Although this example would be left out of the above-cited definition, since it does not involve the "conjunction of two or more autonomous cultural systems," I argue that the depopulation that occurred as a result of the indirect introduction of epidemic disease is of relevance to the process of culture and social change that followed.

Dobyns (1983) and Ramenofsky (1987) showed that profound cultural changes accompanied the introduction of European diseases in many parts of North America, before the mention of Indian cultures in the historic and ethnographic record. Because of this, Dobyns argued, acculturation studies of American Indians that assumed that the indigenous cultural systems first encountered and described by the Europeans represented their prehistoric conditions are incorrect (Dobyns 1983:25–26; see also Ferguson and Whitehead 1992:8–9).

This implies that anthropologists' reconstructions of Indian cultures at contact with Europeans may represent already altered conditions of these prehistoric cultures *before* their documentation in historic records. This issue is in part relevant to the Caribbean area, where some of the most relied upon historic accounts of the Indians are based on observations carried out, in Hispaniola, years after initial contact (Fernández de Oviedo 1959). In the case of Puerto Rico, colonization did not officially begin until 1508, 15 years after its "discovery" and 16 years after the first Spanish enclave in the New World.

Acculturation studies in the New World have mainly been carried out by anthropologists studying the effects of contact with Europeans upon native populations of the Americas. Most stress the conditions of inequality that characterized the majority of the contact scenarios between indigenous groups and Europeans. The cultural and political dominance of the Europeans over natives is emphasized, and the importance of this factor in determining the ability of Europeans to impose their culture upon "weaker" or "less complex" native groups is considered.

The use and continued relevance of the concept of acculturation to explain the processes of culture change in contact situations have been subject to intense criticism (see, for example, Cusick 1998). Whether justified or not, acculturation studies are perceived as inadequate because they assume cultures consist of a list of traits that are then modified (or not), depending on the conditions of contact; because they underestimate or fail to consider the power relations inherent in contact situations; because they assume a one-sided transmission from the dominant to the subordinate culture; because they fail to consider human agency (i.e., the active participation of individuals making choices); and because they fail to explain the genesis of new cultures.

An alternative concept, which is not new but has not been used extensively in North America, is that of transculturation (see Deagan 1998: 23–43). Coined originally by the Cuban scholar Fernando Ortíz (1947), in his study of the contrasting economic, social, and cultural dimensions of tobacco and sugar production (*contrapunteo* in the original Spanish), it emphasizes the dialectical relationship, the give-and-take between two different systems, that combined to produce modern Cuban society and culture. Ortíz was well aware of the acculturation concept (he corresponded regularly with Bronislaw Malinowski, who wrote the introduction to his 1947 volume), but he thought that transculturation clearly articulated the two-way, dialectical, rather than unidirectional, process of contact, and the resulting creation of new cultural and social systems. Ortíz wrote,

> I have chosen the word *transculturation* to express the highly varied phenomena that have come about in Cuba as a result of the extremely complex transmutations of culture that have taken place here, and without a knowledge of which it is impossible to understand the evolution of the Cuban folk, either in the economic or in the institutional, legal, ethical, religious, artistic, linguistic, psychological, sexual, or other aspects of its life. . . . *Transculturation* better expresses the different phases of the process of transition from one culture to another because this does not consist merely in acquiring another culture, which is what the English word *acculturation* really implies, but the process also necessarily involves the loss or uprooting of a previous culture, which could be defined as a deculturation. In addition, it carries the idea of the consequent creation of new cultural phenomena, which could be called neoculturation [Ortíz 1947:98–103; emphasis in original].

Another related concept applied to the study of culture change in the Americas is that of ethnogenesis. This refers to the emergence of new ethnic and cultural identities from the contact scenario. Kathleen Deagan (1998) applies this to the study of early Spanish settlements in the Caribbean and Florida and the development of Spanish-American cultures. Jonathan Hill (1998) uses the term in conjunction with ethnocide in his discussion of long-term contacts and their effect on indigenous populations in South America. He stresses the violent, conflictual interactions among groups that, depending on the historical circumstances, could result in ethnocide (i.e., the disappearance of an ethnic group or groups) or ethnogenesis (the creation of new identities). In his words, "Ethnogenesis is a creative adaptation to a general history of violent encounters—including demographic collapse, forced relocations, enslavement, epidemics and ethnic soldiering—imposed during the expansion of colonial and national states in the Americas" (Hill 1998:166). The creation of new ethnicities and sociopolitical structures such as new tribes resulting from the violent expansion of European states into indigenous New World territories is also discussed by Ferguson and Whitehead (1992:12–15) within the framework of the concept of the tribal zone and the genesis of indigenous warfare.

These approaches certainly apply to the Caribbean, the birthplace of violent encounters between expanding European states and indigenous populations. As mentioned, Deagan (1998) applies the term "ethnogenesis" to describe the development of a distinct Spanish-American culture derived from the Spanish adaptation to New World environments (including interaction with Native Americans; see also Ewen 2000). Based on overwhelming historical documentation describing the disappearance of Indian communities in the Spanish Caribbean, it could be argued that ethnogenesis, as applied to Indian populations, did not occur (in fact, "ethnocide" may be a more accurate term to describe what happened here; see, for example, Mira Caballos 2009). However, the persistence of Indian communities in the Spanish Caribbean (as documented by archaeological research in Hispaniola and Cuba) and the historically small Spanish populations remaining on these islands during the later sixteenth and early seventeenth centuries point to the possibility that small isolated Indian communities continued to exist for a longer period of time. In addition, the conflictive nature of the encounter, the heterogeneity of Indian populations, and the movement of Indians among islands provided the conditions for the creation of native political alliances in which new ethnic identities may have coalesced. This certainly was the case in the Lesser Antilles, where native communities resisted European expansion well into the seventeenth and eighteenth centuries and developed a distinct identity as Island Caribs (Whitehead 1995; Hoff 1995; Sued Badillo 1995; Hulme and Whitehead 1992). Ethnogenesis may have occurred in the Spanish Caribbean after all, but more archaeological research on rural colonial period settlements is needed.

Also relevant as possible models to understand the early history of cultural interactions in the Spanish Caribbean are studies about the emergence of creole societies (creolization). As is the case with the concept of acculturation, the terms "creole" and "creolization" have meant different things to different people at different times (Stewart 2007:8). The term "creole" comes from the Spanish term *criollo,* referring to individuals of Spanish descent that were born and raised in the New World, many of them of mixed racial origin. According to Cañizares-Esguerra, "Creoles saw themselves as the product of the biological, racial amalgamation of Amerindian and Spanish elites that took place during the first years of colonization" (2007:32). In other words, there was the condition of being creole, which was the product of transformation processes occurring to transplanted populations in the New World.

From the late seventeenth century onward the term "creole" acquired a linguistic connotation, referring to mixed languages or nonstandard versions of an accepted language. Then, "in the mid-twentieth century linguists reached a consensus view of creole as a type of language that emerged when pidgins (contact languages facilitating trade between Europeans and locals) were learned as mother tongues by subsequent generations" (Stewart 2007:2). Creole languages also developed among African slaves in the sugar plantations of the Caribbean and in the southeastern United States, where slaves from different linguistic backgrounds were forced together and needed to communicate with each other (Mintz 2010:195).

Borrowing from linguistics, Mintz and other Caribbeanists coined the term "creolization" to refer to the process of "creative cultural synthesis undertaken primarily by the slaves, interacting with each other and with free people, including the master class, particularly in the tropical New World sugar plantation colonies. By this synthesis, new social institutions furnished with reordered cultural content, were forged to provide the basis for continuing cultural growth" (Mintz 2010:190). Mintz argued, then, that the creolization process was a unique cultural synthesis occurring specifically in Caribbean colonies whose founding conditions were slavery and plantations established in places emptied of their native inhabitants and that it should not be applied to other processes of culture change (2010:190–191). He sees creolization, and the particular historical circumstances in which it occurred, as contributing to anthropologists' study of cultural theory:

> My claim that the phenomenon of creolization contributes to our study of cultural theory rests on the concept of culture, as anthropologists have used the term: culture, first, as a universal, uniquely human possession; second, culture as understandable in terms of social organization of behavior within distinguishable human groups. In the whole of world history I know of no destruction, both of cultures and institutions, whose consequences can vie in scale or intensity with those of Atlantic slavery. The American anthropologist Alfred Kroeber wrote that how culture comes to be is really more distinctive of culture than what it is [Kroeber 1948:253]. Creolization, the process by which slaves dealt with the immediate postenslavement trauma, gets as close to understanding how culture comes to be as anything else in the human record that I know of [Mintz 2010:205].

Despite Mintz's recommendation to limit the use of creolization to the cultural syntheses resulting from African peoples' struggles to communicate and create new meanings within the social and economic institution of slavery, the term has been widely applied to other contexts of cultural change, including the emergence of creole identities resulting from resistance and adaptation of subordinate peoples affected by global economic processes (Vergès 2007:133–152; Eriksen 2007:153–177; Roth 2007:201–219; Gallagher 2007:220–236).

Historical archaeologists have applied the concept of creolization in their studies of African peoples' lives in plantation societies (Ferguson 2000:5–9; Wilkie 2000:10–26; Loren 2000:85–98; Groover 2000:99–106; Delle 2000:56–72). This concept has been applied to other archaeological contexts as well (Burley 2000:27–35; Dawdy 2000:107–123; Gundaker 2000:124–133; Ewen 2000:36–45; Cusick 2000:46–55; Mullins and Paynter 2000:73–84). One of the most interesting archaeological studies of a creole community is Douglas Armstrong's volume on the East End creole community in St. John, in the U.S. Virgin Islands, a settlement that began in the 1720s and was abandoned in the early twentieth century (2013:3). His approach looked at the distribution of house sites through time for insights into the changing cultural landscape, what he terms "community level," and excavation of individual house residences, what he terms "household level" (2013:10). He then applied an assemblage-based activity analysis aimed at examining the actions implied by the material remains recovered. In his words, "Activity analysis analyzes the complete assemblage of artifacts in order to examine similarities and differences between contexts" (2013:11). Due to the excellent preservation of the site, the meticulous approach to artifact analysis, and the wealth of historical documentation available, he was able to reconstruct how the East End community's structure differed from the larger Danish colonial plantation society, and how they developed fishing and navigational skills that allowed them to participate actively in the broader economy and maintain a viable community for more than 100 years.

In his study, Armstrong introduces the concept of cultural transformation to explain culture change. He points out that while this concept shares with transculturation and ethnogenesis the recognition that all people, not just the "dominant" ones, are active agents of change, the transformation model "is most reflective of the process of change and includes but does not limit itself to specific conditions involving the definition of distinct or separate cultural identities" (2013:61–62). He further points out that "the transformation model breaks from traditional acculturation and assimilation models based on the 'whole culture' concept, and from assumptions of cultural replacement" (2013:63). It appears to me that, in recognizing the fluidity of relationships, the role of human agency, and the diversity of possible outcomes in situations of culture change resulting from contact between different peoples, and by taking into consideration the wider economic and social contexts in which change occurs, the cultural transformation model developed by Armstrong provides a much broader framework for the study of cultures in contact.

To summarize, acculturation, transculturation, ethnogenesis, creolization, and cultural transformation have been applied by scholars interested in how different interacting cultures change over time. Acculturation is viewed by many as assuming a static view of culture and the outcome of eventual assimilation of subordinate cultures by dominant Western cultures. Transculturation is, in its essence, very similar to acculturation, but it denotes the many-sided aspects of contact and the creation of new social and cultural patterns as a result of active human interactions. Ethnogenesis describes the emergence of new ethnic or cultural identities as a result of sustained contact and adaptation to new social and cultural environments. Creolization, as defined by Mintz (2010), describes the creation of new cultures and institutions by enslaved Africans of different cultural and linguistic backgrounds as they strive to find meaning within a hostile, dominant plantation culture. Cultural transformation emphasizes the role of human agency in the contact scenario and the choices people make when confronted with changing conditions, which "allows us to examine how people utilized their own creative solutions to the problems of daily life, and thus developed their own cultural identities" (Armstrong 2013:76–77).

Contact in the Spanish Caribbean

In the case of Spanish-Indian contact in the Caribbean islands, two or more culturally and ethnically distinct peoples were forced together in situations of conflict that produced changes in the respective cultures. The contact scenario was one of inequality in which the Europeans quickly assumed the dominant role and the indigenous populations, both native and those brought in from neighboring areas, were forced into a wider social and economic system of exploitation. This conspired to make this particular case one of marked stress and inequality.

However, despite this, it must be kept in mind that at the initial phases of contact, Spanish superiority and dominance, although clearly intended, was not well established. Viewing it from a perspective of 500 years, we assume that the outcome was inevitable. Nevertheless, although not so in the Greater Antillean islands, there are numerous examples in the New World where Indian groups were able to survive as viable social and cultural entities for long periods of time after the Spanish conquest. Even in the case of the Caribbean, the early historic documents attest to periods in which Spanish population was minimal, due mainly to extraneous circumstances relating to the expansion into other areas of the New World. As will be seen, in such periods, the Indian population that still survived in the islands rebelled and took advantage of Spanish weakness in order to improve its situation.

In this volume I study indigenous culture change during the early contact period within the rubric of Armstrong's (2013) more inclusive concept of cultural transformation. This term highlights the role of human agency in culture change and serves as a more open-ended model to understand various possible outcomes of the contact scenario in the Caribbean. This approach also acknowledges the historical specificity of culture change, and stresses that the choices individuals make are varied and mediated by the social and political contexts in which they operate. This is important, because Spanish-Indian interaction in Hispaniola and Puerto Rico and the cultural transformations that occurred among the native peoples of these islands must be understood within the wider arena of Spanish policy toward the Indians, the particular histories of conquest and colonization of the two islands, and their relationship with the Caribbean area as a whole. This involves an analysis that contextualizes culture contact on these islands within the broader perspective of colonial state formation and the economic, social, and political processes that developed as a result, including the institutionalization of forced Indian labor (De La Luz-Rodríguez 2003, 2004). The conflictual nature of this contact, which involved peoples of disparate sociocultural and economic histories, the expanding Spanish empire versus the native tribal chiefdoms, also informs this analysis (see also Ferguson and Whitehead 1992:1–30).

To facilitate the narrative, I divide the history of the contact scenario for each island into three phases: initial contact (1492–94 for Hispaniola; 1493, 1506–1508 for Puerto Rico), conquest/pacification (1494–1504 for Hispaniola; 1509–1515 for Puerto Rico), and colonization/enslavement (1504–1550 for Hispaniola; 1509–1550 for Puerto Rico). I focus on five main variables of the contact scenario: the nature of the groups in contact, their points of origin, the geographical/physical framework in which contact occurs, ecologic and demographic factors, and the institutional, political, and economic frameworks that structure contact.

A Porous Frontier, Movement of Indians among the Islands

This factor is critical in understanding the early contact period in the Caribbean. Voluntary movement occurred when affected indigenous populations chose to move away from the source or cause of conflict in a contact situation. It is voluntary in the sense that it is initiated as a strategy of avoiding conflict or further confrontation with an unwanted adversary. One consequence of this strategy can be the disintegration of the indigenous society, if the movement involves individuals and not viable organizational networks (for example, an entire village or a larger segment of one), or a reorientation and restructuring of social networks in another locality. If the movement happens to a locality that is open for settlement and is sufficiently similar in its environmental characteristics to support the displaced population under similar technological and organizational strategies, then there is a better opportunity for the group and its culture to survive, albeit with modifications. If the movement is made into already inhabited areas, then it becomes more difficult for the migrating group to recreate its society in a new place. Conflict between competing groups, and environmental and nutritional stress, may occur (see Colombres 1977). Another consequence of this strategy, which appears to have occurred in the case of movement between Puerto Rico and the Eastern Caribbean, may be the creation of new interethnic political alliances to raid Spanish camps and settlements (Sued Badillo 1995).

There was also forced movement of Indians, that is, the deliberate displacement of Indian individuals and/or populations exercised by the Spanish as a means of obtaining labor for the developing West Indian colonies. This is a historical fact. It will be shown to have had a significant impact on the contact scenario in Hispaniola and Puerto Rico, because it altered the ethnic and cultural composition of the actors.

The processes of forced and voluntary movement are amply documented among various Indian communities in many areas of the New World. Publications that attest to their importance in the culture-contact scenario are numerous (see, for example, Cardoso de Oliveira and Castro Faria 1971; Colombres 1977; Friede 1953; Linton 1940; Acosta Saignes 1946, 1961; Dobyns 1983; Ramenofsky 1987; Smith 1984; Milanich and Proctor 1978; among others). In the case of the Caribbean islands, Indian population movements, whether voluntary or forced, although documented by historians, have not been considered as critical factors in studies of Indian culture change during the early historic period.

Historical Sources Used

I make use of ethnohistorical research to reconstruct the contact scenario in Hispaniola and Puerto Rico. As does Orme (1973:482–483), I consider ethnohistory to be a specific method by which historical documentation is used to study a particular ethnic group. Although it can also include a combination of the historic and ethnographic method (Aguirre Beltrán 1970:14), the former is more applicable to the study area than the latter, since no contemporary Indian communities are recognized to exist on these islands.[3] In this case, the historical documents shed light on the nature of the Indian inhabitants of these islands at the time of contact, of changes occurring as a result of prolonged contact, and of the presence of other Indian groups in the islands during the first half of the sixteenth century (Alegría 1983b).

Ethnohistorical research corroborates the presence of more than one Indian ethnic group, but it does not provide details about their culture. In this respect, the historical record is silent. The ethnohistorical method differs from the historians' method in that it focuses on extracting information on subjugated peoples, in this case Indians, from documents produced by the dominant society.

The ethnohistorical method implies an anthropological orientation. Its use, in the cases where it is merited, contributes significantly to anthropological interpretations, and it has been applied extensively in acculturation and culture-contact studies (Friede 1953; Aguirre Beltrán 1970; Colombres 1977; Linton 1940; Spicer 1961b; Mandelbaum 1967; Tax 1952). I apply it extensively here, relying mainly on primary sixteenth-century firsthand accounts and on documentary sources as available from published compilations of documents.[4] Some are better than others, and discrepancies in the same document published in different sources are not uncommon. These problems cannot be avoided. Published sources are accessible and are relatively easy to read, compared with the original manuscripts housed mainly in Spanish archives. For the benefit of English speakers, all citations from Spanish documents, whether published or not, that appear in this volume are quoted in my English translation. For consistency and clarity and the benefit of Spanish speakers, the original Spanish citations are provided either in endnotes to each chapter or in the applicable appendixes.

Lastly, another type of data was amply consulted: historical demography. This data is necessary to understand the relationship between Indian population loss in Hispaniola and Puerto Rico, on the one hand, and the influx of Indians from other areas, on the other.[5] This data is critical in any discussion of Indian response to contact and needs to be kept in mind when we consider the broader context of discourse on indigenous identity in the contemporary Spanish Caribbean.

1
The Inhabitants of the Caribbean at the Time of Columbus

When Columbus made landfall on October 12, 1492, in the New World, he encountered islands whose human inhabitants and natural environments were very different from what Europeans had seen before. This encounter, which marked the beginning of one of the most tragic episodes of human history, forever transformed the Old World and the New. In the words of Todorov, "The discovery of America, or of the Americans, is certainly the most astonishing encounter of our history" (1984:4).

Any study of what happened during those first years of Euro-Indian contact begins with understanding the nature of the native peoples encountered by Columbus. This statement appears simple enough, but as discussed here, there is a growing consensus that the native peoples of the Caribbean were a more varied lot than previously believed, and that the simple dichotomy of Taíno (referring to the native inhabitants of the Greater Antilles) and Carib (referring to the native inhabitants of the Lesser Antilles) is no longer tenable.

Early historic sources provide synchronic information on Indian society and culture at the time of contact and in the years immediately following, and archaeological and linguistic data provide a diachronic view of the origins and historical development of the peoples who unwittingly erupted onto the European scene and consciousness at the end of the fifteenth century. When Columbus and his men set foot in America, it was the reward of a purposeful voyage to discover new lands. Although the peoples of America were initially foreign to the Europeans, both they and their lands were swept into the sphere of European expansion. However, in the case of the Indians, their "discovery" by Europeans was an intrusion into their separate cultural development for which they had no antecedents, and they had to develop novel responses in an effort to survive. This is a pivotal difference between the two sides of conflict. Despite the hardships that individual Spaniards also had to endure in the process of conquering and settling the New World, they were there with a purpose and because, in a certain sense, they had chosen to come. The Indians had no choice in the matter and had to endure and find ways to respond to the destruction of their world.

The inhabitants encountered by Columbus in the Bahamas, Cuba, Jamaica, Hispaniola, and Puerto Rico were originally known simply as Indians by the Spanish. Although we are all very much aware that this is a misnomer brought about by Columbus's mistaken belief that he had arrived at the eastern lands of the Great Khan of China, the term stuck and was applied generically to all the native inhabitants of the New World. It is still used today.[1] During the early decades of Spanish colonization, the Spanish began distinguishing between the more developed Indian chiefdoms encountered in the Greater Antilles (with the exception of Western Cuba) and the Indians inhabiting the Lesser Antilles, which they called Caribs.

The term "Taíno," in reference to the Greater Antillean inhabitants, was never used by the Spanish.[2] However, starting in the late nineteenth century and becoming prevalent in the twentieth, Taíno entered the lexicon as a term to describe the people of the Greater Antillean chiefdom societies at the time of contact (Lovén 1935; Sauer 1969:37; see also Curet 2014:417–472). It is ironic that the widespread use of the term "Taíno" by Caribbean scholars to name the inhabitants of the Greater Antilles is as much a misnomer as the Spaniards' use of the term "Indians" to refer to the inhabitants of the New World.[3] The term, in my view, served to identify a group of peoples who shared a chiefdom level of social and political organization, as well as what appears to have been a shared tradition of material culture traits and religious/ritual beliefs.

However, as stressed by Wilson (1993), Curet (2014), Oliver (2009), and Rodríguez Ramos (2010), the term "Taíno" masks the diversity and variability of the late prehistoric peoples in these islands and the myriad of influences that shaped them, or what Wilson has called "the cultural mosaic of the indigenous Caribbean" (1993:37). In fact, Curet (2014: 475–476) calls this the Taíno Paradox—the cultural variability demonstrated in the archaeological record and the obvious strong similarities in material culture and cultural practices. These strong similarities, especially in ritual and cosmology, are called "Taínoness" by Oliver (2009) and Rodríguez Ramos (2010).[4] Curet (2014:480) borrows the concept of "symbolic reservoir," developed by scholars studying African cultures and defined as "the assemblage of symbols, beliefs, and myths from which groups or subgroups obtain the ideological tools necessary to 'create' a cultural tradition to legitimize their own interests" (McIntosh 1998:61, quoted in Curet 2014:480), as one with wider application than Taíno or Taínoness "in explaining the similarities in the assemblages from the Greater Antilles and Bahamas and even from the 'Taíno' sites reported outside the traditional Taíno culture area in the Leeward Islands" (2014:481). Curet further argues that since this concept is not constrained to a particular set of cultural characteristics, as implied by Taíno or Taínoness, it could be more widely applied in the Caribbean area.[5] He does not believe it is appropriate to keep using the term "Taíno," except to refer to the "Arawak language spoken in the Greater Antilles" (2014:482; see also Rodríguez Ramos 2010:201).

Curet makes a compelling argument, but this still leaves us with the question of how to refer to the Indians of the Greater Antilles at the time of contact. Taking into consideration what we now know about the ethnic variability that existed in the precolonial Caribbean (and, by the way, still exists today; see Wilson 1993), I will use the first Spanish misnomer of Indian to refer to the native inhabitants and, when appropriate, will apply the term "Caribbean chiefdoms" to refer to the broad sociopolitical characteristics of Indian societies of the Greater Antilles at the time of contact.

The origins and historical development of the prehistoric peoples of the Antilles have been summarized by many scholars, most comprehensively by Irving Rouse (1948:IV:495–565; 1952:VIII, parts 3, 4; 1986; 1987), whose influence on the methods, theory, and practice of Caribbean archaeology in the twentieth century is undisputed. His reconstruction of Caribbean culture history based on ceramic styles, subseries, and series, especially his reliance on migration and diffusion as the main explanatory processes, however, has been challenged by a new generation of scholars (Rodríguez Ramos 2010; Curet 2005; Chanlatte and Narganes 1986; Keegan 2000, 2013). My summary, although necessarily general for the purposes of this volume, incorporates some of these new perspectives.

The Indians encountered by Columbus in the Greater Antilles were descendants of migratory waves of ceramic agriculturalists who entered the Lesser Antilles and traveled up the island chain, the earliest ones arriving in Puerto Rico, the easternmost island of the Greater Antilles, around 300 to 400 BC.[6] Most scholars agree that the chiefdoms encountered by Columbus in Puerto Rico, Hispaniola, Jamaica, and Cuba were a product of centuries of local development. However, local development does not imply isolation, as there were also influences from the South American mainland (Veloz Maggiolo et al. 1981:309–310), as well as interactions of Caribbean peoples with Central Americans (Rodríguez Ramos 2013; Wilson 2007; Dacal Moure and Rivero de la Calle 1996; Hofman et al. 2011; Callaghan 2011). The origins of material characteristics described for the late prehistoric chiefdoms, such as the sculpting of *zemis* and the construction of public works such as ball courts and plazas, are traced at least as far back as A.D. 700 to the Ostionoid series in Puerto Rico (Moscoso 1986:281–282; Alegría 1983a:117).[7] However, the chiefdom societies encountered by the Spanish developed during the period of A.D. 1000–1500 in Hispaniola and Puerto Rico (Moscoso 1986:296) and correlate with the Classic Taíno, in Rouse's terminology (Rouse 1986:149; 1987:300, 305).[8] Different ceramic styles and series of styles have been identified for this period in the Antilles (see Rouse 1988) and indicate local variations within a wider cultural ceramic tradition.

Subsistence and Technology

The Indians of the Greater Antilles at the time of contact were agricultural peoples, inheritors of the South American tradition of manioc cultivation. They cultivated the bitter variety of manioc, which constituted their staple food, cassava bread. Archaeological and ethnographic accounts support the conclusion that these were sedentary peoples who practiced intensive cultivation methods. In addition to manioc, the Indians grew a variety of other crops that, although secondary in importance, were also widely used. Among these were arrowroot, sweet potatoes, pineapple, *ají* (pepper), avocado, maize, various fruit trees, root crops such as *yautía* and *leren*, calabashes or gourds, and cotton (see Lovén 1935:350–409; Sturtevant 1961, for a detailed discussion of these; Petersen 1997). Despite the variety of crops planted, except for manioc, historic sources do not specify cultivation techniques. It is assumed that many of the other cultigens were intercropped in the manioc fields, as is the case with many contemporary South American tribes and in current subsistence farming in Hispaniola (Sauer 1969:52), although the sources are silent on this matter.[9]

Historical descriptions of manioc cultivation are derived mainly from Las Casas (1951, 1985), Fernández de Oviedo (1959), and Mártir de Anglería (1944). Manioc was intensively planted in large fields called *conucos.* These were artificial earth mounds in which various tubers were planted. The basic process consisted of clearing the forest either by felling or girdling trees (Sauer 1969:51), burning the resultant brush, and piling up the mounds by means of the *coa,* or digging stick. The work of clearing the fields and constructing the mounds was labor intensive and was carried out by the men; women contributed in the planting of the tubers and in the harvest one to three years later. Although the extent of the manioc fields and the fallow period, if there was any, is unknown, historical sources attest to widespread areas under cultivation in both the coast and the interior of the islands (Varela 1982; Las Casas 1951, 1985; Mártir de Anglería 1944).

Information concerning crop yields is difficult to assess, although Moscoso, using Las Casas' figures, notes the correlation between sources indicating a dense sedentary population for the Greater Antillean islands and the probable yields of cassava during the early historic period (1986:423–426). Comparative evidence of high yields provided by manioc cultivation under the slash-and-burn method characteristic of South American tropical forest cultures has been documented by Carneiro (1961). Although manioc alone is not sufficient for a balanced diet despite its high-yield potential, its presence in combination with other Caribbean cultigens, and supplemented with fresh water and marine faunal resources, provided adequate nutrition. Manioc continued to be cultivated in the early historic period, and was heavily relied upon by the Spanish as a source of food for themselves and for feeding the Indian labor force.

Agricultural yields must have varied locally in the islands and may have been quite productive in the northern valleys of Hispaniola, along the Río Verde and Río Yaque del Norte, where cultivation of the fertile floodplains, termed *cultivo de várzea* is reported (Veloz Maggiolo et al. 1981:328–329). The possible use of irrigation in Xaraguá, in southwestern Hispaniola, is suggested by historical references (Mártir de Anglería 1944, cited in Sauer 1969:53, note 14), but, to my knowledge, it has not been corroborated archaeologically. More recently, agricultural terraces correlated with the late prehistoric period in the mountainous interior of Puerto Rico suggest intensification of agricultural practices (deFrance and Newsom 2005:183; Oliver et al. 1999).

Besides agriculture, the native inhabitants of the Greater Antilles relied upon a variety of faunal resources, including both marine and land animals, to complement their diet. Although the technological implements for agricultural endeavors consisted mainly of the digging stick and stone celt for felling and clearing vegetation, a great variety of techniques and implements for the harvesting of marine resources is documented in the historical literature. The relative importance of these techniques and their possible yield is unknown.[10]

Apparently, in basic technology, the Caribbean chiefdoms did not differ much from their early agricultural predecessors. The large populations and increased productivity of agriculture suggested generally by the historical accounts were accomplished by the reorganization of the productive forces of society, and not by any technological breakthrough.

Sociopolitical Organization

The consensus among historians and archaeologists of the Caribbean is that the Greater Antillean Indian societies were organized into a series of polities known as chiefdoms of various degrees of complexity.[11] The Spanish sources describe a society divided into chiefdoms or *cacicazgos* of varying importance with hierarchically ranked categories of *caciques* (chiefs), *nitaínos* (nobles), and *naborías* (commoners and slaves). They describe the *cacicazgos* as comprising multiple *yucayeques* (villages) under the leadership of a paramount chief, or *cacique*, with social, economic, and ritual authority (Torres 2013:348). These Spanish terms are still in use today, and the Spanish chroniclers' descriptions of Indian society as they viewed it still form the main body of evidence for analyzing the nature and distribution of Caribbean chiefdoms at the time of contact.[12]

Caribbean chiefdoms have been studied within the wider context of neo-evolutionary theories seeking to describe and explain the evolution of social complexity and consolidation of political power (Earle 1989, in Torres 2013:348; see also Service 1968, Earle 1997). Divergent opinions within this neo-evolutionary perspective include Alcina's (1983:69) contention that the Taíno polities were more than just tribal groups but still not full-fledged chiefdoms and Moscoso's (1986) argument that they were well on their way to becoming a class-structured society when their development was thwarted by the Spanish invasion. Both authors' positions are based mainly on their interpretation of the historical record as gleaned from ethnohistoric sources.

Within an evolutionary continuum, Alcina (1983) interprets the Taíno chiefdoms as transitional between tribal societies and fully developed chiefdoms. Following Harris (1982), Alcina considers the redistributive character of chiefdoms as critical in their development, because it allows the expansion of administrative functions, differing access to resources, and the hierarchy of social groups (Harris 1982:110 quoted in Alcina 1983:69).[13] However, Alcina argues that the Taíno chiefdoms do not exhibit these characteristics (1983:75). He also argues that although the Taíno chiefdoms were apparently capable of supporting dense populations, they had a more dispersed type of settlement pattern than the "urban" or "semiurban" populations characteristic of fully developed chiefdoms (1983:73). According to Alcina, the Taíno lacked slaves, a differentiated priest or temple cult, and a militaristic class, all prerequisites of more complex, stratified chiefdoms. The lack of evidence in the historical sources for artisan specialization and tribute also suggest to him that the Taínos had not yet developed into true chiefdoms at the time of contact with the Spanish.

In contrast to Alcina, and relying on a cultural materialistic, Marxist interpretation, Moscoso (1986) argues that the Taíno chiefdoms were well on the way to becoming a class-structured society at the time of Spanish contact. He argues that the reliance on the hierarchical divisions of Taíno society by the Spanish authorities in their organization of forced Indian labor under the *encomienda* system, and the persistence of the distinctions between *caciques, nitaínos,* and *naborías* (commoners)[14] well into the historic period, mimics the pre-Columbian situation as much as it does the Spaniards' hierarchical viewpoint.

According to Moscoso (1983:309–489), the Taíno chiefdoms' mode of production was tribal-tributary.[15] The Taínos lived in relatively dense, sedentary villages capable of producing an agricultural surplus, which was appropriated by a chiefly class. The chiefly class included the *caciques, nitaínos* (who assisted the chiefs in the organization of agricultural and artisanal productions), and *behiques* (medicine men or shamans with ritual and religious authority). The rest were *naborías.* The sociopolitical organization was of hierarchical, pyramidal chiefdoms that governed specific territories of varying importance. Moscoso argues that the ethnohistorical accounts of the kingdoms of *cacique* Behecchio and the list of tribute goods collected by Columbus (1986:446–447) attest to the productive capabilities of the Taíno chiefdoms and the existence of a class of artisans; only this could account for the richness and technical mastery required to fabricate some of the items. He follows Fernández de Oviedo and Las Casas in accepting the existence of five territories or provinces within aboriginal Hispaniola and of a paramount chief in Puerto Rico (*cacique* Agüeybaná) (figure 1.1).[16]

Alcina's and Moscoso's contrasting interpretations of the same phenomenon may be attributed to their emphasis on different threads of a cultural tapestry. Alcina focuses on data from the thread that reinforces his interpretation of relatively simple, nondifferentiated polities, while Moscoso emphasizes the data that points to stratification, craft-specialization, and intensification of production (see also Moscoso 2003). However, it is important to point out that, despite their different conclusions, both authors are seeking to explain the nature and origin of the Caribbean polities at the time of European contact by assuming that these polities reflect an evolutionary continuum from more egalitarian tribal societies

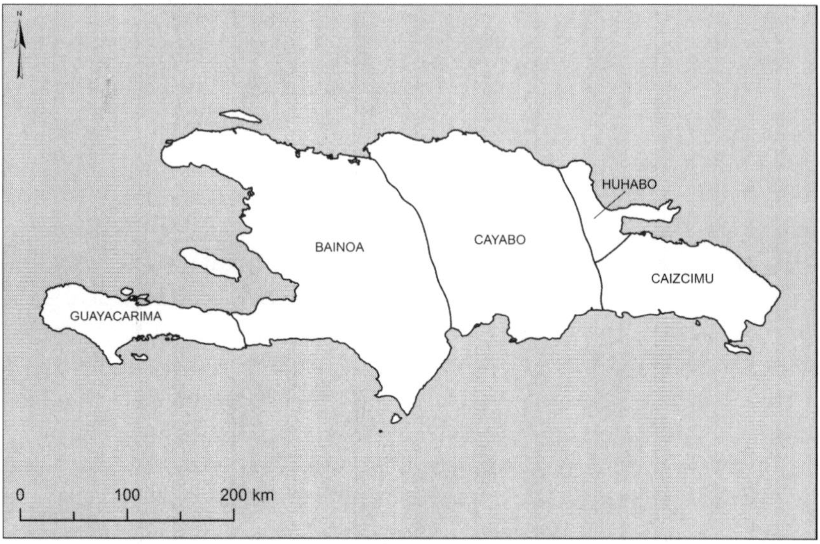

Figure 1.1. Taíno chiefdoms of Hispaniola (based on Sauer 1969:46, figure 7; Vega 1980, map 4; Anderson-Córdova 1990:56).

to more complex and socially stratified ones (see De La Luz-Rodríguez 2004:77–83 for a critique of Moscoso's position). They are using an admittedly ambiguous historical record to explain the development of prehistoric Caribbean polities within this evolutionary framework and are arriving at very different conclusions. A more plausible explanation is that there was considerable cultural variability in the Greater Antilles at the time of contact, which can now be traced back to the late prehistoric period, and that Caribbean polities varied widely as well. Rather than trying to portray all Caribbean chiefdoms as homogenous entities based mainly on the early-sixteenth-century chroniclers' descriptions of these polities, let us look at how they varied and try to explain why. To do so, we must also consider the archaeological record.

Although there appears to be a consensus among most historians and archaeologists that highly developed chiefdoms existed in Hispaniola at the time of contact (see Wilson 1990), emphasis on this point obscures the cultural variability within them, as evidenced by different contemporaneous ceramic styles and local variability in subsistence sources (Veloz Maggiolo et al. 1981). This is further reinforced in Ulloa Hung's (2014) recent archaeological study of the northern area of Hispaniola, where ceramic analyses and settlement patterns point to considerable cultural variability in the late prehistoric and early historic periods. The polities in Puerto Rico, in comparison, appear to have been organized into smaller competitive groups (Torres 2013:350, also Torres 2005; Siegel 2004).[17]

In summary, rather than conceptualizing Caribbean chiefdoms as homogenous entities and relying heavily on necessarily limited historical sources,[18] it is more productive to ask new questions about how Indian communities were organized and to develop more sophisticated theoretical and methodological practices to study how they developed and interacted. As pointed out by Torres, it is time to go beyond the "neo-evolutionary paradigms," which tend to simplify the complex origins of chiefdoms, to "engage the linkages between political centralization and power, ideology, social structure, regional social diversity, local and regional histories, and the production of space and place" (2013:358).

The anthropological comparative approach also provides insight into the nature of Caribbean chiefdoms. The islands of Polynesia serve as an excellent case for comparison (see Kirch 1989 for a synthesis of the genesis and evolution of the Polynesian chiefdoms). Kirch demonstrates that Polynesian chiefdoms, although derived from a similar "Ancestral Polynesian Society" that developed as a result of the process of migration and adaptation of the original inhabitants of the Polynesian islands, differed considerably in their local manifestations. These differences depended on such factors as population density, environmental constraints, development of each society's productive base, and the specific manner in which they organized themselves to cope with each island environment. The fact that differences in the level of chiefly organization are found sometimes within a relatively small island in the Polynesian chain reinforces current research that suggests this is the case in the much larger and environmentally diverse islands of the Greater Antilles.

Archaeological and historical evidence supports the contention that the Indian societies that developed in the Greater Antilles never reached a point in which population and productive capacity resulted in environmental stress (see also Curet 1996:116–117). This may account for the fact that highly stratified, warlike chiefdoms, which are characteristic of many of the Polynesian societies, did not develop in the Greater Antilles. The expansion of the Caribbean chiefdoms and the consolidation of certain chiefly lineages into larger polities was still in full swing at the time of Euro-Indian contact. The picture that emerges from recent research points to a diverse mosaic of cultures that interacted over a wide area. Indian polities differed within each island and between islands, and there were also significant connections and strategic alliances among islands (Torres 2005, 2013; Heckenberger 2011; Mol 2011; Wilson 1993, 1997a; Ulloa Hung 2014; Siegel 2005; Keegan 2013).

Although I believe that the concept of chiefdom can still serve as a heuristic device to categorize the sociopolitical formations that existed in the Greater Antilles during late prehistoric times and at contact, this should not obscure the variability that existed as well. This is important to keep in mind as we delve into the historical record in the following chapters of this volume.

The Caribs

Starting with Columbus's earliest descriptions of the Indies, the historical record documents what appears to be a dichotomy between two distinct peoples: those who inhabited the Greater Antilles and the Bahamas, later called Taínos, as discussed previously, and those who inhabited the Lesser Antilles,[19] whom the Spanish referred to as the Carib. Carib (in Spanish *caribe*) is a corruption of "Caniba," or "Canima," the term supposedly used by the Indians of Hispaniola in 1492 to refer to the inhabitants of the eastern islands (Davis and Goodwin 1990:37). Thus, since the first contact between the Spanish and the Taíno, inklings of the existence of native peoples distinct from the Taíno are noted in the historical literature (Wilson 1993; Dunn and Kelley 1989; Hulme 1986). Although not originally interpreted as such by Columbus (Ramos Pérez 1975; Sued Badillo 1978, Keegan 1996), the term "Carib" later became synonymous with "cannibal" and was used by the Spanish to categorize all hostile Indians as justification to enslave them. The original term "Caniba" as mentioned by the Taíno may have been a valid ethnic categorization of the Indians inhabiting the eastern West Indies. However, its corruption and general usage in sixteenth-century Spanish sources in reference to all hostile Indians blurs the ethnic distinctions that surely existed among the inhabitants of the Lesser Antillean Islands at the time of contact.[20]

Sixteenth-century primary sources do not provide detailed information about the inhabitants of the Lesser Antilles. Since the Spanish did not colonize these islands (although, as discussed in subsequent chapters of this volume, they were subject to numerous Spanish raids to capture slaves for the Greater Antillean mining operations), there are no early accounts comparable to the chroniclers' descriptions of the Greater Antillean Indians. Therefore, the controversy about the nature of the so-called Caribs and their interactions and cultural relationship with the Indians of the Greater Antilles continues to this day.

For example, in his classic study on the historical Caribs, Sued Badillo (1978) argued that the Carib as such never existed but were a mythological construction of the Spanish. He discounted as superficial the differences among the Indians of the Greater and Lesser Antilles noted by the Spanish and argued that all of them were Taíno. Alegría (1981) presents historical evidence against this argument, and Figueredo (1978) uses documentary sources to conclude that the island of St. Croix was an important Carib center during the early sixteenth century (Figueredo 1978, cited in Allaire 1987:128). However, the late prehistoric–early historic settlement of Salt River Bay on St. Croix is interpreted by Morse (1997:45) as an eastern outpost of the Puerto Rico Taíno. With respect to this issue, Sued Badillo has more recently argued that the Spanish may have actually picked up on native political/ethnic boundaries that existed between Puerto Rico and the eastern Lesser Antilles inhabitants (1995:77). However, he also documents historical evidence suggesting "that very strong ties of both kinship and political alliance did exist between Puerto Rico and the Eastern Caribbean" (1995:78). In other words, both historical and archaeological evidence seems to indicate that there was a fluid boundary between Puerto Rico and the eastern Caribbean islands that cannot be adequately explained within the traditional framework of Taíno and Carib.

To further complicate the scenario, seventeenth-century French sources provide quite detailed ethnographic descriptions of Indian communities in the islands of Dominica and Guadeloupe (Breton 1665; Breton and de la Paix 1926; La Borde 1674; Du Tertre 1667, cited in Davis and Goodwin 1990) and, following the Spanish nomenclature, referred to them as Caribs. These descriptions included linguistic information that emphasized, in the case of Dominica, the gender dimorphism of the Island Carib, wherein the men and women spoke different languages, Callínago (male) and Callíponam (female) (Breton 1665; Whitehead 1995a:16–18). Although this alleged dichotomy obscured the fact that the so-called male language was only a jargon (Whitehead 1995a:18, citing Taylor 1954:32–33 and Hoff 1995:38–39), this gender language difference, and the fact that the Island Carib language includes elements from both the Arawakan and the Cariban language families (Hoff 1995: 37–38), has helped fuel the argument for a mainland Carib invasion into the Antilles.

Therefore, the origins and historical relationship, if any, of the seventeenth-century Caribs—as observed by the French—to the earlier sixteenth-century inhabitants of the Lesser Antilles are open to various interpretations.[21] In his recent summary of Carib ethnohistory, Allaire

(2013) interprets the historical and ethnographic sources as indicating clear ethnic differences between the Caribs and the Taínos and points out that seventeenth-century accounts depict communities that self-identify as Caribs.[22]

In addition, archaeologists coined the term "Island Carib" to distinguish the Lesser Antillean Indians from the South American mainland Carib (Rouse 1948; Davis and Goodwin 1990:38).[23] It appears that at the time of Columbus the Island Caribs inhabited only the Windward Islands from Guadeloupe southward (Davis and Goodwin 1990; Allaire 1987:130–31, 1996:43–46; Rouse 1986:112) and that the Leeward Islands were either partially uninhabited (Davis and Goodwin 1990:45; Rouse 1986:114) or essentially an eastern extension of the Taíno. Allaire viewed the Leeward Islands, including the Virgin Islands and St. Croix, as a Taíno-Carib frontier whose inhabitants were distinct from both the Taíno and the Island Carib (1987:131), while Rouse emphasized their cultural affiliation with the classic Taíno of Hispaniola and Puerto Rico and called them "Eastern Sub-Taínos" (1987: figure 4).

When comparing the prehistory and early history of the Greater and Lesser Antilles, it is clear that the use of ethnic labels derived from Spanish accounts have not only obscured the variety of peoples and cultures who inhabited these islands at the time of contact but also further muddied the archaeological interpretations of the precolonial period. Wilson (1993) summarized the various points of view concerning the nature and origins of the Lesser Antillean populations as falling under two broad models: the "Carib invasion" model and the "Arawakan continuity" model (1993:53), both of which oversimplify the area's prehistory (see also Allaire 1997).[24]

Wilson argued that neither model completely fits the facts, especially since no unequivocally "Carib" sites had been identified in the Lesser Antilles (1993:54; also Allaire 1980, 1990; Davis and Goodwin 1990; Rouse 1986, 1992). However, more recent archaeological evidence of ceramic complexes that appear to be unrelated to the previous inhabitants, whose pottery (Suazey) and culture appear more related to the Taíno, are interpreted as being the result of a recent Carib invasion (Allaire 2013:106). For example, according to Boomert (1995:27–29) the protohistoric Cayo ceramic complex first identified in St. Vincent, but now found in almost all of the Windward Islands, is of South American origin and can be considered an Island Carib ceramic assemblage. He traces it to the Koriabo ceramic tradition of the northwest Guiana coastal zone and estimates its introduction to the Antilles at around A.D. 1250 (1995:29).

When taken in combination, the archaeological evidence pointing to a new late prehistoric/protohistoric ceramic complex whose origins can be traced to coastal South America (Boomert 1995; Allaire 2013), the linguistic data of gender-based language differences among the Windward Island Caribs, and the ethnographic descriptions of historic period and contemporary Carib peoples whose mythology traces their origins to migrations from the mainland of men who married the native women (Boomert 1995; Hoff 1995) all appear to favor the model of a Carib invasion. However, there are other ways at looking at the data. As pointed out by Whitehead (1995b:96–104), the ethnographic data concerning kinship and marriage alliances among the Island Carib and among various ethnic groups of coastal South America alludes to the importance of women in these alliances and does not support the argument of invasion from the mainland and subordination of women by men.

In conclusion, until recently, reliance on ethnohistorical sources extrapolated back into the precolonial period resulted in a narrative that established a dichotomy of at least two major culturally distinct ethnic groups in the West Indies at the time of contact: the Taíno[25] and the Island Carib. They spoke different languages,[26] the Taíno occupying the Greater Antilles and the Bahamas (and possibly the eastern Leeward Islands), and the Island Carib the Windward Islands. This narrative tended to gloss over evidence for cultural diversity present in the historical and archaeological record and at the same time focused on the differences between the Greater and Lesser Antilles (the more complex and sedentary Taíno versus the less complex, more mobile and hostile Caribs).

Archaeological investigations reveal a much more nuanced and complex history. The chiefdoms of the Greater Antilles were not homogenous. They varied in apparent complexity (consolidation of smaller territories into larger ones in Hispaniola, less centralized and more fluid in Puerto Rico), structural features (larger settlements with earthworks in Hispaniola, and ball courts in Puerto Rico), and ceremonial/ritual paraphernalia (elaborate ceremonial vessels in Hispaniola, and elbow stones and stone collars in Puerto Rico). Communities with different ceramic traditions existed contemporaneously within Caribbean chiefdoms of the Greater Antilles, and their influence extended into the Eastern Caribbean, specifically Vieques, the Virgin Islands, and the Leeward Islands.

The denomination of Carib or Island Carib to identify the inhabitants of the Lesser Antilles also obscures their cultural diversity. Processes of cultural continuity and interisland emigration and mobility are evident in both the archaeological and the historical record. The inhabitants of the Leeward Islands appear to have had more interaction with the Greater Antilles, and this interaction involved kinship and marriage alliances that appear to have persisted into the beginning decades of the sixteenth century (Sued Badillo 1995:82–84). The inhabitants of the Windward Islands appear to have had more interaction with the South American mainland, specifically the coastal zone of the Guianas.[27]

The Taíno/Carib dichotomy no longer holds. The indiscriminate Spanish use of the term "Carib" to refer to any hostile Indians, be they from St. Croix, Vieques Island, Guadeloupe, Dominica, Trinidad, mainland South America, or elsewhere, invalidates its use as an ethnic category. Furthermore, we must keep in mind that the term "Island Carib" refers to a "post-Columbian culture" with inherited cultural traditions from the native Caribbean, as well as from Europeans and Africans (Whitehead 1995b:105–106). Its existence and persistence (as Garifuna in current Central America, and in the islands of St. Vincent and Dominica) are examples of the process of ethnogenesis in the Caribbean. It should not be confused with the term "Carib" as used by the Spanish in the early sixteenth century. Therefore, I use the term "Carib" in the rest of this volume to refer only to Indians foreign to the islands of Hispaniola and Puerto Rico who either were brought in as slaves or participated in raids against the Spanish settlements of these islands. This is how the term is traditionally used in sixteenth-century sources.

2

The Spanish Conquest and Colonization of Hispaniola and Puerto Rico

Hispaniola

In late 1492, after making initial landfall on the island of Guanahaní (likely El Salvador, one of the Spanish-named Lucayas Islands, now known as the Bahamas) and skirting the northeastern coast of Cuba, Columbus arrived off Hispaniola with his fleet of three ships. Columbus and his crew spent several months exploring the island's northern coast before returning to Spain early in 1493. The descriptions of the island and its inhabitants follow the pattern of Columbus's previous accounts of the passage through the Bahamas and along Cuba. He describes it as a bountiful, beautiful land, larger than Spain, with majestic mountains, rivers larger than the Guadalquivir, which flowed past Seville, and densely populated areas and cultivated terrain (*tierras labradas*). He speaks of the Indians as peaceful, timid creatures who are afraid of the Spanish and believe them to be gods. He also mentions their physical and linguistic affinity to those he had previously seen in the Bahamas and Cuba (Tyler 1988:70–96; Varela 1982; Varela and Gil 1984).

After the wreck of the expedition's flagship the *Santa María* on the north coast of Hispaniola on Christmas Eve of 1492, it was impossible for all the men to make the return voyage. The Spanish were forced to build a garrison to shelter the 39 crewmen who remained (Moya Pons 1992:130). This structure, known as Fort La Navidad, constituted the first Spanish settlement in the New World (Deagan 1990:241). The men were left in the territory (called Marien by the Spanish) of an Indian chief called Guacanagarí and were instructed to prospect for gold and generally to explore the newfound land (Sauer 1969:33).[1] Columbus's second voyage fleet arrived at Hispaniola late in 1493 and boasted 17 ships carrying 1,500 men (Sauer 1969:71) (figure 2.1). He found no survivors at Fort La Navidad.[2]

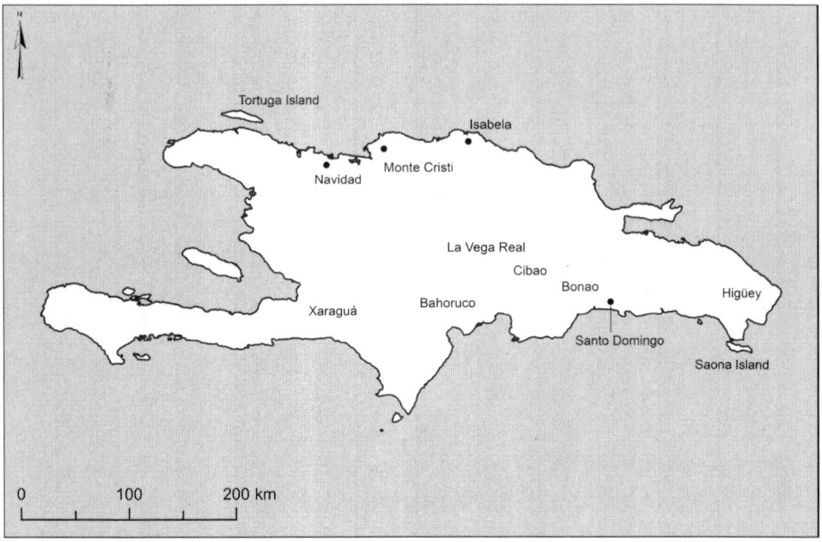

Figure 2.1. Hispaniola, late-fifteenth-century geography (based on Anderson-Córdova 1990:67).

After a brief reconnaissance of the north coast, in January 1494, Columbus ordered the construction of the town of La Isabela at the mouth of the Bajabonico River (Sauer 1969:75; Deagan 1990:241). Columbus wasted no time in dispatching two of his captains south into the interior in search of gold. Upon their return to La Isabela, they indicated that there were many large Indian settlements along the way and that they understood there was gold as well. Columbus decided to go personally, leaving La Isabela on March 12. Sauer (1969:79–80) describes Columbus's route to the interior Cibao region and summarizes his descriptions of the great valley, which he named La Vega Real, an interior valley densely settled by Indian villages.

Archaeological research indicates as well that this fertile valley was densely populated in prehistoric times. Wilson (1986: figure 22) correlates various late-period archaeological sites in the Río Verde area as forming part of the territory of another Indian *cacique,* named in the historical sources as Guarionex. Guerrero and Veloz Maggiolo (1988:88–94, 105) discuss the route followed by Columbus from La Isabela to the interior and correlate various archaeological sites along this route with the Indian villages mentioned in the historical sources (see also Veloz Maggiolo 2002; Ortega 1988; Vega 1980; Ulloa Hung 2014).

Spanish activities during this early period (1493–1494) focused on this area from La Isabela on the north coast south to the interior valley of La Vega Real due to the proximity of gold deposits. The effects of Spanish prospecting and coercion of the Indians to acquire food and labor for the construction of the various forts were quickly felt by the peoples of this area. Sauer (1969:84) relates an incident that occurred during the spring of 1494 at the Yaque River crossing, in the heart of the Vega Real. Captain Alonso de Hojeda captured a *cacique* and members of his family and cut off the ears of the Indians because they allegedly stole clothes from the Spaniards. Irrespective of whether they stole clothes or not (which itself is suspect, since they had no use for such articles), the punishment inflicted upon them must have had a chilling effect on the Indians and set the tone for what was to follow.

In 1494, Hojeda, following Columbus's instructions, set out to capture another *cacique*, Caonabo, *cacique* of Maguana, a region located in the central mountain area south of La Vega Real. The story of his capture is well known (Sauer 1969; Wilson 1986:173; Las Casas 1951:I:406–407; Fernández de Oviedo 1959:I:56). The Spanish considered Caonabo to be dangerous, since they were led to believe by Guacanagarí, *cacique* of Marien and his rival to the north, that he was responsible for the death of the Spaniards left at Fort La Navidad during the first voyage. This apparently sealed Caonabo's fate as the first major Indian *cacique* captured and imprisoned by the Spanish.[3]

Spanish prospecting for gold, demands for food and labor, and actions against Indian leaders led to the first Indian uprising, which occurred late in 1494. Indians of the Macorix area attacked one of the Spanish forts, called Magdalena, on the Yaque River crossing (Sauer 1969: 87).[4] The Spanish retaliated by raiding the Macorix area and taking 1600 Indians as slaves. Miguel de Cuneo, who was a direct observer, gives a vivid description of how 550 of these were taken on board four caravels that left La Isabela on February 17, 1495, and how many were thrown overboard on the trip to Spain, having succumbed to disease (Varela and Gil 1984:257–258). This first incident of raiding Indian territories and enslaving Indian captives was to become widespread in the Caribbean and was later legally justified by the Spanish Crown (Royal Provision of December 20, 1503; in Rumeu de Armas 1975:75–6).

On March 24, 1495, Columbus began a mission of conquest into other areas of the interior of the island (Las Casas 1951:I:414). With a force of 220 men, plus the *cacique* Guacanagarí and his Indians as allies, he embarked on a ten-month march beyond La Vega Real during which, after various battles[5] and skirmishes, he subjugated the Indians and captured the *cacique* Guarionex (Las Casas 1951:I:413, 416). He built fort Concepción de la Vega close to Guarionex's village (Sauer 1969:89) and imposed tribute in gold, cotton, and foodstuffs (Moya Pons 1978).

This was the beginning of a period of famine among the Indians (1495–1496), and scarcity among the Spanish as well (Moya Pons 1992: 131). Las Casas attributed it to the fact that many Indians fled the fields and purposely discontinued planting, as a tactic to force the Spanish to leave (Las Casas 1951:I:419). Wilson (1986:184–185) argues that it possibly had to do with the disruption of native food production due to Spanish intervention. He argues that the effects of the famine were greater in 1496, the year after the ten-month rampage by the Spanish into the interior of the island, which is when the manioc tubers that should have been planted the previous year would have been harvested. Another factor may have been the Spanish demands for food that further strained the indigenous subsistence base.

Upon Christopher Columbus's return to Spain in 1496, the administration of the incipient colony was left in the hands of his brother Bartolomé, who was often called "El Adelantado" (Fernández de Oviedo 1959:I:60). Bartolomé continued in his brother's footsteps, exploring new areas and constructing another fort, Bonao, close to the newly discovered San Cristóbal goldfields (Sauer 1969:91). He also founded the town of Santo Domingo at the mouth of the Ozama River (Sauer 1969:92; Deagan 1990:241).

Bartolomé Colón marched west to the Indian province of Xaraguá (in present-day Haiti), seat of an important chiefdom led by *cacique* Behecchio. Here he was received by the *cacique* and his sister Anacaona (wife of Caonabo). Ethnographic descriptions of this encounter (Las Casas 1951: I:441–443, 447–448) attest to the complexity of Indian social and political organization and to the power of authority over subordinates that the leading chiefs exercised. Offerings of large quantities of food, including *hutías* and iguanas, considered choice items by the Indians, and of other prestige goods suggest the productivity of this area and its ability to generate an agricultural surplus.

The hierarchical character of the Indian chiefdoms of Hispaniola is also evident in this encounter. Bartolomé Colón required that *cacique* Behecchio provide tribute, and an agreement was reached that it would be in cassava bread and cotton, since gold was unavailable in the Xaraguá region. This incident also shows that the famine and depopulation alluded to for the central region under Spanish authority did not extend to Xaraguá. Here, if the description of the encounter is accurate, indigenous social structure and subsistence were intact. It also suggests that Behecchio's authority as *cacique* included the ability to influence his people to provide the required tribute, and illustrates how the Spanish used the native political structure to leverage this tribute.

Meanwhile, in the area of La Vega Real, 14 *caciques* subordinate to Guarionex rebelled (Wilson 1986:186–187) under the strain of the imposed tribute (Sauer 1969:93; Las Casas 1951:I:445). They were quickly suppressed by Bartolomé Colón in a night raid in which all, including Guarionex, were captured (Wilson 1986:186). Bartolomé Colón released Guarionex and again demanded the resumption of tribute. By this time, Guarionex apparently was unable to exert authority over the other *caciques* in the area and fled north to the neighboring territory of another *cacique*, Mayobanex (Las Casas 1951:I:458; Sauer 1969:93).

Some scholars have argued that Guarionex's reluctance to participate in the rebellion is an indication that there were no powerful hierarchical chiefdoms headed by supreme chiefs (Wilson 1986:187). However, it can equally be argued that Spanish actions eroded the chief's authority and ability to control the actions of his people to pay tribute and conduct warfare. Guarionex, by fleeing to the territory of his ally Mayobanex, may have been attempting to recruit additional manpower to confront the Spanish.

Both Mayobanex and Guarionex were captured by Bartolomé Colón (Las Casas 1951:I:461), and many of their subjects were enslaved and shipped off to Spain (Sauer 1969:93; Wilson 1986:199–200). It is not clear why Mayobanex, at the risk of having his territory subject to Spanish retaliation, gave asylum to Guarionex. Las Casas (1951:I:462) mentions that Mayobanex was indebted to Guarionex for teaching him a special *areito* (ceremonial song usually accompanied by music and dance), which suggests a ritual obligation. The fact the chiefs were of different ethnic groups (Mayobanex was identified as a Ciguayo by the Spanish) but appear to have shared social or ritual obligations suggests that the chiefdoms, although they may have been competing for power and territory, shared kinship, trade, and/or other ties.

Meanwhile, at the beginning of 1497, Bartolomé Colón returned to the province of Xaraguá to collect the expected tribute. Chief Behecchio and Anacaona again received him. The tribute of various types of food, cotton, and numerous prestige goods was transported overland to the coast, where a waiting Spanish ship transported it to La Isabela (Moya Pons 1978; Las Casas 1951:I: 447–448). The disruption of native life occurring in the central part of the island apparently had no effect on the Xaraguá area or on its ability to produce enough surplus to satisfy Spanish demands. This supports the Spanish chroniclers' claims that Xaraguá was the most developed of the Indian chiefdoms in Hispaniola (Las Casas 1967:II:308–310).

At the same time in 1497, upon El Adelantado's return to La Isabela from Xaraguá, Spanish men under the leadership of Francisco Roldán, *alcalde mayor* (district governor or Mayor) of La Isabela, revolted against the rule of the Columbus family.[6] Roldán and his followers took refuge in the food-rich Xaraguá area and dispersed to live among the Indians (Las Casas 1951:I:456). According to Moya Pons's account (1978:24), upon Christopher Columbus's return to Hispaniola on August 31, 1498, two separate Spanish factions controlled different areas of the island: his brothers and those who remained loyal to him in the environs of La Isabela, south through the La Vega Real to the newly founded city of Santo Domingo; and Francisco Roldán and his followers in the Xaraguá area to the west. The Indians were thus exploited on two fronts, but in very different ways. In the case of Roldán and his men, they were able to persuade their way into the native villages and live among them in small groups, while Bartolomé and his men continued to demand tribute from the *caciques* whose authority and power the Spanish had already undermined.

When Columbus returned to Hispaniola he came with the Crown's authority, a Letter of Patent of July 22, 1497 (Moya Pons 1978:26; Sauer 1969:100–101), to distribute lands to Spaniards who would settle in the island and work. Roldán demanded as one of the conditions for peace that he and his followers be given *repartimientos* (allotments) of Indians with their respective lands, which were to be worked by the Indians for the benefit of the Spanish settlers. Columbus conceded this. It effectively sanctioned Roldán's previous actions by extending as official privilege what he was already doing in Xaraguá. This apparently harmless concession formed the basis for the system of forced labor imposed upon all of the Indians of this island and other Spanish colonies, known as the *encomiendas* (Sauer 1969:100–101; Las Casas 1985:II:87; Moya Pons 1978: 28–29; Hanke 1951:15–16).[7]

In the period of the late 1490s Spanish settler unrest continued, as Columbus was unable to effectively reestablish his authority. Meanwhile, the Spanish Crown, under the influence of the powerful Bishop Juan Rodríguez de Fonseca,[8] instituted measures designed to limit the Columbus family's original concessions in the Spanish Indies and to establish the incipient colony under direct Crown administration.[9] Fonseca named Francisco de Bobadilla governor of Hispaniola. When Bobadilla arrived at Santo Domingo in the year 1500 and found Spanish settlers again in revolt against Columbus and his brothers (Bartolomé and Giacomo, also known as Diego), he had the latter jailed and sent to Spain in chains (Las Casas 1985:II:202; Sauer 1969:103; Moya Pons 1978:32; Pietschmann 1999:100; Haring 1947:12).

Under Bobadilla, the situation on the island stabilized. No new Spanish revolts occurred. He allowed the Spanish settlers to continue exploiting the Indians' labor, and gold prospecting began in earnest (Las Casas 1985:II:204; Sauer 1969:105–106; Mira Caballos 1997:100).[10] The Spanish continued to live among the Indians and to take the Indians' labor and lands for their own benefit. No new towns were settled, and no further expansion into as yet unconquered areas of the island occurred. Roldán and his followers continued as the dominant force on the island.

Las Casas's description of this period (1500–1502) (1985:II:202–204) portrays a caricature of Spanish society whose members' roles have been inverted—a society that had disintegrated to its most primitive level. The Spanish, who had been members of the common class in Spain and now had been living in rags for lack of clothes and almost any type of commodities, were here assuming the position of nobles and rulers over entire Indian communities (Moya Pons 1978:38–39). In the remote wilderness of a foreign territory, Spanish men—inferior subjects in their own land—became the dominators, internalizing the ideology of the dominant class in Spain and trying to reproduce it in Hispaniola.

As this situation transpired in Hispaniola, Fray Nicolás de Ovando arrived on the island in 1502 as the newly appointed governor.[11] He disembarked with 2500 persons (Moya Pons 1978:43), far in excess of the mere 300 Spanish who were then living dispersed among the Indians in Hispaniola.[12] Fray Bartolomé de Las Casas was a member of this expedition. According to him, many of the newcomers immediately rushed to the goldfields, where at least a thousand of them died from disease shortly after arrival (Las Casas 1985:II:226; Sauer 1969:148).

Ovando's mission was to institute a viable colony on Hispaniola for the benefit of the Crown, based on the exploitation of Indian labor to extract gold (Moya Pons 1978:50). He was instructed to assemble the Indians into villages close to the gold-mine fields, which were to be exploited for the Crown. Following the Crown's instructions, he ordered that no Spaniard could force any Indian to work without just compensation (Mira Caballos 1997:101). However, Ovando was faced with the reality of Spanish settlers who had no interest in working themselves and were already accustomed to depending upon native labor for everything they needed, especially in prospecting for gold (Sued Badillo 2003:278), and Indians who were not inclined to serve the Spanish and fled when they could (Mira Caballos 1997:101).

However, Ovando realized that he could not follow his instructions to the letter if the Spanish were to make productive use of Indian labor, so he opted to continue the practice of *repartimiento* begun by Columbus. He expanded the system to cover the entire island; and to do so, he had to gain control over the chiefdoms that were still independent as of 1502 (Moya Pons 1978:44–45).

Las Casas, a direct observer of this period, described the following events: the destruction and depopulation of Saona Island, off the southeastern coast of Hispaniola, where the Indians had produced cassava bread for Spanish consumption; the march to Higüey (southeastern Hispaniola); the peaceful reception given to Ovando and his men by Anacaona (sister of Behecchio and widow of Caonabo) at Xaraguá, only to be massacred along with 84 *caciques* (Las Casas 1985:II:229–233; Sauer 1969:148–149);[13] Diego Velázquez's (later the first governor of Cuba) subjugation of the western section of Hispaniola by marching southwest to the "province" of Guacayarina (Las Casas 1985:II:240; Sauer 1969:149); and Juan de Esquivel's and Juan Ponce de León's (the latter to become the first governor of Puerto Rico) participation in the conquest of Higüey in 1504, known as the Wars of Higüey (Las Casas 1985:II:269; Sauer 1969:149).[14]

Ovando was thus unsuccessful in his attempt to induce the Indians to congregate in villages close to the mine fields, as required by the Crown (Moya Pons 1978:51; Mira Caballos 1997:108). Furthermore, the newly arrived settlers who had come with Ovando were demanding that they be provided with Indians as well. The extraction of gold required native labor; hence native submission was necessary. As mentioned previously (Moya Pons 1978:44–45), this was the real motive for the infamous wars of this period. When the wars were over, the Spanish controlled the entire island and the *encomienda* system was firmly in place. These actions received official sanction by the Queen in the famous Decree of December 20, 1503 (Moya Pons 1978:51; Rumeu de Armas 1975:77; Mira Caballos 1997:102), which permitted the use of Indian labor in exchange for a nominal salary.

Another important aspect of Ovando's governorship (1502–1509) was the establishment of 15 Spanish *villas* (figure 2.2).[15] Concepción de la Vega, La Buenaventura, and San Juan de la Maguana were located close to the gold mining areas.[16] Some, such as La Vera Paz and Salvaleón de Higüey, were founded in the vicinity of former Indian villages.[17] Oth-

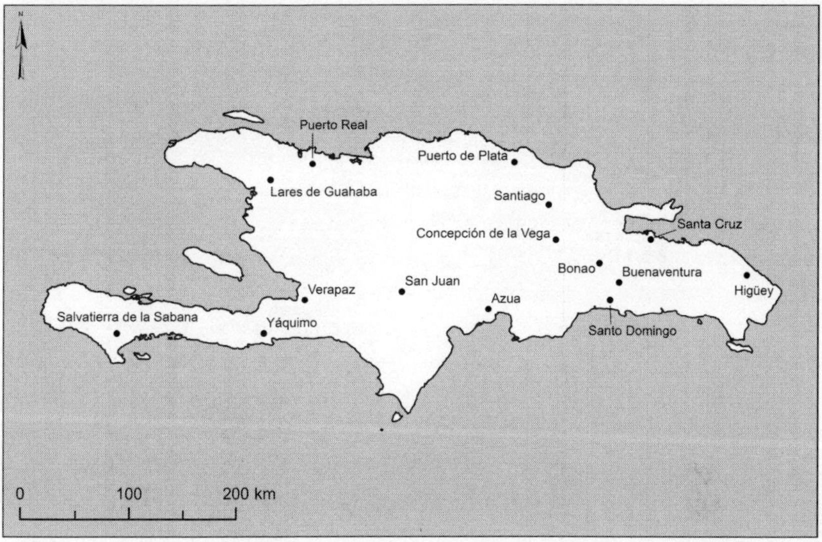

Figure 2.2. Hispaniola, Spanish settlements under Ovando (based on Sauer 1969:152, figure 20; Anderson-Córdova 1990:80).

ers, such as Puerto Plata, Puerto Real, and Salvatierra de la Sabana, were located far from the mining areas. This distribution contributed to the exploitation of the Indians and the institution of the *demora* system, whereby groups of natives from outlying villages were transported for months at a time to work in the mining areas (Moya Pons 1978:56). Historical documents attest to the effectiveness of the gold exploitation and smelting system established by Ovando. Between 1505 and 1506 there was a 220 percent increase in gold production and between 1506 and 1507 it increased by 112 percent (Mira Caballos 2000b:34, table I), all based on the exploitation of native Indian labor.[18]

The effects of Ovando's policies on the Indian population began to be felt as early as 1506 (Moya Pons 1978:67). The first general *repartimiento* was in 1505, in which Ovando favored his friends, Spanish officials, and members of the elite on the island, and was carried out without the express consent of the Crown (Mira Caballos 1997:104–105, 2010:49). Due to the decline in the number of Indians, other *repartimientos* were carried out to redistribute the remaining population.[19] The need to acquire Indians from other areas to supplement the declining native population was brought to the attention of the King and sanctioned by the Crown in 1508 (Moya Pons 1978:72). This provided a new enterprise for the burgeoning aristocracy of the island; slaving expeditions were first started to

Cuba and the Bahamas (known at the time as the Lucayan Islands) from the north coast Spanish towns of Puerto Plata and Puerto Real (Moya Pons 1978:73; Sauer 1969:159; Las Casas 1985:II:348–351).

Hispaniola served as the center for the expansion of colonizing efforts to the Greater Antillean islands of Jamaica, Puerto Rico, and Cuba. In 1509, Ovando, whose sojourn on the island made him probably the richest man in the Americas at the time (Mira Caballos 2000b:128–131), was replaced by Diego Colón (Columbus's son) as governor of Hispaniola. However, the Crown appointed Miguel de Pasamonte as treasurer and alcalde mayor (district governor or district mayor) of the Fortaleza de La Concepción, and, in order to finance the Crown's mounting European debt, King Ferdinand instructed the Spanish officials on the island to increase gold production (Moya Pons 1978:92–93). This only caused greater hardship to the Indians, contributing to further depopulation. The need to find new labor sources to counteract the native Indians' declining numbers provided continued incentive for the colonists' raiding expeditions.

On October 5, 1511, the Crown appointed three men—Lucas Vázquez de Ayllon, Marcelo de Villalobos, and Juan Ortíz Matienzo—to take care of judicial matters on the island, establishing the first Real Audiencia (Court of Appeals) of Hispaniola (Moya Pons 1978:103).[20] The ten-year period between 1502 and 1511 had seen the consolidation of the *encomienda* system in Hispaniola. The entire economy depended on the production of gold, and this in turn depended on Indian labor.[21] An island elite was forming, in which political and economic power was held by those who had the authority to allot Indians and those who had gained their favors (Moya Pons 1978:55–58, 68–69). During this decade the Spanish population of the island declined as well; many of the towns founded by Ovando were abandoned (Sauer 1969:200).

The first public outcry denouncing the condition in which the Spanish had placed the Indians occurred in 1511, with the famous sermon by the Dominican Friar Antonio de Montesinos. The uproar, both on the island and in Spain, that followed this sermon has been recounted many times and brought to bear what proved to be an unsolvable contradiction between evangelizing Indians that were purported to be free vassals of the Crown and exploiting them in the gold mines and Spanish *haciendas* (country estates) under the *encomiendas.* Suffice it to say here that a series of meetings took place at the Spanish Court to address the issue of the treatment of the Indians, resulting in the enactment of the Laws of Burgos (Murga Sanz 1971:92–97; Konestzke 1953:I:38–57).[22]

Almost all scholars of this period agree that these laws were largely ignored and had no influence on the well-being of the Indians of the Antilles. In fact, Moya Pons argues that the Crown's declaration that the Carib Indians could be justifiably enslaved ensured that they could be kept to work in the mines under Disposition 27, which stipulated that enslaved Indians were exempt from the protection of the law. He further argues that King Ferdinand's decrees allowing Indians brought from other islands to be used as slaves, and the transfer of Indians from Hispaniola to Puerto Rico and vice versa, were just excuses to circumvent the legal effects of the Laws of Burgos by increasing the indigenous populations exempt from its application (Moya Pons 1978:131–132; 136–138).

The text of the Repartimiento of 1514 offers a glimpse into Spanish colonial society and the plight of the Indian peoples of the island during the middle years of this decade. The document provides irrefutable evidence of the drastic reduction of the Indian population. It also attests to the continuation of the policies begun by Ovando—the concentration of economic and political power on the island in the hands of a limited number of individuals (Moya Pons 1978:158–159)—and the atomization of the original Indian communities. As a consequence of the 1514 Repartimiento, this decade witnessed the continued abandonment of the original Spanish settlements, as those Spaniards who had been deprived of Indians sought to leave the island to continue their search for gold elsewhere (Moya Pons 1978:172–173).

King Ferdinand died in 1516, and the Crown's affairs rested briefly with Cardinal Francisco Ximénez de Cisneros. At this time, the plight of the Indians of Hispaniola and of other recently settled islands was being openly discussed in court. Cardinal Cisneros appointed three friars of the Hieronymite order to take charge of the affairs of Hispaniola. Their authority extended to the islands of Puerto Rico and Cuba as well. They were instructed to inquire into the status of the Indians and determine one of three possible actions: freeing them and placing them in permanent villages; creating villages under the tutelage/protection of a Spaniard; or keeping the *encomiendas* but requiring strict adherence to the Laws of Burgos (*Ordenanzas de Burgos 1512–1513*; Mira Caballos 2010: 345–346). The three friars arrived on December 20, 1516 (Moya Pons 1978:225).[23] Licenciado (attorney) Alonso de Zuazo was also appointed to carry out the official *juicio de residencia* (judicial review or proceedings of an administrative investigation) of the three previously appointed judges of the Audiencia Real of Santo Domingo.[24]

The friars proceeded to carry out an inquiry in which 14 of the longest-established residents of the island were queried as to the nature and disposition of the Indians and their capacity to live in freedom. Their opinions concerning how best to protect the Indians from further destruction were also solicited. This document, known as the Hieronymite Interrogatory, has been analyzed by Hanke (1935) and others (see also Mira Caballos 2010:343–370). Despite the almost unanimous opinions expressed by the Spaniards concerning the Indians' inability to live in freedom, which was to be expected since all the witnesses of the Interrogatory had vested interests in preserving the status quo, their answers provide insight into the natives' response to the Spaniards and indicated that remnants of their previous way of life were still being manifested a generation after conquest.

After hearing the arguments and traveling to the Indian communities and mining areas of Hispaniola, the friars, contrary to the opinions of those questioned in the Interrogatory, decided to end the *encomiendas* and establish free Indian towns (Mira Caballos 2010:348–349). They started to group Indians into 30 planned towns (Sauer 1969:204–205). These did not prosper, due in large part to the 1519 smallpox epidemic, which caused further decimation among the Indians (Sauer 1969:205), and to the vociferous opposition of the island's residents and officials (Mira Caballos 2010:348–349). This brief period of reforms ended with the death of Cardinal Cisneros and the ascension to the throne of King Charles I. The reins of government in Hispaniola returned to the three previous judges (Vázquez de Ayllon, Villalobos, and Ortíz Matienzo) and Licenciado Rodrigo de Figueroa became the new *juez de residencia* (administrative judge) (Moya Pons 1978:225).

During the 1520s, with the government again in the hands of Diego Colón but subject to the judicial authority of the Audiencia Real, the expansion of the Spanish into large areas of the New World, including the north coast of South America, Central America, and Mexico, broadened the base of operations for a lucrative Indian slave trade (Otte 1956, 1977; Las Casas 1985:II:551). Despite the change of emphasis from gold to a more diversified production based on the cultivation of sugarcane and livestock, trade in Indian slaves remained a profitable business. This trade gradually declined in importance, with the depopulation of many areas from which the Indians were being brought and with the increased reliance upon African slaves to replace the Indian population.

Toward the end of the 1520s, the Spanish population of Hispaniola continued to be depleted as it became the source of manpower for the expanding New World frontier. The Spanish who stayed behind lived mainly in dispersed settlements across the island. Various documents that mention Indian uprisings begin to appear in the historical record at this time. These were the first rebellions to occur since the beginning of the colonial period. Rather than full-blown rebellions, these were mostly incidents of groups of Indians fleeing, or attempting to flee, to areas outside Spanish control—Indians whom the Spanish termed *indios alzados.* The most notorious was the group led by Enriquillo, a former *encomienda* Indian who in 1519 (Fernández de Oviedo 1959:I:124) escaped and took refuge in the hills of Bahoruco (see figure 2.1).[25]

The disruption of Indian communities caused by the smallpox epidemic and the reallocation of Indians into villages under the Hieronymites may have been factors, but the actual trigger for his actions is unknown (Altman 2007:595–598). However, Enriquillo and his followers, which throughout the years grew into the hundreds and included women, children, fugitive Africans and Indian slaves and servants, and some mestizos (Altman 2007:598), were never captured by the Spanish. They were able to live independently in the mountains and evade many Spaniards' attempts at capture, establishing an almost self-sustaining, mobile community. Negotiations for a truce began in 1528, and five years later, in 1533 (Fernández de Oviedo 1959:I:124, 127), the King of Spain himself sent word to Enriquillo requesting that he accept peace (Peña Battle 1948:105). A few months later, Enriquillo agreed and returned with his followers to live independently in a village close to the town of Azua, where he lived until his death in 1535, dying as a Christian and buried at his request in the village church (Altman 2007).

Other Indian groups that had taken to the hills during this period were apparently operating independently of Enriquillo. As part of the peace accord, Enriquillo and his community were granted their complete freedom, but in exchange, Enriquillo agreed to assist the Spanish in the capture of other insurgents. The extent to which he did this is not entirely clear, but, as pointed out by Altman (2007), Enriquillo probably thought that he had to accommodate the Spanish in this respect in order to come to terms with them (see also Mira Caballos 1997:317–320). This incident illustrates the complexity of Spanish-Indian interactions in this early period and the fact that native peoples were still able to negotiate and were active agents in their own lives.

By the 1530s, historic documents indicate that few native Indians remained in Hispaniola.[26] Importation of Indian slaves from other areas continued. When the New Laws for the Protection of the Indians were enacted in 1544, Licenciado Alonso López de Cerrato, who was sent to the New World colonies to ensure compliance with these laws, which categorically declared all Indians to be free, still found Indian slaves in

Puerto Rico and Hispaniola (Sherman 1971:27–28; AGI Patronato 173, no. 1, p. 11).[27]

Puerto Rico

The island of San Juan Bautista de Puerto Rico was discovered by Columbus on November 19, 1493, during his second voyage. Previous reference to this island had been obtained by the Spanish from Indian women and juveniles of Puerto Rico (called Borikén by the Indians) encountered in the islands of Guadeloupe and St. Croix, respectively (*Relación de Miguel de Cuneo* in Varela and Gil 1984:240–241; Las Casas 1951:I:353, 355).[28] The stopover somewhere along the west coast of Puerto Rico was brief, and apparently no Indians were encountered (Las Casas 1985:I:355).

After this brief sojourn in 1493, Puerto Rico disappears from the historical record until 1504, when the Crown authorizes Vicente Yáñez Pinzón to explore the island and build a fort (Murga Sanz 1971:34), an authorization that was not acted upon. The official beginning of the conquest and colonization was in 1508, when Juan Ponce de León was allowed by Governor Nicolás de Ovando to explore the island and to prospect for gold (HDPR 1973:II:519). This was an extension of Ovando's efforts to increase gold production for the Crown.

There is one important document, known as the *Probanza de Juan González*,[29] which places Juan Ponce de León's first voyage to Puerto Rico in the year 1506 (Tió 1961:30–109). Witnesses testifying in this document indicate that a Spaniard named Juan González Ponce de León (Juan Ponce de León's cousin) participated in this first voyage, serving as an interpreter.[30] He apparently had mastered the Indian language of the Higüey region of Hispaniola and was able to communicate with the Indians of Puerto Rico. Thus, the exchange of information between Spanish and Indians occurred within a context of better communication than did the first encounters 14 years earlier. The encounter occurred somewhere along the south coast of the island, and the witnesses indicated that it was peaceful. The customary exchange of gifts took place. Upon Juan Ponce de León's inquiry about the location of a good bay, the Indians indicated that there was an excellent one on the north coast but that they had never been there, since they were at war with the Indians who inhabited that area (Tió 1961:47–48, 69–70). Juan Ponce de León stayed in the village of a *cacique* known as Mabo el Grande (Tió 1961:49), while Juan González and others (including the witnesses testifying in the *Probanza* document) crossed the island through the interior to the Bay of

San Juan. Many Indian villages were found along the way. As in previous reports of the first Spanish encounters with the Indians of Hispaniola, the Indians are described as providing gifts. The initial march through the interior was peaceful at this time (Tió 1961:70).

Further testimony in this document refers to what happened during Juan Ponce de León's second visit to Puerto Rico in 1508. Ponce de León informs about this in his 1509 *Relación*, given in the Villa de la Concepción, Hispaniola (HDPR 1973:II:519–522). Ponce de León sailed for San Juan on July 12, 1508, with a crew of 50, from Salvaleón de Higüey where he resided at the time. He mentions a storm on August 3, in which he lost some of the food being transported for this new venture. He stopped over at Mona Island, where he found Indians and *caciques* living (HDPR 1973:II:530). He landed on the south side of the island of Puerto Rico, in the territory of *cacique* Agüeybaná, on August 12. He also mentions another storm on August 10.

According to Ponce de León's testimony, he asked Agüeybaná to prepare a *conuco* for the Spanish, to which the *cacique* agreed (HDPR 1973:II:520). Fernández de Oviedo (Fernández Méndez 1981:40) indicates that Agüeybaná's mother advised him to treat the Spanish well, in order to avoid being killed, as had happened to the Indians of Hispaniola.[31] This clearly shows that the Indians of Puerto Rico were aware of the events in Hispaniola, which is not surprising, due to the proximity of the two islands, the commonality of language and culture, and the evidence for communication between the Higüey area of Hispaniola and the island of Puerto Rico, especially its south and west coasts. There is also evidence of close kinship ties between Agüeybaná's chiefly family and the chiefly families in eastern Hispaniola (Sued Badillo 2008:33).

From the land of Agüeybaná, Ponce de León proceeded along the coast until he arrived at the Bay of San Juan (figure 2.3). He mentions talking to island *caciques* and Carib Indians along the coast, although he does not specify whether it was the west or north coasts: "After provisioning the said vessel, I left the place bordering the said Island and talking with the *caciques* along the coast as well as the Caribs that I found there, and giving them presents, as a safeguard, until I arrived at the bay that is on the north."[32]

Ponce de León further indicates that he explored some of the rivers along the north coast and established a settlement (later named Caparra). He sent the ship back to Mona Island for food. He also sent men to prospect for gold but could not proceed because of lack of food. This is puzzling, since there were only 50 men with him and they had twice

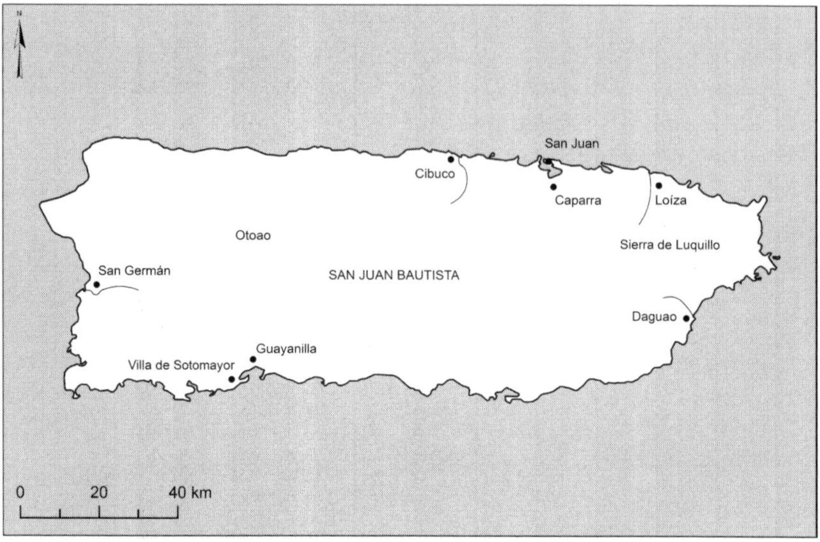

Figure 2.3. Puerto Rico, early-sixteenth-century geography (based on Anderson-Córdova 1990:92).

acquired food on Mona Island. Ponce de León implies that he could not acquire food from the Indians because he had been instructed not to do so (HDPR II:521; Murga Sanz 1971:37):

> I got gold with a crew, but was unable to use three as I planned, because there was no food for the people, and because I was unable to avail myself from the Island, nor from the Indians of said Island. . . . [33]
>
> Because up to now we have been unable to do more than to require the *caciques* to plant crops for His Highness, and there are five *caciques* that have been required to plant crops in their houses for His Highness; and this is all that we have been able to do for now, and no more, because we have moved the town three times, and because we have no food to eat and there is no food in this island, even if I wanted to take it, and because I have not been able to take advantage of the Indians of the said Island as it should be, because of this nothing else can be done.[34]

This testimony contradicts his previous statement, since it indicates that there was no food available for the Spaniards, even if they had wanted to take it from the Indians. Maybe what Ponce de León was observing was the effect of the two storms or hurricanes that delayed his sailing for Puerto Rico and may have struck the island before his arrival.

In the *capitulación* (contract of exploration) presented by Juan Ponce de León on May 1, 1509, he again indicates the lack of food on the island of Puerto Rico, as well as the lack of food in Hispaniola and Mona Island that could be transported to Puerto Rico (HDPR 1973:II:523–524). He requests permission to purchase food from the *caciques* of Puerto Rico or from neighboring islands, if any is available (HDPR 1973:II:524).

This document also mentions the return of Carib Indians whom Ponce de León had captured on the island of St. Croix. He inquires whether he should insist that they plant *conucos* for the Spanish and release the Indians from Puerto Rico whom they held captive (HDPR 1973:II:524). Ponce de León's request that Indian canoes at Higüey, Mona Island, and Puerto Rico be burned to avoid the movement of Indians and/or Spaniards into Puerto Rico suggests that such movement was occurring (HDPR 1973:II:525). This request was denied by Ovando (see HDPR 1973:II:528).

The beginning of the colonization of Puerto Rico coincides with the period in which Nicolás de Ovando is replaced by Diego Colón as governor of Hispaniola. According to Murga Sanz (1971:46), King Ferdinand named Juan Ponce de León governor of Puerto Rico on September 15, 1509, although the decree was not received in the New World until much later. However, settlement of the island continued, following the pattern of Hispaniola. The King extended authority to Ponce de León to allot *repartimientos* to colonists wishing to settle on the island, and this process began in earnest in 1509 (Mira Caballos 1997:193). Colonists from Hispaniola were involved, as well as many who came directly from Spain, carrying decrees authorizing them an allotment of lands and Indians upon their arrival (Murga Sanz 1971:46). Although, as was the case for Hispaniola, the official document pertaining to this first Repartimiento did not survive, judicial lawsuits of the period indicate that only 5,000 Indian men and 500 Indian women were allotted, that government officials received the largest number of Indians (up to 100 per official), followed by settlers and *conquistadores*, and that married men were preferred over single men (Mira Caballos 1997:194–195).

Shortly thereafter, Diego Colón named Juan Cerón alcalde mayor of the island of San Juan. Cerón took over his post on October 28, 1509, and proceeded to carry out another *repartimiento* of all the Indians, taking away from established settlers those Indians previously allotted by Ponce de León (Murga Sanz 1971:47; *Colección de documentos inéditos relativos al descubrimiento, conquista y organización de las antiguas posesiones es-*

pañolas de América y Oceanía, hereafter CODOIN 1864–1880:I:35:457–526). Meanwhile, on March 2, 1510, King Ferdinand named Ponce de León captain governor of the island of Puerto Rico. An identical decree dated June 15, 1510, arrived at San Juan de Puerto Rico at the time when Miguel Díaz was arriving from Hispaniola to occupy the post of alguacil mayor (municipal chief justice or high sheriff), which had been given him by Diego Colón (Murga Sanz 1971:51), much as Bobadilla had done with the Colón brothers years before on Hispaniola.

The power struggles between Diego Colón and his interests and those of the Crown, as represented in Puerto Rico by Juan Ponce de León, adversely affected the Indian communities, who were reshuffled among various *encomiendas*. Juan Ponce de León had allotted *repartimientos* to the first settlers, as he had been authorized to do by the Crown, only to have these superseded by Juan Cerón when he took over as alcalde mayor under the authority of Diego Colón. Las Casas (1985:II:376) indicates the manner in which the Indians were given out in *repartimientos* as the cause of the rebellion that began in February 1511 (Murga Sanz 1971:63).[35]

Fernández de Oviedo (Fernández Méndez 1981:45–49) and Las Casas (1985:II:388) report that the *caciques* of the island formed a confederation to fight the Spanish. The rebellion started in the land of *cacique* Agüeybaná.[36] The Spanish had settled in their *haciendas*, dispersed over the countryside in small numbers, and the Indians attacked them (Fernández Méndez 1981:45; Las Casas 1985:II:388; Tió 1961:52–53). Agüeybaná, whom most authors indicate was the leader of the rebellion, attacked and killed Don Cristóbal de Sotomayor and his men, who, warned about the Indian plot to kill them, were attempting to flee Agüeybaná's village.[37] Then Agüeybaná and his followers proceeded to burn the town of Sotomayor. In this skirmish, Juan González Ponce de León was injured but managed to escape and make his way through the island's Central Cordillera to the Toa area on the north coast, where he informed Juan Ponce de León of what had happened (Fernández de Oviedo [1959], in Fernández Méndez 1981:49).

Upon receiving word of the uprising, Ponce de León retaliated by marching to the land of Agüeybaná, surprising the Indians gathered there by attacking at night (Fernández de Oviedo (1959), in Fernández Méndez 1981:57). Fernández de Oviedo indicates the Carib Indians participated in the uprising,[38] but Murga Sanz (1971:66, 129) discounts Carib participation. However, various witnesses testifying in the *Probanza de Juan González*, cited previously, allude to a general uprising of most of the Indians in the island and mention the presence of either Carib Indians or Indians from neighboring islands (Tió 1961:92–93, 57–58, 75).[39] Sued

Badillo also acknowledges Carib participation but stresses that this was a widespread rebellion that originated with and was led by *caciques* from Puerto Rico (Sued Badillo 1978:144–145, 2008). The *Probanza* document mentions a trip by Juan González Ponce de León to one of the neighboring islands[40] where many Carib Indians were captured, allegedly because of their participation in the rebellion and in the killing of Cristóbal de Sotomayor. Indians from the island of Puerto Rico were also found there and were gathered by the Spaniards and returned as slaves (Tió 1961:58, 75–76).

Fernández de Oviedo's account of the Indian rebellion is sensationalistic in its description of the valor of the Spanish captains, especially Diego de Salazar and the exploits of the infamous mastiff Becerrillo (Fernández Méndez 1981:58–59). The battles between Spaniards and Indians were imprecisely confused and merged into the first one at Yagüeca and the later burning of the town of Caparra. Murga Sanz (1971:66–67) discounts most of this account. He argues (1971:65) that, after this first encounter of the Spanish and Indian forces in the land of Agüeybaná, Juan Ponce de León delivered an ultimatum for the other *caciques* of the island to surrender (the infamous Requerimiento)[41] but that the Indians refused. Fernández Méndez (1984:26) indicates that only two of the island *caciques* surrendered: *cacique* Caguas, of the Turabo area, and *cacique* don Alonso, of the Utuado area. What followed was a series of retaliatory actions by various Spanish captains, which are mentioned in the documents as *guerra postrera de Ponce de León.* Evidence of Indian slaves taken in these raids, termed *cabalgadas,* is present in various Treasury documents, published in Murga Sanz (1971:280–288) and in DRHPR (1971:I; n.d.:II).These actions by the Spanish resulted in an exodus of Indians from the island of Puerto Rico to the neighboring ones of Vieques, Culebra, and maybe others of the Virgin Islands.[42]

While these events were unfolding in Puerto Rico, Diego Colón was again appointed Viceroy of the Indies, and he proceeded to reappoint Miguel Díaz and Juan Cerón as alguacil mayor and alcalde mayor, respectively, of the island of Puerto Rico (Murga Sanz 1971:73). According to their royal instructions for the government of the island (July 25, 1511), they were to carry out a new *repartimiento,* to assure that the Indians were put to work in the goldfields, and to pacify any who remained recalcitrant. They were authorized to persecute, capture, and send rebellious Indians to work as slaves in the gold mines of Hispaniola (Murga Sanz 1971:75).[43]

Cerón and Díaz founded a new settlement in the southwestern part of the island, in the general vicinity of where the villa de Sotomayor had once stood (Murga Sanz 1971:81). They informed King Ferdinand that the Indians were in rebellion (*alzados y alborotados*) (Murga Sanz 1971:86) and proceeded to authorize a series of raids in various sections of the island. The Treasury documents mentioned previously (AGI *Contaduría* 1071; in DRHPR 1971:I and n.d.:II) detail many of the raids (referred to in the documents as *cabalgadas* or *entradas*) made by the Spanish at this time, as well as many occurring later as the rebellion persisted. Probably many others occurred that do not appear in the relevant documents. This tactic of entering Indian villages to capture and pillage had its antecedents in Hispaniola. The argument to the effect that the Indians had rebelled against the Spanish and could therefore be captured and reduced to slavery provided a justification for acquiring slaves. It was also profitable for the Crown, since it received a fifth of the value of each slave taken. This explains why these raids appear in the Treasury documents.[44]

On December 23, 1511, King Ferdinand authorized general war against the Carib Indians. Expeditions from Hispaniola and Puerto Rico were thus allowed, with the purpose of capture and enslavement of these Indians. Incidents describing raids by the so-called Carib Indians (see chapter 1) in the territory of Puerto Rico begin appearing in the historical record after this date. These include skirmishes along the north coast, where many Spaniards and local Indians were killed, including the *cacica* Luysa; the entrance of the Caribs into the Daguao area; and the burning of the city of Caparra during the summer of 1513 (Murga Sanz 1971:133). Murga Sanz (1971:134) lists a series of Spanish raids that occurred in 1513 in lands of the *caciques* of the central and eastern mountainous area of Puerto Rico as probably carried out under the excuse of the "Carib invasion."[45] Sued Badillo documents 18 raids against the territories of rebel *caciques* in the mountainous interior of the island in 1512 and another 23 that occurred in the month of March 1513 (2008: 132–133).[46]

On September 22, 1514, *fiscal* (Crown attorney) Sancho Velázquez arrived in San Juan with authority to carry out a new *repartimiento* (Mira Caballos 1997:198). He did so, with the predictable results of those settlers not benefiting by the allotments of Indians objecting vigorously (Murga Sanz 1971:169–170).

When the Hieronymite friars began their governorship in 1517, Puerto Rico was in a situation similar to that described previously for Hispaniola. The *repartimientos* of 1514–15 had benefited the established royal authorities and had removed many Indians from long-established settlers, just as had happened with the 1514 Repartimiento in Hispaniola

(Mira Caballos 1997:198–202). The Repartimiento of Sancho Velázquez in Puerto Rico took place amid pockets of Indian resistance, and many errors were committed with respect to the numbers of Indians allotted to various *vecinos* (see, for example, *Memoria de Melgarejo* 1582 in Fernández Méndez 1981:112–113). Although the text has been lost, related documents appear to indicate that only about 6,000 Indians were allotted, and of those only three-fourths were able to be located, the rest apparently being absent (Mira Caballos 1997:199). The residents refused to comply with the 1513 Laws for the Protection of the Indians (Murga Sanz 1971:186, based on documents published in Serrano y Sanz 1918; see also Mira Caballos 1997:196–197, 204).

Both *encomienda* Indians and Indian slaves were used extensively in the mining operations that were the main source of income for settlers and the Crown during the first years of Puerto Rico's conquest and colonization. As was the case in Hispaniola, large quantities of gold were extracted from Puerto Rico, and this quest for gold fueled the Indian slave trade, as the native Indians succumbed from overwork, disease, and lack of food. Sued Badillo (2001) documents the critical importance of gold mining for the early economy of the island and the horrendous conditions under which the Indians labored, and shows how the decline of the gold economy was due not to the depletion of gold sources but to the scarcity of Indian labor (see also Anderson-Córdova 2005). Gold mining activities, which were concentrated in the interior mountains of Puerto Rico (Sued Badillo 2001; Anderson-Córdova 2005), were occurring as pockets of rebellion and flight from the Spanish continued. This was a period of increased uncertainty and disruption of Indian social and community life.

After the second decade of the sixteenth century, only sporadic mention of the Indians of Puerto Rico appears in the historical record. The period of Indian rebellion, extending off and on from 1511 to 1515, was considerably longer than in Hispaniola, or anywhere else in the Caribbean (Sued Badillo 2003:282). After the 1520s, references concerning Indians relate to Carib raids, which continued at a reduced rate throughout the sixteenth century. These raids involved native Indians as well as Caribs, the former having left the island as a response to Spanish exploitation (Brau 1966:258; Sued Badillo 1978:152, 157). The relatively small Spanish population of the island since the beginning of the colonization effort may have allowed the Indians to maintain pockets of resistance longer than in Hispaniola. Other possible factors may have been the Puerto Rico Indians' prior knowledge of Spanish tactics (Sued Badillo 2003:282), and the more fluid, less hierarchical nature of Indian chiefdoms on the island, and their kinship and social connections with surrounding island populations.

The accessibility of neighboring islands as refuge spots and the dispersed nature of the Spanish population of Puerto Rico may also have contributed to the persistence of Indian raids. The timing of these raids in relation to major hurricanes that hit the island of Puerto Rico, especially in the years 1526 and 1530, may be an important indication of environmental hardship (Salivia 1972; Sued Badillo 1978:159–162). Sued Badillo (1978:142) points out the major impact that a storm can have on a small island, such as Vieques or St. Croix, for example, compared to the more localized impact on larger islands such as Puerto Rico. (The 1989 hurricane that ravaged Guadeloupe, St. Croix, Vieques, and Culebra islands and then struck the northeastern section of Puerto Rico, sparing the rest of that island, is a case in point.) It may not be a coincidence that the raids may have been due in part to the need to acquire food and other necessary resources from Puerto Rico in times of environmental stress (Sued Badillo 1978).

Despite the official ban on Indian slavery in 1530, the exemption of the Caribs from this ban meant that islands such as Puerto Rico and Hispaniola could continue to legally acquire Indian slaves from the Lesser Antilles. The 1530 census carried out by Governor Francisco Manuel de Lando (Ramírez de Arellano 1934:20–64) attests to the very small Spanish population living in the two towns that existed at the time (see also Lluch Mora 1986), as well as the existence of a majority of Indian slaves, when compared with the free Indians listed.[47] When Alonso de Cerrato visited the West Indies in 1544 it is probable that Indian slaves were still held in Puerto Rico, although the numbers, to my knowledge, have not been documented.[48]

Although most sources cease to mention Indians after this period, there is sporadic reference to the persistence of small numbers of Indians well into the latter part of the sixteenth century. These specify that the survivors were not natives of the island but rather Indians brought as slaves from other areas.

Cuba and Jamaica

As was the case for Puerto Rico, expeditions from Hispaniola under the Ovando administration set out to conquer the other two Greater Antillean islands; the conquest of Jamaica occurred in 1509, and Cuba in 1510

(Valcárcel Rojas 2012:40). With the Spaniards' firsthand knowledge of the sociopolitical and religious characteristics of the indigenous chiefdoms, and with the experience of Hispaniola still fresh in their minds, the conquest of these two islands was swift indeed. Also, the early economic system of exploitation of Indian labor under the *encomiendas* was already being institutionalized in Hispaniola, which made it easier for the Spanish to quickly establish their presence on these islands. Therefore, Diego Velázquez, one of Hispaniola's early settlers and *encomenderos*, who participated in the subjugation of the western part of Hispaniola and became the first governor of Cuba, wasted no time in distributing the Indians in *encomienda*. The *encomienda* system was officially recognized in Cuba in 1513 and in Jamaica in 1515 (Valcárcel Rojas 2012:40).

As in Puerto Rico, the indigenous inhabitants of Cuba and Jamaica were already aware of the Spanish presence in their neighboring islands. They knew about the fate of their brethren on these islands and developed their own strategies of resistance and/or accommodation. For example, in Cuba rebellion started quickly (although it was short-lived compared to that in Puerto Rico) (Valcárcel Rojas 2012:41; Sued Badillo 2003:280–282). *Cacique* Hatüey, who was originally from western Hispaniola and fled to Cuba in the wake of the Xaragá massacre, led the first resistance until he was captured and burned at the stake (Sued Badillo 2003:281, citing Las Casas 1965:II:507). Within two years, the conquest of Cuba was complete (Mira Caballos 1997:281).

The reasons for the lack of widespread rebellion against the Spanish invaders in the cases of Cuba and Jamaica have been attributed to the lack of hierarchical organization of their chiefdoms (Valcárcel Rojas 2012:40; Sued Badillo 2003:281), which made it more difficult for them to coalesce into a more focused resistance. However, the Spaniards were also much more experienced in the nuances of Indian politics and kinship and they wasted no time in exploiting this knowledge to their strategic advantage. Therefore, the period of initial contact was short on these islands, giving way to the quick establishment of a colonial system based on the exploitation of their labor (Valcárcel Rojas 2012:41).

The pattern of various *repartimientos* occurring to benefit the Spanish elite on the islands with the expected effect on Indian communities occurred much more rapidly in Cuba, although the Spaniards' control of the island was much weaker than in the rest of the Greater Antilles (Sued Badillo 2003:281). Pockets of Indian resistance occurred in the decade of the 1520s among the first generation of Indians born under Spanish rule, the most important one mentioned in the sources being *ca-*

cique Guamá in the region of Baracoa (extreme eastern Cuba) (Sued Badillo 2003:282).[49] In Cuba, the use of Indian labor for gold prospecting and mining continued to be important for a much longer time than in the other islands (Mira Caballos 1997:185–186), while in Jamaica, where there was no gold, Indian labor was used in agricultural and textile production to fuel Spanish expansion into the mainland (Tierra Firme) (Bryan 1992:23–24; Morales Padrón 2003).

What is most interesting about Cuba is the abundance of historic, ethnographic, and archaeological sources that document the persistence of native peoples throughout the colonial period and even up to the present. There are numerous historic archaeological sites in Cuba where there is clear evidence of European-Indian interaction and of historic period Indian and mestizo communities (Valcárcel Rojas [2012, 2016] offers an up-to-date summary of this research). Cuba is almost unique in the Greater Antilles in this respect (although there is evidence of historic Indian communities in Hispaniola as well). It is possible that the more dispersed settlement of the indigenous populations and their less hierarchical organization may have allowed them to be more flexible in their responses to contact and colonization, but most important, I think, is the much larger territorial area of Cuba, which allowed the Indians ample places to hide and persist independently. This may explain why Indian communities, albeit small, persisted in Cuba and not Jamaica.

The Organization of Labor in the Spanish Caribbean Colonies

As we have seen in this chapter, the early colonial economy of these islands was based on the forced exploitation of Indian labor under two distinct but interrelated institutions: the *encomienda* system and slavery. Both had devastating effects on the islands' native populations and were the main cause of their eventual demise. Under the *encomienda* system, groups of Indians and their respective *caciques* were allotted to individual Spaniards, or to the Crown, to work in the gold mines or in Spanish *haciendas* or households. Most of the *encomienda* Indians were Island natives and are referred to as service Indians and *naborías* in the early Spanish documents.

The second institution of forced Indian labor was outright slavery. Indian slaves also worked in the gold mines and *haciendas*. However, as slaves they could be bought and sold and were not subject to protection under the laws that governed the use of *encomienda* Indians. Indian slaves were mainly foreign Indians brought into the islands to supplement the dwindling native populations but also included native Indians who had rebelled against the Spanish.

These two systems of forced labor cemented the early economy of these islands and made Spanish colonization possible. As will be seen, they were an integral part of early colonial state formation and socio-political culture. Enslaved Africans became the substitute labor force as Indian populations decreased.

3
Cultural Transformations
Indian Response to Contact

When carefully read and analyzed, the historical narratives of the early Spanish exploration and colonization of the Greater Antillean islands offer clues as to how these islands' native populations responded to and were transformed by these events. In addition, historic archaeological investigations of early-sixteenth-century Spanish and/or Indian settlements have unearthed material evidence not available from written sources that shed light on how these transformations occurred. A perusal of this early history that focuses on teasing out the Indians' strategies in dealing with the Europeans provides an opportunity to flesh out Indian/Spanish interactions from the Indians' perspective.

This chapter summarizes the historical literature on Indian response to contact within the framework of three time periods, which, as we have seen, varied in their beginning and length as the different islands of the Greater Antilles were explored and colonized by the Spanish. Initial Euro-Indian contact occurred in Hispaniola from 1492 to 1494, and in Puerto Rico in 1493 and from 1506 to 1508. Conquest and pacification followed in Hispaniola from 1494 to 1504, and in Puerto Rico from 1509 to 1515, and resulted in changing historical circumstances that affected the Indian communities' social, cultural, and physical environment. This was followed by the imposition of a system of forced labor (*encomienda* and slavery), during which the processes of disintegration of Indian communities were put in motion and set the state for the influx of foreign Indians into the islands. In Hispaniola this occurred from 1504 to approximately 1550, and in Puerto Rico it began in 1509, concurrently with the conquest and pacification phase.

Besides specific references to Indian behavior under Spanish rule (obviously biased toward the Spanish perspective), which shed light on the strategies employed by the Indians to deal with their situation as subject peoples, the historical record also provides information on the social transformations that occurred in the Indian communities as a result, first, of conquest and pacification and, later, of being subject to various forms of forced labor.

Documentation, though scant, provides information on the distribution of Indians during the historic period, the organization of Indian labor for work in the mines, fields, and households, and the relationship between the *encomienda* Indians and those subject to outright slavery. The 1514 Repartimiento of Hispaniola and the 1517 Hieronymite Interrogatory documents are particularly important in this respect. They permit inferences concerning the processes of social and cultural change among Indian communities during the historic period.

Hispaniola

Initial Contact: 1492–94

The strategies developed by the native Indians as a response to the sudden arrival of the Spanish consisted of flight, exchange of food and other items, and accommodation.[1] Columbus's diary of the first voyage (Varela 1982:15, 146) provides information on these strategies. The descriptions that follow are taken from the above-cited Varela edition. The pages consulted are listed after the source, and the equivalent passage from Las Casas (1951:I) follows.

Columbus sighted the island of Hispaniola on December 5, 1492, arriving on the north coast at Point San Nicolás on December 6 (72–73; 250–253). His first mention of the Indians occurs on December 6: "All the Indians fled, and continued to flee when they saw the ships" (75).[2] The same response is recorded at Puerto de la Concepción on December 7 (76; 255). On December 12, while still in this area and unable to communicate with the Indians, the Spanish captured one woman, who, after being clothed and returned to shore, indicated the location of a village (78; 285–259).[3] Upon arrival at the village, the Spanish found it deserted. Its inhabitants were coaxed into returning by the Indian guide that accompanied them. The Indians proceeded to their dwellings (*ivan todos a sus casas*) and brought food for the Spanish. Parrots (*papagayos*) were also presented, apparently because the Indian interpreter indicated that they were prized by the Spanish (79–80; 259).

Columbus quickly saw the benefit of capturing Indians to serve as interpreters. On December 16 he captured a solitary Indian found in his canoe in the waters between the north coast of Hispaniola and the island of Tortuga and sent him ashore to an Indian village bearing trinkets obtained from the Spanish (82). Indians flocked to the ships and exchanged minuscule amounts of gold. The village chief also boarded the vessel and partook of food with the Admiral (83; 262). This partaking of food on Columbus's ship by Indian *caciques* and their closest followers and the reciprocal offering of food by the chiefs in their villages are repeatedly mentioned in the narrative of the first voyage.[4] The same chief returned the next day and again ate with Columbus (85, 86). He also gave him a belt (*cinto*) and two thin pieces of gold.[5] The presentation by the chief of these two types of offerings indicates that the Indians, despite their lack of understanding of the Spanish language, recognized the status of Columbus vis-à-vis the other Spaniards. The presentation of prestige items associated with the Caribbean chiefs, such as beaded belts, masks, and gold pieces, attests to this. The Indians' initial impression that the Spanish were powerful individuals (or gods) and that some had more status than others is reflected in the types of goods the chiefs offered. More mundane gifts, such as cassava bread and water, were brought to the Spanish ships by the general populace, who came in droves to see them (88, 89, 93, 94; 273).

The distinction between the type of goods given to Columbus and his emissaries by the *caciques* and those given by the commoners to the rest of the Spanish sailors is apparent in the following entry of December 23 (95; 273):

> This king (Guacanagarí) gave much honor to the people on the ships, and each of the common folk brought them something to eat and drink. Afterward, the king gave to each one some cotton cloths worn by the women and parrots for the Admiral and certain pieces of gold; the common folk also gave the sailors the same cotton cloths and other things from their dwellings, and even the smallest thing that they received they seemed to treasure as relics.[6]

The diary also documents what appears to be competition between neighboring villages for the favor of Spanish company, as noted below in the entry for December 21 (91):

> After the six Christians had left, certain canoes came with people who pleaded with the Admiral, in the name of another chief, that he come to his town when he left that place. And since the chief's town was on the way, on a point of land, waiting for the Admiral with many people, the Admiral went there. And before he took leave, many folks, men, women and children, came loudly calling for him not to go, but to stay with them. The other chief's messen-

> gers who had come with the invitation were waiting in their canoes, to make sure that he did not leave without seeing their chief. And he did so; and when the Admiral arrived where the chief was waiting for him, there were many things to eat, and the chief ordered all his people to sit, and ordered that the food be taken to the Admiral's ships, at the seashore.[7]

The remaining time spent by Columbus in this area of the north coast, under the hospitality of chief Guacanagarí, is occupied in the reciprocal exchange of gifts and visits between the ship and the Indian village. These Indians assisted the Spaniards in the storage of goods recovered from the *Santa María*. Contacts remained peaceful. The Spanish could not afford to upset the Indians of an island where they were forced to leave 39 of their own, and the Indians had no reason to attack the Spaniards. The relationship was apparently one of reciprocity and a certain degree of accommodation on the part of the Indians to Spanish requests for food and gold. The encounter up to this point was one of two very different but still autonomous and independent groups assessing each other on their own terms.

The only evidence of conflict between the Spanish and Indians occurred in an area on the north coast called by Columbus *El Golfo de las Flechas* (Gulf of Arrows) (118; 305), where they had stopped to gather food and water for the return journey. Columbus speculated that they may have been Caribs (114), and he also mentions that they spoke a different language (115). Apparently the Spaniards tried to acquire more of the bows and arrows than the Indians were willing to give, and a brief skirmish ensued, resulting in the flight of the Indians (115; 303–304). The following day, the pattern of exchange of gifts is established with these Indians as well (117).[8]

Upon Columbus's return late in 1493, he found Fort La Navidad burned and his men dead. It seems that chief Guacanagarí sought to appease Columbus, since he knew that he would be upset at the fate of his men. Guacanagarí sent messengers with gifts to Columbus (Las Casas 1951: I:356). Guacanagarí's version of the Spaniards' demise, as interpreted by Columbus, was that the men had been killed by Indians subject to another chief called Caonabo.[9] Whether this was what truly happened is not known, but the incident does attest to the existence on the island of other chiefs of equal or greater authority than Guacanagarí.

The Indians of the territory governed by chief Guacanagarí and those who inhabited the interior villages of the island continued to assume a friendly attitude as the Spanish marched into the interior in search of gold. Las Casas (1951:I:372) relates how they came to greet the Spaniards along the way, and brought food and small trinkets of gold. This situation quickly deteriorated into Indians' flight from the villages, either because the Spaniard's demands for food were becoming excessive (Las Casas 1951:I:375) and individual Spaniards were raising havoc in the villages or because the threat of war with Caonabo was real (Las Casas 1951:I:378). It thus appears that in these initial encounters, the rules of reciprocity and exchange among Indian chiefs and the Spanish worked effectively until the Spanish, from the Indians' perspective, exceeded their demands. The Indian's killing of the Spaniards left at Fort La Navidad indicates both a response to Spanish excesses (which included the abuse of Indian women), and perhaps also the conflict between the competing chiefdoms of Guacanagarí and Caonabo.[10]

Conquest-Pacification: 1494–1504

Whatever the actual trigger of events, the relationship between the Spanish and Indians deteriorated from the initially friendly contact based on reciprocity to conflict. According to Las Casas (1951:I:402), the Indians rebelled because the Spanish made excessive demands for food, took their women and enslaved their children, and did not respect the power and authority of the *caciques.* The Spaniards were no longer in Hispaniola to exchange with the Indians and look for the sources of gold. They knew gold was available and where to exploit it. Their attitude and actions with respect to the Indians changed, and the Indians responded accordingly. Whether they actually rebelled against the Spanish at this time, as implied by Las Casas, or simply opted to flee from their villages, is not clear in the sources. Las Casas (1951:I:402) indicates that the four *caciques* of the island rebelled, which does not seem possible, since most of the native territory of the island was still outside direct Spanish influence. As discussed previously, Columbus proceeded to carry out a pacification campaign throughout just the interior of the island, which lasted nine or ten months, and imposed tribute on these conquered Indians (Las Casas 1951:I:416–417).

According to Las Casas (1951:I:419) and Mártir de Anglería (1944:45), and accepted by Cassá (1979:63), the Indians' response, upon seeing that outright confrontation was ineffective, was to quit cultivating their *conucos* in order to force the Spanish out of the island by starvation. Cassá (1979:63) believes that the plan backfired and caused starvation among the Indians, because they were a sedentary population unable to subsist solely on gathering, fishing, and hunting.[11] The possibility that the Indians' actions were not premeditated but rather a result of the collapse of the Indians' agricultural base under the "pacification" and tribute system imposed by Columbus was discussed in the previous chapter.

Elsewhere in Hispaniola the Indians presumably continued their livelihood more or less independently of the events of the north-central area of this island. The Indians were most certainly aware of the Spanish presence and its consequences, since communication among different parts of the island must have continued. The fact that no general rebellion occurred may be an indication that the various chiefdoms were politically independent. Las Casas's descriptions of the "kingdom" of Xaraguá in northwest Hispaniola, where chief Behecchio and Anacaona reigned, in the context of Bartolomé Colón's two visits and Ovando's later massacre of Anacaona and numerous subordinate chiefs are the most detailed surviving accounts providing insights as to how the native elite functioned and exercised regional chiefly authority. This has been discussed in detail elsewhere (Wilson 1986) and was briefly mentioned in the previous chapter. Suffice it to say here that the elite class of Xaraguá received the Spaniards in about the same way as chief Guacanagarí had three years earlier: by welcoming them to the village and offering food and gifts. The fact that the food was plentiful and varied and that the prestige items were more elaborate only attests to the relative wealth of the Xaraguá area in comparison to Marien. The Xaraguá offerings suggest that the events unfolding in nearby areas had not affected the ability of the Xaraguá chiefdom to produce food and a variety of prestige goods.[12] The willingness of the Xaraguá chiefdom to provide the tribute imposed by the Spanish may indicate the chiefdom's realization that confrontation was useless, or its confidence in its ability to provide the tribute and thereby avoid Spanish encroachment into its territory.

Forced Labor: 1504–1550

During the governorship of Nicolás de Ovando, the Indian population was violently subjugated and survivors distributed among the Spanish settlers, officials, and absentee owners under a system known as *encomienda.* The Indians' response to their violent suppression and to being parceled out to work in the gold mines far from their native villages is described in a very general way by most of the early chroniclers. Their primary response after the "wars" of Xaraguá and Higüey was to flee, which resulted in their persecution by horse-back-riding Spaniards in raids (*cabalgadas*), who captured and enslaved many (see chapter 2 this volume, and Las Casas 1985:II:232–233). The principal *caciques* were killed (Las Casas 1985:II:240, 269) and the rest were given out in *repartimientos.*

The Indian response to their condition as subject peoples also included suicide, by drinking the poisonous juice of manioc (Las Casas 1985:II:337) or by inhaling the poisonous smoke of certain leaves (Mártir de Anglería 1944:456); abortion and infanticide (Las Casas 1985: II:250); and flight to marginal areas of the island or to other islands (Mártir de Anglería 1944:500). Although these actions on the part of the Indians may be construed as acts of desperation from helpless people, I believe they also demonstrate a conscious decision to escape from their oppressors at any cost. Even in these extreme actions, the Indians were not passive receptors of Spanish oppression but active agents in their own right.

During the 1520s, when the gold economy of Hispaniola suffered from a scarcity of Indian laborers and the island was turning toward the cultivation of crops such as sugarcane and relying on the importation of African slaves, *encomienda* Indians escaped and persisted as "rebels" in marginal areas of the island. As discussed previously, this coincided with the decrease in Spanish population, as people sought riches elsewhere in the conquests of the northern coast of South America (Tierra Firme), Mexico, and later Peru. No historical evidence exists concerning other types of Indian response to continued contact at this time. However, archaeological research in early Spanish and Indian settlements indicate that Indian communities persisted on the island, although they were not reported nor described in the historical records. We shall return to this issue later.

Puerto Rico

Initial Contact: 1493, 1506–1508

The initial Indian response was very similar to the pattern already discussed for Hispaniola. The island was discovered during the 1493 voyage, but this did not result in an encounter between Spanish and Indians, since the latter apparently fled upon seeing the vessels approach. Upon later contact, they did not flee (*Probanza de Juan González* in Tió 1961; *Relación de Ponce de León 1509* in HDPR 1973:II), apparently because they already knew of the existence of the Spanish in neighboring Hispaniola.[13] The Spanish were well received and escorted to the north coast by Indians from the south part of the island. The exchange of names between Juan Ponce de León and chief Agüeybaná is mentioned (HDPR 1973:II:520), something that is not described in the early accounts of Hispaniola.[14] The *Probanza* document, as described previously, suggests that the Spaniards' march through the interior to the north coast was greeted by the Indian inhabitants in much the same manner as the natives of Hispaniola had received Columbus and his men in their first march to the interior of that island in 1493. Indians of the south area of Puerto Rico served as escorts, and along the route many came to greet them and exchange gifts of food and other items.

Conquest Pacification and Forced Labor: 1509–1550

In Puerto Rico, Juan Ponce de León wasted no time in requiring the Indians to plant *conucos* for the Crown's benefit (*Relación de Ponce de León 1509* in HDPR 1973:II:520–521). On September 24, 1510, Ponce de León established eight agricultural plots or *conucos* in various areas of the island, seven of which he sold publicly among the settlers (Fernández Méndez 1984:16–19). Gold prospecting began almost immediately, and the Indians were promptly parceled out to Spanish settlers. Thus, the *encomienda* system was quickly instituted on the island. The initial contact, characterized by the exchange of food and gifts and certain accommodation on the Indians' part to the requests for gold, quickly deteriorated into outright exploitation.

In February 1511, the Indians of Puerto Rico rebelled. Contrary to what occurred in Hispaniola, where Ovando and his men thought it necessary to subdue the entire island in order to establish Spanish settlements and institute the *encomienda* system, in Puerto Rico the Spaniards were few in number and opted to establish themselves in small *haciendas* dispersed across the island. No "pacification" occurred in Puerto Rico before the establishment of the *encomiendas*. Apparently, the Spanish did not consider the Indians too much of a threat, and, taking advantage of their prior knowledge of indigenous sociopolitical hierarchies and the important role played by *caciques*, began to use them immediately for agricultural work and gold prospecting.[15] This situation quickly intensified until the natives, perhaps taking advantage of the dispersed pattern of Spanish settlement, rebelled. Indian rebellion was relatively more successful (in the short run) than was the case in Hispaniola. As previously discussed, this may have been due to the opportunity that the Indians had to escape to neighboring islands and to return to raid Spanish settlements.

Puerto Rico, in contrast to Hispaniola and Cuba, has very few first-hand historical accounts of its conquest and colonization. Despite this, the limited evidence available suggests that there was one important difference between events in Hispaniola and in Puerto Rico. The chiefdoms of Puerto Rico appear to have been less hierarchically organized than those of Hispaniola (although this may be more an artifact of the lack of historical descriptions of these chiefdoms).[16] However, alliances between chiefs of different areas of the island are implied in the accounts of the rebellion (see Fernández de Oviedo [1959], in Fernández Méndez 1981, the *Probanza de Juan González* in Tió 1961, and Sued Badillo 2008, as discussed previously). It is possible that the much smaller geographical extent of the island of Puerto Rico may have made such alliances easier than in the much larger island of Hispaniola. The existence of Carib Indians from outside the island is mentioned in the earliest accounts of the *Probanza* document and in Ponce de León's *Relación* (in HDPR 1973:II:519–530). The persistence of Indian raids on Puerto Rico, probably originating from Vieques, Culebra, St. Croix, and other neighboring islands, as well as the retaliatory raids by the Spanish, in which Indians from San Juan were found and returned to the island, have been mentioned. It appears, then, that a considerable number of Indians of Puerto Rico opted to flee the island rather than face defeat.

The establishment of the *encomienda* system resulted in the Indians either accommodating the Spanish demands or fleeing to neighboring islands. If the above-quoted historical accounts are true with respect to the role played by the Carib Indians as allies in the rebellion, it may be an indication that strong ties of kinship, trade, and/or ritual considerations existed between them (Sued Badillo 1978, 2008). As discussed in chapter 1, archaeological evidence, such as found at Salt River Bay on St. Croix, suggests that the Indians of Puerto Rico were expanding into the neighboring Virgin Islands before Spanish contact. Similarities between the late prehistoric ceramic complexes of eastern Puerto Rico and the U.S. Virgin Islands suggest that the latter were part of the Caribbean chiefdoms' sphere of influence.[17] It is possible that the Puerto Rico Indians were able to utilize their close ties with the Indians of the smaller islands in their strategies to cope with the Spanish conquest of their territory. They were thus able to utilize the fleeing strategy more effectively than were their kin in Hispaniola.

Transformation of Native Social and Political Organization and Persistence of Cultural Traditions

The above discussion provides a general picture of the Antillean Indians' response to contact with the Spanish from the period of initial encounter to the period of colonization and the imposition of forced labor. Historical sources also provide information on the transformation of native social and political organization and suggest the persistence of certain native cultural manifestations. Las Casas (1967:II:175) describes the *cohoba* rites in Hispaniola, which he observed firsthand. He mentions *behiques* (shamans), the use of *duhos* (ceremonial chairs), and the inhalation of snuff. The date of his observations is not known but must have been sometime after 1502, when he arrived at Hispaniola. Fernández de Oviedo (1959:I:114) witnessed the performance of *areitos* in Hispaniola in 1515, although he did not think much of them, compared to the ones he had observed on the South American mainland (Tierra Firme).

In addition to the records of the early chroniclers, there are other sixteenth-century documentary sources that provide clues to the persistence of Indian cultural traits among the remnant populations of the islands. These consist mainly of accounts concerning proposed remedies to check the vertiginous decline of the native population, which became a growing concern during the second decade of the sixteenth century. Documents dating from the period of the regency of Cardinal Cisneros are revealing in their practically unanimous appraisal of the nature of the Indians and why they were so diminished in number. All informants seemed to be keenly aware that the *encomienda* system was responsible for the demise but were unable to arrive at the only logical solution, which was to free the Indians from further servitude. This contradiction was woven into the very fabric of colonial society and economy.[18] As argued by De La Luz-Rodríguez (2003:9–11; 2004:83–99), the *encomienda* system was more than a system of forced labor. It served as a colonial social structure that legitimized the economic exploitation of the Caribbean's native peoples within an ideological and political rubric that formed the basis of the emerging colonial society in these islands.[19]

The Hieronymite Interrogatory of 1517

The documents for this period include several accounts of colonists, clergy, and officials from the islands that address the issue of the Indians and their demise.[20] One of the most important documents of this period is the Hieronymite Interrogatory of 1517 (in Rodríquez Demorizi 1971: 273–354), which provides information on the condition of the Indians and their actions under the Spanish. As mentioned previously, this document consists of a collection of the responses of various long-term residents of Hispaniola to the questions posed by the Hieronymite governorship. Two main issues queried were whether the Indians had the ability to live as free vassals of the Spanish Crown and whether they should be collected and placed to live in villages close to the Spanish settlements or permitted to remain under the system of *encomiendas.*

This document has been analyzed by historians (see, for example, Hanke 1935) in the context of the evolution of Spanish policy concerning the Indians and the philosophical and theological questions posed by their servitude and quick demise. My interest in analyzing this document is for what it can tell us about the Indian response to contact. Information on various aspects of Indian culture at this point in time (25 years after discovery) is provided, albeit from the dominant culture's point of view. The testimony of the various witnesses is illuminating, despite the fact that all had something at stake in legitimizing the Indians' continued servitude and all had *encomiendas* or served the Crown in an official capacity.

Their testimony is unanimous in asserting the Indians' inability to govern themselves following the Spanish model of free laborers and in stressing the persistence of cultural traits that reflect their previous way of life. In addition to the cultural survivals mentioned, the testimony touches on the social aspects of the relationship between Spanish and Indians and on the organization of Indian communities and their relationship with each other. The basic pattern of *caciques* with their Indians (sometimes referred to as *naborías*) inhabiting separate villages is mentioned, as well as the persistence of a dispersed settlement pattern of villages located far from the centers of Spanish control. The disintegration of Indian communities under the *encomienda* system and the decrease in population are evident in the witnesses' description of Indian behavior and references to the lack of authority and control of many *caciques* over their Indians. The testimony suggests differences and antagonisms among Indian communities and the existence of both large and small native villages. The cultural and social characteristics of the Indian peoples of this period, as viewed by the Spanish informants in the Hieronymite Interrogatory, are discussed below.

Persistence of Cultural Traits

Cohoba rites. Various witnesses mentioned Governor Ovando's experiment (the Spanish term is *experiencia*, which literally means experience in English) in which he took certain Indians who lived among the Spanish and were fluent in the Spanish language and gave them *repartimientos* of their own. The witnesses indicate that these Indians spent their time in vagrancy and reverted to their ancient customs, including the preparation of *cohoba*.[21]

Areitos and ballgames. The persistence of *areitos* and ballgames among the Indians is mentioned by various witnesses, both within the context of Ovando's earlier "experiment" and in other examples. All consistently mention that they would practice their *areitos*, ballgames, and *cohobas* upon returning to their villages after working in the gold mines and the Spanish *estancias*; all witnesses argue that if given their liberty, this would be all that they would do.[22]

Bohites or *behiques* (medicine men, shamans) in the Indian communities. This is mentioned by one witness in two different contexts. Marcos de Aguilar (Rodríquez Demorizi 1971:346–347) states that old *behiques,* who knew how to prepare a poisonous concoction that when burned and inhaled produced death, were interviewed by him in 1511, in relation to an alleged conspiracy by the Indians of the Higüey region upon knowing about the rebellion of the Indians of Puerto Rico. Aguilar also mentions the existence of *behiques* in his general testimony regarding the activities of the Indians in their villages.[23] *Behiques* had extensive knowledge of herbal remedies and cures for different maladies and held a privileged position in Indian communities before contact. It appears that the Indians tried to keep this knowledge from the Spanish, as a means of passive resistance (Mira Caballos 2010:428).

Ritual vomiting, cleansing, and feasting. Various witnesses mention having observed the practice of food gorging among the Indians and interpret it as proof of their inability to take care of themselves. What these witnesses describe[24] is clearly the persistence of the practice of ritual feasting characteristic of the Indians before contact, examples of which abound in the ethnographic literature of chiefdoms. In aboriginal times it may have served as a mechanism for redistributing surpluses and of reinforcing the *caciques'* authority and prestige.

Shifting of villages. One witness, Pedro Moreno (Rodríquez Demorizi 1971:334), mentions the custom of abandoning a village, taking all possessions, and establishing a new settlement elsewhere. He indicates that he was informed by his Indian wife that this was also practiced before the arrival of the Spanish. This practice is common among horticulturalists practicing slash and burn agriculture, and may still have been customary in the Greater Antilles despite the increased productivity of *conuco* agriculture. The disruption of native agricultural production resulting from the Spanish colonial enterprise may have required the Indians to rely more on shifting cultivation.

Indian Settlements, Social Relationships, and Response to the Spanish

The Interrogatory document also provides information concerning Indian settlements, social organization, and psychological responses to the conditions of forced labor. Various witnesses indicate the persistence of Indian villages dispersed throughout the island, some quite removed from the centers of Spanish population and the gold mining areas. They are also unanimous in their opinions concerning the Indians' strong reactions about moving their villages close to the Spanish, suggesting that they fled to the woods and threatened to commit suicide if forced to abandon their villages. It appears that under the conditions of exploitation in which they lived, the Indians clung to the last remnants of their way of life, which could only be recreated or reenacted in their own villages. The historical evidence indicates that the conditions of forced labor and the long periods of proximity to the Spaniards, which occurred during the *demoras* (the time that they were away from their villages working in the gold mining areas), were not conducive to Indian acculturation. Despite the extreme conditions under which they labored, the Indians did not assimilate. On the contrary, all consulted sources that mention the Indians at this time indicate that they rejected contact with the Spanish and would "forget" the Catholic doctrine immediately upon returning to their villages.

Apparently, the strategy adopted by the *encomienda* Indians was to work for the Spanish since they could not do otherwise, and then return to their villages and perform their traditional customs. In this respect, it is comparable to the ethnographically documented response of the Pueblo Indians, termed "compartmentalization" by Spicer (1961a:533).[25] Under a colonial system based on forced labor, inequality, and extreme exploitation, the "cultures in contact" became "cultures in conflict." The strategy of compartmentalization allowed the Indians to reinforce their values and worldview within the context of their villages, however reduced they may have been in number and population.

The Interrogatory document also suggests that there were still relatively large (actual size unknown) Indian villages on the island. Witness Jerónimo de Aguero (Rodríquez Demorizi 1971:289) indicates that the larger villages that still had legitimate *caciques* would be more difficult to move into towns close to the Spanish, presumably because they were still able to recreate some measure of their former life. Conversely, he argues that it would be easier to reduce scattered Indians into villages (presumably because these remnant groups lacked the social cohesion of the larger settlements): "The difficulty of moving them is only with the major *caciques*; the minor ones are easier to bring into towns because they do not have vice-ridden villagers like the larger ones, because they hide in the hills or in solitary and sterile places and not in places where their vices make them hesitant to come to the Spaniards' *haciendas*."[26]

Another witness, Lucas Vázquez de Ayllon (Rodríquez Demorizi 1971: 308–328), provides key information on how important maintaining native social and village ties was for their biological and cultural preservation. He indicates that the "naborías de casa," who were Indians employed in Spanish households, were more acculturated and had some rudimentary knowledge of Spanish customs, language, and of the Catholic religion.[27] He also mentions that the Indian villages that were located farther away from Spanish settlements had the largest populations, in contrast to those located in close proximity to the Spanish (Rodríquez Demorizi 1971:316). (This is also mentioned by another witness [1971: 335], although it is in contradiction with the 1514 Repartimiento document.) Another aspect of Vázquez de Ayllon's testimony that tends to corroborate the importance of maintaining ties with native communities for the biological survival of the Indians is his impression that Indian women who were married to Spaniards and those who lived with Spanish women, although generally better treated than those who worked in the fields, suffered high mortality and morbidity (1971:328).[28]

Evidence for the disintegration of chiefly authority within the surviving Indian villages, as well as rivalry among existing villages, is also apparent in the Interrogatory testimony (Rodríquez Demorizi 1971:309, 315). The loss of population in the villages and the usurpation of the traditional authority of the *caciques* may have created conditions for insubordination (Rodríguez Demorizi 1971:312–313). Under these conditions, traditional kinship ties and relations of reciprocity among villages must have been affected, resulting in increasing intergroup rivalry.

The Interrogatory testimony thus provides the following scenario: dispersed Indian villages of varying sizes, some with bona fide *caciques* and others with none, which had lost most of their intervillage social and cultural ties. The Indians who lived in these villages maintained their rituals in an effort to survive as communities but were isolated one from the other. No widespread rebellions were possible (although the Spaniards continued to raise the possibility of Indian rebellion as justification for maintaining the *encomiendas*); only the isolated flight of small groups into the hills and other marginal areas of the island occurred. This pattern continued into the 1520s and 1530s, as already mentioned.

Summary

The historical sources allow tentative conclusions concerning Indian response to contact. It followed a distinct pattern that was repeated, albeit with certain differences, first in Hispaniola and then in Puerto Rico. This pattern suggests different ways to conceptualize Euro-Indian contact on these islands, beginning with autonomous individuals interacting according to different cultural and social values, allowing contact to be sporadic and the Indian communities to have choices, followed by violent conquest and colonization, in which the unequal power relations offered a very different scenario wherein Indian communities had limited choices.

Initial contact was characterized by a) flight, b) exchange or barter, c) presentation of gifts and prestige items, and d) accommodation to Spanish requests. The contact scenario under which individuals of at least two distinct peoples related to each other in more or less equal terms gave way to the imposition of one over the other in an inherently unequal manner.

This was followed by the conquest-pacification phase. In this phase, the Spanish were able to impose their will by force. The Indians responded first by flight and rebellion, then by submission under the force of Spanish domination and nominal acceptance of Spanish ways. As discussed previously, in the case of Puerto Rico the period of rebellion persisted for a longer time, due in part to the opportunity of flight to neighboring islands from which raiding of the few Spanish settlements was carried out. The phase of prolonged contact with the Spanish under the system of *encomiendas* began between 1502 and 1504 in Hispaniola. In Puerto Rico, the establishment of the *encomienda* system coincided with the period of rebellion.

Historical evidence of Indian response under prolonged contact is available mainly for Hispaniola. It included reactive mechanisms such as flight and suicide. The strategy of compartmentalization, that is, the tacit acceptance of Spanish ways when forced to do so and the recurrence of traditional ways when in their own villages, was also employed. The strategies were not homogenous among all Indians. Those who elected to flee from the Spanish, either by interning themselves in the inaccessible areas of their own islands or by taking up residence in others, remained outside direct Spanish interference and presumably differed in their strategies vis-à-vis the Spanish.

The descriptions of Indian responses to Spanish policy already noted indicate that the Indians of Hispaniola (and perhaps also of Puerto Rico), despite proximity to the Spanish during long periods of the year, did not accept Spanish ways.[29] They "forgot" Catholicism when not in the company of Spaniards, returned to their villages, practiced their *areitos*, ballgames, and *cohobas*, preferred to eat their own food rather than what was provided by the Spanish, never understood European-style tribute or the value of transactions, and generally shunned contact with the Spanish. It appears that the conditions under which they lived were so extreme that they were not conducive to the Indian's acceptance of Spanish ways and that any acceptance was more apparent than real. The *encomienda* Indians were neither "assimilated" nor "acculturated." As their numbers diminished and their communities shrunk in size, they apparently responded by separating their actions into two categories: those that were acceptable to the Spanish and those that were not, the latter to be renewed and reinforced in their villages. This process may have continued until the last native Indian communities ceased to exist or finally became part of the larger colonial mestizo society. As pointed out by Deagan and Cruxent, Taíno, African, and Spanish traits and traditions survived and developed into what became a new society, neither Spanish, African, nor Native American (2002b:227).

In the case of foreign Indians who were brought in as slaves, they were probably placed to live within the Spanish settlements, although they did interact with native Indians during the periods of labor in the fields and mines. It is also possible that foreign Indians were able to live among native communities. The foreign Indians also established separate communities, or were so placed by the Spanish, if later sources indicating the presence of these villages are correct.

It is important to point out, however, that the documentary evidence discussed in this section relates to the native Indians' response to contact. The response of foreign Indians is practically unknown. Sporadic mention to the effect that these Indians were more acculturated to Spanish ways than the *encomienda* Indians is found in the Interrogatory document (Rodríquez Demorizi 1971:340). Mártir de Anglería (1944:500) indicates responses similar to those of the native Indians among the Lucayan Indians brought to Hispaniola, that is, suicide, flight to inaccessible areas of the island, and attempts to return to their homeland. It is probable that acculturation among foreign Indians subject to slavery occurred at a much faster rate, and that they may have eventually replaced the native inhabitants of the islands.

The historical record clearly indicates the complexity of the culture-contact processes that occurred as the early colonial society developed on these islands. Native Indians that were able to return to their villages rejected Spanish ways and struggled to maintain at least a semblance of their rituals and way of life, while enslaved Indians who lived in the proximity of Spaniards appear to have become more assimilated. The processes of assimilation, compartmentalization, cultural transformation, and ethnogenesis were all happening at this time, as can be seen as well in the archaeological record.

Archaeological research in Hispaniola and Cuba has provided irrefutable evidence of historic-period Indian communities. For example, the site of El Cabo, located in coastal south-eastern Hispaniola, was occupied from about A.D. 600 to A.D. 1500 and includes a small historic component in which European artifacts were found within house structures associated with Chicoid ritual paraphernalia (Hoffman et al. 2014: 597–598). The site was probably occupied until around 1504 and is an example of a still-autonomous Indian community that chose to incorporate European artifacts (mainly beads and fragments of metal, glass, and earthenware) acquired probably through native networks, as part of their native value system (Hoffman et al. 2014:598; also citing Oliver 2009, Samson 2010, Valcárcel Rojas et al. 2013; Keehnen 2011). Rather than direct Euro-Indian interaction, what we see here is an independent community that acquired a limited number of European artifacts but was not directly affected by a Spanish presence at the site. These artifacts may have been viewed by the Indians as novel items that, because of their uniqueness or scarcity, were handled by the religious leaders in charge of ritual objects.[30]

Another contact-period site in Hispaniola is the En Bas Saline site, located on the northeastern coast of Haiti, close to where Columbus built Fort La Navidad and about two kilometers from the Spanish town of Puerto Real (Deagan 2004:605). Kathleen Deagan led extensive excavations at this large village site, which she believes was the seat of the chiefdom of Guacanagarí at the time of contact (Deagan 2004:605, citing also Deagan 1989; Hodges 1983; Morison 1940). Her investigations of discrete precontact and postcontact deposits, structured within the framework of gender relations and sociopolitical dynamics, demonstrate that despite the site's proximity to a Spanish town and its submission under the *encomienda* system, native lifeways—as revealed in food consumption and preparation, ceramic traditions, ritual/feasting behavior,[31] and the maintenance of social differentiation and hierarchy—persisted and that evidence of Spanish material culture is rare. It further indicates how the explicit look at gender can inform the archaeological record and provide important insights into how Indian communities were able to maintain their lifeways despite the Spanish. In addition, it provides archaeological evidence that supports my analysis of the historic record as indicating the Indians' rejection of Spanish culture and religion.

Another aspect of Spanish-Indian interaction informed by archaeology is the role played by Indian women in the adoption of elements of native culture into Spanish households. Although the historical record seems to indicate that Indians who lived among the Spanish were more acculturated than those still living in their communities and laboring under the *encomiendas*, it appears that the contrary was happening: as a result of the domestic chores carried out by native women, Spanish households were influenced by native lifeways. In the words of Kathleen

Deagan, "From an archaeological perspective, Taíno cultural continuity and Spanish cultural transformation in sixteenth-century Hispaniola suggests that contact-induced cultural change in household domestic practice was largely unidirectional—from Taíno to Spaniard" (Deagan 2004:622).

Indigenous survival and cultural transformation during the early colonial period is also documented for Cuba. There are numerous historic-period indigenous sites that show evidence of Euro-Indian contact that have been studied by Cuban scholars (Domínguez 1978, 1983, 1987, 2008; Pichardo Moya 1945; Tamames 2009). A particularly interesting one is the site of El Chorro de Maíta, a large Indian village site located in the province of Holguín, in northeastern Cuba, where extensive excavations were carried out in the 1980s under the direction of José Manuel Guarch Delmonte. Analyses of the site's collections were carried out by Roberto Valcárcel Rojas and formed the basis for his 2012 doctoral dissertation (Valcárcel Rojas 2012), as well as additional works by him and others published in recent years. Like the En Bas Saline and El Cabo sites in Hispaniola, El Chorro de Maíta is a large village site occupied from late prehistory into the early colonial period, where Indian cultural survival is evident. Like the Indian inhabitants of En Bas Saline, El Chorro de Maíta inhabitants were under the influence of the Spanish *encomienda* system. Unlike En Bas Saline, El Chorro de Maíta was not in the proximity of a Spanish town but was nevertheless affected by interactions with the Spanish system of forced labor.

Archaeological investigations and analysis concentrated on the extensive burials found at the site, where 133 individuals and 108 graves were excavated (Valcárcel Rojas 2012, 2016; Guarch Delmonte 1996; Hofman et al. 2014). Described as "one of the earliest inter-cultural interment contexts in the Americas" (Hofman et al. 2014:599), the site indicates a mixture of both Indian (the majority of internments) and European mortuary traditions (9.7 percent of individuals were interred in an extended position, which is characteristic of Christian burials), as well as individuals, many of them female, buried with European metal objects, and some with gold and gold-copper alloys originating from Colombia and Europe (Hofman et al. 2014:599; Martinón-Torres et al. 2012; Cooper et al. 2008).

The tentative identification of non-native Indians interred at the site includes a female Amerindian individual possibly from Yucatán, as well as the presence of mestizos and Africans (Hofman et al. 2014:599; Valcárcel Rojas 2012, 2016). The fact that exotic burial goods are associated mainly with historic-period female interments, and the authors' comment that there appears to have been more male mobility during the historic period, may indicate the increasing importance of women in the community, since they were more prone to remain there while their male counterparts were taken away to work for the Spanish. This appears to be similar to what Deagan (2004) described for En Bas Saline. El Chorro de Maíta, then, provides another tantalizing glimpse of how an Indian community persisted under the Spanish *encomienda*, maintaining its cultural autonomy while incorporating some aspects of Spanish material and religious culture. It also provides concrete evidence of the presence of foreign-born Indians, as well as mestizos and Africans, within a native Indian *encomienda* town, a fact that is mentioned repeatedly in the sixteenth-century documentary sources.

In conclusion, a careful perusal of historic sources to study Spanish-Indian interaction during the early colonial history of the Greater Antilles allows certain inferences about the Indian response to contact. The Indians acted in a variety of ways, including various degrees of resistance and accommodation. However, it appears that the native inhabitants insisted in maintaining their communities and way of life and continued to practice their ball games, *areitos*, and other rituals, preferring to live independently from the Spanish. Documentary sources, when scrutinized carefully, point to the persistence of Indian communities well into the sixteenth century, especially in Hispaniola and Cuba. Recent archaeological research provides concrete, material evidence for the persistence of viable Indian communities, where rituals and community life rooted in their prehistory continued into the historic period. There is evidence from archaeological burial contexts of the presence of foreign Indians, and of mestizos and Africans in at least one historic-period Indian community in Cuba. The processes of interaction among native Indians, foreign Indians, Spanish, and Africans that formed the basis for the genesis of New World Caribbean societies are therefore beginning to be discerned through detailed historic and archaeological research.

4
Aboriginal Demography in the Antilles

The debate regarding the size of New World native populations at the time of European contact and the cause for the rapid decline of these populations throughout the New World has been controversial for decades.[1] Today there is a general consensus among scholars on the decline of New World native populations and, in the specific case of the Greater Antilles, their virtual extinction by the latter part of the sixteenth century, and that the causes of the decline were varied. Archaeological and historical research provides rich comparative data on the differential impact of European colonization on New World peoples and the myriad ways these populations interacted and changed in response to contact with Europeans (Boomert 1985; Deagan 1985a, 1985b, 1987, 1988; Domínguez 1983, 1987; Mathers et al. 2013; Mendoza 1980; Ortega and Fondeur 1978b; Romero Estébanez 1981; Smith 1986). This research demonstrates Indian communities continued into the sixteenth century, in spite of Spanish conquest and colonization. There is also controversy over whether remnants of these native populations persisted in secluded areas of the Greater Antilles well into the late colonial period, as advocated by individuals who self-identify as Taíno (Veloz Maggiolo 1974; García Molina et al. 2007; Haslip-Viera 2006; Castanha 2011). The demographic aspects of European-Indian interaction continue to be critical for an understanding of the processes of cultural transformation that occurred in the Greater Antilles during the sixteenth century.

This chapter considers the aboriginal demography of the islands of Hispaniola and Puerto Rico within the context of New World population estimates and the factors that contributed to population decline within a comparative framework. The section on Hispaniola includes an analysis of the 1514 Repartimiento (also known as Repartimiento de Albuquerque). The section on Puerto Rico analyzes the 1530 census carried out by Governor Francisco Manuel de Lando. These are the only two surviving documents of this period that provide specific counts of the aboriginal populations of these islands. The incorporation of data on the demographic history of the Indians of Hispaniola and Puerto Rico is summarized here for the information it may bring to bear on the particular issue of the relationship between contact numbers, rate of population decline, and native cultural transformation. It is also included because of its bearing on the question of Indian emigration and immigration, that is, the relationship between the native Indians of Hispaniola and Puerto Rico and foreign Indians, and the significance of this relationship in the culture-contact scenario of these islands.

Aboriginal Historical Demography in the New World

A good deal has been written on this complex subject because of its relevance to how we interpret the consequences to New World peoples of the European conquest. Accurate numbers matter, as there is a difference between, on the one hand, assuming the inevitability of the decline and decimation of small populations confronted with the European invasion and, on the other, attempting to explain how large populations could have succumbed so quickly. This is especially true in the Caribbean, whose native populations bore the brunt of first contact with the Spanish.

In the 1970s, the historical demographer Woodrow Borah (1976:14) discussed how estimates had shifted from the sixteenth-century accounts of very dense populations that fueled the arguments for high figures for many areas of the New World, especially Mesoamerica and Peru, to the low estimates of the nineteenth and early twentieth centuries, and back to the higher estimates of scholars in the middle of the past century (Denevan 1970, 1976; Cook and Borah 1971–1974; Lipschutz 1966; Rosenblat 1954, 1967; Dobyns 1966, 1983; Kroeber 1939; Steward and Faron 1959; Friede 1963; Sauer 1969; Sánchez-Albornoz 1974). Since the 1990s, the pendulum has swung again toward lower estimates, based on a deeper appreciation of the complex variety of New World populations.

Sixteenth-century estimates relied on firsthand accounts of travelers, official reports to the European colonial authorities, and upon various censuses carried out for the purposes of determining tribute or apportionment of labor under the *encomiendas*. These early accounts generally indicate large aboriginal populations at the beginning of contact (in the cases in which historical accounts coincide with first contact) and the rapid decline thereafter. These accounts were mainly impressionistic and must be analyzed within the historical context in which they were written.

In his analysis of the causes of depopulation in Hispanic America after the Spanish conquest, Livi-Bacci (2006:200, table 1) summarizes twentieth-century scholarly estimates for New World native populations. One of the earliest scholarly estimates was Kroeber's (1939) low number of 8.4 million for the Western Hemisphere. A decade later, Steward (1948) estimated 15.5 million; five years later Rosenblat (1954) estimated 13.4 million, and in the 1960s and 1970s, Dobyns (1966) and Borah (1976) (see Denevan 1992 and Livi-Bacci 2006:200, table 1) estimated more than 100 million. These very high mid-twentieth-century estimates were based in part on assumptions about the accuracy of the early-sixteenth-century historic accounts of very large aboriginal populations in the Americas, as well as on the various statistical methods and assumptions used to derive these estimates.[2] Denevan's (1992) estimate of 53.9 million falls about halfway between the low and high estimates. As pointed out by Livi-Bacci (2006:200), there is a 12:1 ratio between the lowest and the highest estimates.

The lack of consensus among scholars about this issue is not surprising, and some may argue that it may be best not to pursue the issue further. However, new data and theoretical approaches provide much more sophisticated interpretations of sixteenth-century aboriginal demography (and for later aboriginal historic populations as well). For example, archaeological studies such as those of Ramenofsky (1987) and Smith (1984) have documented the existence of large, complex, and densely populated polities in various areas of the Americas before contact. Recent archaeological research in lowland South America (Mann 2005; Moore 2014) provides corroborating evidence for previous ecological studies on the productivity of lowland tropical areas and their capacity to support large populations (Carneiro 1967; Denevan 1970).

Aboriginal historical demography is also relevant for the study of the relationship between rapid depopulation and culture and social change. An important example of the use of historical and archaeological data to document cultural change caused by depopulation is that of Smith (1984) in his study of the sixteenth-century chiefdoms of the southeastern United States. He concludes that the rapid cultural change observed in this area during the early historic period cannot be explained as acculturation; rather, it must be explained as deculturation brought about by massive population losses (Smith 1984:179). More recent data indicate that there was considerable variety in the population densities of aboriginal populations in the southeastern areas of the United States and in their response to contact with Europeans (Larsen 1994).

Although the drastic decline of native populations across the Americas after European contact is an undisputed established fact, we know that the process was not homogenous and that to understand what happened to different populations and why requires careful reconstructions of local areas and a comparative approach.

Epidemic Disease and Native Depopulation

Historians have postulated numerous explanations for the rapid depopulation and actual extinction of many New World peoples. In the case of scholars of colonial Latin America, there is a consensus that points to the *encomienda* system and other systems of forced or coerced labor as the culprits. Lipschutz (1966) argues as much in his comparison of the rate of population decline among central Mexicans, the Quimbaya Indians of Colombia, the Taínos of Hispaniola, and the Uru and Aymara of Peru. He believes the drastic rate of population decline evidenced in the case of the first three, as opposed to the slower rate of the last two (1966:242: figure 3), can be explained by the fact that the former were subjected immediately to the rigors of the *encomienda* system and the latter were not. Other scholars, such as Cassá (1979) and Moya Pons (1978), in the case of the Taínos of Hispaniola, and Brau (1966) and Fernández Méndez (1984), in the case of Puerto Rico, have advanced arguments along similar lines.

Another proposed cause for rapid population decline across the Americas were Old World diseases that, when introduced to the New World, reached epidemic proportions (Dobyns 1966; Denevan 1976:2–3). Many studies of historic populations (based on historic and archaeological research), as well as of current aboriginal groups, document the catastrophic effects of epidemics of what in the Old World were endemic diseases on the immunologically susceptible New World populations (Crosby 1976; Dobyns 1963, 1983; Ewers 1973; Krech 1978; Schleiser 1976; Wright 1981; Wagley 1940).

The most important epidemic diseases that struck Native American populations were smallpox, measles, whooping cough (pertussis), chicken pox, mumps, influenza, pneumonia, scarlet fever, epidemic typhus, and bubonic plague (see Ashburn 1947; Crosby 1972; Deutschmann 1961; McNeil 1976 for general discussion on the role of disease in the New World depopulation and on the ecology of the major diseases). Ramenofsky (1987:140, table 45) has classified some of the epidemic diseases that affected New World populations. Of all the diseases noted above, smallpox was apparently the most dangerous, because of its high mortality and its longer period of infection. The fact that the smallpox virus can survive for many years in a dry state illustrates the potential. This particular disease accounts for the first historically documented pandemic in the New World, which started among the Indians of Hispaniola in 1519, 27 years after initial contact.

It is easy to understand why the spread of epidemic disease has been considered by many scholars as the principal factor in the rapid decline of native populations. The sheer number of Old World diseases to which native peoples had little or no biological immunity is staggering, and the historical accounts describing their effects on susceptible populations are chilling. However, although very important, disease must be viewed as one variable among many others. As pointed out by Larsen (1994) in his overview of contact and postcontact Native American biology, population density was not uniform across the Americas (this is especially well documented for North America), and neither was population decline.[3] Larsen also cites archaeological studies that document different precontact populations in regions of the southeastern United States, including areas that appear to have been unpopulated well before contact with Europeans (such as the Savannah River basin of Georgia and South Carolina) and unpopulated regions between different aboriginal groups, as well as areas where population appears to have increased after contact (Upper Oconee watershed in Georgia) (see also Anderson 1994). He argues that unpopulated areas between aboriginal groups would have served as culturally induced buffer zones against the rapid spread of epidemic disease in some areas, that the conditions for the spread of introduced infectious diseases were not ideal, and that the spread of disease was not inevitable (Larsen 1994:123).

Therefore, a much more nuanced approach to the effects of disease on aboriginal demography that takes into consideration the variable size of initial contact populations, the social and cultural ties that bound communities together or kept them apart, the geography of contact, the sociopolitical complexity of populations, and the intensity of contact is merited. These variables apply to the contact period throughout Spanish America and the Greater Antilles as well (see also Livi-Bacci 2006) and help to explain the difference between the disappearance of Greater Antillean populations and polities in the sixteenth century and the persistence of aboriginal populations (known historically as Caribs) in the Lesser Antilles (see also Wilson 1997a).

The Case of Hispaniola

Archaeological Evidence

As the discussion on the historical evidence here will make clear, it is only through archaeology that we will ever be able to come up with more accurate estimates for contact population numbers. There is a certain irony in the fact that this Caribbean island, which first experienced the onslaught of Spanish conquest and colonization and whose native populations were the source for most of the early historic documents about the Indians in this early period, has a dearth of archaeological research focusing on aboriginal chiefdoms, and much less on their demography (there is more data now for Puerto Rico and Cuba, see Keegan 2013:75).

We have already discussed the nature and development of Caribbean chiefdoms, stressing how recent archaeological research is asking new questions and providing data that contradicts the homogenous descriptions of the Spanish chroniclers in favor of a much more varied social and cultural landscape. Studies by Dominican archaeologists Veloz Maggiolo et al. (1981) and Guerrero and Veloz Maggiolo (1988) have suggested a correlation of numerous late prehistoric sites discovered along the river valleys of the Yaque and Verde rivers in north and central Hispaniola with those mentioned in the historic accounts, which may indicate a considerably dense population. Remnants of *conuco* fields, the cultivation of periodically inundated river floodplains (*cultivo de várzea*), and intensive cultivation in areas of productive karst soils have all been physically documented for this area of Hispaniola (Veloz Maggiolo 1991:209; 1993:148–150). These studies support the case for intensive agricultural practices in selected areas of the island, and hence for dense population of these areas. However, no specific evidence on which to base demographic estimates is available; this will have to await further archaeological investigations.

Historical Evidence

Sixteenth-century sources are unanimous in their depiction of a very large aboriginal population in Hispaniola at the time of contact. With the exception of Bishop Fonseca, as cited in the December 4, 1519, letter of the Dominican friars, and Nicolaus Federmann, all other sources estimate a population of 1,000,000 or more. Table 4.1 summarizes the sixteenth-century sources. Historians, however, have argued for decades about the value of these estimates. Arguments fall into two main camps: those who accept the early estimates as probably true (Dobyns 1983; Cook and Borah 1971–1974; Chaunu 1963; Sauer 1969; Denevan 1976) and those who stress the tendency of most sixteenth-century Spaniards

Table 4.1. Aboriginal Population of Hispaniola based on Sixteenth-Century Sources.

Year	Indians	Date of Source	Source
1492	3–4 million	1552, 1527–60	Las Casas (1945, 1951:II)
	2 million	1535 report to the King 1540	Fray Tomás de Angulo, Benzoni (Saco 1932:II)
	1.2 million	1516	P. Mártir de Anglería (1944)
	1.13 million	January 22, 1518	Alonso Zuazo (CODOIN I:1)
	1.1 million	December 4, 1519	Dominican friars (CODOIN I:35; Las Casas 1951:III)
	1 million	1516–17	Oviedo (1851:I), Hieronymites (CODOIN I:1)
	600,000	December 4, 1519	Bishop Fonseca (CODOIN I:1)
	500,000	1532–33	Federmann (1945)
1495–1497	1.1 million	June 4, 1516	Bartolomé Colón (CODOIN I:7)
1508	60,000		Pasamonte census, in Las Casas (1951:II)
1509	33,528–40,000	1516	Diego Colón census, Las Casas (1951:II); (CODOIN I:7)
1510	46,000	1517	Fray Bernardino, in Las Casas (1951:III)
1512	40,000–20,000	December 4, 1519	Hieronymites Las Casas (1951:III)
1514	25,540	1514	1514 Repartimiento (CODOIN I:1; Rodríguez Demorizi 1971)
1517	15,000–16,000	1517	Hieronymites (CODOIN I:1)
1518	11,000	January 18, 1518	Hieronymites Alonso Zuazo (CODOIN I:1; Incháustegui 1958:I)
1519	12,000	December 14, 1519	Dominican friars (CODOIN I:35)

Continued on the next page

Table 4.1. *Continued*

Year	Indians	Date of Source	Source
1529	2,340	July 18, 1529	Ramírez de Fuenleal (Utrera 1951: I)
1542	200	1552	Las Casas (1945)
1547	150	July 25, 1547	Dr. Montalvo (Utrera 1951:I)
1548	500		Oviedo (1959:I)
1565	150		Benzoni (Cook and Borah 1971–1974:I)
1671–1674	100		López de Velasco (Cook and Borah 1971–1974:I)

Sources: Rosenblat 1954, appendix V:294–295; Lipschutz 1966:236–237, tables 3 and 4; Cook and Borah 1971–1974:380–401; Cassá 1979:191; Anderson-Córdova 1990:191–195, table 4.

toward exaggeration and the basically illustrative or symbolic nature of the figures provided (Rosenblat 1954, 1967; Moya Pons 1976; Cassá 1979; Henige 1978).

In the case of Hispaniola, the more contemporary arguments for or against a large aboriginal population are based almost exclusively on the same historic sources that have remained unchanged for decades. The only detailed document that exists is the text of the 1514 Repartimiento. Since by this time the native population of the island was greatly reduced, it is not relevant for an estimation of native numbers at the time of contact. However, the small number of remaining Indians mentioned in this 1514 document has been used to bolster the argument for a small initial contact population. Table 4.2 summarizes the principal estimates that have been made by twentieth-century scholars. Almost without exception, these estimates are based on extrapolations of figures derived from the sixteenth-century sources. It is critical, therefore, to keep in mind the context in which the sixteenth-century estimates were provided and the motivations behind the Spaniards' providing these counts. They cannot be taken at face value and must be carefully interpreted (Curet 2006).

I begin with the most generous estimate: the Cook and Borah conclusion that there were probably at least 8,000,000 in 1494 (1971–1974:I: 376–410). Their approach has been critically discussed by others, espe-

Table 4.2. Contact Aboriginal Population of Hispaniola, Later Estimates.

Estimate	Source
60,000	Verlinden (1973:453–62)
100,000	Rosenblat (1954:102, 105–116; 1967:9–23)
250,000	Cassá (1979:198)
300,000	Morison (1948:393)
377,529	Moya Pons (1976:87)
500,000	Córdova (1968)
1,300,000	Sauer (1969:65–69); Chaunu (1963:76–77)
8,000,000	Cook & Borah (1971–1974:I:408)
100,000	Mira Caballos (1997:34)
200,000 to 300,000	Arranz Márquez (1991); Livi-Bacci (2003:49)

cially Rosenblat (1967), Moya Pons (1976), Henige (1978), and Arranz Márquez (1991). The procedure followed by Cook and Borah to arrive at the 8,000,000 estimate for aboriginal Hispaniola is summarized below:

1. They begin by presenting a series of quotes from Columbus's Diary of the First Voyage and other documents relating to this and other early voyages, which indicate the Admiral's impressions of the high density of aboriginal population of the island. However, as pointed out by Henige, they neglect to present opposing evidence from the Diary for low population densities (1978:220–221).
2. Cook and Borah present an analysis of the 1514 Repartimiento, because "this report of the *repartimiento* constitutes first-hand evidence that the sixteenth-century Europeans did indeed know how to count" (1971–1974:I:380). However, the purported accuracy of this document is not comparable with the very large estimates given by Columbus, the Dominican friars, and Las Casas, since the latter were not based on actual counts but on necessarily vague impressions of large numbers. In addition, their analysis of the 1514 Repartimiento was based on a flawed earlier transcription of the original manuscript (see Arranz Márquez 1991:198–199).
3. After summarizing the contemporary sixteenth-century sources for the 1492–1497 population estimates, they conclude that since these are consistent in estimating 1,000,000 to 1,130,000 Indians, the historical references to a census or count carried out for tribute purposes by Bartolomé Colón (Columbus's brother) must be accurate. They accept Sauer's argument to this effect and his date of

1496 as the most probable for when the census took place (1971–1974:I:393–394).

4. As part of the acceptance of this count as valid, they make a series of adjustments to the figure, arguing that the census included only areas subject to the Spanish (which is correct to assume, since in 1496 the Spanish had not gained control of the entire island). Furthermore, they also assume that the count did not include the children or aged and thereby arrive at a range of 2,500,000 to 5,000,000, with a midpoint of 3,770,000 for the population of Hispaniola in 1496 (1971–1974:I:396).
5. They then proceed to list the later population estimates (for the period 1508–1574), present a graph plotting the rate of population decline, and interpret the resulting population curve as representing two distinct populations (the native Indians and the influx of Spanish-introduced foreign Indians).
6. Finally, they apply the methods developed in their study of Central Mexico to estimate the 1494 population (which marks the beginning of native population decline) as a midpoint figure of 8,000,000. They argue that these numbers are plausible, given the demonstrated productivity of manioc cultivation and the fertility of the island, and explain the catastrophic depopulation that these figures imply by postulating that disease must have been the cause.

These estimates, so extreme in retrospect and viewed from the vantage point of half a century later, are of value because they forced scholars to reassess assumptions about native Caribbean populations and because they demonstrate the importance of using historic sources carefully and critically. I believe most historians, and archaeologists for that matter, would agree that the Spanish chroniclers' accounts, although of obvious importance to understanding early sixteenth-century history, have to be interpreted in context. Columbus's writings cannot be taken literally, and Las Casas was also notoriously inconsistent in his estimates. Many historians of this period have pointed out the dichotomy between Las Casas's early letters and memorials, which give a figure of 1,000,000 Indians at the time of initial colonization, and his later works, in which he begins to give figures of 3,000,000 to 4,000,000 Indians (Henige 1978; Rosenblat 1967; Arranz Márquez 1991, Livi-Bacci 2003).

The issue of how historic sources are interpreted is critical in arriving at population estimates. This is clearly the case with Cook and Borah's estimates for Hispaniola, whose statistical extrapolations hinge upon the 1 to 1.3 million figures for 1494–1496. These depend not only on accepting the existence of Bartolomé Colón's count but also on how this supposed count is interpreted. Cook and Borah make the assumption in the absence of any documents that an actual count must have been made in order to collect tribute. Henige (1978), Moya Pons (1976), and Rosenblat (1967) were of the opinion that there is no historical evidence for such a count, and that the figures cited by various sixteenth-century authors are probably part of an oral tradition handed down since the first years of colonization and indeed probably traceable to Columbus himself.[4]

More recent estimates (see table 4.2) have come up with consistently lower figures. Two estimates particularly relevant to our discussion are those of Arranz Márquez (1991) and Livi-Bacci (2003). As part of their analyses, both relied on well-known historical sources and assumed the existence of Bartolomé Colón's tribute count. However, their interpretation of the sources and who was actually counted is completely different from Cook and Borah's interpretation. Arranz Márquez dismisses the early accounts of 1,100,000 Indians in the tribute area (which was limited to the Vega Real and Cibao areas) as attributable to the euphoria and exaggerations that were part of the initial Columbus enterprise, and gives credit to an anonymous 1496 account of an individual returning to Spain with the Admiral's (Columbus's) party that specifically mentions a tribute of more than 60,000 gold pesos to be paid by the Indians in three installments, of which only 200 pesos were collected (1991:34). Arranz Márquez infers that the tribute was collected in 1495, and that, irrespective of what was actually collected, the 60,000 gold pesos imposed as tribute must have been based on an estimated number of Indian tributaries.

The author assumes that if these were supposed to be paid in three 20,000 peso installments, and each tributary was required to pay one Flanders hawk's bell (which would be about 3–4 gold pesos' worth of gold) every three months, then there would have been 6,000 tributaries in the region (Arranz Márquez 1991:36). He further estimates, based on chroniclers' descriptions of Taíno settlements, the probable number of *bohíos* (houses) per settlement, and number of persons per *bohío*, that the 6,000 tributaries represented heads of households and that there were then 6,000 *bohíos* in the Vega Real/Cibao area in 1495 (1991:37). He concludes that for the years 1492–1494, the population of this area was 90,000 (6,000 *bohíos* x 15 persons per *bohío*), and that by the period 1494–1496, when the population was already declining due to the imposition of tribute, abandonment of agricultural fields, and general starvation, it had been reduced by a third, to 60,000 (6,000 *bohíos* x 10 persons) (1991:62, table). Following this analysis, the author then estimated the population of the entire island to be about approximately three times the size of the Vega Real/Cibao area, or 270,000 in 1492–1494 and 180,000 in 1494–1496 (on the assumption the Vega Real/Cibao area represented roughly one quarter of the island's population and was probably one of the most populous regions).

Livi-Bacci, in his reassessment of the causes for the catastrophic population decline in Hispaniola, uses historical records relating to the amount of gold extracted in the decade following Bartolomé Colón's tribute count (1500–1510) to estimate the labor force used in the mines, and then estimates a total population of not more than 120,000 at mid-decade (ca. 1505) (2003:14–20). This figure, when compared with Arranz Márquez's estimates of 1494, indicates that close to half of the population had perished, a rate that accelerated when one considers that only 26,000 were left to be distributed 10 years later in the 1514 Repartimiento. The careful analysis of the historical sources by these two authors offers a plausible number for the native population of Hispaniola at the time of contact, compared to the high estimates of the sixteenth-century chroniclers that Cook and Borah took at face value.

Another way of looking at this issue is to use the comparative approach with other areas of the world that were also organized as chiefdoms and where there is sufficient archaeological data on population demographics. This provides an independent way at arriving at population estimates that can then be compared with those provided by the authors just cited. A comparison of historians' estimates for Hispaniola and what they may imply in terms of population density and level of sociopolitical organization with the figures derived from various Polynesian chiefdom societies provides insights into plausible aboriginal population figures for Hispaniola (table 4.3).

In the case of Polynesia, Kirch (1989:99) points out that there is a consistent correlation "between the degree of stratification, as measured by Sahlin's (1958) criteria, and the population size of the maximal political unit" and "between population density per square kilometer of arable land and degree of stratification," although he does not indicate that the relationship is causal. While the Caribbean and Polynesian chiefdoms were obviously very different, a comparison between the two, using the different estimates that have been derived for Hispaniola and the possible size of the maximal political units, does provide interesting insights.

In Polynesia, and without postulating causal relationships, there is evidence to conclude, following Kirch (1989), that the highly stratified chiefdom societies were densely populated and required an intensive use of available resources. The highly stratified islands of the Hawaiian ar-

Table 4.3. Population Densities in Hispaniola versus Selected Polynesian Chiefdoms.

Island or Group of Islands[a]	Total Population	Population of Maximum Political Unit[b]	Total Land Area (km2)[c]	Density per Total Land Area (km2)[d]
Hawaiian Islands	200,000	30,000	16,633	12
Tongan Islands	40,000	40,000	696	57
Society Islands	45,000	9,000	1,535	29
Samoan Islands	80,000	25,000	2,829	28
Easter Island	7,000	3,500	160	44
Uvea	4,000	4,000	59	68
Mangaia	3,000	3,000	70	43
Marquesas Islands	35,000	1,500	1,058	33
Futuna	2,000	2,000	62	32
New Zealand	115,000	3,500	256,146	0.43
Hispaniola[e]	60,000?	12,000	76,500	0.78
	100,000?	20,000		1
	250,000?	50,000		3
	300,000?	60,000		4
	377,529?	75,506		5
	500,000?	100,000		6
	1,300,000?	260,000		17
	8,000,000?	600,000		106

[a] Data on Polynesian chiefdoms based on Kirch (1989:98, table 10)
[b] Column 3 numbers based on assuming that the five provinces mentioned in the historical sources for Hispaniola refer to the maximum political unit
[c] Column 4 total land area based on Cook & Borah (1971–1974:I:408)
[d] For the sake of comparison, the population densities listed in column 5 for Polynesia and Hispaniola are computed on the basis of total land area, and not on arable land as was done by Kirch (1989:98:10)
[e] Data on Hispaniola based on table 4.2

chipelago, Tonga, Society Islands, and Samoa exhibit high population densities and intensive agricultural practices. All islands presented in table 4.3, with the exception of New Zealand, had high population densities and varying degrees of intensive agricultural practices.

When the population figures for Polynesia are compared with the hypothetical figures of Hispaniola, the latter indicate much lower population densities (except when the high estimates of Cook and Borah are used). Although the correlation between population density and social stratification that exists in Polynesia may not apply in Hispaniola, it is apparent that the 8,000,000 figure of Cook and Borah must be discarded. It is inconceivable that a population density of 105 p/sq. kilometer could have been sustained on Hispaniola, irrespective of the productivity of manioc cultivation, when the highly stratified chiefdoms of Polynesia that practiced intensive agriculture and animal husbandry had consistently lower densities.

Table 4.3 also presents estimates of what may have been the maximum population units of Hispaniola under the various postulated estimates, assuming the division of the island into five polities (called provinces in the historical sources). This exercise produced some interesting results. If the ethnohistoric evidence for the existence of five Indian provinces has any validity whatsoever and if maximum political units of more than 20,000 to 30,000 individuals correlate with highly stratified chiefdoms, as has been demonstrated in Polynesia, then Rosenblat's 100,000 population estimate for Hispaniola at the time of contact may still be the most plausible. However, the low population density figure of 1 p/sq. kilometer that a 100,000 population entails seems more indicative of seminomadic societies or at best shifting cultivators than of the chiefdom societies described by the chroniclers for Hispaniola. The evidence for agricultural intensification on this island, although not as great as what has been amply documented for Polynesia, does suggest a higher population density than Rosenblat's low estimate. We have already discussed the ethnohistorical and archaeological evidence that support the assumption that the chiefdoms of Hispaniola were capable of producing an agricultural surplus and of the power of the chiefly class. Evidence for social stratification, intensive agricultural practices, and developed artisanal production of prestige items has also been presented. Based on the above, I estimate an aboriginal population for Hispaniola of between 250,000 to 500,000. This estimate, which rests on the comparative analysis just discussed, is similar to the estimates based on historical sources of Cassá (1979), Arranz Márquez (1991), and Livi-Bacci (2003).

This comparative analysis also suggests that the traditional picture of the island divided into five provinces, each one governed by a chief, is probably incorrect. If it were true, the maximum political unit would have consisted of 50,000 individuals (with an estimated population of 250,000) to 100,000 individuals (with an estimated population of 500,000), much higher than those of the Polynesian chiefdoms. The existence of a population between 250,000 and 500,000, organized into chiefdoms of various sizes, seems to fit better with the ethnohistorical and archaeological evidence.

Based on data from their analyses of the 1514 Repartimiento, Arranz

Márquez (1991) and Livi-Bacci (2003) came to the same independent conclusion. This contact population still demonstrates a drastic rate of population decline, but one that could be explained without having to postulate an undocumented catastrophic epidemic to account for the decline of millions as suggested by Cook and Borah.[5]

The 1514 Repartimiento

As noted, this Repartimiento is the only surviving document of the early sixteenth century that provides actual numbers for the aboriginal population of Hispaniola (demonstrating a population in drastic decline only 22 years after contact with the Spanish). In addition to providing total numbers of allotted Indians and their *caciques*, it provides data on age groups (adult, aged, and children), sex (but only for the *encomiendas* in the towns of La Concepción and Puerto Plata), labor categories (*indios de servicio* or service Indians, and *naborías*), and the distribution of Indians throughout the island.

Because of its unique character and undeniable importance, it has been subject to the scrutiny of scholars for many years. In addition to information on the *encomienda* Indians, the document also discusses the Spanish population: who the *encomenderos* were, where they lived, whether they were married, whether they were *vecinos* (residents), *moradores* (inhabitants), and so on. This aspect has been studied by Moya Pons (1976, 1982) and more recently by Arranz Márquez (1991). These authors discuss how the largest number of Indians were allotted to the members of the Spanish elite and study the relationship between these allotments and the distribution of economic and political power on the island (see also Mira Caballos 1997:126).

Arranz Márquez (1991) also provides information on two additional documents that he located in Spanish archives that shed special light on Spanish politics and the colonial society of Hispaniola at this time: the Royal Instructions provided to Rodrigo de Albuquerque and Ibarra in 1513 regarding how to carry out the Repartimiento, and a *probanza* (court deposition) carried out in Santo Domingo in 1515 related to the abuses of the 1514 Repartimiento.[6] In his masterful analysis of the Repartimiento and these two documents, Arranz Márquez demonstrates how Albuquerque, and the Spanish elite allied with him, benefited greatly, and how most of the earliest settlers and the Spaniards who had been in the camp of Diego Colon (Columbus's son and the former governor) were deprived of Indians. He points out how the rampant dissatisfaction among the Spanish population on the island resulted in the widespread migration of those who did not benefit from the allotments.

Table 4.4. 1514 Repartimiento: Total Number of Indians Allotted by Categories and Town

Town	CQ[a]	ISR	ISRA	VO	NO	NY	NB	NBA	Totals
Mining towns									
La Concepción	55	2,094	(21)[b]	228	226	1	700	132	3,436
Santiago	39	1,283	(25)	158	130	27	869	118	2,624
Santo Domingo	77	4,239	(1)	607	534	3	1,541	271	7,272
La Buenaventura	30	1,066	(26)	78	97	—	358	83	1,712
San Juan de la Maguana	33	1,101	(1)	204	153	—	343	120	1,954
Nonmining towns									
Puerto Plata	13	279	(1)	37	45	3	280	41	698
Salvaleón de Higüey	5	863	—	4	8	3	263	33	1,179
Azua	19	676	(3)	85	60	—	131	39	1,010
Villa del Bonao	16	719	(10)	22	50	—	317	55	1,179
Puerto Real	13	541	—	55	48	—	261	52	970
Lares de Guahaya	10	266	—	8	9	—	158	36	487
La Vera Paz	24	559	(10)	33	97	(1)	606	108	1,427
La Sabana	21	696	—	34	111	—	138	37	1,037
Yáquimo	37	730	—	17	51	1	250	4	1,090
Totals	392	15,112	(98)	1,570	1,619	38	6,215	1,129	26,075

[a] CQ = Caciques; ISR = *Indios de servicio*; ISRA = *Indios de servicio allegados*; VO = *Viejos*; NO = *Niños*; NY = *Nitainos*; NB = *Naborías*; NBA = *Naborías allegados*

[b] Numbers in this column are those specified as *indios de servicios allegados* in each town and are included in the *indios de servicio* count

The 1514 Repartimiento text followed in my analysis is the one published by Rodríguez Demorizi (1971:73–248). I examine the Repartimiento text in terms of the following: pattern of distribution of the Indians throughout the island, organization of Indian communities, relationship between *indios de servicio* (service Indians) and *naborías*, and Indian mobility.[7]

The Repartimiento text uses the following categories to describe the allotted Indians: 1) *caciques y nitaínos* (chiefs and close kin); 2) *indios de servicio* (service Indians, associated with *caciques* and always allotted with them); 3) *naborías* (servants); 4) *allegados* (relatives or "hangers-on" associated with either a *cacique* or a Spanish *encomendero*); 5) *viejos* (aged); and 6) *niños* (children). In my analysis I study the relationship between *indios de servicio* and *naborías* in each town and between these groups in the mining towns versus those in the nonmining towns. I also focus on the relationships between *indios de servicio* and *allegados* and between *naborías* and *allegados* to see whether there were significant patterns in their distribution in each town.[8]

It is important to note at the outset that there is discrepancy in the figures that different scholars cite in their studies of the Repartimiento document (for a summary of various historians' estimates, see Arranz Márquez 1991:196). This depends in part on which transcription of the original manuscript was used, and also how each author may have defined the various categories counted. I use my figures here (table 4.4).[9]

Table 4.4 is organized by town; the first five listed are mining towns, and the nine that follow are nonmining towns. This organization facilitates the comparison between these two basic categories of towns (these numbers are the basis for the computations presented in subsequent tables, with the exception of table 4.9). According to my calculations, the total number of allotted Indians is 26,075.[10]

The majority of the Indians allotted in the Repartimiento were *Indios de Servicio* (15,112, or 58 percent), followed by *naborías* (6,215, or 24 percent), and *naborías allegados* (1,129, or 4 percent). A comparison between mining and nonmining towns indicates that the majority of the Indians (16,998, or 65 percent) were distributed among the five mining towns of La Concepción, Santiago, Santo Domingo, La Buenaventura, and San Juan de la Maguana. The rest (9,077, or 35 percent) were allotted among the nine nonmining towns of Puerto Plata, Salvaleón de Higüey, Azua, Villa del Bonao, Puerto Real, Lares de Guahava, La Vera Paz, La Sabana, and Yáquimo. The largest single allotment of Indians (7,272, or 28 percent) was for the capital city of Santo Domingo. The smallest individual allotment (487, or 2 percent) went to the town of Lares de Guahava, one of the least populated of the island. The total number of allotted Indians also includes the aged (1,570) and the children (1,619)—3,189, or 12 percent, each one constituting 6 percent of the total. The majority of the aged (1,275, or 81 percent) and the children (1,140, or 70 percent) were allotted in the mining towns.

Historians, including Moya Pons and Arranz Márquez (see also Mira Caballos 1997, 2000a, 2000b, 2010), assume that the *indios de servicio* allotted along with their respective *caciques* to different *encomenderos* reflect the remnants of the original Taíno communities that existed before contact. It is an accepted fact among most historians of the period that the Spanish followed their understanding of the Indians' social categories, especially the distinction between *caciques* (chiefs or leaders of a settlement or group of settlements), *nitaínos* (the *caciques's* close kin), and the rest of the Indians, who "belonged" to a *cacique*, as basis for allotment of *encomiendas*. Usually, *caciques* were allotted along with their people, who the Spaniards referred to as *indios de servicio*, to particular *encomenderos*. I concur with this assumption. Therefore, a careful analysis of the 1514 Repartimiento can provide insights on the transformations of Indian communities resulting from contact and the establishment of the *encomienda* system.

I start by focusing on the numbers of *naborías* and *indios de servicio*. In general, of the total number (22,457) of *naborías* and *indios de servicio* allotted, 15,112, or 67 percent, were *indios de servicio* and 7,345, or 33 percent, were *naborías*. This indicates that, despite the destruction of Indian communities that accompanied the depopulation of the Indians of Hispaniola, a considerable majority of those allotted in *encomienda* were still associated with their *caciques*. Table 4.5 tabulates the percentage of *indios de servicio* (ISR) and of *naborías* (NB) by town and compares mining and nonmining towns. The proportions of ISR and NB are similar: 68 percent ISR and 32 percent NB for the mining towns; 65 percent ISR and 35 percent NB for the nonmining towns. Therefore, apparently no significant difference exists between the proportion of ISR versus NB in the mining and nonmining towns.

Table 4.5 also presents the average number of Indians per *cacique* allotted in *encomienda*. This was done to determine the approximate number of Indians per community at the time the Repartimiento was made. This average follows Moya Pons, who did something similar in his analysis of the Repartimiento. Table 4.6 tabulates these averages as computed for each town and groups them in terms of those towns that had more than 79 percent service *encomienda* Indians (ISR), those that had 79 percent to 70 percent, 60 percent to 69 percent, and 59 percent to 40 per-

Table 4.5. Percentage of Service *Encomienda* Indians and *Naborías* per Town and Average Number of Indians per Community.

Town	Percentage (%) Service *Encomienda* Indians	Percentage (%) *Naborías*	Community Average (%)[a]
Mining towns			
La Concepción	72	28	38.07
Santiago	57	43	32.89
Santo Domingo	70	30	55.05
La Buenaventura	71	29	35.53
San Juan de la Maguana	70	30	33.36
Totals	68	32	41.80
Nonmining towns			
Puerto Plata	46	53	21.46
Salvaleón de Higüey	75	25	172.60
Azua	80	20	33.70
Bonao	66	34	44.93
Puerto Real	53	37	41.61
Lares de Guahaya	58	42	26.60
La Vera Paz	44	56	23.29
La Sabana	80	20	33.14
Yáquimo	74	26	19.72
Totals	65	35	33.72

[a] Community averages were computed by dividing the total number of service Indians by the number of *caciques* given in *encomienda* in each town

cent. As shown, it appears that there is no significant relationship between the percent of ISR allotted in each town and the community average. The towns with the highest percent of ISR, which are the Indians associated with *caciques* and therefore with remnants of original native communities, do not have consistently higher numbers of Indians per community. In addition, there is no consistent pattern of higher community averages in mining towns compared with nonmining towns, or vice versa. The proportion of ISR to NB may thus be of no relevance to predict the degree of community cohesion that may still have been present among the surviving Indians in 1514.

The reason for the high proportion of *naborías* observed in the case of the nonmining towns of La Vera Paz (56 percent), Puerto Plata (53 per-

Table 4.6. Percentages of Service Indians by Town and Relationship with Community Averages.

Town	More than 79%	79 to 70%	69 to 60%	59 to 40%
Azua	35.70			
La Sabana	33.14			
Salvaleón de Higüey		172.60		
Santo Domingo		55.05		
La Concepción		38.07		
La Buenaventura		35.53		
San Juan de la Maguana		33.36		
Yáquimo		19.72		
Bonao			44.93	
Puerto Real			41.61	
Puerto Plata				41.61
Santiago				32.89
Lares de Guahaya				26.60
La Vera Paz				23.29

cent), and Lares de la Guahava (42 percent) is not clear. It may be that these were towns in which the disintegration of Indian communities was more acute, judging from the low community averages (23.29, 21.46, and 26.6, respectively). However, the data are inconclusive.

The next category examined was that of Indians listed as *allegados.* Moya Pons argues that these probably referred to displaced Indians who were incorporated into existing communities (in the case of service Indians, ISR ALL) or placed as *naborías* (in the case of NAB ALL). According to Moya Pons (1982:131, table 1), the *allegado* category comprises 1,383 Indians, or 6 percent of the total number of Indians allotted (not including the aged and children). Of these, 981 are NAB ALL and 402 are ISR ALL, or 16 percent of *naborías* and 2.6 percent of *indios de servicio,* respectively.

Table 4.7 summarizes my calculations for the number and percentage of service Indians *allegados* (ISR ALL) and *naborías* (NAB ALL) per town. According to my figures, the total number of *allegados* is 1,228, or 5 percent of the total number of Indians allotted in *encomienda* (excluding the aged and children). The mining towns have 6 percent of *allegados* comprising the total allotted and the nonmining towns have 5 percent.

In contrast to Moya Pons's calculations, mine indicate that the great majority of the *allegados* category were *naborías.* In this respect, my analy-

Table 4.7. Relationship between Service Indians and Service Indian *Allegados*, and between *Naborías* and *Naborías Allegados* by Town.

Town	ISR	ISR ALL	Percentage (%)	NB	NB ALL	Percentage (%)	Total ALL	Percentage (%) ALL
Mining towns								
La Concepción	2,094	(21)	1	700	132	19	153	5
Santiago	1,283	(25)	2	869	118	14	143	6
Santo Domingo	4,239	(1)	.02	1,541	271	18	272	4
La Buenaventura	1,066	(26)	2.4	358	83	23	109	7
San Juan de la Maguana	1,101	(1)	.09	343	120	35	121	8
Subtotal	9,783	74	.76	4,535	724	16	798	6
Nonmining towns								
Puerto Plata	279	(1)	.35	280	41	15	42	7
Salvaleón de Higüey	863	—	—	263	33	12	33	3
Azua	676	(3)	.4	131	39	30	42	5
Bonao	719	(10)	1.4	317	55	17	65	6
Puerto Real	541	—	—	261	52	20	52	6
Lares de Guahaya	266	—	—	158	36	23	36	8
La Vera Paz	559	(10)	2	606	108	18	118	9
La Sabana	696	—	—	138	37	27	37	4
Yáquimo	730	—	—	250	5	2	5	2
Subtotal	5329	24	.45	2,810	406	14	430	5
Total	15,112	98	.65	7,345	1,130	15	1,228	5

ISR = service Indians; ISR ALL = service Indian *allegados*; NB = *Naborías*; NB ALL = *Naborías allegados.*

Table 4.8. Indian Population Displacement by Town.

Town[a]	Service Indians	*Naborías*	Total	Total Remaining in Town
Salvaleón de Higüey[b]	452		452	1159
Yáquimo[c]	176	100	276	985
Azua[d]	168		168	846
La Vera Paz[e]	75	170	245	1273
Santo Domingo[f]	33	12	45	6061

[a] The 1514 Repartimiento document does not provide concrete evidence for Indian population displacement in the other towns
[b] All moved to Santo Domingo
[c] 148 moved to Santiago, 28 to San Juan de la Maguana, and 100 to Santiago
[d] 88 moved to Santo Domingo, 80 to San Juan de la Maguana
[e] 75 moved to San Juan de la Maguana, 163 to San Juan de la Maguana, 7 to La Concepción
[f] All moved to Santiago

sis is in line with Arranz Márquez (1991), who calculates 1,256 *allegados* and stresses that these were in their majority *naborías*. He also notes that the great majority of the *allegados* (1,127) were associated with *encomenderos* and that some (129) were associated with *caciques* (1991:253, 529).

The percentage of ISR ALL is less than 1 percent of the total, both in the mining and the nonmining towns, and in combination. If this is true, it may imply that the remnant Indian communities that were allotted along with their respective *caciques* did not incorporate stray Indians into their structure. Apparently, they continued to exist in a depleted state, maintaining ties with a *cacique* until only a few Indians remained. When *indios de servicio* strayed from Spanish control, they did so along with their *caciques*, if the case in the town of Yáquimo is any indication. Here, *encomenderos* were given *caciques* and Indians who were "lost" (*ausentes*) if they could manage to find them and put them to work.

As noted, it is in the *naboría* category that most of the *allegados* are found. Of the total number of *naborías* allotted (7,345), 113, or 15 percent, were *allegados*. In the mining and nonmining towns, these are 16 percent and 14 percent, respectively. Despite the higher numbers of NAB ALL in the mining towns, percentage-wise there were apparently slightly more *allegados* in the nonmining towns. Since the percentages are so close, this is probably not significant.

The analysis so far does not support the hypothesis that the *allegados* were more prevalent in the mining towns, thereby reflecting the high

Table 4.9. Displacement of Service Indians by Town.

Town[a]	ISR	Total ISR Removed
Salvaleón de Higüey	452	863
Yáquimo	176	730
Azua	168	676
La Vera Paz	75	559
Santo Domingo	33	4,239

ISR = service Indians.
[a] The 1514 Repartimiento document does not provide concrete evidence for Indian population displacement in the other towns.

level of disintegration of Indian communities subject to the rigors of the gold mines. On the contrary, as noted, the percentage of *allegados* is slightly higher in the nonmining towns, which may mean that these were either receiving displaced Indians fleeing from the mining centers or that they were suffering a higher rate of disintegration due to displacement of Indians toward the mining centers. Another explanation, following Arranz Márquez's analysis, is that since most *allegados* were in fact *naborías*, they simply reflect the fact that many Indians were taken by the Spanish from their communities to work as either house servants or field workers in their *haciendas*. It is also important to bear in mind that since this Repartimiento took place during the time of the *demora* (when Indians were away from the mines and fields and back in their communities), the *allegados* included Indians that at the time of the count were moving from place to place and not in their previously known location (see Arranz Márquez 1991:188, 255).

Evidence for population displacement is addressed in tables 4.8 and 4.9. The former summarizes the numbers provided in the Repartimiento document on the provenience of Indians displaced to other areas as a result of the allotments of 1514. As can be seen, four towns lost population—Salvaleón de Higüey, Yáquimo, Azua, and La Vera Paz—the Indians being transferred to *encomiendas* in the mining towns of San Juan de la Maguana, La Concepción, Santiago, and Santo Domingo. The latter summarizes the number of ISR transferred from these towns to the mining towns.

Table 4.10 estimates the Indian population of these five towns before the Repartimiento, by adding the numbers of the displaced Indians to those reported in the 1514 Repartimiento, in order to arrive at an ap-

Table 4.10. Estimated Indian Population of Towns before the 1514 Repartimiento.

Town	Service Indians	Naborías	Total Removed	Grand Total	1514 Total	Percentage (%) Removed
Salvaleón de Higüey	863	296	452	1,611	1,159	28
Yáquimo	730	255	276	1,261	985	22
Azua	676	170	168	1,014	846	17
La Vera Paz	559	714	245	1,518	1,273	16
Santo Domingo	4,239	1,812	45	6,096	6,051	.73

Table 4.11. Estimated Service Indian Population of Towns and Community Averages before the 1514 Repartimiento.

Town	Original ISR	Remaining ISR	Grand Total	Percentage (%) Remaining	Community Average[a]
Salvaleón de Higüey	863	452	1315	34	263[b]
Yáquimo	730	176	906	19	24.48
Azua	676	168	844	20	44.42
La Vera Paz	559	75	643	12	26.41
Santo Domingo	4,239	33	4,272	.77	55.48

ISR = service Indians.

[a] Computed on the basis of the number of *caciques* in the 1514 Repartimiento. See table 4.4.

[b] The two *caciques* whose Indians were divided up in Santo Domingo do not appear in the original 5 *caciques* listed in Salvaleón de Higüey. If we assume that there were originally 7 *caciques*, the community average would drop to 187.85.

proximate figure of the percentage removed in 1514. As can be seen, the town of Salvaleón de Higüey lost 28 percent of its Indian population, followed by Yáquimo with 22 percent, Azua with 17 percent, and La Vera Paz with 16 percent.

Table 4.11 estimates the *indios de servicio* of these same towns before the Repartimiento, in the same manner as was done for table 4.10. The rationale for this estimate was to provide a more accurate figure to gauge the disintegration of the Indian communities of these towns as a result of the displacement of *indios de servicio*, again assuming that these represent the remnants of the original Indian communities. Here again Salvaleón de Higüey leads the group, with 34 percent of its service Indians removed, followed by Azua (20 percent), Yáquimo (19 percent), and La Vera Paz (12 percent). Community averages based on the figures of table 4.10, columns 2 and 3, and table 4.4, column 2, are presented here as well.

When compared with the averages in table 4.5, these towns exhibit a measure of attrition as a result of the 1514 Repartimiento, which is to be expected. The fact that the towns having the lowest community averages had their Indians transported over larger distances to the mining towns may not be a coincidence. Thus, the evidence for displacement from four of the nonmining towns to the mining towns may explain why the community averages computed for the mining towns as a group are consistently higher than is the case for the nonmining towns (excluding the town of Salvaleón de Higüey, since it represents an anomaly compared to all the other towns). However, it may be that the high averages for the mining towns are just a reflection of the higher number of Indians allotted here as opposed to the nonmining towns.

Another issue of interest with respect to the relationship between *naborías* and *indios de servicio* is the degree in which they were allotted together. Information to this effect may provide insights into whether or not these two categories of Indians had any opportunity for social contact within the confines of the Repartimiento allotments.[11] In addition, the manner in which Indians associated with specific *caciques* were distributed among the *encomenderos* can provide information on the effects of the allotments on the integrity of Indian communities. This is addressed in table 4.12.[12]

The total for all towns indicates that 382 *caciques* were allotted in *encomienda*, 33 (9 percent) of which were women.[13] Four hundred and ninety-one (66 percent) of the *encomenderos* received service *encomiendas* (ENC SERV), 366 (49 percent) received only *naborías* (ENC NB), and 322 (43 percent) received both. More significantly, 418 (85 percent) of the ser-

Table 4.12. Total Number of Allotments by Type of *Encomienda*, Number of *Encomenderos*, and Town.

Town	CQ	FCQ	%	Enc Serv	%	Enc Nb	%	Enc Nb/Serv	%	Enc	Rel Enc Serv to Enc	% Enc Serv to Enc
Mining towns												
La Concepción	55	(7)	13	56	65	42	49	(30)	35	86	33 to 12	59 to 14
Santiago	32	(2)	6	46	92	22	44	(24)	48	50	24 to 9	52 to 18
Santo Domingo	74	(13)	18	104	52	115	57	(75)	37	201	32 to 11	31 to 5
La Buenaventura	30	(2)	7	37	57	35	54	(28)	43	65	12 to 5	32 to 11
San Juan de la Maguana	33	—	—	39	89	18	41	(17)	39	44	23 to 10	59 to 23
Subtotal	224	(24)	11	282	63	232	52	(174)	39	446	124 to 47	44 to 11
Nonmining towns												
Puerto Plata	13	—	—	13	65	8	40	(11)	55	20	4 to 2	31 to 10
Salvaleón de Higüey	5	(4)	80	28	62	15	33	(30)	67	45	5 to 28	18 to 62
Azua	19	—	—	24	96	7	28	(17)	68	25	11 to 6	46 to 24
Bonao	16	(1)	6	23	55	24	57	(17)	40	42	6 to 3	26 to 7
Puerto Real	13	(2)	15	18	50	20	56	(16)	44	36	2 to 2	11 to 6
Lares de Guahaya	10	(1)	10	11	48	15	65	(8)	35	23	5 to 2	45 to 8
La Vera Paz	24	(1)	4	27	56	28	58	(20)	42	48	13 to 6	48 to 12
La Sabana	21	—	—	26	118	3	14	(11)	50	22	3 to 2	11 to 29
Yáquimo	37	—	—	39	118	14	42	(18)	54	33	33 to 14	85 to 42
Subtotal	158	(9)	6	209	71	134	45	(148)	50	294	102 to 65	49 to 22
Total	382	(33)	9	491	66	366	49	(322)	43	740	418 to 112	85 to 15

CQ = *caciques*; FCQ = female *caciques*; Enc Serv = *encomiendas de servicio* (service *encomiendas*); Enc Nb = *encomenderos naborías* (*encomenderos* allotted only *naborías*); Enc Nb/Serv = *encomenderos naborías* & *encomenderos servicio* (*encomenderos* allotted both *naborías* and service Indians; Enc = *encomenderos* (all *encomenderos* receiving separate allotments of Indians); Rel Enc Serv to Enc = relationship between service *encomiendas* and *encomenderos*.

vice *encomiendas* (ENC SERV) were allotted among 112 (15 percent) of the *encomenderos*, a clear indication of the concentration of service Indians into a few Spanish hands.

With respect to the relationship between *naborías* and *indios de servicio*, slightly less than half of the total number of allotments made included both *naborías* and *indios de servicio*, and slightly more than half of the Indians being allotted were only *naborías* (ENC NB). When compared with mining and nonmining towns, it appears that the latter provided a greater possibility of contact between *naborías* and *indios de servicio*, since 50 percent as opposed to 39 percent of the former allotted included both *naborías* and *indios de servicio*. In any case, a significant percentage (49 percent) of the *encomiendas* allotted were of *naborías* given to *encomenderos* who had no *indios de servicio* to speak of (52 percent ENC NB in mining towns, 46 percent ENC NB in nonmining towns) and with possibly no opportunity for communication with *indios de servicio*, implying a total loss of community ties.[14]

The service *encomiendas* (ENC SERV) still constitute the majority of the *encomiendas* allotted, which is consistent with the larger number of *indios de servicio*, when compared with the *naborías*, that appears in the totals of the Repartimiento. Since all *indios de servicio* are consistently allotted in association with a particular *cacique*, they probably constitute the true remnants of the original Indian communities, as already argued.

An analysis of what occurred to these communities as a result of the 1514 Repartimiento can be made by studying the relationship between the number of *caciques* allotted per town and the number of *encomenderos* listed as receiving service *encomiendas* (ENC SERV) (table 4.13). In 8 of the 14 towns the number of *caciques* exceeds the number of *encomenderos* listed as receiving service *encomiendas* (ENC SERV). In the towns of La Concepción, Santiago, San Juan de la Maguana, Azua, Lares de Guahava, La Vera Paz, La Sabana, and Yáquimo, *encomenderos* received more than one *cacique* and his or her Indians as allotment. This implies that if these Indians were placed within the same physical and social environment, either in the mines or in the agricultural fields, more than one community of Indians would be placed together, even though they may have originally come from separate villages.

Conversely, in four of the 14 towns, the number of *caciques* allotted is less than the number of *encomenderos*. In the towns of Santo Domingo, Puerto de Plata, Salvaleón de Higüey, and Puerto Real, a *cacique's* Indians were divided among more than one *encomendero*. This implies further dismembering of the *cacique's* original community, by separating the Indians to work in what may have been different areas and further contributing to undermining what little may have been left of the *cacique's*

Table 4.13. Relationship between Number of *Caciques* Allotted and Number of *Encomenderos* Receiving Service *Encomiendas* by Town.

Town	*Caciques*	*Encomenderos* Receiving Service *Encomiendas*	Proportion[a]
La Concepción	55	44	>1
Santiago	32	28	>1
Santo Domingo	74	86	<1
La Buenaventura	30	30	=
San Juan de la Maguana	33	26	>1
Puerto Plata	13	12	>1
Salvaleón de Higüey	5	39	<1
Azua	19	18	>1
Bonao	16	18	<1
Puerto Real	13	16	<1
Lares de Guahaya	10	8	>1
La Vera Paz	24	20	>1
La Sabana	21	19	>1
Yáquimo	37	19	>1

[a] Proportions of more than 1 indicate that there were more *caciques* given in *encomienda* than *encomenderos* allotted service *encomiendas*, which means that some *encomenderos* received more than one *cacique* and his Indians in *encomienda*. Conversely, proportions of less than 1 indicate that there were fewer *caciques* given in *encomienda* than *encomenderos* allotted service *encomiendas*, which means that some of the *caciques*' Indians were allotted among more than one *encomendero*.

authority. Only in the case of La Buenaventura is the proportion of *caciques* equal to that allotted to *encomenderos* listed as receiving service *encomiendas* (ENC SERV). This analysis demonstrates beyond a doubt the disastrous effect of the *encomienda* system upon the integrity of the Indian communities.

The Case of Salvaleón de Higüey

As is evident from the discussion so far, the town of Salvaleón de Higüey stands out as a different case. It is the only one of the 14 towns on the island that continued to have a high average of Indians per community (172.60, table 4.5). The 863 service Indians listed for this town were distributed among five *caciques*, four of them women. These four women *caciques* had 808 of the 863 service Indians listed in the allotment for Salvaleón de Higüey. *Cacica* Isabel de Iguanamí had 304, *cacica* Doña María del Higüey had 416, *cacica* Carolina de Azura had 30, and *cacica*

Catalina de Habacoa had 44. The remaining 55 Indians were allotted with *cacique* Bravo, the only male *cacique* listed in this town's *repartimiento.*

If the relatively larger number of Indians allotted per *cacique* is an indication that in Salvaleón de Higüey the Indian communities were still serving the Spanish more or less intact, then it is logical to assume that the traditional lines of succession of male *caciques* rather than women would also have been preserved. That the opposite occurred may be an indication that the rules of succession among the Hispaniola chiefdoms provided more opportunities for women to succeed than has traditionally been argued (see Alegría 1993:24 for a different perspective).[15] The prominence of Anacaona in the Spanish chroniclers' accounts of the conquest and colonization of Hispaniola may not have been a noted exception to the norm.[16]

The apparent integrity of the Indian communities in Salvaleón de Higüey may explain an anecdote from the Hieronymite Interrogatory of 1517. According to this document, the *caciques* of Salvaleón de Higüey were said to have maintained kinship ties with Indians in southwest Puerto Rico and to have planned a rebellion after the events of 1511 in Puerto Rico. The persistence of knowledge concerning the use of poisonous fumes in warfare and of *behiques* (*curanderos* or medicine men) may also reflect a greater degree of integrity among the Indian communities of the Salvaleón de Higüey region.

Any existing community cohesion ended with the 1514 Repartimiento, when 28 percent of the Indians and 34 percent of the *indios de servicio* of Salvaleón de Higüey (see tables 4.10 and 4.11) were transported to Santo Domingo. In addition, the five *caciques* remaining in Salvaleón de Higüey had their 863 Indians divided among 30 *encomenderos.* The 304 Indians under *cacica* Isabel de Iguanamí were divided among 10 *encomenderos,* in numbers varying from a high of 60 to a low of 10. In a similar fashion, the 416 Indians under *cacica* Doña María del Higüey were divided among 14 *encomenderos,* from a high of 48 to a low of 25. The case of Salvaleón de Higüey may be an indication in 1514 of what happened to the other Indian communities of Hispaniola before this date. Why this did not occur sooner in the case of Salvaleón de Higüey is unknown.

In summary, the 1514 Repartimiento reveals the following:

1. The majority of the Indians allotted in *encomienda* were service Indians; the minority were *naborías.* This pattern holds when the Repartimiento is viewed in its entirety and even when it is analyzed separately, by mining towns versus nonmining towns. The majority of the total number of Indians allotted was that of the allotments in the mining towns. Despite the steep decline in Indian population

evident in the totals of this Repartimiento, the Indians in their great majority continued to be used principally in the mines.

2. There apparently is no relationship between the number of *indios de servicio* allotted per town and the degree of community cohesion exhibited in the averages computed. In other words, a larger percentage of *indios de servicio* per mining town than per nonmining town, or per the Repartimiento as a whole, does not necessarily equate with a higher community average.
3. The *allegado* category comprises a minority of the Indians allotted; and most of these were *naborías.* No significant differences between mining and nonmining towns were found.
4. Evidence for the displacement of Indians from nonmining towns to the mining centers is clear in the case of Azua, Salvaleón de Higüey, La Vera Paz, and Yáquimo.
5. The disintegration of the relatively more intact Indian communities of the region of Salvaleón de Higüey that resulted from the 1514 Repartimiento may be a rather late illustration of how this process had occurred in other areas of the island in previous *repartimientos.* The segmentation of native villages into smaller units was a consequence of the displacement of Indians toward the mining centers and of the division of communities belonging to one *cacique* among separate *encomenderos.* The relentless exploitation of Indian labor in Hispaniola's mining areas was a significant cause of the disintegration of Indian communities and of the associated decline of the native Indian population.
6. Sixteen percent of the total number of *vecinos* allotted Indians were married to Indian women (62 of the 133 marriages reported, or 47 percent, were of marriages of Spanish men with Indian women). Since the Repartimiento does not include the entire Spanish population of the island (only those who received Indians are included), and since the majority of the Indians were allotted to members of the Spanish elite, which probably were not married to Indian women, it is very likely that there were many more mixed marriages than those reported.
7. The higher mortality of women is suggested in the higher number of men as opposed to women registered in the Repartimiento of La Concepción and Puerto Plata (Moya Pons 1982:129). However, this discrepancy may not indicate higher mortality in women but rather the direction in which miscegenation took place: Indian women married to Spanish men, and not vice versa. The Indian wives and/or concubines of Spanish men may not have been included in the Repartimiento totals.[17]

8. The low percentage of children and aged in the Indian communities. As pointed out by every scholar who has studied the 1514 Repartimiento, the small number of children is a clear indication that as early as 1514, only 22 years after initial contact with the Europeans, the reproductive rate of the aboriginal population was too low to allow for their survival (see also Arranz Márquez 1991:250–251, and Livi-Bacci 2003:44–46).
9. The wealth of the settlers and the relative prosperity of the island was tied to Indian labor. Even though it was evident to the Spanish settlers, as well as to the Spanish Crown and other court officials, that the Indians were diminishing rapidly, and that the system of *encomienda* labor and the work in the mines was largely to blame, they continued to distribute the Indians and use them preferentially in the mines. The entire economy was based on forced labor and on the unequal distribution of this labor among the Spanish elite favored by Albuquerque, including many nonresidents who held high positions in the Spanish court. The Repartimiento wreaked economic havoc among the many Spanish settlers that did not receive or received a small number of Indians, and there was considerable backlash from those left without, causing many to leave the island in search of better fortune elsewhere in the newly "discovered" New World. Worse yet, it also wreaked cultural and social havoc among the remaining Indian communities and among the many *naborías*, or house servants, that were taken from Spanish households where they had worked many years and allotted to a different *encomendero* (see also Arranz Márquez 1991:249). Even though it was clear that the Indians were in decline, the Spanish continued the status quo, as if unable to do anything else. The *encomiendas* became the defining economic, social, political, and ideological institution of the early Spanish Caribbean colonies (De La Luz-Rodríguez 2003, 2004), until there were no longer enough Indians to exploit. Africans took the place of the Indians, and outright slavery became the predominant source of labor in the latter half of the sixteenth century.

The Aboriginal Demography of Puerto Rico

Archaeological Evidence

In the 1930s, archaeologist Irving Rouse carried out an island-wide survey of Puerto Rico, including the islands of Mona and Vieques, and he sampled 48 sites. The main purpose of this survey was to establish a cultural chronology for the island, and as such he focused on ceramic period sites. Rouse (1952) postulated an initial settlement of ceramic peoples that spread along the coasts 200 B.C. to A.D. 600 (Period II, Saladoid Series), until A.D. 600 to A.D. 1200 (Period III, Ostionoid Series), when they began settling the central mountainous interior. Rouse indicated an apparent population increase during this period, followed by a decrease in population A.D. 1200 to A.D. 1500 (Period IV, Chican Ostionoid Subseries). He suggested that this decrease may have been due to migration to neighboring Hispaniola in response to raids carried out by Carib Indians, evidence of which persisted during early historic times.

Archaeological research in the Caribbean, and especially in Puerto Rico, has expanded considerably in the last 20-plus years. New syntheses of Puerto Rican prehistory and its relationship with the Caribbean area as a whole have added considerable new data and levels of interpretation that have revolutionized the way we look at the precolonial past (Curet and Hauser 2011; Rodríguez Ramos 2010; Siegel 2005; Oliver 2009; Wilson 1997b; Hofman and Duijvenbode 2011). Surveys and regional studies that expand on those undertaken in the 1980s by Pantel (1982), Solís Magaña (n.d., 1986), Espenshade et al. (1986), Thomas and Swanson (1986), and Rodriguez López (1984, 1985) provide much more detailed cultural-chronological data, as well as data on settlement size and distribution of sites throughout the island, that can shed light on aboriginal populations (paleo-demography) (Curet et al. 2004; Torres 2001; Tronolone et al. 1990; Maíz López 1990; Maíz López and Questell Rodríquez 2002). Although we are still not close to an estimate of absolute population numbers, it is possible to identify general trends through time and have at least a general perspective of population dynamics in Puerto Rico's late prehistoric period.[18]

Most of the information that we have on the prehistoric paleo-demography of Puerto Rico has been synthesized by Antonio Curet (2005). In his chapter on intraisland population trends, he compares the temporal/spatial site distributions (settlement patterns) in four regions where there is sufficient survey and GIS data: the Loíza River Basin, the Salinas River Basin, the Island of Vieques, and the Yauco River Basin (which includes the Guayanilla River as well) (Curet 2005:95–143). The first three regions are within the eastern half of Puerto Rico—northeast coast, south central coast, and the island of Vieques—while the Yauco River Basin is on the southwest of the island (2005:97, figure 5.1). He compares these regions under three main topics: population trends, the abandonment of sites, and settlement patterns and monumental architecture (2005:134). All regions show a gradual increase in population from the early ceramic period (Rouse's Period II) up to the early Ostionoid Series (Rouse's Period IIIa), referred to by Curet, following Rouse, as the Elenan and Ostionan Ostionoid Subseries (2005:134); then there is an apparent decline during the following Chican Ostionoid subseries, especially in the Salinas River Basin (2005:136–137). Within this general trend, Curet points out that the timing of the population increase differed in each area. He also notes that the decline in population during the later ceramic period is clear in the case of the Salinas River Basin but may have been slight in the other areas. Furthermore, he indicates that the Salinas River Basin experienced marked population decline and the abandonment of sites with monumental architecture, and he stresses that in all four regions "the demographic processes involved in the transition between Santa Elena and Esperanza styles were different" (Curet 2005:138).

Curet's analysis of the settlement patterns and monumental architecture in all four regions also demonstrates that, despite being within the same cultural/chronological area (except for the Yauco River Basin), demographic patterns (as may be inferred by settlement patterns and abandonment of sites) in each area varied (2005:134–143). Further comparative research in other areas of the island, especially the mountainous interior and the north and north-west coasts, is necessary to understand the population trends throughout the island, but this analysis clearly shows that the prehistoric populations in Puerto Rico in late prehistoric times, although identified archaeologically by late ceramic styles/subseries/series, and by ethnohistorians as Taíno, were socially and politically diverse. For the areas where information is available, there appears to have been a decline in population in the late prehistoric period, which, if corroborated by more refined paleo-demographic analyses, may explain the consistent sixteenth-century reports of Puerto Rico being less densely populated than Hispaniola.[19]

Historical Evidence

Documentary sources that could shed light on the Indian population of Puerto Rico during the early contact period are even scarcer than for Hispaniola. No document comparable to the 1514 Repartimiento for Hispaniola is available for Puerto Rico. Early chroniclers who mentioned the number of Indians at contact usually compared Puerto Rico favorably with Hispaniola but neglected to provide figures. The consensus at the time was that the island was densely populated by Indian populations very similar to the ones in Hispaniola.

Despite the traditional arguments for a dense native population in Puerto Rico, a closer scrutiny of the early historic sources reveals consistently lower numbers of Indians allotted in the *repartimientos* of this island (Alegría 1993:12–13). Although admittedly this was because the *repartimiento* numbers for Puerto Rico represent partial counts,[20] there is also documentary evidence that Indians from Puerto Rico were already moving out toward the Virgin Islands and/or other islands of the Lesser Antilles in order to avoid contact with the Spanish.

Sixteenth-century estimates for the aboriginal population of Puerto Rico are scarce. Rosenblat (1954:301–303, appendix V) summarized the available sources. Table 4.14 provides a synthesis of the available historical estimates.

As we did with Las Casas's estimates for Hispaniola, we assume his estimate of 600,000 to be exaggerated. However, the estimates of "war Indians" and *encomienda* Indians for the period between 1510 and 1511 provide figures that compare favorably with the population range we discussed for Hispaniola. Assuming that war Indians were able-bodied adult males, we could speculate that the total population would have been at least four times larger. If we take the middle estimate of 11,000 war Indians and multiply it by four, we get a rough total of 44,000; and if we add the 5,500 *encomienda* Indians, we get 49,500. Without these figures, and based on the same analysis that we provided for Hispaniola, we had calculated the population of Puerto Rico at the time of contact to be between 30,000 and 60,000 (Anderson-Córdova 1990, 1995). This estimate is similar to Rosenblat's estimate of 50,000 for Puerto Rico, a figure that is also accepted by Mira Caballos (1997:34).

Another, more recent, attempt to estimate Puerto Rico's contact population is provided by Francisco Moscoso (2008). Moscoso carefully scrutinized the sixteenth-century sources and documented 44 *caciques* that appear to have existed on the island, and he provides a map of the island with their probable locations (2008, appendix). He then uses Las Casas's estimates for the number of persons per household and number of households per village (similar to what Arranz Márquez did for Hispaniola, as previously discussed) to come up with various estimates for the population of Puerto Rico, assuming that there were 44 *caciques* at the time of contact (see 2008 table 11:226). Moscoso concludes with the hypothesis that each *cacique* had an average of 2,500 people, for an estimated population of 110,000. However, in his table 11 (2008:226), he also has lower figures of 1,000 to 2,000 people per *cacique*, which would indicate a total population of between 44,000 to 88,000, closer to the range of estimates discussed above.

Archaeological evidence that seems to indicate a decrease in population during late prehistoric times in Puerto Rico may help to explain the

Table 4.14. Aboriginal Population of Puerto Rico, Historical Estimates.

Year	Estimate	Source
1508–1510	600,000	Las Casas
1510–1511	More than 3,000 war Indians	Fernández de Oviedo (1959:I:470)
1511	11,000 war Indians 15,000 war Indians 5,500 *repartimiento* Indians	Herrera and Oviedo Castellanos *Memoria de Melgarejo* (1582)
1515	Less than 4,000 in *repartimiento*	Lic. Velázquez's letter to King Ferdinand
1530	1,148	Governor Francisco Manuel de Lando 1530 Census
1544	60	Bishop Bastidas

Sources: Brau 1894:312–313; Ramírez de Arellano 1934

consistency of historic sources' descriptions of much lower populations in Puerto Rico than in Hispaniola. In addition, in Puerto Rico the delay between the conquest of neighboring Hispaniola and the colonization of the island provided a hiatus in which native numbers may have been altered. The fact that the Indians of Puerto Rico knew about the existence of the Spanish and their activities in Hispaniola is documented. The Indians, when approached initially by Ponce de León, were apparently wary because of previous experiences with sporadic ships that had come to the island before Ponce de León's expedition (Tió 1961:45–46, 86). It is possible that this reduction in population may have begun before Spanish colonization, although this cannot be documented with the available evidence. What is clear, though, is the rapid movement of Indians out of Puerto Rico once the Spanish colonization process began.

The 1530 Census

This census is the only early-sixteenth-century document that provides detailed counts of the Indian population of Puerto Rico, since none of the *repartimiento* texts have survived.[21] Taken 22 years after the initial conquest of Puerto Rico (1508), the census documents the disappearance of the Indian population of the island. It differs from the 1514 Repartimiento for Hispaniola in that it provides information on both native

Table 4.15. Total Number of Black Slaves, Indian Slaves, and Free Indians, 1530 Census of Puerto Rico.

Town	San Juan	San Germán	Island Total
Black slaves, male	1,626	170	1,796
Black slaves, female	355	61	416
Total black slaves	1,981	231	2,212
Indian slaves	773	266	1,039
Free Indians	333	171	504
Total Indians	1,106	437	1,543

and slave Indians and it allows inferences concerning inter- and intraisland movement of Indians, a topic discussed in the following chapter. It also provides information on African slaves, which formed the majority (69 percent) of the enslaved labor force of the island (Cósimi 1994:9).

I consulted the transcription of the original document published by R. W. Ramírez de Arellano (1934) in this analysis. Summaries of all counts included here are those I computed. The census consists of a listing of colonists and the number of black and Indian slaves owned by each for the two subdivisions (partidos) of the island, San Juan and San Germán. It is followed in each "partido" by a list of the colonists who reported free Indians. There is also information concerning the profession, legal (residential standing), and marital status of the colonists; unfortunately, this is provided for only a minority of cases.

This document was analyzed to address the following: 1) the legal status of the Indians remaining on the island; 2) the relationship between Indian slaves and free Indians; 3) the relationship between black and Indian slaves; 4) the difference, if any, between San Juan and San Germán with respect to these issues; 5) the existence of Indians from other areas within the slave population; and 6) information on the work carried out by the Indians.[22] Tables 4.15 through 4.22 summarize the results of the analysis.

Totals for Puerto Rico indicate 2,212 black slaves and 1,039 Indian slaves (table 4.15). Of the total number of slaves reported (3,251), 68 percent were black and 32 percent were Indian. When the number of free Indians is included (504), the total non-European ethnic category of black and Indian (3,755) reported is 59 percent black and 41 percent Indian.[23]

A comparison between San Juan and San Germán reveals important differences. Most of the black slaves (1,981, or 90 percent of the total for the island) and Indian slaves (773, or 74 percent of the total for the island) are reported in the San Juan District. The total number of slaves, both Indian and black, is much less for the San Germán District. However, in San Germán more Indian slaves (54 percent) than black slaves (40 percent) are reported, and the proportion of blacks to Indians is opposite to what is observed in San Juan. San Germán reports proportionally more Indians than blacks, when compared with San Juan.[24] It is significant that the number of Indian slaves reported is consistently higher than the free Indians when viewed in the totals for the island as well as when separated by district.[25] Since free Indians represent the native *encomienda* Indians of the island, and Indian slaves represent mostly those brought in from other areas, these 1530 figures support my hypothesis that survivors on the island were mainly foreign Indians (see also Cósimi 1994:9). However, it is also possible that many of the Indian slaves documented in this census were surviving native Indians enslaved during the earlier Spanish raids against rebellious Indians within the island of Puerto Rico.[26]

An analysis of the individuals who reported owning both Indian and black slaves, as well as both free and slave Indians, for the island and for each district provides insights into the opportunities for communication between these ethnic groups under the institution of slavery. Taken as a whole, 300 individuals reported owning Indian and/or black slaves. Of these, 184, or 61 percent, reported owning both Indian and black slaves, 62, or 21 percent, reported only black slaves, and the remaining 54, or 18 percent, reported only Indian slaves. When analyzed separately, San Juan reports 149, or 62 percent, of individuals owning both Indian and black slaves, 54, or 22 percent, black slaves only, and 37, or 15 percent, Indian slaves only. San Germán reports 35, or 58 percent, having both, 8, or 13 percent, blacks only, and 17, or 28 percent, Indians only. It appears, then, that the Indian and black slave populations of the island coexisted under the same owners to a significant degree, slightly more so in the case of San Juan. However, since the majority of the owners of slaves had few of them, the opportunities for the coexistence of larger groups of black and Indian slaves was probably minimal.

A comparison of the colonists owning slaves and reporting free Indians is also revealing (tables 4.16 and 4.17). In the case of San Juan, all the individuals that report free Indians also owned Indian slaves. The same is true, with one exception, in San Germán. Although the number of individuals who reported free Indians is much lower than the number

Table 4.16. Details of the 33 Individuals Reporting Free Indians in San Juan, 1530 Census of Puerto Rico.

Name	Personal Information	Black Male Slaves	Black Female Slaves	Indian Slaves	Free Indians
Francisco M. de Lando	Lt. Governor, *vecino* of SJ, single	44	0	4	4
Alonso de Cáceres	Scribe, *vecino*, married to Spanish woman	0	0	3	1
Diego Ramos	*Vecino*, married to Spanish woman	15	1	10	3
Nicolás Alonso	Married to Spanish woman	0	0	3	3
Bartolomé Ramírez	Carpenter, married to Spanish woman	0	1	1	1
Francisco Mejía	*Vecino*, married to Spanish woman	5	2	3	3
Diego de Cuéllar	Mayor, *vecino*, married to Spanish woman	15	5	7	7
Diego Guilarte	Mayor, *vecino*, married to Spanish woman	33	10	8	12
Martín Hernández (or Fernández)	Contador, *vecino*, married to Spanish woman	20	8	7	21
Fernando Labrador	*Vecino*, married to Spanish woman	3	1	1	1
Baltasar de Castro	*Regidor*, married to Spanish woman	30	11	4	17
Pedro Espinosa	*Regidor*, *vecino*, married to Spanish woman	3	0	6	17
Garci-Troche	*Regidor*, *vecino*, married to Spanish woman	52	17	9	32
Francisco Alvarado	*Vecino*, married to Spanish woman	35	14	7	2
Rodrigo (or Francisco) Toscano	Married to Spanish woman	0	0	1	1
Antonio Sedeño	*Contador*, *vecino*	26	3	3	48
Yguiluco	*Vecino*, single	29	0	16	6
Blas de Villasante	Treasurer & *regidor* of SJ, *vecino*, single	60	10	6	45

Diego Muriel	*Vecino*, married to Indian woman	13	4	17	19
Francisco Manso	*Vecino*, single	28	6	9	4
Bishop		34	9	7	10
Angel Alvarez & Juan Castellanos	*Vecinos*	31	0	9	3
Diego de Villareal	*Vecino*, single	8	5	16	1
Juan de Toro	Married to Spanish woman	13	3	2	6
Asensio de Villanueva	Sheriff, Holy Inquisition	8	7	10	8
Cristóbal de Guzmán	Deceased	26	9	10	15
Juan Ruiz	*Vecino*, married to Indian woman	7	4	5	8
Lucas de Sayavedra	Mayor, *vecino*, single	31	12	13	4
Francisco Juancho	*Vecino*, married	17	7	30	6
Pedro de Angulo	*Vecino* of San Germán, married	35	7	50	16
Cristóbal de Zafra	*Vecino*, married	5	2	1	1
Francisco de Aguilar	Single	4	2	8	3
Santo Domingo Monastery		27	—	2	5

Table 4.17. Details of the 24 Individuals Reporting Free Indians in San Germán, 1530 Census of Puerto Rico.

Name	Personal Information	Black Slaves	Indian Slaves	Free Indians
Alonso de Vargas	Mayor, *vecino*, married	18	6	13
Anton de San Miguel	*Regidor*, *vecino*, single	12	8	3
Esteban Martín	*Vecino*, married	1	2	2
Juan de Burgos	*Vecino*, married	1	5	3
Isabel de la Torre	Wife of Lic. de la Gama	18	9	13
Juan Maldonado	*Regidor*, *vecino*, married	15	6	11
Pedro Pabón	*Vecino*, married	1	1	2
Francisco de Ortega	*Vecino*, married	3	7	1
Juan Geniz	*Vecino*, married	0	10	4
Gaspar de Bruxuelas	*Vecino*, single	12	5	7
Vasco de Tiedra	*Regidor*, *vecino*, married	25	13	18
Br. Alvaro Marín	Doctor, *estante*, married	3	2	2
Diego de Avila	*Vecino*, married	1	4	2
Benito Caramao	*Vecino*, married	0	6	3
Gonzalo Rincón	*Vecino*, married	11	22	12
Rodrigo de San Lucar	Mayor, *vecino*, single	19	41	5
Bernardo de Jerez	*Vecino*, married	0	2	11
Rodrigo de Campano	*Vecino*, single	10	9	13
Luis de Añasco	*Vecino*, married	1	3	6
Juan de Cervantes	Scribe, *vecino*, married	2	4	4
Alonso Rodríguez Minaya	*Regidor*, *vecino*, married	10	11	20
Juan Mulero	*Vecino*, married	0	2	2
Francisco de Morales	*Vecino*, single	0	2	2
Juan de Quener	*Vecino*, single	0	0	12

owning Indian slaves (38 versus 238), those who did report free Indians also owned Indian slaves. The free Indians, then, were in all cases except one coexisting with Indian slaves. This provides some indication of interethnic communication between free Indians (presumably those native to the island) and slave Indians (presumably including many brought from other areas). Since almost all of the individuals who reported free Indians also owned black slaves, the possibility of multiethnic communication also existed.

An analysis of the legal and marital status of the individuals who owned Indian slaves and those also reporting free Indians confirms many historians' contention that the free Indians were preferably allotted to established, married *vecinos* (tables 4.18 to 4.21). Ninety-six percent of individuals who reported free Indians, for which information concerning their legal and marital status is provided, were *vecinos* (100 percent of those in San Juan and 92 percent of those in San Germán), and 73 percent were married (71 percent of those in San Juan, and 75 percent of those in San Germán). This contrasts with 65 percent *vecinos* and 52 percent married in the case of Indian slave owners for which information is provided (67 percent *vecinos* and 55 percent married in San Juan, and 62 percent *vecinos* and 43 percent married in San Germán). It appears that the colonists of the island who, because of their legal and/or marital status, did not benefit from the limited number of free Indians available for allotment opted to acquire Indian slaves as an alternative. This allowed them the opportunity for socioeconomic mobility that would otherwise have been unavailable (Wolff 2014:250).

Provenance of the Indians

As mentioned, the census provides information that points to the fact that the majority of the Indians remaining in Puerto Rico in 1530 were slaves. It is probable that many, if not most, of the Indians reported as slaves were brought to the island from outside areas. Although the origin of these Indians is in the majority of cases not specified, when it is, all references to outside Indians are of Indian slaves and not of free Indians. The 81 instances in which Indians from outside the island are specified occur in the section of the census on the Indian slaves in San Germán. These constitute 30 percent of the total number of Indian slaves reported for this town. Of these 81, four are specifically indicated as natives of Yucatán. It is probable that most of the Indian slaves mentioned in the census were not natives of the island. The text of the census specifically refers to the existence of foreign Indians within the slave population (Ramírez de Arellano 1934:54).

Table 4.18. Legal, Marital, and Professional Status of Slave Owners, San Juan, 1530 Census of Puerto Rico.

Legal Status	*Vecinos*	64
	Moradores	21
	Estantes	3
	Ausentes	8
	Not specified	117
Marital Status	Single	58
	Married	4
	Married to Spanish woman	53
	Married to Indian woman	7
	Married to black woman	2
	Married in Spain	12
	Total married	78
	Not specified[a]	76
Profession	Royal & municipal official	12
	Scribe	5
	Miner	12
	Carpenter	3
	Vaquero	9
	Servant	9
	Estanciero	7
	Merchant	12
	Tailor	4
	Clergy	7
	Doctor	2
	Other[b]	17
	Not specified	114

[a] There is also mention of five women slave owners, whose marital status is not specified but may have been widows, as well as one deceased individual still listed as slave owner

[b] Many other professions are mentioned at least once

Table 4.19. Legal, Marital, and Professional Status of the 33 Individuals Reporting Free Indians in San Juan, 1530 Census of Puerto Rico.

Legal Status	*Vecinos*	25
	Not specified	4
Marital status	Single	7
	Married	3
	Married to Spanish woman	15
	Married to Indian woman	2
	Total married	20
	Deceased	1
	Not specified	3
Profession	Royal official	10
	Scribe	1
	Carpenter	1
	Bishop	1
	Sheriff of the Inquisition	1
	Not specified	16

In contrast, the free Indians appear all to be natives of the island, since they are consistently referred to as *naborías*, or *naborías indios libres*, or *indios libres naborías de repartimiento*.[27] In summary, the analysis of the data provided in this census (table 4.22) is consistent with other historical data to the effect that the native Indians survived as free Indians who were distributed among the Spanish colonists in the *repartimientos*, while the Indian slaves included a substantial number, if not a majority, of foreign Indians. Data in this census also demonstrates, as pointed out by Cósimi (1994:24), that the transition from *encomienda* labor to slave labor (both Indian, and to a greater extent, African) was occurring more rapidly in San Juan than in San Germán, and that Puerto Rico was already mainly black in 1530:

> A marked ethnic contrast is observed between the two cities: in the Capital, there are proportionately less Taínos (assuming that the *naborías* were Taínos) in the labor force: 9 percent in the former, and 26 percent in the latter, and the percentage of Amerindians among the allotted slaves is only 27 percent in San Juan versus 48 percent in San Germán. Puerto Rico is already mainly black in 1530, but the indigenous racial presence is much larger in the west than in the rest of the island [my translation].

Table 4.20. Summary of Legal, Marital, and Professional Status of Individuals in San Germán Who Reported Owning Slaves, 1530 Census of Puerto Rico.

Legal Status	*Vecinos*	33
	Estantes	20
	Not specified	3
Marital status	Married	22
	Married in Castille	2
	Total married	24
	Single	28
	Minors	2
	Not specified[a]	4
Professions	Royal official	5
	Clergy	2
	Vaqueros	1
	Doctor	1
	Miner	1
	Scribe	1
	Carpenter	1
	Estanciero	1
	Blacksmith	1
	Not specified	42

Note: Individuals reporting both black and Indian slaves, 35; individuals reporting only black slaves, 8; individuals reporting only Indian slaves, 17; individuals reporting Indians and/or black slaves, 60

[a] There is also mention of 2 women slave owners, whose marital status is not specified, but may have been widows

Table 4.21. Legal, Marital, and Professional Status of the 24 Individuals Reporting Free Indians in San Germán, 1530 Census of Puerto Rico.

Legal Status	*Vecinos*	22
	*Estant*e	1
	Woman	1
Marital status	Single	6
	Married	17
	Married woman	1
Profession	Royal official	6
	Scribe	1
	Doctor	1
	Not specified	15

Table 4.22. Summary of Legal, Marital, and Professional Status of Slave Owners Reporting Indian Slaves and/or Free Indians for the Island of Puerto Rico, 1530 Census.

Legal status of slave owners	*Vecinos*	97
	Estantes	23
	Moradores	21
	Ausentes	8
	Not specified	120
Marital status of slave owners	Married	26
	Married in Castille	14
	Married to Spanish woman	53
	Married to Indian woman	7
	Married to Black woman	2
	Total married	102
	Single	86
	Minors	2
	Not specified[a]	80
Profession of slave owners	All public professions	23
	Clergy	9
	Vaqueros	10
	Doctor	3
	Miner	13
	Servant	9
	Carpenter	4
	Estanciero	8
	Merchant	12
	Tailor	4
	Other	18
	Not specified	156
Total number of Indian slaves		1039
Legal status of those reporting free Indians	*Vecinos*	47
	*Estante*s	1
	Woman	1
	Not specified	4
Marital status of those reporting free Indians	Married	20
	Married to Spanish woman	15
	Married to Indian woman	2
	Total married	37

Continued on the next page

Table 4.22. *Continued*

Marital status of those reporting free Indians	Single	13
	Married woman	1
	Not specified[b]	3
Professions of those reporting free Indians	All public professions	18
	Carpenter	1
	Bishop	1
	Sheriff of the Holy Inquisition	1
	Doctor	1
	Not specified	31

Note: Individuals reporting both black and Indian slaves, 184; individuals reporting only black slaves, 62; individuals reporting only Indian slaves, 54; individuals reporting black and/or Indian slaves, 300

[a] There is also mention of 7 women who owned Indian slaves, whose marital status is not specified, but may have been widows, as well as one deceased individual still listed as owning an Indian slave

[b] There is also one deceased individual still listed as reporting free Indians

The institutionalization of slave labor (both Indian and black) that is clearly evident in this census document for Puerto Rico has its beginnings in the previous enslavement of rebellious Indians on the island, a process that became more prevalent as more and more Indians were brought in from other areas to work in the gold mines and Spanish *haciendas*. Both institutions, the *encomienda* system and outright slavery, were critical to the development of early colonial society and were the essential cause for the destruction of the islands' native peoples (De La Luz-Rodríguez 2003, 2004; Wolff 2014). However, during this early period, as blacks began to substitute for a declining native population, multiple ethnicities coexisted under these dual systems of oppression.

Summary

This chapter critically examined the data available on the historic aboriginal demography of Hispaniola and Puerto Rico. It estimates that the former had a population fluctuating between 250,000 and 500,000 Indians, the latter between 30,000 and 60,000. Both islands suffered rapid population loss beginning early in the sixteenth century due to the unfavorable conditions under which contact occurred, mainly the establishment of two systems of forced labor: the *encomiendas* and outright slavery.

The relationship between depopulation and the social and cultural transformation occurring among the historic Indian population of these islands was explored in the analysis of the 1514 Repartimiento of Hispaniola and the 1530 Census of Puerto Rico. These documents, along with those discussed in chapter 3 concerning native Indian response to contact, provide material for inferences concerning how the process of Indian cultural change occurred within the scenario of rapid population decline. They also provide clear indications on the existence of foreign Indians, their distribution among the colonists, and their relationship with native Indians.

5
The Voluntary and Forced Movement of Indians among the Islands and the Mainland

Archaeological research demonstrates that the 7,000-year human history of the Caribbean archipelago has been one of continuous cultural variation and movement of peoples throughout the islands and surrounding mainland areas. Trade and kinship networks, as well as broader ideological and religious ties among diverse native peoples, were important factors as social groups settled and established themselves on these islands. These networks were inevitably disrupted in the wake of late-fifteenth-century European settlement, with disastrous consequences for the islands' native inhabitants. To understand how native inhabitants coped with the influx of Europeans, it is important to keep in mind that this variation and movement of peoples characteristic of precolonial times continued, albeit in a drastically modified form, during the early years of European colonization. This movement, and the variety of ethnic groups that historically participated in it, must be clearly acknowledged when we study the culture-contact scenario in the early Caribbean.

This chapter presents the results of historical research carried out to document the processes of voluntary and forced movement of Indians among the islands and the mainland that occurred during the period of conquest and early colonization of Hispaniola and Puerto Rico, and the significance of these movements in the processes of social and cultural change among Indian island communities. It includes evidence for movement out of the islands—voluntary out-migration—and offers an interpretation as to why this happened. The movement into the islands—involuntary in-migration—is also discussed. In contrast to the former, the latter was due to the forced transfer of Indians from outside to work as slaves and *naborías*. I discuss the nature of the Spanish Indian slave raids, how they operated, and how the institution of slavery was established and transformed in the Spanish possessions.

Voluntary Out-Migration

Geographical and Cultural Characteristics of the Antilles and Interisland Contact

The Antilles (also known as the West Indies), in contrast to other island chains such as the Polynesian Islands, are relatively compact. They are described by many researchers as stepping stones stretching in a southeast to northwest arc from mainland South America to the Gulf of Mexico (figure 5.1). Except for islands of Tobago and Grenada, which are separated by a large gap, each is visible from its closest neighbor (Rouse 1986:108), which must have offered favorable conditions for quick expansion up the island chain. The larger, more fertile islands are located in the northwestern section of the arc, known as the Greater Antilles. These were the last to be colonized by the migratory waves of ceramic agriculturalists who entered the Antilles beginning sometime around 500 to 200 B.C. (Rouse 1988:10; Haviser 1997:59–69).

In contrast to Polynesia, where vast oceanic distances separated the main archipelagos, opportunities for interisland contact were ample in the Antilles. The processes of settlement, tribal segmentation, and movement to other Caribbean islands that occurred for centuries led to a common cultural heritage. It is possible that the history of the local island migrations may have survived in the form of mythological symbols still in expression in the Indian societies at the time of contact. Mythical geography, which must have had its roots in the prehistoric migration of the local peoples, is present in mythological accounts compiled by Fray Ramón Pané (1974) in Hispaniola and in the discourse of the Indians with the Spanish conquistadors at initial contact (Sued Badillo 1978:68–71).

The similarities in the ceramic styles between contiguous island areas of the Antilles were noted by Rouse (1964) many decades ago. These series of ceramic styles (by which Rouse grouped styles with similar characteristics that may indicate a common cultural tradition) show significant similarities between the ceramics of eastern Puerto Rico and the U.S. Virgin Islands, of western Puerto Rico and eastern Hispaniola, of northern Hispaniola and the Bahamas, and of western Hispaniola and eastern Cuba. The fact that the Caribbean prehistoric peoples were oriented toward the sea, especially with respect to the larger islands, was also pointed out years ago by Rouse (1986) and, as previously discussed, has been corroborated by various researchers. The consensus among Caribbean scholars is that interisland contact existed throughout the pre-Columbian period, during which a variety of ethnic and cultural groups

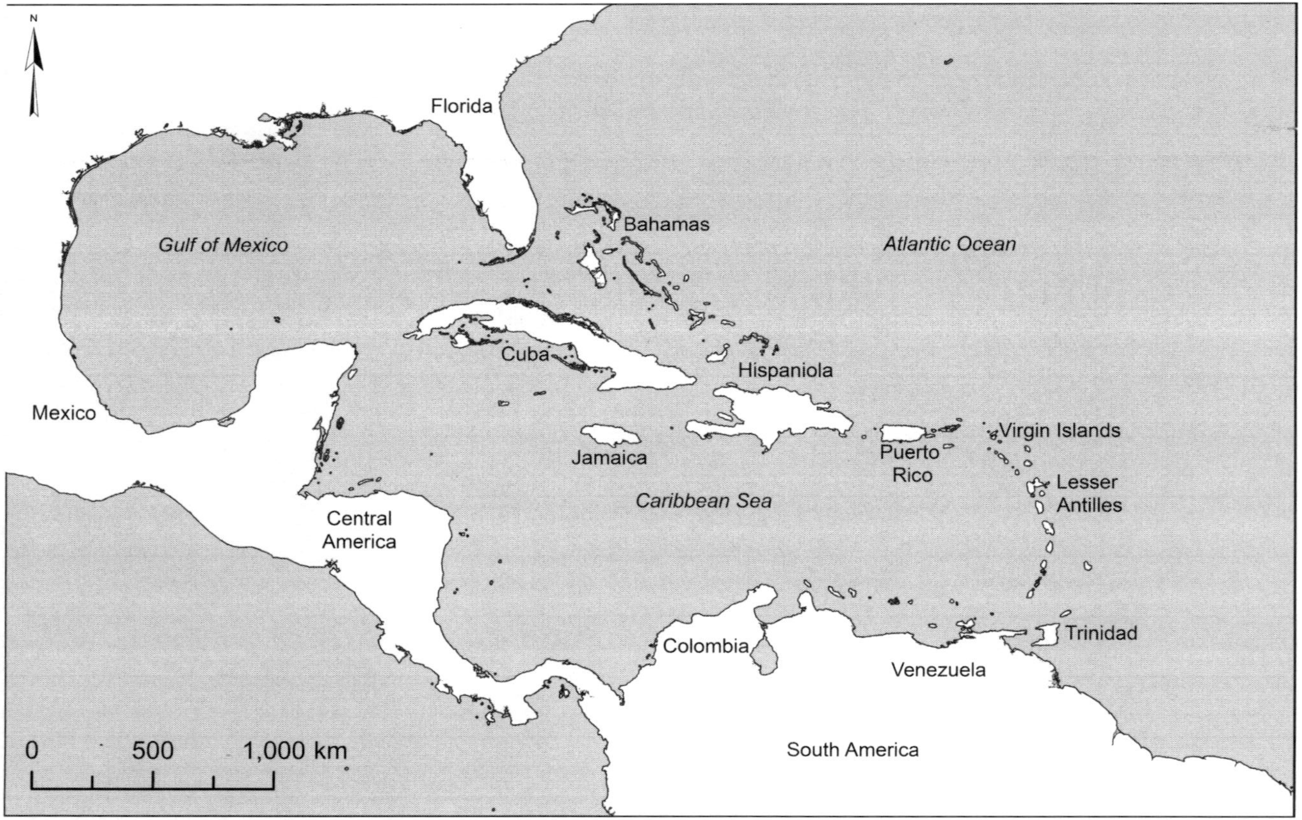

Figure 5.1. The Antillean Islands (based on Anderson-Córdova 1990:221).

interacted over a wide area. Cultural similarities observed between adjacent islands may be the product of the routes of expansion from one island to the other followed in the migrations up the island chain. Alternatively, the earliest historic sources attest to the navigational skills of the native inhabitants of these islands and to the movement of small groups of Indians among islands. Interisland trade networks are evident in the prehistoric archaeological record as well, indicating another avenue for interisland communication (Rouse 1948:130–131; Rose 1987:327–329; Dagget 1980; Sullivan 1980; Cody 1991; Rodríguez López 1991; Watters 1997; Rodríguez Ramos 2010).

Historical Evidence for Interisland Contact in the Contact Period

Columbus's account of the first voyage provides some clues to Indian interisland contacts.[1] The pertinent passages from the narratives of the first voyage are presented in appendix 1. The cited sections of his Diary indicate that the Indians were cognizant of island geographies and that they transported themselves over relatively long distances.

Further evidence for interisland movement is also present in the historical references of Columbus's second voyage. On this voyage, the Spanish arrived first on Guadeloupe. All sources consulted mention the existence of Indians from other islands kept captive there. They refer to the Indians of Guadeloupe as *caribes* (Las Casas 1951:I:353), *cambalos* (Cuneo 1495 in Varela 1982:241), or *caníbales* (Coma in Varela 1982:191; Columbus 1498 in Varela 1982:222). They also concur in indicating that the captives were women and young men from other islands, although only Las Casas refers to them as being captives of Borikén (Puerto Rico).[2]

These descriptions support the fact of pre-Columbian interisland contact, at least between the island of Puerto Rico and the Lesser Antilles. Las Casas's account states that the women who approached Columbus's ships at Guadeloupe mentioned that there were many islands, as well as a mainland "Tierra Firme," and that these women "called each island by name" ("*nombraron a cada una por su nombre*") (Las Casas 1951:I:353). In what probably refers to the same incident, Columbus indicates that Indian cannibals (*caníbales*) had told him "that the mainland was to their south": "I was in the island of Guadeloupe, and I also heard others from the island of St. Croix and San Juan [Puerto Rico], and they said that there was a lot of gold" (Varela 1982:222).[3]

The Carib custom of navigating among the islands of the Lesser Antilles is mentioned by Simón Verde in 1493 (Varela and Gil 1984:210): "And they say that during the summertime these people travel 300 leagues from the coast, going from island to island, navigating in search of booty."[4] Las Casas, in reference to Columbus's second voyage, mentions that upon his passage through Cuba, the Indians indicated the location of Jamaica (Las Casas 1951:I:380). Jamaica is located 150 miles to the south of Cuba over open water.

Sources therefore strongly suggest that interisland communication was a widespread phenomenon in pre-Columbian and early contact times in the Caribbean. The Indians of different islands knew the existence and location of other islands, and some had actually traveled (in some cases unwillingly) among them. The Indians were skillful navigators and were frequently seen by Columbus and his men in waters far from shore. They utilized their canoes as a means of transportation, both within and among the islands and along the major waterways and coasts. Kinship ties may have existed among islands and may be an indication of the expansion of the chiefdoms of Hispaniola and Puerto Rico into surrounding islands (Keegan 1989, 1992, 2007; Oliver 2006). This knowledge must have served the Indians well, both as a strategy of escape from Spanish domination and as they coped with life under the Spanish. This apparently was of more importance in the case of Puerto Rico.

Historical Evidence for Interisland Movement in the Colonial Period

Movement from Hispaniola to Cuba. Indians from the westernmost province of Hispaniola (Guahaba) fled to Cuba to escape the Spanish. Sources mention the Hispaniola *cacique* Hatüey, who settled in Punta Mayarí, Cuba, with some of his people (Las Casas 1985:II:506–507).

Movement from Hispaniola to Florida. There is one reference concerning Juan Ponce de León's voyage of discovery of Florida, which suggests that the Indians of Hispaniola navigated that far. Murga Sanz (1971:110–111), citing Herrera, mentions that on June 4, 1513, as the Spanish were waiting on the south coast of Florida, "a canoe arrived at their vessel, and an Indian who understood the Spaniards and whom they thought must have been from Hispaniola or another of the islands inhabited by Spaniards, told them to wait because the *cacique* wanted to send gold as ransom."[5]

Movement from Hispaniola to San Juan de Puerto Rico. Brau (1966:95–96) indicates that the Mona Channel served as a communication link between these two islands and that movement of peoples and goods continued despite the conquest of Hispaniola. This was first mentioned by Las Casas: "Because since the neighboring Indians of the province of Higüey were the closest to the said island of San Juan, and they were no more than 12 or 15 leagues away, every day they would go back and forth, and they communicated, and could know what was in each other's land" (1985:II:355–356).[6]

The last reference suggests continued contact between the Indians of Higüey (southeast Hispaniola) and those of Puerto Rico, as evidenced by the testimony of Marcos de Aguilar, a longtime resident of Hispaniola, in the Hieronymite Interrogatory of 1517 (see also Alegría 1976:33). This testimony is important, not only because it mentions interisland communication after contact but also because it suggests that kinship bonds that existed before contact may have persisted as well: "He knows how a *cacique* from the island of San Juan killed don Christoval de Sotomayor and other Christians in an area called Xavca in the island of San Juan, and that *cacique* Andres, who now works for his Highness, and was a relative of the other *cacique*, also knew that Don Christoval had been killed" (Rodríguez Demorizi 1971:346).[7]

Movement from San Juan de Puerto Rico to the Lesser Antilles. Contemporary historic sources suggest that movement out of San Juan east into the neighboring islands of Vieques, Culebra, the Virgin Islands, and on into the Lesser Antilles was a common and widespread phenomenon. This is always mentioned in relationship with the Carib Indians, who are placed in San Juan since the first reference to the conquest and colonization of the island.[8]

Historical references that suggest the participation of Carib Indians in the rebellion of the Indians of San Juan and the flight of the latter into neighboring islands to the east have already been discussed. The consistently lower population figures mentioned for the indigenous population of San Juan compared to those for Hispaniola, and the possibility that the exodus toward the Lesser Antilles had been occurring since the beginning of Spanish colonization, has also been considered. As early as 1511, royal instructions to the officials of San Juan concerning the Indian rebellion mention that their canoes should be destroyed to avoid their flight to neighboring islands (CODOIN:I:32:225–230; *Boletín Histórico de Puerto Rico,* hereafter BHPR:1970:292). Many historians agree that the sources point to the alliance of Puerto Rico Indians and Caribs in the rebellion in San Juan, as well as in the so-called Carib raids on the island, which persisted well into the latter half of the sixteenth century (Ramos Pérez 1975:92–99; Brau 1894:140–141, 1966:235, 254–255; Sued Badillo 1978, 2008). As pointed out by Brau, the decline of the Indian population, which accelerated between 1514 and 1530, may have been due in large part to the movement of the Indians from Puerto Rico toward the Lesser Antilles (1966:390).

This flight to the Lesser Antilles is partly confirmed by the information pertaining to the Spanish armadas (raids) against the so-called Caribs. These began in 1510–1511 (Ramos Pérez 1975:92), almost coinciding with the Indian rebellion in San Juan de Puerto Rico, which started in February 1511. They are discussed briefly below, to corroborate the existence of San Juan Indians in Lesser Antillean islands. The issue concerning the influx of Indians from these islands is discussed in a separate section below. Complete references for the data presented are found in appendix 2, unless otherwise noted. All references to San Juan pertain to the entire island of Puerto Rico. This island was called Isla de San Juan Bautista during the sixteenth century.

1. In a Royal Decree of June 6, 1511, addressed to Diego Colón and officials of Hispaniola, the King authorizes Indians to be brought from St. Croix but indicates that any Indians found to be natives of San Juan should be returned to that island.
2. On November 9, 1511, the King authorized the Spanish residents of San Juan to raid the islands of Dominica, Martinique, St. Lucia, La Ascensión, Barbados, Tobago, and Mayo and retrieve the San Juan Indians found among the Caribs. A similar decree of November 22 to Diego Colón concerns the return of the San Juan Indians from Carib islands. There are two versions of this decree, one suggesting that the Indians from San Juan were taken captive by the Caribs, the other suggesting that they fled Puerto Rico to live among the Caribs.
3. In a 1512 decree, mention is made of the discovery of six Indians from San Juan by the Spanish during an expedition to Trinidad (Fernández Méndez 1984:36–37 citing Tapia y Rivera 1970:101). Trinidad is located more than 600 miles to the southwest of Puerto Rico.
4. In 1515, the King instructed Juan Ponce de León that natives from San Juan found in Carib islands were to be returned to the islands as *naborías*, if they gave themselves up voluntarily.

Historical data on the Carib raids on the island of San Juan also indicate movement of Indians between San Juan and the Lesser Antilles. The Miguel Díaz letter cited in note 8 of this chapter mentions the participation of foreign Indians, whom he identified as Carib, in the Indian rebellion. After this rebellion, which continued until 1515, reference to recurring Carib raids on the Spanish settlements and *haciendas* of the island of San Juan appears in the historical record. The target of these raids was the eastern half of the island, especially the northeastern area of the city of San Juan de Puerto Rico (previously Caparra) and the Hacienda Real del Toa (Royal Hacienda at Toa), and the eastern sections of Humacao and Luquillo.

During the raids, the invading Indians usually killed both Spanish and native Indians, though on many occasions they took the latter with them. Whether these Indians left voluntarily is not known, but this practice does point to another way in which native movement outside of the island may have occurred. For example, a November 20, 1520, letter to the Emperor from an official in Santo Domingo, describing a Carib attack on the Humacao area of San Juan de Puerto Rico approximately two months before, mentions that 50 native Indians were taken (Tapia y Rivera 1970:332–333). Another letter dated October 31, 1530, mentions a Carib attack in the Daguao and Luquillo areas in which 25 native Indians were taken (*Santo Domingo en los documentos de Juan Bautista Muñoz*, hereafter SDDJBM 1981:351–352).

Other references to Carib attacks usually have them occurring during the month of September or October (1514 attack to the Toa area Fernández Méndez 1984:44; Murga Sanz 1971:143; 1529 attack on the San Juan area, PRDJBM 1960:260–262; Tapia y Rivera 1970:343), a pattern that did not go unnoticed by the Spanish, as evidenced in a February 16, 1534, letter from the city council of San Juan to the Emperor (HDPR 1973:I:30–31). These recurrent raids provided opportunity for native Indians to abandon the island in favor of settling in areas not yet colonized by any European power.

In summary, historical evidence suggests the following conclusions concerning the movement of Indians among islands during the early historic period:

1. The native inhabitants of the Antilles were knowledgeable about island geography and frequently traveled among the islands for various purposes, including trade, raiding for women and/or goods, and, possibly, maintaining kinship ties.
2. During the early colonial period, the native inhabitants utilized the strategy of flight to other islands in order to escape from the Spanish. This flight occurred toward areas not yet settled by the Spanish, that is, first from Hispaniola to Cuba and Puerto Rico and maybe as far as Florida, and later from Puerto Rico to the neighboring islands of Vieques and St. Croix and into the Lesser Antilles, as far south as Trinidad.
3. This strategy was more effective in the case of Puerto Rico, probably because the neighboring islands to the east and southeast continued

to be unconquered or outside the immediate control of the Spanish or other Europeans during the sixteenth century. Therefore, contrary to Hispaniola, which quickly became surrounded by Spanish settlements in Cuba, Jamaica, and Puerto Rico, the Indians of Puerto Rico continued to have an eastern frontier where they could escape from Spanish encroachment. The strategy for Puerto Rico was of flight out of the island, rather than into the island, as was partly the case in Hispaniola and Cuba. The larger land area of the latter two islands allowed bands of *indios alzados* (rebel Indians) to remain on the islands and to subsist by practicing small-plot horticulture in mountainous or secluded areas and by raiding the Spanish settlements. The smaller area of Puerto Rico may have precluded this strategy. Instead, historical evidence strongly suggests that the Indians of Puerto Rico fled out of the island and then raided the Spanish settlements from the neighboring islands, in alliance with neighboring Indians, referred to as Caribs by the Spanish. Despite the common experience of the native inhabitants of Hispaniola and Puerto Rico under the Spanish and their common ethnic and cultural background, the strategy of flight assumed different characteristics. This, in turn, may explain in part the disparity in terms of numbers of Indians in both islands throughout the historic period and in the ethnic composition of these Indians as well.

Involuntary In-Migration

Forced Movement and the Institution of Slavery

Hispaniola and San Juan de Puerto Rico were the first two New World territories to be settled by the Spanish. They served as centers for an expanding New World frontier that eventually stretched throughout large portions of the South, Central, and North American mainland (figure 5.2).

The movement of the Spanish through this frontier was accompanied by the movement of the native inhabitants displaced by the Spanish as they invaded newly discovered territories. In many cases, this movement was forcefully imposed by the Spanish for the sole purpose of securing labor for the entire range of economic activities that they pursued. The influx of foreign Indians to Hispaniola and Puerto Rico followed the route of exploration and conquest of the Greater Antilles island chain, into the arc from Venezuela and Trinidad to the southeast and extending into the peninsula of Florida to the northwest—what Sauer (1969) called the Spanish Main.

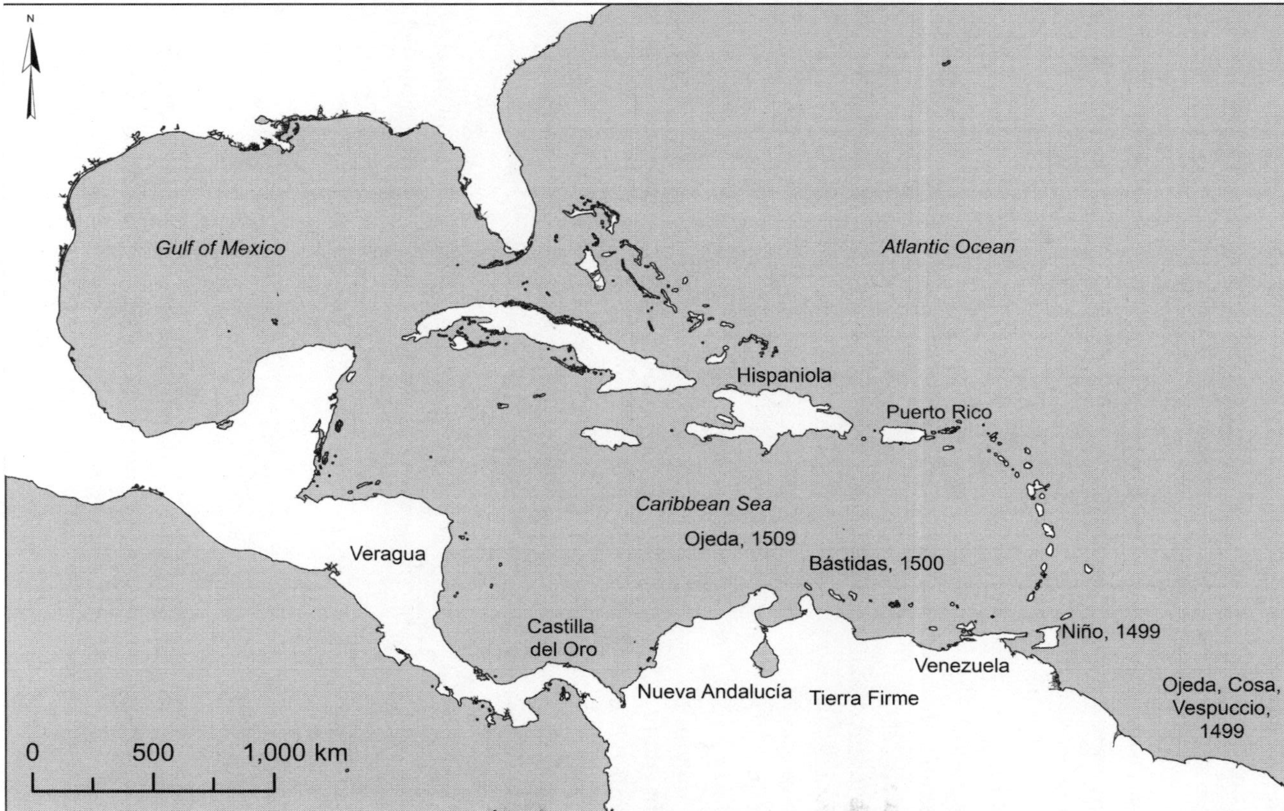

Figure 5.2. Early Spanish explorations of Tierra Firme (based on Alvarez Rubiano 1944:20; Anderson-Córdova 1990:235).

As slavery and other forms of forced labor, such as the *encomienda* system, were imposed throughout this expanding frontier, Spanish policy with respect to the enslavement of Indians and the desirability of transporting them from one colonial area to another developed and changed through time. Appendix 2 summarizes chronologically the pertinent legislation and official correspondence that illustrate the development of Spanish policy concerning this matter. The reader is referred to it for complete citations of the documentation utilized in this discussion, unless otherwise noted.

The institution of slavery was already firmly rooted in Spanish society before the discovery of the New World, and it is therefore not surprising that it was almost immediately incorporated into its emerging societies (Konetzke 1949:441–452; Friede 1961:63).[9] Columbus captured Indians to take back to Spain during his first voyage and noted how easy it would be to enslave them (Konetzke 1949:451–452; Mira Caballos 2010:45, citing from Columbus's diary). The ambiguities of the Spanish Crown concerning the legality of enslaving Indians began early as well (see Royal Decrees of April 12 and 16, 1495, June 20, 1500, and December 2, 1501) and continued throughout the reign of the Catholic monarchs Ferdinand and Isabel and King Charles V (Friede 1961:61–62).

In August 1503 a royal provision authorized the enslavement of the so-called cannibals (*indios caníbales*). Since these Indians inhabited other islands and mainland areas not yet under Spanish control, this implied that any Indians in these areas were determined legally by the Spanish to be cannibals and could be brought to the island of Hispaniola as slaves. In addition, on December 20, 1503, the Crown sanctioned the unofficial *repartimiento* system that began during the tenure of the Columbus brothers, thereby officially legalizing by royal decree the Spanish use of native Indian labor.

On this same date the Crown authorized the residents of Hispaniola to pay only a fourth of their earnings from the raids to acquire Indian slaves, payment that was reduced to a fifth shortly thereafter (*Real Cédula*, hereafter RC, of February 4, 1504). Therefore, by 1503, the Crown had endorsed the use of forced native Indian labor under the *encomienda* system and of forced labor of foreign Indians under outright slavery, and even provided financial incentives for such acts. Native Indians who rebelled or fled the Spanish were also allowed to be taken as slaves.[10]

By 1505 exploration of the Pearl Coast (northern coast of South America) began under the auspices of Spanish impresarios residing in Hispaniola (Otte 1977:102; Mosk 1938), providing further opportunities for the introduction of Indian slaves from the mainland and neighboring islands to Hispaniola. On November 15, 1505, King Ferdinand was authorizing the enslavement and transportation to Hispaniola of so-called *indios caníbales* (cannibal Indians) from the islands of San Bernardo, Fuerte, and Vany, and the ports of Cartagena.

By 1508–1509, the Spanish raids on so-called Carib islands extended to the so-called *islas inútiles* (useless islands), or Lucayan Islands to the north of Hispaniola (Otte 1977:103). The expeditions of Diego de Nicuesa and Alonso de Hojeda were allowed to take up to 400 Indians from islands neighboring Hispaniola in their expedition to Tierra Firme and Veragua (RC and *asiento*, or contract, of June 9, 1508). Official sanction was given to the licenses for raiding both the "cannibal" and "useless" islands being negotiated among Spanish officials and residents of Hispaniola, and the category of slavery was extended to any Lucayan Indians resisting their relocation (RC of May 3 and August 14, 1509). Royal decrees of September 15 and November 13, 1509, reinforced the previous authorization and encouraged the Spanish officials and residents to bring in as many Indians as possible.

By 1510, the Spanish colonization of San Juan de Puerto Rico was well under way, and authorization for Indian slave raids was extended to its residents (RC of April 11, May 18, and June 15, 1510). The official correspondence of this early period demonstrates the Crown's confusion as to which areas could legally and morally be the focus of slave raids.[11] On June 6, 1511, King Ferdinand extended the authority to give out licenses and determine the areas open for slave raids to the officials of Hispaniola (Zavala 1948:123). On July 21, 1511, the residents of Hispaniola were authorized to acquire Indians from areas devoid of gold without having to pay the fifth of their earnings to the Crown, as a further incentive to bring Indians to the gold-producing islands.

There is additional correspondence between the Crown and the royal officials of Hispaniola and Puerto Rico during the year 1511 that relates to the authorization of slave raids, as well as the branding of slaves brought from other areas, the transfer of rebellious Indians from San Juan to Hispaniola, and of *encomienda* Indians from Hispaniola to San Juan (June 21, July 16 and 25, September 9, November 9, 1511). The authorization for slave raids against many of the Lesser Antillean islands was justified in part by the apparent Carib participation in the Indian rebellion of San Juan.[12]

Another important piece of legislation for this year (1511) was the establishment of the Audiencia Real de Santo Domingo, the appellate court, by royal decree of October 5 (*Cedulario cubano*, hereafter CC, n.d.: 383–386; Otte 1975:190). The court's three judges arrived in Hispaniola early in 1512 and, taking advantage of their authority under the June 6 and October 5, 1511, decrees, entered into an agreement with the already established Spanish elite of the island to combine the taking of pearls with the armadas against the Caribs, thereby creating the necessary conditions for an intensification of the slave raids already sanctioned by the Crown (Otte 1977:107–108).

While interest in the Pearl Coast was increasing, the Indian rebellion in San Juan continued. As was the custom, the enslavement of rebellious Indians was sanctioned by the Crown (RC February 22, 1512). At the same time, both the so-called Carib and Lucayan Indians enslaved as a result of the authorized raids were also being brought to San Juan. There is confusion as to the terms used by the Spanish to distinguish among these Indians. The native Indians, although enslaved, were apparently referred to as *naborías*. The Indians brought from the outside were sometimes called *naborías* (probably in reference to the Lucayan Indians) and sometimes slaves (those probably alluding to Carib Indians). To add to the confusion, the practice of exchanging native rebellious Indians and Carib Indians between the islands of Hispaniola and San Juan also received royal sanction (see various Royal Decrees of February 22 and 23 and December 10 and 12, 1512). Apparently, Indian slaves were being transferred from Hispaniola to San Juan and out of San Juan illegally as well, prompting the Crown to suspend all licenses (RC July 4, 1513 and September 27, 1514). However, judging from a 1515 Relación (Narrative) from the officials of San Juan to the King, Carib Indians were still being transported out of the island without authorization (September 6, 1515).

The armadas to the Pearl Coast and other areas of the mainland continued during this period, except for a brief respite from the spring of 1517 to the beginning of 1518, during which no armadas are documented (Otte 1977:137). Testimony in the juicio de residencia (Judicial Review or Proceedings of an Administrative Investigation) of Alonso Zuazo charges that Zuazo was extending illegal licenses for slave trading as early as March 1518, without the knowledge of the Hieronymites, who were in charge of the administration of the Indies at this time (Otte 1977:144). Slave commerce was officially authorized by Zuazo in June 1519 (Otte 1977:147). The Crown also gave license to Miguel de Pasamonte, Royal Treasurer of Hispaniola, to acquire Carib Indians from the coast of Paria for his use in the above mentioned island (RC June 19, 1519).

In 1520, Rodrigo de Figueroa replaced Zuazo as *juez de residencia* (administrative judge) of Hispaniola. Figueroa declared all islands not then inhabited by Europeans as Carib, excluding Trinidad, the Lucayan Islands, Barbados, the Gigantes (Aruba, Bonaire, and Curaçao), and the island of Margarita. The armadas to the Lesser Antilles and Tierra Firme continued throughout the 1520s. By this time, according to a January 22, 1518, letter from Zuazo to King Charles V, the human cargo from the Lucayan Islands had apparently been depleted.[13]

The establishment of Spanish colonies in Castilla del Oro, the island of Cubagua, Pánuco, New Spain, and other mainland areas in Venezuela and Central America opened up vast new territories where Indians could be taken. Therefore, despite the proclamation of liberty given to the *encomienda* Indians of Puerto Rico who were unassigned to Spanish *encomenderos* (RC July 12, 1520 and December 1, 1525), foreign Indians continued to be brought in as slaves (September 3, 1526, *Relación Quinta de Cortés*; August 27, 1529, letter of Bishop Zumárraga to Emperor Charles V).

Because of the widespread abuses committed by the Spanish against the Indians, who were indiscriminately enslaved and taken out of their places of origin to be shipped to foreign areas (Friede 1961:66; Sherman 1979:39), a total prohibition against the enslavement of Indians was issued by the Crown to the authorities of the Indies on August 2, 1530. This proclamation prohibited all armadas but did permit those colonists already owning Indian slaves to keep them. Illegal raiding activities continued despite the prohibition (July 24, 1531, *Probanza* concerning Indians from Trinidad brought to San Juan by Sedeño; and a 1532 letter to the Empress from various officials of San Juan who mention armadas carried out by the residents of Cubagua that brought Indians to San Juan).

Total prohibition against the armadas did not last long. By September 13, 1533, the prohibition against the Carib armadas was lifted, and on February 20, 1534, the general prohibition against the taking of Indians slaves was lifted as well. Although the latter decree established controls by prohibiting the enslavement of women and of children below the age of 14 (except for use as *naborías de casa*) and the transfer of Indians outside of their province of origin, these were not enforced. In addition, the decree permitted the royal officials to make exceptions to the clause concerning the transfer of Indians. Since it is known that the governors and royal officials of the various Spanish provinces in the Indies were actively involved in the promotion of the Indian slave trade, this must have amounted to another carte blanche for the continuation of already established practices.[14]

During the 1530s, Indian slaves from Yucatán were being transported to Cuba (RC July 18, 1534), and the residents of Cubagua and Hispaniola were engaged in armadas to the Venezuelan coast (RC December

11, 1534). Three decrees of October 27, 1535, make reference to the illegal enslavement of Indians taken from Venezuela and sold in Hispaniola. The residents of San Juan even went so far as to request the Crown's permission to bring Indians from Brazil without paying taxes (July 16, 1535, letter from the San Juan City Council to Charles V).

Although the December 11, 1534, decree cited above prohibited the officials of Hispaniola from unilaterally permitting raids to Venezuela, this practice apparently continued, since the Crown again prohibited it in RC of March 19, 1540. Indians were still being transported outside of their places of origin during the 1540s (RC November 28, 1543, and September 23, 1547; December 18, 1547, letter from Alonso López de Cerrato to the Emperor). San Juan and Hispaniola continued to receive transported Indians, as evidenced by the RC of July 14, 1543, and Las Casas's letter to the Council of the Indies of September 15, 1544.

Geography of the Indian Slave Trade

As mentioned, the geography of the slave trade closely followed the route of Spanish settlement of the New World. This expanding network of the slave trade is illustrated in figure 5.3. The main ports involved in the slave trade, the areas subject to raids, and the destinations of the Indians are incorporated in this map.

The first raids were started from Hispaniola, probably as early as 1503, when the enslavement of "cannibal" Indians was authorized (Real Provisión, hereafter RP, of August, 1503). The islands of San Bernardo and Fuerte, the port of Cartagena, and the Vany Islands were apparently the first areas for which authorization for raids was given (RC November 15, 1505). By 1508 these were expanded to encompass the islands neighboring Hispaniola, probably including the Lucayas to the north. By 1510, the Indians of St. Croix had been subjected to raids (RC February 28, 1510; Zavala 1948:123), and by 1511 those of Trinidad probably as well (RC June 6). Hispaniola's north coast town of Puerto Plata served as base of operations for the armadas against the "*islas inútiles*" (useless islands) in which Lucas Vázquez de Ayllon was actively involved (Otte 1977:113–115). Raiding expeditions now originated from San Juan as well as from Hispaniola, and the Gigante Islands were included by the judges of Hispaniola as *islas inútiles* (Otte 1977:116).

By the middle of the 1510s, armadas originating mainly from the ports of Santo Domingo, San Juan, and San Germán were raiding the Pearl Coast as well (Otte 1977:129). These intensified after 1519, and by the middle of the following decade (1520s) they apparently proliferated along the entire northern coast of Tierra Firme (Otte 1977:209).

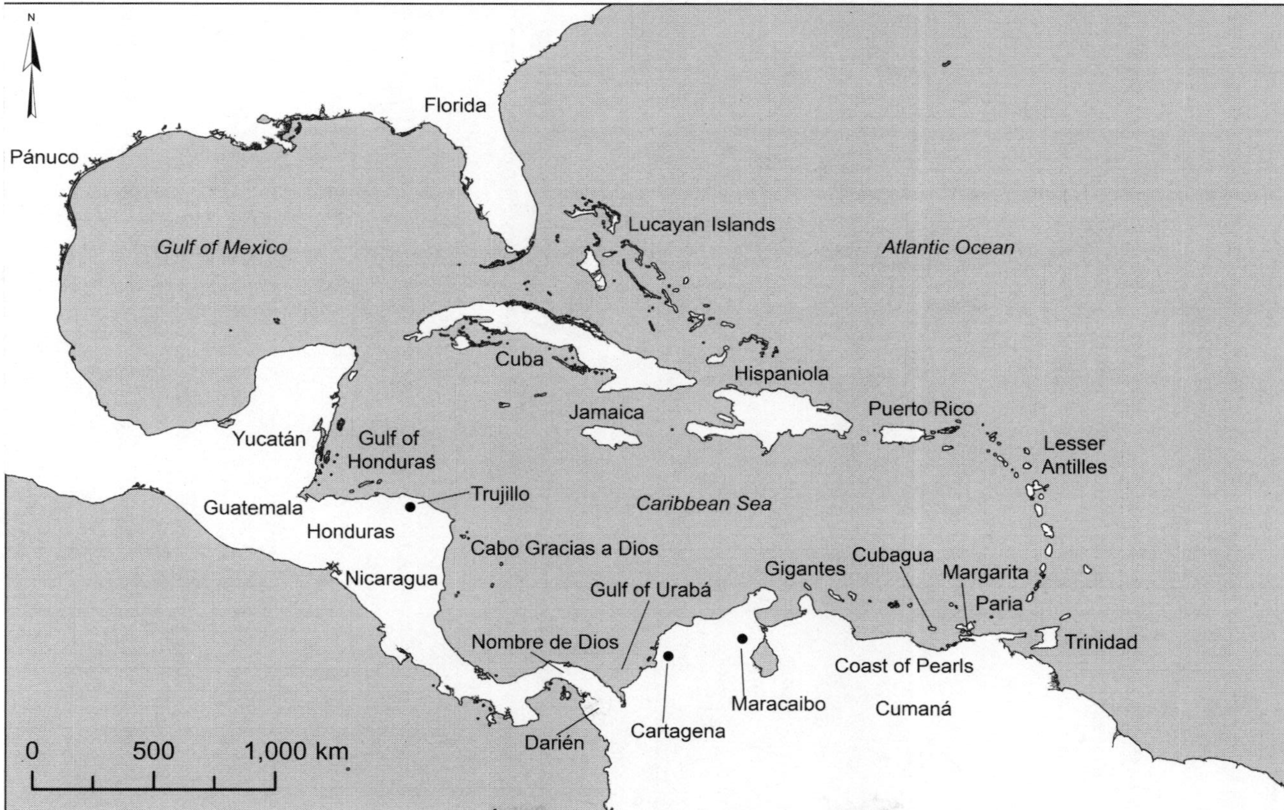

Figure 5.3. Geography of the Indian slave trade (based on Anderson-Córdova 1990:245).

By the end of the 1520s, the new provinces of Nicaragua, Honduras, Panama, Pánuco, and New Spain were also brought into the slave trade (Sherman 1979:41; Zavala 1967:22–25; ENE 1939–1942:I:153–166; Chipman 1967:216–217; Radell 1976:71; Saco 1932:II:107–108, 152, 154). In the 1530s, the port of Higueras (in Honduras) became important as a center from which Indians were shipped to the West Indies (Chamberlain 1953:120–122). Indians from Yucatán were being sent to New Spain and the West Indies as well (Chamberlain 1966:153–154; CODOIN 1885–1932:II:4:325–326). An active slave trade was also in effect between the citizens of Coro, in the province of Venezuela, and the island of Hispaniola (Friede 1961:66–67; *Cedulario de la monarquía española relativos a la provincia de Venezuela*, hereafter CMEPV, 1959:II:13–14).

Provenience of Indians Brought to Hispaniola and Puerto Rico

The historical data on this subject are difficult to assess because of their incomplete quality. Evidence of specific armadas, as well as more general references to the subject of the slave trade, is dispersed in the official documentation of the period. Some of it is nebulous, with only limited information given on the origin of the Indians taken, final destination, and numbers. More detailed data are available from primary sources, such as the Treasury documents for San Juan de Puerto Rico (DRHPR 1971 and n.d.), and from documents of the slave trade between the coast of Paria, Cubagua, and the Antilles (Otte 1956, 1977), as well as comparative evidence from studies on the slave trade in mainland areas of the Spanish colonies (Chipman 1967; Sherman 1971, 1979; Chamberlain 1953, 1966; and Radell 1976).

The historical evidence below is organized geographically. The areas from which Indians were taken to the islands are presented first. Pertinent chronological and numerical data is included when available. This is followed by a more detailed presentation of the evidence for the arrival of armadas in Hispaniola and Puerto Rico, and inferences concerning the dates of major slave trafficking and the number and probable place of origin of the slaves shipped to the islands.

The Lucayan Islands (now known as the Bahamas)

1508 to 1518 or 1519?—General references mention 40,000 Indians transported to Hispaniola (Herrera 1728, cited in Saco 1932:I:162–164). Another indicates that 20,000 Indians arrived and only 800 remained alive (December 4, 1519, letter form the Dominicans to Xevres, cited in Zavala 1948:141). According to the account of Fr. Pedro de Córdova,

30,000 or 40,000 were taken and only 5,000 remained (CODOIN 1864–1889:I:34:140, I:35:231, I:11:216–224).

1518—During the middle part of this year, an armada to the Bahamas and the Gigante Islands was organized from the towns of Puerto Plata and Santiago, and the Indians acquired were used in the mines and other activities in Hispaniola (Otte 1977:143).[15]

The Gigante Islands (Aruba, Bonaire, Curaçao)

1514 May or June—Armada from the Gigantes arrived at Hispaniola. Various references mention this armada. The number of Indians mentioned fluctuates between 500 and 2,000 (Otte 1977:118–120).

1515—September 6 letter to the King from royal officials of Hispaniola mentions 1,200 Indians (SDDJBM 1981:310). It may be referring to the same 1514 armada.

1516—During the fall of this year an armada led by Juan Gil arrived in San Germán with illegally taken Indians (Otte 1977:135).

The Carib Islands (Lesser Antilles)

1508–1509—One hundred and fifty Indians from St. Croix were brought to Hispaniola by Nicuesa. He was instructed to return them, but there is no record that he complied (RC February 28, 1510; Zavala 1948:123).

1512—Armada to the Virgin Islands and Dominica. No details known (Otte 1977:117).

1520—Armada against the Caribs, led by Ponce de León (Saco 1932: I:167–168).

1534—San Juan de Puerto Rico expedition against the Caribs. Returned with 70 Indians from Dominica (February 16, 1534, letter from the City Council of San Juan to the Emperor; HDPR 1973:I:30–31; PRDJBM 1960:296; Brau 1966:448; Fernández Méndez 1984:73).

1539—Armada against the Caribs led by Bartolomé Carreño that brought Indians to San Juan (May 29, 1539, letter from the royal officials of San Juan to the King).

Trinidad

1516—In the fall of 1516 an armada led by Juan Bono de Quexo brought 100 Indians (Otte 1977:133). In December of the same year, this individual brought an additional 180 to 200 Indians from Trinidad to San Juan. Half were sold in San Juan and half in Hispaniola (Saco 1932:I:176–177; Otte 1977:134).

1531—Indians from Trinidad, the coast of Paria, and the province of Turipiani, Venezuela, brought to San Juan de Puerto Rico by Sedeño (Tapia y Rivera 1970:210; Fernández Méndez 1984:69).

Gulf and Peninsula of Paria, Cumaná, Margarita, and Cubagua

1516—On April 23 a caravel from Margarita and the Gulf of Cumaná arrived in San Germán with 40 Indians (Otte 1977:139).[16]

1520—Thirty-one Indians from the Cumaná/Paria area who had been captured by Hojeda were sent to Hispaniola by the mayor of Cubagua (Zavala 1948:129–130).[17]

1521—January to October expedition of Ocampo to the coast of Paria, took 139 Indian slaves (Ojer 1966:52). Otte (1956:51–82) analyzes the results of this expedition in the accounts of Treasurer Miguel de Pasamonte. He indicates that six vessels participated (1956:63) and 118 Indians appear in the document as sold in Hispaniola (1956:66).

1521 (?)—In a period of two months, 600 Indian slaves from Cumaná were brought to Hispaniola and sold by its royal officials (Ojer 1966:56).[18]

1530s (?)—One hundred Indians from Paria captured by Sedeño were sold as slaves in San Juan de Puerto Rico, and, according to Brau (1966:416), those not sold were used as slaves in Sedeño's *hacienda* in Otoao (Utuado).

1534—Approximately 60 or 70 Indians from Paria were shipped by Gerónimo Dortal, governor of this province, to Santo Domingo and San Juan, where they were sold.[19]

Coast of Tierra Firme

This includes the Pearl Coast, from Cumaná west to the Province of Venezuela, including Cumanagoto, Neveri, and Maracapana.

1514—During the summer or early fall, an armada from Hispaniola to the Pearl Coast returned with one *cacique* and 18 Indians (Otte 1977:121; source, Las Casas 1951:II:550).

1518 (?)—Armada to the coast of Tierra Firme by Diego de Salazar, where 2,000 Indians were taken. Some were given to Juan de Ampies, factor of Santo Domingo.[20]

1521—Armada led by Juan Mosquera returned to Hispaniola with Indians from Maracapana (Otte 1977:209).

1524–25—Otte (1977:208), citing the *Probanza* of Juan de Ampies, indicates that in 1524, 800 Indians from the coast of Venezuela bordering the Gigante Islands were taken to Hispaniola and that there was another armada to this same area in 1525.

1532—Cubagua residents sent many slaves from the coast of Tierra

Firme to Puerto Rico (June 2, 1532, letter from officials of San Juan to the Empress; Saco 1932:I:244; Zavala 1948:113).

1534—Three caravels from Hispaniola returned from the coast of Tierra Firme with 600 Indian slaves (Saco 1932:I:274; source April 16, 1534, letter from Bishop Bastidas to the Emperor).

Venezuela (Maracaibo and Coro)

1530—Two hundred and twenty-two Indians from Maracaibo were captured, branded, and shipped to Santo Domingo.[21]

1535—Indians from the vicinity of Coro were being sent as slaves to Hispaniola by the citizens of Coro, with the approval of the governor of the Province of Venezuela.[22]

Cartagena

1535—Indians from this area were being sold to merchants and transported to Hispaniola as slaves (Saco 1932:II:72–73; source May 7, 1535, letter of Fr. Tomás de Angulo, Bishop of Cartagena, to the Emperor).

Gulf of Urabá

1509—Alonso de Ojeda sent a ship with Indian slaves and gold from this area to Hispaniola to be sold for needed supplies (Saco 1932:II:119; source, Herrera 1728, December 1, Bk. VII, Ch. XVI).

?—Five hundred Indians from the area of Cenú, west of the Gulf of Urabá, were sold as slaves in the West Indies (Saco 1932:II:37; source, Fernández de Oviedo 1851, *Historia de las Indias*, Bk. XXIX, Herrera 1728, December 2, Bk. 1, Ch. II).

Castilla del Oro (now Colombia-Panama)

1515—Indians from the area surrounding Santa María de la Antigua (Darién) were being sent to Hispaniola to be sold (Alvarez Rubiano 1944:425–426, appendix 9, January 2, 1515, letter to the King from Bishop Juan de Quevedo).

Honduras

1517–1519—Officials from Honduras branded and sent many Indians to be sold in Hispaniola and San Juan (Sherman 1979:42; source, Díaz del Castillo 1969: 328–329).

1526—Indians from the area of the port of San Andrés, Bay of Honduras, were being taken and shipped as slaves by Pedro Moreno, resident of Hispaniola (*Relación Quinta de Cortés*, September 6, 1526; Saco 1932:II:152; Sherman 1979:41). Residents of Trujillo were trafficking in

Indian slaves with the islands (Saco 1932:II:154; source, Herrera 1728, December 4, Bk 1, Ch. VI).

1539—Numerous Indians from Honduras were enslaved and shipped to Cuba, Santo Domingo, and Jamaica (Sherman 1979:49).[23]

1530s—Active Indian slave trade between Honduras and the West Indies, first from the city of Trujillo and then also from Higueras (Chamberlain 1953:120–122); sources, correspondence between Honduras officials and the Crown, various documents in the Archivo General de Indias (AGI), Audiencia de Guatemala). Sherman (1979:74) estimates that at least 4,000 Indians were taken from Honduras during the slave trade, but he does not have data to estimate how many of these were shipped to the West Indies.

Yucatán

1531–1533—Indians from Yucatán were sent to New Spain and the West Indies, especially Cuba, mostly in the ships of Juan de Lerma. Although not as extensive, the slave trade with the islands was again in place during the period of 1541–1559 (Chamberlain 1966:153–154, 279; Zavala 1948:148–149; Santovenia y Echnide 1939:258).

Pánuco (East Central Mexico)

1521–1533—A review of the sources on the Indian slave trade from Pánuco suggests that at least 10,000 Indians were taken out of this province between these years. The town of Santisteban de Puerto, founded in 1521, had been active in the slave trade since its inception.[24] Zavala (1948:83) cites documents from the AGI *Patronato Indice de Protocolos* (Protocol Index) that provide references to slave agreements between the residents of Hispaniola and the officials of Pánuco.

In one case it is a resident of the town of Salvatierra de la Sabana in Hispaniola who enters into agreement with individuals in Santisteban del Puerto for the transfer of 60 Indian slaves to be traded for goats and calves, and in another the agreement is with a merchant in Santo Domingo. The practice was regulated by Nuño de Guzmán when he assumed the governorship of the province in 1527 (Chipman 1966:142). In his *Memoria* of services as governor of Pánuco, published by Carrera Stampa (1955:39–89), Nuño de Guzmán indicates that he limited the number of slaves allowed per license to 20 for foot soldiers (*peones*) and 30 for horsemen (*los de caballo*), and he acknowledges personally sending only about 20 slaves to the islands in order to exchange them for much-needed horses and other cattle.

The Bishop of New Spain, Zumárraga, in his August 27, 1529, letter to the King (CODOIN 1864–1889:I:13:104–179), estimated that between 9,000 and 10,000 Indian slaves from Pánuco and New Spain were shipped to the islands under the tenure of Guzmán. Zavala (1967:19–21), in his summary of the contents of this letter, indicates that these included Indians from Mexico that were first transported to Pánuco and then shipped off to the islands. He also summarizes the testimony of Jerónimo López that more than 20 vessels had been sent, with the consent and profit of Guzmán, from the ports of Veracruz, Guazacualco, and the Grijalba River.

Chipman (1967), in his book on Nuño de Guzmán and his tenure as governor of Pánuco, utilizes all the above-cited sources, as well as the extensive unpublished *juicio de residencia* of Guzmán, and provides a broader perspective on this slave trade and Guzmán's role in it. He examined the Pánuco slave ship registers from Santisteban del Puerto and indicates that a total of 3,441 Indians were shipped between August 20, 1527, and September 6, 1529, and that there was a gap in the register for a seven-month period from September 26, 1528, to May 15, 1529 (Chipman 1967:216). To cover the gap, he adds 2,420 more slaves mentioned in the 1529 *Información* document cited in end note 24 above, for a total of 5,861 (1967:217). Then he suggests that since this total refers to the Indians transported to the islands as of September 1529 and the slave traffic legally lasted until June 1530, it is probable that Zumárraga's figure was not that far off the mark (1967:218). There is another Zumárraga letter (1533 letter to the Emperor; *Documentos inéditos del siglo XVI historia mexicana* 1914, hereafter DIHM:17–49) that makes reference to the same 1529 document indicating that 15,000 Indians from Pánuco and New Spain were illegally sent to the islands as slaves.

Florida

1514—Four Indians from Florida and six from the Lucayas were brought to Puerto Rico by Captain Juan Pérez de Ortubia and pilot Antón de Alaminos on February 20 (Murga Sanz 1971:114, cited in Fernández Méndez 1984:43).

1517—Three hundred Indians from the Bimini Islands and Florida were allegedly brought to Puerto Rico by Diego Velázquez (RC July 22, 1517; *Cedulario puertorriqueño*, hereafter CP, 1961:I:442–443; Murga Sanz 1971:188).

Brazil

1538—One hundred and forty Indian slaves and some free Indians arrived in Puerto Rico aboard three Portuguese ships from Brazil and were sequestered by the island officials until the Crown determined what was to be done with them (Tapia y Rivera 1970:374; Zavala 1948:120).

Documentary Evidence for the Arrival of Foreign Indian Slaves

The above discussion was based on primary sources that confirm the widespread Spanish practice of trafficking in Indian slaves under government licenses or in lieu of the same. Most of this early traffic was targeted to provide slaves to supplement the dwindling native population of the islands of the Greater Antilles. The next step is to peruse the evidence for the arrival of foreign Indians in the islands. This consists of published primary documents on the movement of vessels among the islands and mainland, and the organization and outcome of the armadas carried out to acquire merchandise and Indian slaves. This information, although limited in scope, is presented below. The available sources include Otte's (1977) extensive tables on the movement of vessels between Cubagua and Hispaniola and Puerto Rico and the armadas carried out to the Pearl Coast. His tables are based on primary documentary sources in the AGI; and the DRHPR 1971:I; DRHPR n.d.:II.

Documentary evidence for the armadas from Hispaniola is available for the years 1519 to 1527. This data is presented in Otte (1977:451–460) and is based on AGI *Contaduría* 1050; *Justicia* 53, 143ss. Twenty-three armadas are listed for 1519–1520. Although the number of Indians is not mentioned, the tax (*centena*) paid for Indian slaves is mentioned in 17 of the 23 cases. There were 4 armadas in 1521, 10 in 1522, 7 in 1523, 5 in 1524, 7 in 1525, 3 in 1526, and three in 1527. Of this total of 62 armadas in an eight-year period, the number of Indians brought is mentioned in only one of the armadas for the year 1524. Eight hundred Indians are mentioned, all apparently from an armada that returned from Tierra Firme on November 4, 1524. If the evidence for the 1519–1520 armadas is any indication, it is probable that most if not all of the armadas listed brought Indians whose numbers went unrecorded.

The AGI *Contaduría* 1050 document also provides data on the arrivals in Santo Domingo of vessels from Cubagua for an eight-year period extending from 1521 to 1529. This is presented in Otte (1977:465–470). A total of 93 vessels are listed. Data on the vessels departing Cubagua during the period 1525–1541 indicates a total of 144 departures, 26 of these to Hispaniola (including one to Puerto Plata), five to Puerto Rico, and the remaining 113 not specified as to destination (Otte 1977:470–477). A comparison of the overlapping years in the documentation of the two tables mentioned indicates that many of the unspecified departures from Cubagua were destined for Santo Domingo. It is well known that the residents of the city of Nueva Cádiz, Cubagua, carried out an active trade in Indian slaves for much-needed merchandise with the residents of Hispaniola and other islands of the Greater Antilles (Otte 1977:234–235). Therefore, it is probable that many of the vessels arriving from Cubagua to Santo Domingo, although not indicated in the sources of the armadas, brought Indian slaves as well as other merchandise.

Evidence for the movement of vessels and armadas to Puerto Rico consists of documents for a decade earlier than what is available for Hispaniola. Data presented in Otte (1977:447–451), which is based on AGI *Contaduría* 1071, 1072, and *Diezmo de Colón, documentos* 1971, indicates a total of 39 armadas for the five-year period between 1515 and 1520. One is listed for 1515, eight for 1516, two for 1517, eight for 1518, 14 for 1519, and six for 1520. Indians are listed only for four of the eight armadas for 1516, for a total of 106 Indians (an average of 26 per armada). Further documentation in DRHPR n.d.:II indicates that at least four of the eight armadas of 1518 and five of the 14 armadas of 1519 were to the Pearl Coast (Doc. 4.1.1.). Document 4.7.4., which consists of a register of deposits of Indians from an armada led by Juan Ponce de León dated from November 25 to November 29, 1515, lists 25 Indians. If this register refers to the one armada registered for 1515, then it demonstrates that Indians were brought in armadas that officially do not list them.

Documents 4.7.2. and 4.7.3. include a list of Indian slaves branded and publicly sold during the months of November and December 1521 who were obtained in the Juan Ponce de León 1520–1521 armada against the Caribs. The November entry mentions 19 Indian slaves, mostly women and children, branded and sold. Of these 19, many are specified as being Indians from Puerto Rico, while others are indicated as coming from Guadeloupe and St. Croix. The December entry is similar, indicating the sale of 27 Indian slaves from this armada, again mostly women and children from Puerto Rico. This is another example of an armada that does not appear in the official armada registry as bringing Indians but which did so, according to other primary documents.

Documents 4.7.3. and 4.7.4. consist of a listing of various deposits of Indians that came in different caravels arriving in 1516 from the Pearl Coast. A total of four vessels are listed, from which 119 Indians were deposited. The number of vessels coincides with Otte's table (discussed above) with respect to the four armadas for this year for which Indians are listed. However, the total of Indians is slightly higher than what his table indicates. Document 4.7.4. also lists 22 Indians deposited from the 1517 armada against the Caribs led by Antonio Cansino.

Other documentation from AGI *Contaduría* published in DRHPR 1971:I provides insight into another aspect of the movement of Indians among islands. The Relación de Navíos (Ship Registry) for the years 1512 to 1513 (DRHPR 1971:I:132–372) includes a total of 20 vessels that arrived in Puerto Rico (19 to the port of San Germán and one to the port of San Juan) from Hispaniola (mostly from the port of Salvaleón de Higüey) in the 15-month period extending from September 1512 to November 1513 and lists Indians as passengers and/or merchandise. A total of 127 Indians are mentioned, including Indian slaves, *repartimiento* Indians, and *naborías*. This corroborates the practice alluded to in the Royal Decree of August 12, 1509, of Spanish settlers and royal officials traveling between the islands of Hispaniola and Puerto Rico with their Indians. All the Indians listed were specified as either accompanying or belonging to particular Spaniards. In other words, these were not Indians that were brought in as slaves to be sold but Indians that already had owners and came along as personal property of the Spanish. Official Crown correspondence that mentions this practice is thus corroborated in the treasury documents for these years.

What does this data indicate concerning the number of Indian slaves transported to these two islands during the period under study? It appears from the documentation that the number of Indians transported per vessel and year varied considerably. The 1524 armada from Hispaniola lists 800 Indians, while the four armadas listed for Puerto Rico in 1516 indicate a total of at least 119 (judging from the documents), which averages about 30 per vessel. The 1517 armada document for Puerto Rico mentions 22 Indians sequestered. Although the number of sequestered Indians does not necessarily coincide with the number of Indians that actually came on board (since the term "sequester" refers to Indians about whom there is some question as to the legality of their slavery), it does indicate at least a minimum of perhaps 30 per ship. Assuming that all the armadas listed arrived with Indians, the total would be 5,050 Indian slaves transported to Hispaniola and Puerto Rico between 1515 and 1529. This total would not include Indians that may have been transported in the frequent movement of vessels between Cubagua and Hispaniola. If these vessels carried a minimum of five Indians each, approximately 500 additional Indians could be added, yielding a figure of approximately 6,000.

How does this compare with the documentation of Indian slave trade from other areas? Of 38 specific references to the transport of Indian slaves from various areas to the West Indies found in the historic literature, only 20 give any indication of the number of Indians transported. The numbers for specific armadas fluctuate from a low of 19 Indians transported in a 1514 armada from Hispaniola to the coast of Tierra Firme to a high of 2,000 mentioned for a 1518 armada, again from Hispaniola to Tierra Firme. Since in the majority of cases it is not known how many vessels participated in each armada, it is not possible to arrive at an estimate of an average number of Indians transported per vessel.

The numbers that appear in the sources add up to 7,334 Indians for the period between 1509 and 1544, most of these specified as destined for Hispaniola or Puerto Rico. These do not include the contemporary estimates for the Lucayan Islands, which fluctuate between 20,000 and 70,000. Neither do they include the estimates for Honduras and Pánuco. Modern historians working with primary unpublished sources for these areas have estimated that 4,000 Indians were transported out of Honduras (Sherman 1979:74) and probably close to 10,000 out of Pánuco to the islands (Chipman 1967:217–218). Assuming that half of these estimated 14,000 Indians were destined to Hispaniola and/or Puerto Rico, an additional 7,000 Indians may be added to the numbers that appear in the sources. Taking the lower figure of 20,000 for the Lucayas, I suggest an admittedly very rough estimate of 34,000 Indians transported to the two islands during the entire period under study.[25]

Evidence for the Survival of Foreign Indians

To address this issue, we need to return to the question of aboriginal demography. As early as the latter half of the first decade of the sixteenth century (1505–1510) the loss of Indian population was already occurring. The transportation of Indians from the Lucayas and other island groups considered useless by the Spanish (Gigantes, for example) had started, and it became widespread during the second decade of the sixteenth century.

By the time of the 1514 Repartimiento in Hispaniola, a large number of Lucayan Indians had been transported to this island. As already indicated, many of these Indians were brought to the islands of the Greater Antilles as *naborías*. Although they labored as slaves and were illegally sold as well (1518 *Memorial* of Fray Bernardino de Manzanedo, from the order of the Hieronymites, to King Charles I concerning the Indians of Hispaniola), most nominally retained the title of *naboría*. As such, it is possible that many of the *naborías* allotted in the 1514 Repartimiento were Indians brought from the Lucayan Islands. The numbers of the 1514 Repartimiento indicate that approximately one-third of the Indians allotted were *naborías* and almost half of them were allotted separately from the *encomiendas* of *indios de servicio* (service Indians).

My analysis of this *repartimiento* suggested that the number of *naborías* allotted per town bore no relationship to the possible degree of community cohesion, as reflected in the average number of Indians per service *encomienda* per town. If the *naborías* reflected Indians displaced from their villages, it would have been expected that the towns with a higher number of *naborías* would exhibit a lower average number of Indians per service *encomiendas,* and this was not the case. The tendency of the native Indians to continue to be associated with a *cacique,* despite their dwindling numbers, suggests that remnants of Indian communities continued to exist until they disappeared by attrition. That these *encomienda* Indians did not incorporate foreign Indians into their midst is suggested by the tendency of most of the *allegado* category to be *naborías* and not *indios de servicio.* Although admittedly a question of interpretation, my analysis of the 1514 Repartimiento suggests as a strong possibility the existence of foreign Indians among the *indios de repartimiento,* although this is disputed by Arranz Márquez (1991).

Research by other scholars, however, tends to support this conclusion. Cook and Borah (1971–1974:I:402–404) interpreted their population curve for the historic aboriginal population of Hispaniola as indicating two distinct populations: the native Indians and the influx of foreign Indians during the period of 1510–1520. Utrera (1973:126–127, 311–312, 402) argues that more than 7,000 *naborías de casa* were registered after the 1510 Repartimiento and before the 1514 Repartimiento, and that probably all of those registered in the latter *repartimiento* were foreign Indians. He also indicates that by including them in the *repartimiento,* the officials were effectively placing them under the *encomienda por dos vidas* (*encomienda* for a term of two lives, which meant that upon the death of the first *encomendero,* his heir could still keep the Indians under *encomienda*) authorized by the King in 1512. If my analysis is correct, it would indicate that a considerable number of foreign Indians listed as *naborías* were surviving long enough in their new environs to be counted among the native Indians of Hispaniola.

After 1519, when 12,000 Indians are mentioned as remaining on the island (see table 4.1), no further reference to the number of Indians appears until 1529, when 2,340 are mentioned (July 28, 1529, letter to the Emperor from Bishop Ramírez de Fuenleal, in SDDJBM 1981:344–345). The Bishop does not specify whether he is referring only to native Indians. In the 1529–1530 *Narración de Nicolás Federman sobre Santo Domingo* (Nicolas Federman's Narrative about Santo Domingo) (Rodríguez Demorizi 1971:19–20, note 13), there is mention of 20,000 Indian slaves. Since this number is at odds with the mostly very low estimates for remaining Indians, slave or otherwise, it may be in error. Supposing that the correct number given by Federman was 2,000, it is possible that most of the 2,340 mentioned by Bishop Ramírez de Fuenleal were slaves.

The pertinent section of Federman's account, as published by Rodríguez Demorizi, reads as follows: "At present they do not inhabit a single independent town, but rather are slaves to the Christians, in other words, the few that remain, because they have almost disappeared . . . there are not even twenty thousand still alive."[26] In the context of this narrative, it is evident that 20,000 must be an error. When compared to the total population of the island, 2,000 Indians were much more than the less than 1,000 Spanish settlers remaining in 1528.[27]

During the 1530s and 1540s there is sporadic mention of Indians. The remaining Indians included *naborías* who were still being used to work the mines[28] and "free" Indians who were being illegally sold.[29] Some of the remaining Indians were working in sugar *haciendas* as well.[30]

Although these sources suggest that hardly any Indians survived up to this period, it is known from the history of the Indian slave trade that Indians from the mainland continued to be transported to Hispaniola during this period. The 1545 investigation carried out by Cerrato concerning the Indian slaves of Hispaniola produced a total of 5,000. This number had not been previously mentioned in contemporary sources, which indicates that probably throughout the early colonization period a considerable number of foreign Indians were living on the island but were officially unaccounted for. The fact that many of them were illegally enslaved may explain why they were not mentioned.

In the case of Puerto Rico, I have alluded to the small number of native Indians documented in the historical record for this island, as well as the probable reasons for this. The historical evidence for the influx of Indians from neighboring Hispaniola, the Lucayas, and the mainland has been discussed as well. The only document that mentions population figures for native Indians as well as Indian slaves in Puerto Rico is the 1530 census carried out by Governor Manuel de Lando, which I analyzed in chapter 4. This census indicates that the majority of the Indians in the island were slaves, and thus in all probability foreign (1,039 Indian slaves, 504 free Indians).[31]

The influx of foreign Indians apparently continued (June 2, 1532, letter from officials of Puerto Rico to the Empress; in BHPR 1970:348; November 29, 1538, letter from officials of Puerto Rico to the King; in Tapia y Rivera 1970:374), but the number of Indians mentioned is very low.[32] There is no indication of the Indian slave population of the island in the middle 1540s to compare with the 5,000 documented by Cerrato in Hispaniola. However, there is reference to Indian slaves in Puerto Rico in 1550 who were set free by Vallejo (December 14, 1550, letter from Dr. Vallejo to the Emperor; in PRDJBM 1960:382–384; Tapia y Rivera 1970:399; see also Brau 1966:478).

There was apparently an Indian town named Cibuco, located in the proximity of the town of Guayanilla on the south coast of Puerto Rico, that was inhabited by Indians set free by Vallejo in 1559 (Brau 1966:479) but had ceased to exist in 1582 (CODOIN I:21:240–286). By all accounts, according to cited historic sources, very few Indians remained on the island, and those who did were probably the remnants of the liberated slave population. However, eighteenth-century census documents cited by Brau (1966:479) mention the existence of 1,759 Indians in 1777, 2,302 in 1787, and 2,312 in 1797. This indicates that a small number of Indians who gradually became ethnically and racially mixed existed undocumented on the island throughout the sixteenth, seventeenth, and eighteenth centuries.

In conclusion, although the narrative of the rapid extinction of the Greater Antillean Indians is consistent throughout most of the available historic documentation of the era, and has been repeated by most modern scholarship, a closer, critical perusal of these sources indicates a much more complex story. A considerable number of foreign Indians from various island and mainland societies were forcibly brought to Hispaniola, Puerto Rico, and Cuba, survived on the islands, and must have interacted with native Indians, as well as with Africans and Spanish. The ethnic/racial categories of what constituted an Indian, or an African for that matter, were inconsistently applied, and as one goes forward in time in the colonial period, Indians were no longer officially counted in the censuses. As pointed out by Guitar et al. (2006:48) in their article about what they consider to be Taíno survival in the Dominican Republic, the Spanish consistently under-reported the number of Indians in order to justify the importation of African slaves, who they believed could better resist European-introduced diseases. In addition, later censuses in Hispaniola include a large category of "others" that probably incorporated individuals of mixed Indian-European-African descent (2006:50–51).

Based on the many accounts in the historical record for these islands of maroon Indians (*indios cimarrones*) who fled to the hills, it appears that remnants of the original native Indians persisted. In addition, there were foreign Indian slaves who may have intermarried with native Indians and who also interacted with the increasing population of African slaves. There is archaeological evidence for this in Cuba (as discussed in chapter 3) and Hispaniola. There is also genetic, DNA evidence for the persistence of native genes in the modern populations of these islands, including Puerto Rico, as well as ethnographic evidence for the persistence of native cultural and religious values, rituals, and beliefs among modern rural populations on these islands; and finally, there is a resurgence of individuals and groups claiming their indigenous heritage (Forte 2006; Guitar et al. 2006; Palacio 2006; Barreiro 2006; García Molina et al. 2007; Martínez Cruzado et al. 2001, 2005). This new way of interpreting the colonial history of the indigenous Caribbean, and what we can anticipate as future research on this subject, remains to be discussed in the final chapter of this volume.

6
Spain's First New World Frontier and "Taínoness" Today

The momentous events brought about by the contact of Europeans and Native Americans in the New World have been the subject of inquiry for generations of scholars in fields too varied to count. I have always been fascinated by the early time period in the Caribbean, where the first encounters between individuals of vastly different cultural, political, social, economic, and religious worldviews occurred, with catastrophic results for the indigenous peoples. Why dwell on what happened more than 500 years ago? Can we really know what occurred or are the facts too obscure or contentious? What relevance could it possibly have to the present-day Caribbean? Why should we still be interested in what happened to the Caribbean's indigenous inhabitants so long ago? These are some of the questions that I address in this last chapter. I start by summarizing the basic assumptions and results of the research presented in this volume and explore their implications for current and future investigations. I end with a discussion of this research within the current context of contemporary Caribbean indigenous survival and/or resurgence.

A basic assumption of this study was that information concerning how the Indian populations responded to contact with the Spanish could be obtained from a careful perusal of the historic documentation of the early colonization period in Hispaniola and Puerto Rico (the two main islands examined in this volume). The research relied on the ethnohistoric method to gain insight into the processes of culture contact on these islands and utilized the concept of cultural transformation, as developed by Armstrong (2013), to better understand these processes. This concept allows for a better appreciation of the role of human agency in culture contact and avoids the assumption that so-called recipient cultures do not have much choice but to adapt to the demands of the dominant culture.

The role of conflict and the basically coercive nature of the relation-

ship between the Spanish and Indians in the contact scenario of these islands was also emphasized, but, again, within the context of human agency. In this respect, specific research goals related to the role played by the movement of Indians into and out of the islands within the culture-contact scenario were discussed as well. I suggested that the processes of Indian voluntary out-migration and involuntary in-migration, which occurred during the first 50 years of Spanish colonization of the Greater Antilles, played an important role in Indian cultural transformation, because they effectively altered the cultural and ethnic composition of the Indian communities on the islands. I also suggested that if we could demonstrate that the historic native population of the islands consisted of an ethnic mix of Indians, this would have important implications in the archaeological interpretation of historic Indian sites as well as in culture-contact studies in general, as it implies a much more complex contact scenario.

Using the Ethnohistoric Method to Interpret Indian Response to Contact

Documents analyzed in this volume necessarily reflect the Spanish point of view. However, my careful scrutiny of the colonial historical record to glean data on Indian response to contact with the Spanish demonstrates that interpretive insights are instructive and relevant. My analysis of the Hieronymite Interrogatory (1517) document supports the conclusion that native Indian acculturation was only superficial. Despite prolonged contact with the Spanish, it appears that the native Indians did not assimilate Spanish religious beliefs; nor were they willing to abandon their villages except under duress. The strategy employed appears to have been one of acquiescence to Spanish customs when in the presence of the Spanish and reversal to native customs when allowed to return to their villages. The celebration of *areitos* and ballgames, which served to cement chiefly authority and maintain community cohesion and continuity of customs and beliefs during prehistoric times, continued to be critical for the native Indians during the historic period. These were performed by the Indians until the last vestiges of native village life disappeared.

My analysis of the 1514 Repartimiento indicates that at this time the majority of the native Indians of Hispaniola were still living in association with their respective *caciques* almost a generation after initial contact. The basic native Indian social distinction between *caciques* and commoners was still in effect. The Indians, although subject to the *encomiendas*,

chose to remain in their villages when not engaged in the mines or *haciendas*. Despite the atomization of Indian villages resulting from the *encomienda* allotments and the decrease in native population numbers revealed in the *repartimiento* document, native villages continued to exist under *caciques'* authority.

The persistence of native ritual practices alluded to in the 1517 Hieronymite Interrogatory is consistent with the earlier data of the 1514 Repartimiento. The *encomienda* system of forced Indian labor established by the Spanish effectively divided the emerging colonial society into two separate classes. The Indians were reduced to serving as laborers for the Spanish, and only lip service was made to the latter's responsibility under Crown policy to indoctrinate them into the Catholic faith. The Indians were not assimilated into colonial society.

The 1514 Repartimiento document provides clues on how this process occurred. The Indians still under *caciques*, who constituted the majority of the Indians allotted, were parceled out among the *encomenderos*. They were transported to the work areas and were allowed to return to their villages when their cycle of work was completed. The accelerated rate of depopulation suffered by the Indians, as well as the practice of allotting Indians belonging to one *cacique* among more than one *encomendero*, meant that the Indian villages eventually disappeared by attrition. But, until this occurred over some decades, the Indians returned to them and, judging from Spanish accounts, reenacted their rituals. Following Spicer (1961a), I used the term "compartmentalization" to describe this response. I suggest that this response of the Indians under the *encomienda* system occurred as a strategy for dealing with the extreme conditions under which they were forced to live, and the Spanish attitude of viewing them as nothing more than a source of labor. This response would be sustained as long as they were allowed to return to their villages.

Separate Indian villages continued to exist apart from Spanish settlements and are mentioned in historic sources well into the sixteenth century, and into the next century in some areas of the Caribbean. The reduction of Indians into villages established by the Spanish in close proximity to Spanish settlements and the sporadic attempts by the Crown to grant the Indians their freedom, in order that they should work as free vassals, were not successful. Thus, the conditions under which Indians would have maintained prolonged contact with the Spanish under noncoercive situations that may have allowed for Indian assimilation into colonial Spanish society did not materialize. The colonial society "compartmentalized" the Indians by limiting their participation to that of forced

laborers; the Indians in turn "compartmentalized" their behavior between their role as laborers in the Spanish enterprises and their traditional roles under village life. Minor exceptions to this would have been Indian women who married or were mistresses to Spaniards and those Indians removed from village life to serve Spanish households and *haciendas.*

Movement of Indians among islands and the mainland

Voluntary Out-Migration

The historical evidence for Indian out-migration from the two islands is sparse when compared with the data for in-migration. This is because in-migration was the result of a deliberate Spanish policy of raiding other areas to supply the dwindling native labor in the islands, and was therefore mentioned repeatedly, though not completely, in official documents; out-migration, on the other hand, was a voluntary native response to the Spanish and therefore less likely to be officially noted in the historical record.

It appears that the process of voluntary movement, or out-migration of Indians from their place of origin, although a strategy employed by native inhabitants of both islands, was more prevalent in Puerto Rico than in Hispaniola. Flight in Hispaniola may have been more effective into areas of the island not yet settled by the Spanish, due to its larger size (in comparison to Puerto Rico). It may also have been more difficult for the Indians of Hispaniola to relocate to the neighboring islands of Cuba and Puerto Rico, since these, while populated by indigenous peoples, were being settled by the Spanish as well. The Indians of Puerto Rico may have been able to take advantage of the strategy of flight more effectively than the Indians of Hispaniola, by fleeing out of the island eastward to the Lesser Antilles. The much smaller size of Puerto Rico (compared to Hispaniola and Cuba), may have made flight within its borders impractical. The fact that the smaller islands east of Puerto Rico remained largely unsettled by Europeans throughout most of the sixteenth century would have allowed the Indians of Puerto Rico more opportunity to emigrate.

Historical documentation relating to the conquest and colonization of Puerto Rico presented in this volume suggests that the native population of the island was small compared to Hispaniola. The presence of foreign Indians (whom the Spanish referred to as *Carib*) among the native Indians when the Spanish arrived between 1506 and 1508, and their possible role in the Indian rebellion that started in 1511 and continued for various years, suggests that the boundary between Puerto Rico and its eastern neighbors was a fluid one. Puerto Rico's native population's strategy of out-migration was followed by the strategy of raiding Spanish settlements on the island, in coordination with Indians from the Leeward Lesser Antilles. In contrast to the Indians of Hispaniola, who raided from within the island, the Indians of Puerto Rico and their "Carib" allies apparently raided from the outside.

These Indians were thus able to exercise the option of avoiding the Spanish by moving away from the centers of Spanish population. Although there are no numbers available on how many Indians may have participated in this strategy, it is evident that it had a twofold effect: 1) it removed an unknown number of the native population of the islands (especially Puerto Rico), which was already suffering from increased morbidity and mortality; and 2) it divided the native population into at least two groups—those outside the Spanish sphere of influence and those subject to it under the *encomienda* and other forms of forced labor. The latter were more vulnerable to acculturation than the former.

Forced Movement (In-Migration)

The Spanish practice of raiding neighboring islands and the mainland for Indians to be used in the mines and *haciendas* of Hispaniola and Puerto Rico was widespread during their early colonization and throughout the sixteenth century. I suggested that a minimum of 34,000 Indians were transported to Hispaniola and Puerto Rico during the first half of the sixteenth century. Although it is difficult to determine how these Indians were distributed chronologically and geographically, it is likely that the first immigrants came from the Bahamas and the Gigante (Aruba, Bonaire, and Curaçao) Islands. These were followed quickly by Indians from the Lesser Antilles, the peninsula of Paria, and the Pearl Coast of the mainland (Tierra Firme), and later by Indians from the province of Venezuela, Castilla del Oro (Colombia-Panama), Honduras-Higueras, Pánuco, Yucatán, and New Spain. Some may have come from Nicaragua, although most of the Nicaraguan Indians appear to have been transported to Panama and Peru (Radell 1976).

The analyses of the 1514 Repartimiento of Hispaniola and the 1530 Census of Puerto Rico provide historical documentation for the survival of foreign Indians. It is possible that some of the *naborías de casa* mentioned in the Repartimiento document were foreign Indians from the Lucayas and Gigante Islands, who were usually placed under the category of *naborías perpetuos* (perpetual servants) rather than outright slaves. In the case of Puerto Rico, the 1530 census reflects the drastic decline in the Indian population, and the fact that the majority of the remaining Indians were slaves. Although the document specifies only 86 of the Indian slaves as being foreign Indians, it is probable that the majority of them were by 1530. However, the slave category may still have included at this date natives recovered from neighboring islands or natives remaining from those enslaved during the Indian rebellion.

We know that during the 1530s, Indians were still being transported to the islands. Most post-1530 documents that mention Indians refer to them as being foreign Indians. As late as 1544, five thousand Indian slaves were reported for Hispaniola, not a negligible number when compared to the two thousand or so supposedly native Indians mentioned as surviving in 1529.

Implication of Indian Voluntary (Out-Migration) and Forced (In-Migration) in the Culture Contact Scenario

Many scholars, especially modern Latin American and Caribbean historians of the sixteenth century, have extensively researched the Spanish Indian slave trade during the first decades of this century. They emphasize the importance of this trade in facilitating Spanish expansion in the New World and how the early colonization efforts were invariably accompanied by raiding for Indians. This became an important source of income for the residents of the early Spanish settlements in the mainland, as well as the island entrepreneurs who supplied Indian slaves to counteract the dwindling numbers of native Indians. Hispaniola and Puerto Rico were at the receiving end of this trade, and, I suggest, this influx of foreign Indians is an important factor to consider in the study of the Spanish-Indian culture-contact scenario in these islands, because it demonstrates the complex nature in which this contact occurred. It was contact not only between the Spanish and the native Indian population of the islands but also between different groups of Indians.

A comparison of the data on historic aboriginal demography with that of the influx of foreign Indians clearly indicates that both populations suffered steep decline in numbers. As the native population continued to diminish, it may be that the percentage of foreign Indians increased in comparison. This is because an influx of foreign Indians continuing for many years would replenish the Indian slaves who died on the islands, while the native population who died received no such influx. This tendency may have been compounded in Puerto Rico, where the out-migration of native Indians added to the decline in numbers. The replacement of the native Indian population with foreign Indians may have occurred more readily in Puerto Rico than in Hispaniola.

What were the chances of interaction between foreign and native Indians within the framework of the emerging colonial society? Irrespective of the categories that the Spanish assigned to them (*encomienda* Indians, *naborías, naborías perpetuos*, slaves, Lucayos, Caribs, etc.), they carried out similar work: in the gold mines, in gold foundries, and in the Spanish *haciendas* and households. There is no record that foreign Indians were segregated or destined to work only at particular tasks. This means that interaction between both groups of Indians probably occurred on a regular basis. The 1514 Repartimiento revealed that most of the *encomenderos* who were allotted service *encomiendas* (*encomiendas* of Indians along with their *caciques*) were also allotted *naborías*. If these *naborías* included some foreign Indians, and if the *encomenderos* also owned Indian slaves, it is probable that there was interaction between native and foreign Indians. Furthermore, the 1530 census document for Puerto Rico reveals that all the residents that had free Indians (presumably native Indians) also had Indian slaves, thereby permitting interaction to take place. Conversely, many had only Indian slaves, who then would have had less of an opportunity for contact with native Indians.

The historic sources do not address the living conditions of the Indian slave population of the islands. We know that the *encomienda* Indians resided in the mining areas and Spanish *haciendas* during most of the year, after which they were allowed to return to their villages. Indian slaves labored in similar chores and presumably interacted with native Indians. However, Indian slaves were subject to work the entire year, since the laws for the protection of the Indians did not apply to them. Indian slaves resided either in Spanish settlements or in close proximity to them. They formed a heterogeneous group under continuous contact with their Spanish owners and may have been more readily assimilated into the bottom rung of the emerging colonial society. The survival of aboriginal material culture or the reenactment of rituals was probably negligible in such a group, given the conditions of contact and the various ethnicities transported to the islands.

During the early historic period of Hispaniola and Puerto Rico, two different Indian populations existed: the native Indians and the heterogeneous group of foreign Indians imported since the first decade of the sixteenth century. Both were in a subordinate position with respect to the Spanish and were subject to similar working conditions. Historical data suggests that interaction between these groups was possible but may have been limited to the common work areas in the mines, *haciendas*, and, to a lesser extent, Spanish households. I suggest that despite the similar conditions of contact and the subordinate nature of both groups vis-à-vis the Spanish, the strategies employed by both groups in the culture-contact scenario differed. I have already commented on the strategy of flight, and, if this was not successful, of compartmentalization by the native Indians. I argued that this was possible because the Spanish continued to rely on native social categories in dividing the native labor force and allowed the Indians to return to their villages.

In the case of foreign Indians brought to the islands as slaves, although flight was possible and did occur, compartmentalization was not. The heterogeneous nature of these Indians and their constant proximity to the Spanish made this option more difficult. Thus, they may have become more quickly absorbed into the Spanish communities, and those that survived were assimilated into the colonial culture.

In summary, historic sources analyzed in this volume allow the following conclusions about Indian cultural transformations during the early sixteenth century. Initial contact occurred between the island Indians and the Spanish of the first two Columbian voyages. The relationship that developed among the two groups was initially peaceful and consisted mainly in the reciprocal exchange of gifts. Despite the technological advantage of the Spanish, the contact relations occurred on more or less equal terms. The institutional framework of colonization and forced labor was not yet in place.

This quickly changed as the Spanish returned in greater numbers to establish settlements and extract gold. The contact relations became coercive and unequal, as Spanish warfare, tribute, and slavery were imposed on the Indians. Indian response to this situation consisted of flight or other means of avoidance, accommodation to Spanish demands, and, especially in the case of Puerto Rico, outright rebellion.

As the Spanish consolidated their hold over the new colonies during the colonization/enslavement phase, the Indian strategies of flight, accommodation, and sporadic rebellion continued. Accommodation apparently took a different turn. The Indians compartmentalized their behavior by accommodating to Spanish ways when under their authority and reverting to native ways when back in their villages. During this period, the processes of cultural and social disintegration of Indian communities accelerated, due mainly to the rate of population loss among Indian communities, and not because of Indian acculturation.

Within this scenario, the processes of Indian out-migration and in-migration played an important part. Flight out of the islands contributed to population loss, and this in turn affected the social and cultural fabric of Indian communities. In-migration of Indians into Hispaniola and Puerto Rico contributed ethnic and cultural diversity to the contact scenario by incorporating new actors. The geographical and cultural boundaries in which the contact scenario occurred were thus expanded to include a diversity of Indians. The native Indians continued to live in separate villages until the last remnants disappeared, while the imported Indians probably resided in or in close proximity to Spanish settlements, at least until they were finally given their freedom.

The strategies developed by both groups in their interaction with the Spanish were probably very different. The processes of cultural change or transformation were thus complex and varied and cannot easily be categorized as Taíno versus Spanish. This, in turn, has implications for archaeological research of the contact period in these islands, and also for how we interpret the role of indigenous cultures in the formation of colonial island societies. The complexity and variety of peoples who interacted in the early sixteenth century and who were the genesis of new island cultures included native Indians, foreign Indians, Africans of various ethnicities, and Spanish Europeans. These populations formed the basis of the creole/*criollo* cultures that developed on these islands, incorporating new ethnicities throughout the centuries that followed. Present-day Dominicans and Puerto Ricans are the product of these centuries of cultural transformations.

Where Do We Go from Here?

Further Ethnohistorical Research

Cuba and Jamaica, the other two sixteenth-century Spanish Antillean colonies, had native Indian populations similar in cultural complexity to Hispaniola and Puerto Rico, and they were subject to similar processes of colonization and enslavement. Future studies that focus on the sources for these two islands could provide relevant comparative data on Indian culture contact and ethnic heterogeneity.

In the case of Cuba, the processes of Indian movement in and out of the island were also taking place. Since Cuba is such a large island and may not have been as populated as Hispaniola, the establishment of Indian communities outside of Spanish influence was more plausible. Sources indicate the survival of Indians, both native and foreign, throughout and possibly beyond the sixteenth century (Romero Estébanez 1981, appendixes A–H; Zerquera y Fernández Lara 1977; Morales Patiño 1947; Mira Caballos 1997; Sued Badillo 2003; Guitar et al. 2006). In fact, the survival of communities whose members self-identify as Indians is documented for the twentieth century (Rivero de la Calle 1978), as well as cultural traditions and folklore in rural communities that may be traced back to indigenous practices mentioned in Spanish documents (García Molina et al. 2007). Therefore, a more detailed focus on Cuba in future studies on Spanish-Indian culture contact in the Caribbean should provide valuable comparative information (see Valcárcel Rojas 2012, 2016 on the use of ethnohistoric sources in the study of the Indian *encomienda* village of Chorro de Maíta, and Valcárcel Rojas 2015 on Indians in colonial Cuba).

Although there appears to be less historical documentation dealing directly with Jamaica, this island should also be considered in future comparative studies. Historical records indicate that Jamaica had no gold deposits to speak of; however, the Spanish nevertheless established the *encomienda* system of forced labor and utilized its Indian inhabitants, as well as foreign Indians, in agriculture and cattle raising (Morales Padrón 2003). The colony served as a bread basket for the Spanish incursions into Tierra Firme. There is historical evidence for the persistence of Indian villages in Jamaica well into the seventeenth century (Morales Padrón 2003:35, 306). Since the gold mining economy was particularly harsh on the Indian populations of Hispaniola and Puerto Rico (Sued Badillo 2001), an interesting research question is whether there were significant differences in Indian survival or response strategies in Jamaica as a result of their being used as agricultural laborers rather than in mining activities.

Archaeological Research

Research on the archaeology of early Spanish colonization in the southeastern United States and the Caribbean has focused on a variety of research interests. Archaeologists have located and identified many types of early Spanish sites (forts, missions, settlements, trails) as well as historic Indian sites that show material evidence of European-Indian contact (Boomert 1985; Brown 1979; Deagan 1985a, 1985b; 1995; Deagan and Cruxent 1993, 2002a, 2002b; Domínguez 1978, 1980, 1983, 1984; García Arévalo 1978; García Castañeda 1949; Loucks 1979; Lyon 1981; Fairbanks and Marrinan 1982; Morales Patiño 1947; Ortega 1982; Romero Estébanez 1981; Smith 1956; Williams 1986; Willis 1976, 1980; Cooper et al. 2008; Valcárcel Rojas and Martinón-Torres 2013). Broad research questions concerning Spanish lifeways and adaptation to different New World environments, including Spanish interaction with the native inhabitants, and the transformation of native cultures resulting from Spanish colonization have been addressed (Cusick 1987; Deagan 1985a, 1987, 1990, 1996, 1998, 2004; Domínguez 1983; Ewen 1987, 1991; García Arévalo 1978; Loucks 1979; Marrinan 1982; McEwan 1983, 1986; Mendoza 1980; Ortega and Fondeur 1978b; Smith 1986; Willis 1976, 1980; Valcárcel Rojas 1997, 2012). The variety of early-sixteenth-century historic-period sites studied in Florida and the Caribbean and the methodological and theoretical tendencies of historic archaeological research at these sites were summarized in excellent essays by Deagan (1988; and again in 2004). Here I will limit discussion to those of relevance to the issues in this volume.

I have demonstrated that the contact situation in the Greater Antillean islands included a heterogeneous group of Indians, both native and foreign, who were subject to similar labor conditions and who must have interacted both among themselves and obviously with the Spanish. It should be possible to identify the presence of foreign Indians archaeologically. Recently, Valcárcel Rojas (2012) identified at least one individual as native of Yucatán among the burials at the site of Chorro de Maíta, province of Holguín, Cuba, as well as individuals of *mestizo* (mixed) and African descent at this same site. This important find provides archaeological evidence of the ethnic mix of individuals that had interacted on the island since the outset of Spanish-Indian contact and corroborates the historical record.

Historic archaeological work in Hispaniola has uncovered evidence of historic Indian remains, both in Spanish and Indian contexts. Most of the research has been on Spanish sites such as Puerto Real, La Isabela, and La Vega Vieja. Greg C. Smith (1986, 1995) analyzed the non-European pottery of three loci in the settlement of Puerto Real, a site occupied from 1503 to 1578 (Deagan 1988:211). He found that the Chican-Ostionoid ceramic tradition characteristic of late prehistoric Indian sites of this area was negligible at Puerto Real (only 1.4 percent of the non-European pottery was of this type), and that the more prevalent Meillacan-Ostionoid pottery (22.3 percent of the non-European pottery) was a result of redeposition from an underlying prehistoric midden at the site (Smith 1995:362–364). It was rapidly replaced by undecorated Colono wares that Smith defined as Unidentified Plain and Christophe Plain (Smith 1986:109; 1995:373). He concluded that the Unidentified Plain ware was produced by Indians and Africans during the early occupation of Puerto Real and represents a transition between earlier aboriginal ware and the later Christophe Plain ware, which he attributed to African manufacture (Smith 1986:54, 108; 1995:368). That this transitional ware may have been produced by foreign Indians brought to Puerto Real during the early phases of the Indian slave trade is not suggested by Smith, but it is a possibility.

Although Deagan (1988:211) suggests that the Indian laborers residing in Puerto Real came from the neighboring Indian village of En Bas Saline, it is possible that there were also foreign Indians among them. As previously noted, many of the early slave raiding expeditions to the Lucayan Islands were organized by Spaniards from Puerto Real. As far as I am aware, comparative analyses of transitional aboriginal ceramics from Puerto Real with other early Spanish sites where aboriginal cultural components have been identified have not been carried out. This type of study could help to identify the presence of foreign Indians archaeologically. For example, historic-period aboriginal ceramics found at the Spanish sites of La Vega and Santo Domingo, although not originally identified as such (Ortega & Fondeur 1978), appear to be of Central or South American origin (Deagan 2002).

Comparative archaeological analyses of historic aboriginal ceramics recovered from both Indian and Spanish settlements could therefore be of relevance in determining the presence of foreign Indians. They could also shed light on the process of Indian cultural transformation and how it differed among Indians who remained in their villages and those who lived among the Spanish. Apparent differences in the rate of cultural change in the postcontact Indian components of village sites as opposed to Spanish settlements have been noted in studies carried out at En Bas Saline and Puerto Real. The historic Indian assemblages of En Bas Saline exhibit less change and more continuity with prehistoric assemblages than do the aboriginal assemblages from the Spanish site of Puerto Real (Deagan 1987:349, 1988). Although these differences may be due to the earlier (and shorter) historic Indian occupation at En Bas Saline as opposed to the longer occupation at Puerto Real, as has been suggested by Deagan, the differences may also reflect the disparate rates of culture change among the Indian populations of both sites and/or the presence of foreign Indians at Puerto Real.

At present, archaeological research provides concrete, tangible data that indicates the persistence of Indian lifeways and rituals into the historic period, which supports the interpretation of Indian response to contact provided by the historical record. Much more detailed investigations along the lines of research followed by Deagan at En Bas Saline at other early-contact-period Indian sites are necessary to confirm this and to better grasp the changes occurring among these populations as the sixteenth century progressed.

Another issue that continues to be a historical puzzle is the lack of archaeological evidence for contact-period Indian sites or for historic Indian cultural remains in Spanish sites in Puerto Rico, especially since these have been identified in the rest of the Greater Antilles. No Spanish sites comparable to those excavated in Hispaniola (Puerto Real, La Isabela, La Vega Vieja, Azua, and Santo Domingo), Cuba (La Habana Vieja), Jamaica (Sevilla la Nueva), and Cubagua (Nueva Cádiz) have been excavated in Puerto Rico. Ruins associated with the early settlement of Caparra of 1508 to 1521 were partially excavated by Adolfo de Hostos (1938), but no historic Indian material was reported. Archaeological surveys in southwestern Puerto Rico reported surface material that may be early sixteenth century (Elliott 1987). Some test excavations in the vicinity of the church of Porta Coeli in San Germán by Irizarry et al. (1982) suggest that this was an area of Spanish-Indian interaction in the early sixteenth century.

Cultural resources survey reports on file at the Puerto Rico State Historic Preservation Office make sporadic references to early colonial materials, but no testing or large-scale excavations have been carried out aimed at identifying contact-period Indian and Spanish settlements on the island. In a previous publication (Anderson-Córdova 2005) I addressed the dearth of early-historic-period sites in Puerto Rico and how difficult it is to explain, given the significant increase of archaeological investigations that have been carried out there in the past 20 years (2005:350–351). I also suggested that surveys of the mountainous interior of the island, where Sued Badillo (2001) documented historical references to gold mining operations carried out with Indian labor, could potentially identify early period sites. Ten years later, the same question remains. To my knowledge, no early-historic-period contact sites have been identified in Puerto Rico. This does not mean that they do not exist, just that it has not been a priority research interest among archaeologists working in Puerto Rico.[1]

It may also be that many of these sites have been destroyed by now. Puerto Rico is the most densely populated and urbanized of all the Greater Antillean islands, and we may never have a historical archaeological database to compare Puerto Rico with the other Spanish colonial islands. Or it may just be that the survey methods and excavation techniques being employed are not what we need to identify these early types of sites. Deagan (2004) points out that archaeologists have traditionally searched for evidence of European artifacts in native Indian sites as an indicator of historic-period occupation; but, based on empirical data from sites that have been excavated, it appears that many of these sites have negligible or no European artifacts at all. She argues that remains of introduced fauna may be a better indicator and that larger-scale excavations and recovery of discrete archaeological deposits may be necessary in order to identify historic-period Indian sites.

Indigenous Survival and Identity in the Modern Caribbean

During the past 10 to 15 years there has been a growing interest in indigenous survival in the Caribbean, and there are many individuals who self-identify as Taíno (neo-taíno in Curet's 2015 assessment). This was started by individuals of Puerto Rican, and to a lesser extent, Dominican descent living in urban centers in the United States, and coincided with indigenous rights movements among Native Americans in North America (Jiménez Román 2006:104).

Currently, one group of scholars interprets Taíno survival or resurgence as a phenomenon that has nothing to do with the actual survival of Taíno populations throughout the islands' colonial histories and everything to do with the politics of racial and cultural identity (Jiménez Román 2006; Duany 2006; Dávila 2006; Haslip Viera 2006). Other scholars, as well as members of the Taíno revival movement, counter that the extinction of the Taíno is a myth that started with the Spanish as a way of justifying the importation of African slaves into the islands, and has been perpetuated by historians who have uncritically accepted Spanish historical accounts of their disappearance (Guitar 1998; Guitar et al. 2006; Castanha 2011).

These contrasting views are manifested in two edited volumes on the topic: Haslip-Viera's *Taino Revival: Critical Perspectives on Puerto Rican Identity and Cultural Politics* (2006), and Maximilian Forte's *Indigenous Resurgence in the Contemporary Caribbean* (2006). As pointed out by Curet (2015), there are valid arguments on both sides of the debate. Regarding this debate, I stress the following points:

1. The overwhelming repetition in the Spanish historic sources regarding the native Indian population's rapid decline and extinction has resulted in most scholars' acceptance of this as fact, thereby ignoring documentary evidence for the persistence of at least small numbers of Indian populations in various Caribbean islands;
2. It is possible that small groups of Indians survived well into the sixteenth century, and there is archaeological evidence for this at least in Cuba and Hispaniola;
3. The relatively small Spanish population on these islands throughout the sixteenth and seventeenth centuries may have allowed Indian communities to persist in certain isolated areas;
4. Ethnographic research of mountain communities in Hispaniola and Cuba documents native folklore that may be traced to Indian practices and beliefs (use of medicinal plants, leadership roles of head-

men or medicine men, religious rituals that resemble *areitos*, and mythical tales and beliefs attributed to Indian ancestors) (Veloz Maggiolo 1974; García Molina et al. 2007; Poole 2011);

5. What has been interpreted by some scholars as native folklore may also reflect the influence of African beliefs and of foreign Indians;
6. Limited DNA studies of modern populations in Puerto Rico, the Dominican Republic, and Cuba show genetic indicators associated with native Indian populations (Martínez Cruzado 2002; Martínez-Cruzado et al. 2001, 2005; Luna Calderón 2002), and although this has been frequently cited as proof of Indian survival, the interpretation of these results is controversial, and more comparative research is needed;
7. As late as 1898 visitors to Puerto Rico were informed of the Indian and Spanish heritage of the rural *jíbaro* population of the island (Dewell 1898:30, 83–84).

In conclusion, I believe that it is counterproductive to dismiss the claims of individuals who consider themselves to be Taíno. The thread connecting them with their prehistoric and early historic predecessors cannot be established with the empirical evidence currently at hand. However, in the case of Puerto Ricans either from the island or from the United States who self-identify as Taínos, I see their claims of "Taínoness" (borrowing a term from archaeologists Oliver 2009 and Rodriguez Ramos's 2010) as part of an ongoing ideological process of appropriating the imagery of the native inhabitants of these islands into the national identity. The image of the Taíno Indian and its iconography as a national symbol is ubiquitous in Puerto Rico. It is on its coat of arms (Curet 2015), on T-shirts, on all kinds of artisanal crafts, in books for children, in popular songs, in museum displays, in school books, in art and paintings, and so on. Rather than criticizing this perspective and arguing, as some have done, that it ignores the history of African contributions to Puerto Rican culture and society, I believe it persists because, in an island whose colonial history is so contentious and ever present, the Taíno symbolizes what is indigenous and singular about the island.[2]

It is probable that Indian communities survived undetected or under the radar on the islands for a considerable time, and I would agree that these islands' rural populations, called *jíbaros* in Puerto Rico, *campesinos* in Hispaniola, and *guajiros* in Cuba, are the product of cultural and biological interactions among native, African, and Spanish peoples. All peoples should have a right to call themselves what they want and to believe what they want, including those who currently claim their heritage as Taíno. However, this volume clearly demonstrates certain aspects of the interaction among native, African, and Spanish peoples: a variety of Indian cultures existed in the Greater Antilles at the time of Spanish-Indian contact, and the term "Taíno," a later invention, does not do justice to this variety of peoples; foreign Indians were brought into the islands in relatively large numbers and must have interacted with the native Indians; and the culture-contact scenario, which included the influx of African peoples from the earliest years of Spanish colonization, was extremely complex. May future studies elaborate on this and provide focus and perspective on the present.

Appendix 1

Historical Evidence for Interisland Movement of Indians, from Columbus's Diary of the First Voyage

Indian Knowledge of Antillean Geography

1. "As many of them showed me, they said that there was land to the South and Southwest and Northwest, and that from the Northwest they came to fight with them many times____, and to the Southwest you find gold and precious stones." (October 13, 1492, while on the first island Columbus discovered, which he named San Salvador; Que según muchos d'ellos me enseñaron dezían, que avía tierra al Sur y al Sudueste y al Norueste, y qu'estas del Norueste les venían a combater muchas vezes___, y así al Sudueste a buscar el oro y piedras preciosas; Varela 1982:32; also in Las Casas 1951:207.)
2. "And as we were halfway between these two islands, namely, from Sancta Maria to this large one, which I name Fernandina, I found one man in a small canoe that was going from the island of Sancta Maria to Fernandina, and he brought about a fistful of water in a gourd, and a piece of red earth pulverized and kneaded, and some dry leaves, which must be very valuable to them, as gifts; and he brought a small basket with a small bunch of glass beads and two white ones, by which I knew that he had come from the island of Sant Salvador, to Sancta Maria and then to Fernandina." (October 15, 1492; Y estando a medio golpho d'estas dos islas, es de saber, de aquell Sancta María y d'esta grande, a la cual pongo nombre la Fernandina, fallé un hombre solo en una almadía que se passava de la isla de Sancta María a la Fernandina, y traía tanto como un puño y una Calabaza de agua, y un pedaco de tierra bermeja hecha en polvo y después amassada, y unas hojas secas, que debe ser cosa muy apreciada entr'ellas en presente; y traía un cestillo a su guise en que tenia un ramalejo de cuentezillas de vidro y dos blancas, por las cuales cognoscí qu'él venía de la isla de Sant Salvador y aví (a) pas-

sado a aquella de Sancta María y se passava a la Fernandina; Varela 1982:35; also in Las Casas 1951:I:211.)

3. "To proceed to circle all of the island and work to find Samaet, which is the island or city where there is gold, which is what all these that come to the ship are saying, and what those from the island of San Salvador and Sancta María also said." (October 16, 1492; Para pasar a rodear toda la isla y trabajar hasta que halle Samaet, que es la isla o ciudad el donde es el oro, que así lo dizen todos estos que aquí vienen a la nao, y nos lo dezían los de la isla de San Salvador y de Sancta María; Varela 1982:44.)
4. "Tonight at midnight I pulled anchor from Isabela Island, which is on the North part, to go to the island of Cuba, which I heard from these people was very big and had much gold and spices and big ships and merchants." (October 24, 1492; Esta noche a media noche levante' las anclas de la isla Isabela del cabo del Isleo, qu'es de la parte del Norte, adonde y (o) estaba posado para ir a la isla de Cuba, adonde oí d'esta gente que era muy grande y de gran trato y avía en ella oro y especierías y naos grandes y mercaderes; Varela 1982:44.)
5. "The Indians that I had onboard said that it took one and a half days in their canoes to navigate from these islands to Cuba, which are canoes made of one tree trunk that have no sails." (October 26, 1492; Apparently, he was on islands of the Bahamas, which he called *islas de Arena;* Dixeron los indios que llevava que avía d'ellas a Cuba andadura de día y medio con sus almadías, que son navetas de un madero ddonde no llevan vela; Diary, October 27, 1492, in Valera 1982:45).
6. "The Indians said that in that island (Cuba) there were mines of gold and pearls and the Admiral saw that it was an adequate place for them and he also saw oysters, which is a sign of them. And the Admiral understood that large ships from the Great Can came there, and that it was a journey of ten days from there to the mainland." (October 28, 1492; Dezían los indios que en aquella isla (Cuba) avía minas de oro y perlas y vido el Almirante lugar apto para ellas y almejas, qu'es señal de'ellas.Y entendía el Almirante que allí venían naos del Gran Can y grandes, y que de allí a tierra firme avía jornada de diez días; Varela 1982:46.) Note by Varela referring to Las Casas 1951:144—"The mainland was not even a five days journey, but it was not the mainland that he thought, but the one we now call Florida." (La tierra firme no estaba de allí jornada de cinco días, mas no la que él pensaba, sino la que hoy llamamos la tierra Florida; Varela 1982:46:note 50).

7. "He left the port and river of Mares at 4:00 AM, to go to another island that the Indians on board said was called Baneque." (November 12, 1492; Partió del puerto y río de Mares al render del cuarto de alva, para ir a una isla que mucho affirmaron los indios que traía que se llamava Baneque; Varela 1982:54:note 67 indicates that this may refer to Inagua Grande).
8. "And because the Indians on board told him yesterday (Tuesday) that it took three days to get from the Mares river to the island of Baneque, and we should understand that they refer to days in their canoes, which can navigate seven leagues." (November 14, 1492; Y porque los indios que traía le dixeron ayer martes que avría tres jornadas desde el río de Mares hasta la isla de Baneque, que se deve entender jornadas de sus almadías, que pueden andar 7 leguas; Varela 1982:57.)
9. "As he went, he looked to the Southeast and saw land and it was a very large island, which he had learned from the Indians was called Bohío, full of people. The people of Cuba or Juana and of all the other islands are said to be very afraid of these people, because they ate men." (December 5, 1492; Yendo así, miró al Sueste y vido tierra y era una isla muy grande, de la cual ya tenía diz que información de los indios, a que llamavan ellos Bohío, poblada de gente. D'esta gente diz que los de Cuba o Juana y de todas estas otras islas tienen gran miedo poque diz que comían los hombres; Varela 1982:72.)
10. "And because, according to the Indians on board, from there you could go to the island of Baneque, which they said was a very large island with very large mountains and rivers and valleys, and they said that the island of Bohío was larger than Juana, which they call Cuba, and that it is not surrounded by water, indicating that it was the mainland, which is here behind Hispaniola, which they call Caritaba, and it is something infinite, and they are right to say that these are inhabited by astute people, because all of these islands live in great fear of the Caniba." (December 11, 1492, in Hispaniola; Y porque, según le dezían los indios que traía, por allí se avía de ir a la isla de Baneque, los cuales le dezían que era isla muy grande y de muy grandes montañas y ríos y valles, y dezían que la isla de Bohío era mayor que la Juana, a que llaman Cuba, y que no está cercada de agua, y, parece dar a entender ser tierra firme, qu'es aquí detrás de'esta Española, a que ellos llaman Caritaba, y que es cosa infinita, y cuasi traen razón qu'ellos sean trabajados de gente astuta, porque todas estas islas biven con gran miedo de los de Caniba; Varela 1982:78.)

11. "All these Indians that came with that Indian woman supposedly came in one canoe, which is their caravel in which they navigate, from somewhere, and when they came to the entrance of the Port and saw the ships, they went back and left the canoe somewhere in the area and went back to their village." (December 12, 1492, in Hispaniola; Todos estos indios que venían con aquella india diz que venían en una canoa, qu'es su caravela en que navegan, de alguna parte, y cuando asomaron a la entrada del Puerto y vieron los navíos, bolbiéronse atrás y dexaron la canoa por allí en algún lugar y fuéronse camino de su población; Varela 1982:79.)
12. "In the afternoon, a canoe with forty men came from the island of Tortuga." (December 17, 1492, in Hispaniola; En la tarde vino allí una canoa de la isla de la Tortuga con bien cuarenta hombres; Varela 1982:84.)
13. "While the Admiral was speaking to him, another canoe came from another area bringing certain pieces of gold, which they wanted to trade for a hawksbell." (December 26, 1492; En tanto que el Almirante estava hablando con él, vino otra canoa de otro lugar que traía ciertos pedacos de oro, los cuales quería dar por un cascavel; Varela 1982:99.) Here Columbus is in the land of Marien, of the *cacique* Guacanagarí, on whose lands the mishap of the *Santa María* occurred on Christmas Eve.
14. "And this he supposedly knew from many people, and that the said island of Hispaniola and the other island Yamaye were ten days journey by canoe from the mainland, which may be sixty or seventy leagues, and that the people there wore clothes." (January 6, 1493; Y esto diz que de muchas personas lo sabía, y que aquella isla Española (y) la otra isla Yamaye estava cerca de tierra firme diez jornadas de canoa, que podría ser sesenta o setenta leguas, y que era gente vestida allí; Varela 1982:109–110.)
15. "And he, when he knew from the Indians that the Admiral was on the coast of the same island of Hispaniola and that it was not a mistake, he came to him." (January 10, 1493; El cual, después que supo de los indios que el Almirante estava en la costa de la misma isla Española y que no podia errar, se vino para él; Varela 1972:112.) This passage refers to Columbus's encounter with Martín Alonso and the caravel La Pinta at the Gracia River, suggesting that the Indians knew the location of the Spanish and communicated with both parties.

Appendix 2

Chronology of the Indian Slave Trade

Legislation and Other Pertinent Documentary Evidence

1495, April 12: Royal Decree (*Real Cédula, RC*) from the Catholic monarchs to Bishop Fonseca. Mentions that Indians brought in the caravels can be sold in Andalucía. CODOIN 1864–1889:I:24:18; I:30:331.

1495, April 16: RC from the Catholic monarchs to Bishop Fonseca. Not to sell the Indians sent by Columbus until it is determined whether they can be slaves. CODOIN 1864–1889:I:24:25; I:38:335.

1500, June 20: RC from the Catholic monarchs to Contino Pedro de Torres. Instructed to turn over the Indians to Bobadilla for return to the Indies. CODOIN 1864–1889:I:38:439.

1501, December 2: RC from the Catholic monarchs to Diego Gómez de Cervantes. Concerning the Indians brought and sold by Miguel Guerra. They should be given to Ovando and returned to the Indies. CODOIN 1864–1889:I:31:104–107; SDDJBM 1981:33.

1503, August: Royal Provision (*Real Provisión, RP*) "cannibal Indians," CODOIN 1864–1889:I:31:196–200; SDDJBM 1981:51. There is correspondence from officials in Puerto Rico to the captains that were traveling to the mainland concerning this same matter in CC n.d.:49–52.

1503, December 20: RC from Queen Isabela authorizing the Spaniards to utilize the Indians of Hispaniola as laborers. Important document that legalized and sanctioned the servitude of the Indians. SDDJBM 1981:52–53; CC n.d.:85–87.

1503, December 20: RP from the Catholic monarchs to the authorities of the Indies. Authorizing the *vecinos* (residents) of Hispaniola to pay only a fourth, rather than a third, of their earnings from the *rescates* (raids) of Indians. CODOIN 1864–1889:I:31:206–208.

1504, February 4: RC from the Catholic monarchs to the governor of the Indies. Authorizing the *vecinos* of Hispaniola to pay only a fifth of their earnings in the war against the Indians. CODOIN 1864–1889: I:31:214; SDDJBM 1981:53 (with February 5 date).

1505, November 15: RC from Don Fernando to Governor Ovando. Informs Ovando that the Indians who can be taken as slaves and brought to the island are the "cannibal Indians" from the islands of San Bernaldo and Fuerte, the ports of Cartajena, and the Vany islands. CODOIN 1885–1932:II:5:110–113.

1508, April 30: RC authorizing the *vecinos* of Hispaniola to use the Indian slaves as individuals subject to servitude. Refers to the Indians taken as slaves during the rebellion in the island. CDHFSHA 1953:17–18.

1508, June 9: RC to Governor Ovando. Explains that Diego de Nicuesa and Alonso de Hojeda may take 400 Indians from the neighboring islands in their expedition to the mainland. CODOIN 1864–1889: I:36:245.

1508, June 9: *Asiento* (contract) between the King and Nicuesa and Hojeda concerning the colonization of the mainland and Veragua. This *asiento* permits them to take Indian slaves from Cartajena and the islands of "vain," "Sant Bernabé," and "fueita" to be sold in Hispaniola. Also allows 400 Indians from the neighboring islands to be taken in the expedition. CODOIN 1864–1889:I:22:13–26; I:32:29–43.

1509, May 3: RC to Ovando. Sanctions the transfer of Indians from other areas to Hispaniola, since this island had so few Indians. Indicates that they should be used in the King's holdings (*granjerías*) and that any remaining ones be given out as accustomed. Instructs Ovando to complete the *asiento* with the Spaniards that are going to raid for cannibal Indians, without this costing anything to the Crown. CODOIN 1864–1889:I:31:424–431; SDDJBM 1981:63; Tapia y Rivera 1970:266 (with date of March 3).

1509, August 14: RC to Treasurer Miguel de Pasamonte. Indicates that he should meet with the Admiral (Diego Colón) and Gil González Dávila concerning the *asientos* to bring Indians to Hispaniola. Indicates that the Crown would retain three-fourths of the Indians and that the individuals who carried out the raids would keep one-fourth. Indicates that the Indians who resist transfer can be taken as slaves and those who do not resist can be taken as *naborías*. CODOIN 1864–1889:I:31:440–442; CC n.d.:172–173; SDDJBM 1981:70. There are two additional letters of the same date and subject written by the King to Gil González Dávila and Diego Colón, respectively. The letter to Diego Colón indicates that the best Indians should be used in the mines. The letter to González Dávila indicates that the Indians should be given out not for life but for a few years, since otherwise it would appear that they were being enslaved and that would be a pang of conscience (*cargo de conciencia*). These two letters (or decrees) are published in SDDJBM 1981:71–72.

1509, September 15: RC to Ovando. Indicates royal approval of this order to bring Indians from the surrounding islands and that as many as possible should be brought. SDDJBM 1981:73–74.

1509, November 12: RC to the Admiral Diego Colón. Instructs him to hurry in the expeditions to bring outside Indians, due to the great need for them. SDDJBM 1981:74–75.

1510, February 28: RC to Treasurer Miguel de Pasamonte concerning the expedition of Nicuesa and Hojeda. Again mentions authorization for taking 400 Indians to the mainland. Also indicates that 150 Indians taken by Nicuesa from St. Croix should be returned. Also that as many Indians as possible should be put in the mines. CODOIN 1864–1889: I:31:529–533; SDDJBM 1981:83–84. Cited in Zavala 1948:123.

1510, February 28: RC to the Admiral and officials of the Indies. Mentions four caravels that went for Indians, and the two that arrived with Indians, and indicates the King's approval, but specifies that Indians should not be brought from Jamaica, Cuba, and the islands bordering San Juan. Again mentions the 150 Indians brought by Nicuesa from St. Croix and instructs that these be returned and taken from elsewhere. PRDJBM 1960:15; SDDJBM 1981:83.

1510, April 11: RC to Jerónimo de Bruselas in San Juan de Puerto Rico. Extending a license to have a caravel to be used exclusively to bring Indians from other areas to Puerto Rico. CP 1961:I:25; Tapia y Rivera 1970:279.

1510, May 18: License from the King to Miguel Díaz to bring and commerce in the island of San Juan with two caravels. PRDJBM 1960:34.

1510, June 15: RC to the Admiral and royal officials of Hispaniola. Indicates that persons from Hispaniola cannot have Indians in San Juan, except in the case of special decrees given out to royal officials. Also indicates that for the time being, no Indians should be brought from Trinidad or from the islands neighboring San Juan, or from Jamaica and Cuba. Mentions that Indians can be taken from the northern islands (the Lucayas) and those areas at war. Authorizes the *vecinos* of Hispaniola to raid for Indians, paying a fifth of their earnings to the Crown. CC n.d.:269–281; SDDJBM 1981:86–87.

1510, June 15: Royal license to Don Cristóbal de Sotomayor to have two caravels to bring Indians and merchandise to the island of San Juan. PRDJBM 1960:21; CP 1961:I:32; Tapia y Rivera 1970:281.

1510, July 3: RC to the Admiral and royal officials of Hispaniola. Indicates approval of the *asiento* with Bastidas to bring Indians to Hispaniola. CC n.d.:283–285; SDDJBM 1981:88.

1511, June 6: RC to Diego Colón and officials of Hispaniola. Long decree answering various official letters. Indicates that they should be very careful about bringing Indians from Trinidad; they should inquire whether there is gold in said island and whether Indians could be brought without affecting the Indians of the Pearl Coast. Leaves it up to the officials to determine this. Authorizes that Indians be brought from St. Croix, since San Juan (Puerto Rico) has received attacks from this island, but instructs them to return any San Juan Indians that may be captured in St. Croix. Most important, this decree gives leeway to the officials of Hispaniola to determine and extend licenses for the raiding of outside areas for Indians. CODOIN 1885–1932:II:5:312–328; CC n.d.:309–322; SDDJBM 1981:89–91. Cited in Zavala 1948:123.

1511, June 21: RC to the Admiral and officials of Hispaniola. Authorization to grant Miguel Díaz the transfer of 40 Indian slaves to the island of San Juan. PRDJBM 1960:40; CP 1961:I:76; ENE 1939–1942:I:17–18; Tapia y Rivera 1970:291.

1511, June 21: RC to Governor Diego Colón. Prohibits Indians from Hispaniola to be sent to Castille without special license from the King. CODOIN 1885–1932:II:5:266; CC n.d.:361–362.

1511, July 16: RC to the Admiral, governor of San Juan. Instructs him to let Juan Ponce de León keep the 200 Indians from the *repartimiento* of Hispaniola in San Juan. Tapia y Rivera 1970:295.

1511, July 17: RC to the Admiral. Instructs him to let Juan Bono keep in San Juan the 20 house *naborías* (*naborías de casa*) and 50 mine *naborías (de minas)* from the *repartimiento* of Hispaniola. Also, an identical one in favor of Juan Velázquez. Tapia y Rivera 1970:295.

1511, July 21: RC to the *vecinos* of Hispaniola. Authorizing them to bring Indians from areas where there is no gold, with the permission of the governor and royal authorities of Hispaniola, and without having to pay a fifth on their earnings. CODOIN 1885–1932:II:5:262–264; CDHFSHA 1953:26–27; CC n.d.:363–364; SDDJBM 1981:93.

1511, July 25: RP authorizing the branding on one leg of the Indians brought to Hispaniola from other areas. CODOIN 1885–1932:II:5:271–273; CC n.d.:369–370; SDDJBM 1981:96–97.

1511, July 25: RC to the Admiral Diego Colón. Long decree in answer to various letters. Mentions the following: approval for those who want to raid for Indians to do so without having to pay a fifth on their earnings; that the Carib Indians must be destroyed, and specifically mentions the

Caribs of St. Croix; instructions sent to Díaz and Cerón in San Juan concerning the Indian rebellion and authorizing Indians enslaved in San Juan to be taken to Hispaniola. CODOIN 1864–1889:I:32:257–266; CC n.d.:371–380; SDDJBM 1981:95,100.

1511, July 25: RC to the *vecinos* of the island of San Juan. That they should unite with Cerón and Díaz in the war against the rebellious Indians. CODOIN 1864–1889:I:32:222–225.

1511, July 25: RC to Juan Cerón and Miguel Díaz, San Juan de Puerto Rico. Instructions concerning the Indian rebellion: that they should destroy their canoes; that they should try by whatever means to pacify the Indians; and that if the Indians continue to rebel, to make war and enslave them. Authorizes Cerón and Díaz to send 40 or 50 of the *caciques* who participated in the rebellion to work as slaves in the gold mines of Hispaniola. CODOIN 1864–1889:I:32:225–230; Tapia y Rivera 1970:292.

1511, September 9: RC to Juan Cerón and Díaz. Concerning the Indian rebellion. Instructs them to try to pacify the Indians without enslaving them. If the Indians do not submit, they can be taken as slaves. Instructs that as many outside Indians as possible be brought to San Juan. CODOIN 1864–1889:I:32:275–280.

1511, November 9: RC to Cerón and Díaz. Authorizes them to give license to the *vecinos* of San Juan to raid the islands of Dominica, Martinique, St. Lucia, La Ascensión, Barbados, Tobago, and Mayo and take the Indians as *naborías*. The justification given is that the Caribs from these islands have attacked San Juan and taken many natives. The *vecinos* are thus allowed to go to these areas and retrieve the Indians taken by the Caribs, whom they can have as *naborías*. PRDJBM 1960:63; CP 1961:I:105–106.

1511, November 22: RC to the Admiral and Governor Diego Colón. The Indians from San Juan stolen by the Caribs are to be returned to San Juan. CODOIN 1864–1889:I:32:292–293; PRDJBM 1960:65. Note: the version published in CODOIN (1864–1889) states "that the Indians found in these other islands that were taken by the Caribs from the island of San Juan" (qye los yndios que se fallasen en cualesquiera yslas que obiesen llevado los caribes de la Isla de Sant Xoan). The version in PRDJBM (1980) states "that if Indians from San Juan who fled to the Carib islands are found" (que los indios huidos de San Juan a isla de caribes, si se tomaren).

1511, December 23: RP to all the authorities of the Indies. Provision that permits the Carib Indians to be taken as slaves. Includes the following areas: Trinidad, San Bernardo, Fuerte Island, port of Cartajena, Barú Island, Dominica, Martinique, St. Lucia, l'Ascension, Barbados, Tobago, and Mayo. CODOIN 1864–1889:I:32:304–309; SDDJBM 1981:101. Another decree extending the same privilege to the *vecinos* of San Juan, in PRDJBM 1960:66; CP 1961:110–112.

1512, February 22: RP authorizing the officials in San Juan to bring Carib Indians as slaves to be passed on to the owners' inheritors. The text of the document says *naborías* rather than slaves. CODOIN 1864–1889:I:32:319–322.

1512, February 22: RC to the *vecinos* of Hispaniola authorizing them to take the rebellious Indians as slaves and have them as *naborías* to be passed on to their descendants. The text states: "Decree allowing the residents of Hispaniola to take without cost all the rebellious Indians from the surrounding area and make them slaves and have them as *naborías* for themselves and their successors in perpetuity." (Cédula para los vecinos de la Española puedan tomar sin pagar nada a todos los indios rebeldes de la comarca y hacerlos esclavos y tenerlos por naborías ellos y sus sucesores perpetuamente; SDDJBM 1981:102).

1512, February 23: RC to the Admiral and royal officials of the Indies. States that Indians brought from outside to the islands of Hispaniola and San Juan are to be kept in perpetual servitude: "*sean para quien los truxiere e para sus herederos para siempre jamás.*" Authorizes the selling and trade of Carib Indian slaves between the islands of Hispaniola and Puerto Rico. CODOIN 1864–1889:I:32:329–340; CC n.d.:417–424; CP 1961:I:116; SDDJBM 1981:107–108.

1512, February 23: RC to Cerón and Díaz concerning the Indians of San Juan. Authorizes war on the Caribs and their enslavement without paying a fifth of their income; authorizes the taking of native Indians as *naborías*, with the consent of their *caciques*. CDHFSHA 1953:36–38; SDDJBM 1981:105–106; CP 1961:I:117.

1512, July 3: RP allowing the *vecinos* of Hispaniola and San Juan to carry out slave raids against the Caribs of certain islands. CODOIN 1885–1932:II:5:258–262; CP 1961:I:131.

1512, December 10: RP indicating that the Indians taken in "just war" in the island of San Juan be *naborías* and not slaves. PRDJBM 1960:86; CP 1961:I:177–178; Tapia y Rivera 1970:304. Another one with the date of January 23, 1513, concerning the same matter in PRDJBM 1960:90; CP 1961:I:204–205.

1512, December 10: RC to Diego Colón, appellate judges and royal officials of Hispaniola. To inform concerning the areas from where Caribs can be taken; to organize armadas to rescue pearls as well as Caribs; indicates that the island of St. Croix is an *isla inútil* (useless island) and has no objection to the granting of licenses to bring Indians from said island. Again mentions the exchange of Carib Indian slaves between Hispaniola and San Juan. Grants permission for the sailors and other men involved in the armadas to transfer Indian slaves to the *armadores* (armada leaders) and also that the latter may transfer Indians slaves to the *vecinos* of Hispaniola up to half a year after having been taken. CP 1961:I:151–165.

1512, December 12: RC to Diego Colón and officials of San Juan. Authorizes the exchange of the rebellious Indians taken as slaves in San Juan to Hispaniola. The justification given for this is to avoid the tendency of the Indians to escape from Spanish custody and return to their *caciques*. PRDJBM 1960:87–88; SDDJBM 1981:113–114.

1512, December 16: RC to Treasurer Miguel de Pasamonte. Authorizing the transfer of Indians from Jamaica to Hispaniola, since there is no gold in the former. SDDJBM 1981:114.

1513, January 23: Valladolid. Royal Ordinances concerning the good treatment of the Indians. PRDJBM 1960:92–97; CP 1961:I:183–203; SDDJBM 1981:115–119.

1513, June 2: Royal license to Andrés de Haro to transfer from Hispaniola to San Juan two Indian slaves and two *naborías* from the Lucayan Islands. PRDJBM 1960:103–104; CP 1961:I:229–230.

1513, July 4: RC to the officials and justices of the island of San Juan. To inquire about the Indian slaves transferred from Hispaniola to San Juan without license from the justices and the Admiral or with license from the Admiral only. The officials are to retain custody of these Indians until the matter is investigated. CP 1961:I:241–242. Another one with the same date to the Admiral, appellate justices, and royal officials of Hispaniola indicating that no licenses are to be given to transfer Indian slaves to San Juan, in CP 1961:I:242–245.

1513, September 26: *Traslado* (notification) confirming royal authorization whereby the residents of Hispaniola may keep in perpetuity (*naborías perpetuos*) the Indians brought from the neighboring islands. CDHFSHA 1953:57–60; Fernández de Navarrete 1945–1946:II:354.

1514, September 27: RC naming Juan Ponce de León captain of the armada against the Caribs. Tapia y Rivera 1970:308.

1514, September 27: RC to the officials of San Juan, responding to their letter of February 12, 1514. Indicates approval of the deposit of Indian slaves from Hispaniola who had been taken to San Juan. Revokes the license to bring Indians to San Juan previously given to Miguel Díaz. Indicates that no Indians should be brought to or taken out of San Juan, since there are so few of them and they die when moved from one place to another. PRDJBM 1960:116–118; Tapia y Rivera 1970:308–309; CP 1961:I:280–283.

1514, September 27: RC to Lieutenant Mendoza and officials of San Juan. Prohibiting the transfer of native Indian slaves to Hispaniola or elsewhere. PRDJBM 1960:126–127; CP 1961:I:279–280.

1514, November 28: RC to the admiral, judges, and officials of Hispaniola, in answer to theirs of September 1. Indicates approval of the armada that brought 200 Indians from the Gigante Islands. Approves of two other small armadas against the Caribs. CP 1961:I:355–356.

1515, August 8: *Relación* (Narrative) of the officials of San Juan to the King. Indicate compliance with royal instructions concerning the deposit of the Indian slaves taken in war in the island of San Juan and sent to Hispaniola to be sold. Inform the King that in the future only Carib Indian slaves would be taken from the island. CODOIN 1864–1889:I:36:384–392; PRDJBM 1960:150–152; Tapia y Rivera 1970:322.

1515, September 6: *Relación* from the royal officials and the Audiencia (court) of Hispaniola to the King. Indicates that of the Indians brought to the island, the Caribs are the best, but that of the 1200 Indian slaves brought from the Gigante Islands, many have died. CODOIN 1864–1889:I:36:412; SDDJBM 1981:310.

1515: RC to Juan Ponce de León. The natives of San Juan found in the Carib islands who give themselves up voluntarily are to be taken to San Juan as *naborías*. CP 1961:I:376–377.

1518: Memorial of Fray Bernardino de Manzanedo, from the Hieronymite order, to King Charles I concerning the Indians of Hispaniola. Long *Memoria* that provides interesting information on the social and economic conditions of Hispaniola, especially the plight of the Indians. Inquires about the legal ambivalence of the perpetual *naboría (naborías perpetuos)* category in which the Lucayan Indians are placed. Mentions that these have been sold and bought numerous times among the settlers, even though it is prohibited. Mentions the Carib Indians that attack San Juan periodically. CODOIN 1864–1889:I:11:298–321; 34:287–319; RCCGSD 1958:I:35–48; SDDJBM 1981:242–247; Tapia y Rivera 1970:244–249.

1518, January 14: Royal Commission to Licenciado (attorney) Alonso de Zuazo concerning the Indian captives from Cumaná. Relates the incident where a Spanish ship arrived at the Pearl Coast, specifically the area known as the valley of Chiribichi, and had taken captive a *cacique* known as Alonso along with 16 or 17 of his *naborías* and shipped them to Hispaniola. Indicates that after this, many other ships came from Hispaniola to capture Indians. Mentions the area where captives have been taken: "especially from the valley of Chiribichi and Cumaná and Paria and Curiacoa and Maracapaná, which are provinces of Castilla del Oro, in the coast of pearls." (especialmente al valle de Chiribichi y Cumaná y Paria y Curiacoa y Maracapaná, que son provincias de Castilla del Oro, en la dicha costa de las perlas.) Instructs Zuazo to find out what happened to these Indians and arrange for their return at the expense of those who took them. CRV 1963:100–103.

1518, January 22: Letter from Licenciado Zuazo to Charles I. Mentions, among other topics, how the Lucayan Islands became depopulated as a result of the Spanish armadas to capture Indians, and how this was done under the initiative of the judges of Hispaniola, Treasurer Pasamonte, and with the approval of King Ferdinand. Indicates that 15,000 Indians were brought from the Lucayas, Gigantes, Barbados, and other islands, and at least 13,000 have died. RCCGSD 1958:65–79.

1519, March 3: RC from King Charles I to Antonio de la Gama, *juez de residencia* (administrative judge) of San Juan. Concerning various issues concerning the Indians. Mentions Indians from the mainland and some islands brought to San Juan as slaves, but are *naborías*. CP 1961:II:56–66.

1519, June 19: RC to Miguel de Pasamonte. Extends exclusive license to Pasamonte to obtain Carib Indian slaves from Paria to work for him in Hispaniola. CRV 1963:122–123.

1519, June 19: RC to Licenciado Figueroa, *juez de residencia* of Hispaniola, to decide concerning the transfer of Francisco de Barrionuevo's Lucayan Indians from Hispaniola to San Juan. CP 1961:II:108.

1519, September 14: Letter of the *oidores* (judges) of the Audiencia of Santo Domingo (Pasamonte, Dávila, and Ampies) to the King. Among other issues, this letter alludes to the fact that black and Indian slaves, as well as Indians from the Lucayas and Gigante Islands, work in the gold mines of Hispaniola: "that his highness allow that the gold taken from the mines with black and Indian slaves, lucayans and gigantes pay only the tenth." (que nuestra alteza mande que del oro que se cogere en las minas con esclavos negros e yndios e yucayos e gigantes pagen la diesma parte; RCCGSD 1958:I:134–139).

1520: Declaration of Licenciado Rodrigo de Figueroa concerning the Carib Indians and the *guatiaos* (friendly Indians). Figueroa declares as Carib islands all the islands not inhabited by Christians, with the exception of Trinidad, the Lucayan Islands, Barbados, Gigantes, and Margarita. Tapia y Rivera 1970:415–420.

1520, July 12: RC to *Licenciado* Antonio de la Gama, *juez de residencia* of San Juan, declaring the liberty of the Indians. This refers only to the

Indians that became free of *encomiendas*, "*indios que vaquen.*" The ones under *encomiendas* would continue to be subject to servitude. CODOIN 1864–1889:I:7:413; Tapia y Rivera 1970:262–264.

1521, June 22: *Probanza* (proof, evidence document) of the services of Rodrigo de Bastidas, carried out under Gonzalo de Ovalle, lieutenant governor of Hispaniola. All 15 witnesses presenting testimony in this *probanza* indicate that Bastidas financed and participated in various armadas against the Carib Indians and to other areas, and as a result many Indians were brought to Hispaniola as slaves. CODOIN 1864–1889:I:2: 366–467.

1525, December 1: RP to fray Antonio de Montesinos concerning the liberty of the Indians. Again, declares that the Indians that are free or become free of *encomiendas* are to be granted their freedom. Similar ones sent to Cuba and Hispaniola. CDHFSHA 1953:78–80; CP 1961:II:402–405; CODOIN 1885–1932:II:9:235.

1526, February 10: Two decrees, one to the officials of San Juan and the other to the Audiencia Real (Appellate Court) of Santo Domingo, prohibiting the taking of Indians from San Juan to the Pearl Coast. CRV 1963:168–170.

1526, September 3: *Relación Quinta de Cortés* (Cortés's Fifth Narrative or Memoir) to Emperor Charles V. Mentions his encounter in the port of San Andrés (near Trujillo, Honduras) with Pedro Moreno, a resident of Hispaniola. Indicates being informed by the residents of Trujillo as to Moreno's practice of taking Indians from the surrounding villages and shipping them off as slaves to Hispaniola. Indicates that the Guanajo Indians, located just off the coast of Honduras, have been depopulated as a result of slave raiding from the islands, particularly from Cuba and Jamaica. CDIHE 1844:4:124–145.

1526, November 9: RC to the Audiencia and royal officials of Santo Domingo. Among other things, prohibits the sending of Indians to Spain. CODOIN 1885–1932:II:9:248–256.

1526, November 26: RC to the governor and royal officials of San Juan, granting the liberty of an Indian *cacique* of San Juan de Puerto Rico. The King orders that complete liberty be given to *cacique* Juan de Humacao, who had been unjustly branded as a slave since the time when Juan Cerón was alcalde mayor (district governor or district mayor) of the island. CDHFSHA 1953:96–97.

1526: Letter from Juan de Ampies, factor of Santo Domingo, to the King informing what he did with the Indians brought to Hispaniola from the islands near the mainland and how many were returned to Curacao. CODOIN 1864–1889:I:1:431–436.

1529, August 27: Mexico. Letter from Fr. J de Zumárraga to Emperor Charles V. Indicates that Nuño de Guzmán, while governor of Pánuco, fomented the commerce in Indian slaves by giving out individual licenses for 20 to 30 slaves each. Mentions the testimony of various witnesses to the effect that 21 ships had traveled from Pánuco to the islands carrying human cargo. Estimates that between 9,000 and 10,000 Indian slaves from Pánuco and New Spain had been shipped to the islands while Guzmán was governor. CODOIN 1864–1889:I:13:104–179.

1530, August 2: RP from the Empress to the *audiencias* (courts) of Santo Domingo and Mexico. Prohibits the enslavement of the Indians under any circumstances. Reasons given are the abuses committed against the Indians and the illegal enslavement of many. Indicates that those already owning Indian slaves must register them. CODOIN 1885–1932:II: 10:38–43; CDHFSHA 1953:134–136.

1531, July 24: *Probanza* concerning Indians brought by Sedeño, given in the presence of Gaspar Troche, *alcalde ordinario* (magistrate) of Puerto Rico. Indicates that Sedeño brought free Indians from Trinidad and the province of Turipiani in the mainland, as well as Indians given to him as Caribs in the Paria Coast. Tapia y Rivera 1970:210.

1532, June 2: Letter to the Empress from Francisco Manuel de Lando, Baltazar de Castro, Martín Equiluz, and Juan de la Puente, Puerto Rico. Indicates that the royal prohibition against the taking of Indian slaves had been announced, but that *vecinos* from Cubagua had brought many Indians from the mainland coast. They indicate that these are Caribs and should be slaves. Tapia y Rivera 1970:348.

1533: Letter to the Emperor from Fr. Juan de Zumárraga. Includes mention of the Pánuco slave trade. Mentions the *probanza* made under him concerning this matter. According to Zumárraga the *probanza* proves that more than 15,000 Indians from Pánuco and New Spain were shipped illegally as slaves to the islands. DIHM 1914:17–46.

1533, January 13: Asunción, Cuba. *Visita* (visit) of Governor Manuel de Rojas to Asunción. Indicates that among the Indians found there, there were 60 from Yucatán and Pánuco. CODOIN 1885–1932:II:4:309.

1533, September 13: RC to the President and *oidores* (judges) of the Audiencia of Santo Domingo concerning the war against the Caribs. Lifts the previous prohibition of organizing raids against the Caribs. Authorizes the Audiencia to determine the areas that can be raided and extends permission to the residents of San Juan to take Carib slaves. CDHFSHA 1953:145–146.

1534, February 20: RP from the Emperor to the *audiencias* of Santo Domingo and Mexico. Lifts the 1530 prohibition against the taking of

Indian slaves. Authorizes the enslavement of Indians obtained in "just war" or by *rescate.* States that they are not to be taken outside their place of origin and that women and children under 14 are not to be enslaved but may be used as household *naborías* (*naborías de casa*). In addition, it allows the royal officials of each province to make exceptions to the clause prohibiting the transfer of Indian slaves out of their provinces of origin. CODOIN 1885–1932:II:10:192–203; CDHFSHA 1953:153–159.

1534, July 18: Santiago, Cuba. Letter from the royal officials to Emperor Charles V. "The pending lawsuit in Hispaniola regarding the slaves brought from New Spain to be sold, please resolve the case: female and male Indians arrive every day from the conquest of Montejo (Yucatan), and the import duties are being deposited during the lawsuit." (El pleito pendiente en La Española sobre los esclavos traídos á vender de Nueva España, suplican mande a determinar: cada día llegan de la conquista de Montejo (Yucatán) indios é indias y los derechos se depositan durante el pleito; CODOIN 1885–1932:II:4:325–326.)

1534, December 11: RC prohibiting the governors and other justices of Hispaniola and Cubagua and all areas of the mainland to send armadas to Venezuela. Text indicates being informed by the governors of the province of Venezuela and Cabo de la Vela that the *vecinos* of Hispaniola and Cubagua engage in armadas against the Indians of the province of Venezuela, to its detriment. Instructs the royal officials to desist from these practices unless they have the approval of the governor of said province. CMEPV 1959:I:184–185.

1535, July 16: Letter from the San Juan City Council to Charles V. Request license for the *vecinos* to bring Indians from Brazil without having to pay taxes. HDPR 1973:I:155–156.

1535, October 27: Two decrees from the Queen: one addressed to the governor and royal officials of Venezuela instructing them to investigate the illegal enslavement of Venezuelan Indians by the governor of the province and their transfer to Hispaniola; the other addressed to the royal officials of Hispaniola concerning the same matter. It mentions that Indians from Venezuela were publicly sold in Hispaniola and to investigate. There is a third decree of the same date and subject addressed to the governor of Venezuela that indicates that the Indians were being taken from the vicinity of the city of Coro. CMEPV 1959:II:13–14.

1536, March 17: RC from the Empress to all the authorities of the Indies. Prohibits the sending of Indian slaves to Spain without the license of the governor of the province from where they are being sent. CODOIN 1885–1932:II:10:317–319.

1538, October 25: RC to the Audiencia of Santo Domingo. Alludes to the existence of many Indian and black slaves in the city of Santo Domingo who have not been instructed in the Catholic faith. CODOIN 1885–1932:II:10:442.

1539, May 29: Letter to the King from the royal officials of San Juan. Mentions that Bartolomé Carreño led an armada against the Caribs and brought some Indian slaves that were sold in San Juan. Request permission to brand them as is done in Hispaniola and Cubagua. PRDJBM 1960:332–333; Tapia y Rivera 1970:376.

1540, March 10: RC to the Audiencia of Santo Domingo. Indicates that they should stop the practice of giving out licenses to take Indian slaves from the mainland coast to residents of Santo Domingo and other areas. This is done at the request of the authorities of Nueva Cádiz in Cubagua, since the practice thwarted their attempts at the same. Sanctions the licensing from Cubagua and prohibits it from Santo Domingo. CMEIC 1961:I:165–166.

1543, June 23: Seville. Colonial information concerning the liberty and treatment of the Indians. Information provided to Gregorio López, Council of the Indies. Includes the testimony of Luis de Morales, a clergyman who resided eight to ten years in Santo Domingo and visited San Juan, Cuba, and many areas of the mainland. Eyewitness and participant in the raids to the mainland and transport of Indians to Hispaniola and other islands. *Informaciones coloniales sobre libertad y tratamiento de los indios,* 1951, in *Revista del Archivo Histórico de Cuzco* (Journal of the Historic Archives of Cuzco) 2:225–269.

1543, July 14: RC commissioning the Audiencia of Hispaniola to investigate the bad treatment of the Indians of Venezuela, Paria, Cubagua, and Margarita. Mentions the practice of slave raiding in these areas to supply the islands of San Juan and Hispaniola, among others. CRV 1963:371–374.

1543, November 28: RP from Prince Phillip (in the name of Emperor Charles V) prohibiting the transfer of Indians, whether free or slaves, outside of their province. CODOIN 1864–1889:I:18:467–470 (with date of November 23); CDHFSHA 1953:227–228.

1544, September 15: Santo Domingo. Letter to the Council of the Indies from Fr. Bartolomé de Las Casas. Mentions that Indian slaves are still being brought into Hispaniola and Cuba at this date. Text of the letter, which is an extract taken from the Muñoz Collection (see Catalogue of the Muñoz Collection 1954–1956), indicates that Las Casas witnessed the arrival of two or three vessels in Santo Domingo some days before writing this letter. Indicates that the vessels also went to Cuba. CODOIN 1864–1889:I:7:431–437.

1545, April 23: Letter to the Emperor from Licenciados Cerrato and Grajeda, Santo Domingo. Mentions that there are very few native Indians left in the island and that they freed them; that there were 5,000 Indian slaves in the island; that while they were in Hispaniola two caravels arrived from Cubagua and Margarita with more than 250 branded Indians, whom the attorneys deposited until a declaration could be made. Mentions that the island had no *indios de repartimiento* (*repartimiento* Indians). SDDJBM 1981:407.

1547, September 23: RP from King Charles to the officials of the Indies. Prohibits the transfer of Indian slaves outside of their province. CDHFSHA 1953:244–245.

1547, December 18: Letter to the Emperor in the Council of the Indies from Licenciado Cerrato, Santo Domingo. Mentions that despite royal prohibition, Indians, especially women, were being sent from the mainland and sold publicly in Seville. SDDJBM 1981:418.

Notes

Introduction

1. These processes, especially the latter, have been studied mainly by historians (Moya Pons 1978; Rodríguez Demorizi 1971; Alegría 1976; Chipman 1966; Fernández Méndez 1984; Otte 1956, 1975, 1977; Saco 1932; Sherman 1971; Zavala 1948) but have not, to my knowledge, been the focus of anthropological studies of the early contact period in the Caribbean.

2. The concept of social and cultural disintegration used by Patterson (1966) in his study of African slavery and the formation of Jamaican society is of relevance here. As argued later in this introduction, cultural and social disintegration is a recurrent process in the early stages of contact between disparate cultures. A clear instance of this occurred in the early days of colonization in Hispaniola, when the forces of Francisco Roldán and his approximately 300 followers literally took over the island (Moya Pons 1978).

3. Currently, there are individuals who have identified themselves as Taíno. This issue is discussed later in this volume.

4. For a detailed discussion of the primary sources used in this volume and the biases inherent in their interpretation, consult the bibliographic essay in this volume.

5. Two important documents are analyzed in detail: the 1514 Repartimiento of Hispaniola and the 1530 Census of Puerto Rico.

Chapter 1

1. "Native American" is another more recent term used to refer to the indigenous inhabitants of the New World. Both terms, "Indian" and "Native American," are broad categories that serve mainly to contrast native peoples to those of European, African, or Asian descent, but have no value as identifiers of ethnicity. It is like calling people of Spanish descent in the United States by the generic term "Latino" or "Hispanic," disregarding the variety of cultures and peoples included in the term.

2. The first historical reference to the term "*taíno*" (not capitalized) is in Columbus's second voyage, where in Guadeloupe they encountered "Carib" Indians who had captured Indian women and children from Puerto Rico. According to Diego Alvarez Chanca (a physician who was a member of this expedition), the women told the Spanish that they were *tayno*, meaning good or noble, to distinguish themselves from their captors (see Curet 2014:470; also Keegan 2013:70). As pointed out by Curet, the term was an adjective to describe a condition, not an ethnic term as used later by scholars.

3. The term "Island Arawak," used by Sauer (1969:37) to distinguish these Indians from the Carib of the Lesser Antilles and from their Arawak cousins in the South American mainland, is no better, because the Caribbean chiefdoms encountered by the Spanish differed considerably from their Arawak origins.

4. For a more detailed discussion of these authors' use of the term "Taínoness," see Curet 2014:476–481.

5. This concept of symbolic reservoir could be applied to the Hopewellian Interaction Sphere as well (Brose and Greber 1979).

6. Earlier Archaic peoples (called pre-Arawak by Rodríguez Ramos 2010) already existed in Puerto Rico and the rest of the Greater Antilles at this time but are not discussed here.

7. Keegan (2013:77) indicates the start of stone-lined plazas in Puerto Rico around A.D. 900. See also Oliver 2005:238.

8. Keegan postulates the Taíno culture originated in the area of eastern Dominican Republic and spread into Puerto Rico "through incorporation of the peoples of this island whose local practices were encapsulated in a wider social formation" (2013:77).

9. See Pagán-Jiménez 2011:87–116 for information on recent archaeobotanical studies in the Circum-Caribbean.

10. For detailed information on the exploitation of land and marine resources in the Caribbean, see Newsom and Wing 2004.

11. Within the anthropological framework of cultural evolutionary studies, chiefdoms are ranked, hierarchically organized societies placed in a continuum between tribal societies and class-structured societies. Chiefdoms are further classified into different categories, depending on their degree of complexity.

12. Historical documentation also forms the basis for inferences regarding the rules of descent and post-marital residence in Caribbean chiefdoms. As pointed out by Oliver (1997:145), the evidence is ambiguous. Most scholars argue for matrilineal descent (Keegan 1992; Sued Badillo 1975), and Keegan (1989, 1997) has argued for avunculocal residence.

13. This theoretical perspective starts with the premise that environmental/ecological factors that put stress on social institutions are the main factors in the development of social complexity (see also Curet 1996:115 for a dis-

cussion of the principal archaeological models to explain this complexity in the Caribbean).

14. The term *naboría* and what it may have referred to in Taíno society is subject to varied interpretations. Sixteenth-century Spanish descriptions seem to imply that the *naborías* were a special category of commoner who worked exclusively for the *caciques* and other members of the chiefly class. Many scholars (see, for example, Rouse 1948; Sauer 1969:50; Moya Pons 1973) have traditionally assumed that the *naborías* were servants or slaves. Here I am following Moscoso's (1983:339) interpretation—that is, the *naborías* were commoners, not slaves or servants. Also, the term *naboría* assumed various meanings during the historic period. As noted in subsequent chapters in this volume, it was used later by the Spanish to mean Indians who worked in Spanish households (*naborías de casa*) and to distinguish between Indian slaves (*esclavos*) and foreign Indians who could not be legally enslaved but were compelled to work for the Spanish (*naborías perpetuos*).

15. De La Luz-Rodríguez disagrees with this and views the Taínos of Hispaniola and Puerto Rico as polities that exhibited both kin and prototributary modes of production; he argues that this was obscured by the "fact of conquest," which essentially "resulted in the elimination of kin-based productive relations and solidified whatever forms of tributary processes already existed" (2004:82–83).

16. This point has been contested by many. Chiefdom boundaries appear to have been much more fluid, and there appear to have been many more *caciques* in Hispaniola than the ones mentioned in the early chroniclers' accounts. In the case of Puerto Rico, archaeological evidence suggests a decentralized system of village alliances, in contrast to Hispaniola. Agüeybaná may have been able to form alliances with other *caciques* to fight the Spanish, but this does not imply that he was a paramount chief. The historical *cacicazgos/caciques* are discussed further in chapters 2 and 3.

17. Cuba, Jamaica, and the Bahamas chiefdoms were also different. The Bahamas chiefdoms had close ties with the chiefdoms of Hispaniola (Berman et al. 2013:268, also Keegan 2007, Keegan et al. 1998). The relationship of Jamaican chiefdoms to those of the other Greater Antillean islands is one that requires further investigation (see Wesler 2013:259). The native inhabitants of the eastern two-thirds of the island of Cuba were also loosely organized into chiefdoms (Rouse 1992).

18. I agree with Wilson (1986:206) that historical and archaeological evidence cannot establish clear boundaries for the chiefdoms of Hispaniola. The boundaries most probably fluctuated with the ability of the respective chiefs to exert authority over a particular territory, and chiefdoms also exhibited different levels of economic productivity. The degree of sophistication attributed to the chiefdom of Xaraguá cannot be assumed for the entire island.

19. The Lesser Antilles include all of the West Indian islands east of Puerto Rico.

20. For detailed discussion on how these terms were interpreted and misinterpreted in the historical record, see Hulme 1986.

21. The Indian communities described by French, and later English, sources were removed by 100 years or more from those that inhabited these islands at the beginning of the sixteenth century. Ethnographic descriptions exist, but these reflect communities that had already had long-term, albeit sporadic, contact with Europeans (see Wilson 1993:51). Although called Caribs by the French and English, they may bear little or no resemblance to the sixteenth-century inhabitants. However, Allaire considers the seventeenth-century Caribs described by the French ethnographers as similar to the populations described for the sixteenth century: "By 1493, 'ethnic' Caribs, in many ways similar to the later populations encountered and described in the seventeenth century, had occupied the islands at least as far north as Guadeloupe from where they raided the Lesser Antilles" (2013:99).

22. As also noted by Allaire (2013:100), the French ethnographers who documented the Carib in the seventeenth century had no knowledge that the Taíno Indians had ever existed in the Greater Antilles, and neither did the Carib they studied.

23. This term has persisted in the literature, but, as pointed out by Whitehead, it obscures the fact that "the Island Carib were, and are, part of a *continental* context, and cannot be analyzed as if they were solely an insular population." (1995:12).

24. Interestingly, they parallel the cultural continuity versus migration models postulated to explain post-Saladoid cultures in the Greater Antilles.

25. Although, as noted previously, Spanish sources never used the term "Taíno," and were cognizant of ethnic differences. They mention the Macorís in northern Hispaniola, the Ciboneys in the rest of Hispaniola, the Ciguayos in the Samaná Peninsula, and the Guanahatabeys in Western Cuba. The Spanish referred to the inhabitants of the Bahamas as Lucayos.

26. Granberry (2013:61) identifies seven indigenous speech communities in the Caribbean: 1) Ciboney Taíno in Hispaniola (central and southern Haiti), central Cuba, the Bahamas, and Jamaica; 2) Macorís (Dominican Republic section of northern Hispaniola); 3) Ciguayo in the Samaná Peninsula of northeastern Hispaniola; 4) Guanahatabey in the Pinar del Río province of far western Cuba; 5) Classic Taíno in Hispaniola (primarily in what is now the Dominican Republic), Puerto Rico, Vieques Island, and the Virgin and Leeward Islands; 6) Kalíphuna in the Windward Islands, and 7) Karina Carib, also in the Windward Islands.

27. According to Boomert, "in protohistoric times the southern portion of the Lesser Antilles, Trinidad, and the littoral zone of the Guianas should be conceived of as forming one sphere of interaction, closely knit by ties of kinship, ethnicity, language, exchange, war, and culture" (1995:32–33).

Chapter 2

1. Thus, since the beginning of Spanish intervention in the Antilles, the discovery of gold was of paramount importance. It was the economic engine that fueled the early colonial economies of the New World (see Sued Badillo 2001, 2003).

2. According to Moya Pons (1992:130), citing Las Casas, they were all killed by the Indians for abusing their women (see also Sued Badillo 2003:280).

3. Once the Spanish ascertained the indigenous political structure and recognized the importance of the *cacique*, they began to either kill or capture them, effectively ending Indian resistance (see Sued Badillo 2003:280–281). Sued Badillo (2003:287) also documents a partial list of 36 *caciques* in Hispaniola at the time of contact.

4. However, according to Wilson, this battle occurred at the Vega Real area in March 1495, and Indians of various chiefdoms participated (1986:174).

5. The first battle occurred at a place known as Santo Cerro (Holy Hill), located just west of Maguá, in *cacique* Guarionex's territory and northeast of the modern town of La Vega (Guitar 2009). This was a major battle in which Guarionex and various other *caciques* and their warriors participated (Guitar 2009).

6. Roldán took care to point out that they were rebelling against the Columbus family and not against the Crown (Moya Pons 1992:131).

7. There is a distinction between *repartimiento* and *encomienda*. The first term refers to the early distribution of Indians among Spanish settlers but did not involve the distribution of land. The *encomienda* was the legal institution that legitimized the use of Indian labor and lands under specific Spanish *encomenderos*, who had, at least on paper, the responsibility of feeding the Indians and instructing them about Christianity. For detailed information about the *encomienda* system established in the Spanish Indies, see Córdova 1968; Kirkpatrick 1939; Zavala 1948; Mira Caballos 1997, 2000a, 2000b.

8. Fonseca, archdeacon of Seville, was a member of the Royal Council of Castille and was the first minister appointed by the Crown to oversee the affairs of the Indies (Sued Badillo 2003:19).

9. Columbus's vision of the colony being a *factoría* (factory), modeled after the Portuguese enterprises in Africa, where he and his family would share the profits with the Crown was completely unraveling. The model contemplated by Roldán and his followers was more like the Spanish *Reconquista*, in which Spanish settlers would occupy the land and have the subjected peoples work for them as serfs (Moya Pons 1992:130). See also Pérez de Tudela Bueso 1955a, 1955b.

10. When Bobadilla left the island in the year 1502, he was carrying more than 200,000 pesos in gold (Sued Badillo 2003:275, citing Herrera 1944: II:10). As pointed out by Sued Badillo, this amounted to more than 2,000 pounds of gold, all collected before the *encomienda* system was fully estab-

lished (2003:275). Neither the gold nor Bobadilla made it back to Spain, the entire fleet being lost in a hurricane just off Hispaniola in the Mona Passage.

11. The Crown extended almost absolute power to Ovando, giving him jurisdiction over almost all of the known Spanish possessions, and including not only the governorship of Hispaniola but judicial powers as well, as he was also appointed *juez de apelación* (apellate judge) (Mira Caballos 1997:100, citing Lamb 1977, Armas Medina 1957, and García Gallo 1987).

12. Pietshmann describes this as follows: "Many of the Spaniards spread out over the islands and went on to live among the natives, adapting in many respects to their customs and habits. As a grotesque derivation of the seigneurial customs of their homelands, they caused themselves to be treated as 'lords' by the natives. They set up a Spanish-inspired noble 'court' staffed by Indians, had themselves carried around in hammocks wearing rags or half-naked and held orgies with the natives. They married the daughters of Indian *caciques* and neglected their religious obligations or even profaned the Christian religion. As these Spaniards also adopted the language of their environment, from the standpoint of the Crown there was not just the threat of a process of hybridization but also that of complete assimilation of the Europeans by the natives" (1999:100).

13. According to Sued Badillo, also citing Las Casas, 80 *caciques* of Xaraguá were burned alive, and Anacaona was later hanged by Ovando (2003: 281). Mira Caballos (2000b:71) indicates the discrepancies concerning these numbers and cites Irving (1851:192) for a summary of this issue.

14. The Spanish took advantage of the divisions among competing chiefdoms (divisions that would have been exacerbated by the Spanish presence) and recruited Indians from enemy chiefdoms in these wars. Sued Badillo (2003:280), citing Las Casas, indicates that hundreds of Indians from Ycayagua participated with Juan de Esquivel in the conquest of Higüey; just as 3,000 Indians had allied with Bartolomé Colón against *cacique* Guarionex and the ciguayos.

15. Although many of these did not survive for long, they served to consolidate Ovando's political power over the entire island (Mira Caballos 2000b:103).

16. San Juan de la Maguana was founded in the area where *cacique* Caonabo had resided (Altman 2007:592).

17. La Vera Paz was founded in the site of Anacaona's village (Altman 2007:592).

18. Mira Caballos's (2000a:34–35) data on gold production between 1505 and 1507 is based on an unpublished manuscript located in the General Archives in Seville (AGI): *Información del Tesorero Cristóbal de Santa Clara*, Santo Domingo, 13 octubre de 1531. AGI, *Justicia* 990, no. 1.

19. See Mira Caballos (1997:35) for a summary of the decline of the indigenous population of Hispaniola from 1492 to 1548. See also Córdova (1968) for a discussion of the effects of the *repartimientos* on Indian society and culture (and more on these issues in chapters 3 and 4 of this volume).

20. This court served as intermediary between local government officials and the Crown (later with the Council of the Indies, which was established in 1523). It was the first in the New World and "for more than a decade had under its jurisdiction all of the territory discovered thus far" (Sued Badillo 2003:19).

21. For a detailed account of the gold economy that was at the core of the early colonization of the Indies, see Sued Badillo 2001, 2003.

22. See Hussey (1932) for the complete Spanish text of the Laws of Burgos, with English annotation. See also De La Luz-Rodríguez 2004:192–194.

23. The friars were Fray Luis de Figueroa, Fray Alonso de Santo Domingo, Fray Bernardino de Manzanedo, and a servant, Fray Juan de Salvatierra (Mira Caballos 2010:345, note 178).

24. The Juicios de Residencia (Judicial Reviews or Proceedings of an Administrative Investigation) that were carried out at the end of a Spanish official's tenure as a way of taking stock of his deeds and accomplishments while in office were a standard Spanish practice. An official appointed by the Crown or its delegate would hold court and carry out an official inquiry wherein any resident under the official's jurisdiction could publicly testify for or against him. This performance review of an official's term in office was documented in voluminous detail. The many documents of this type that have survived offer a wealth of information about Spanish colonial society, and in some cases, provide clues about the Indian populations as well.

25. Enriquillo was originally a native of the province of Xaraguá, where he apparently had been a *cacique* (Peña Battle 1948:73). He was born around 1500, was a grand-nephew of Anacaona, and, as member of the Indian chiefly class, was educated in the monastery of the town of La Vera Paz (Altman 2007:589). He was later allotted to an *encomienda* in the town of San Juan de la Maguana. When he rebelled, he returned to his place of origin, the Bahoruco hills north of the native seat of the chiefdom of Xaraguá, which had been one of the principal chiefdoms of Hispaniola. The description provided by Fernández de Oviedo (1959:I:127) concerning Enriquillo includes references to the use of canoes by Enriquillo's people and to the use of old and abandoned Indian villages as refuge areas. Knowledge of ancient sites and the art of canoe building and canoe transportation persisted 40 years after contact, if Oviedo's 1533 description is accurate.

26. In Alonso de Zuazo's 1532 report to the King he indicates that there were hardly any *encomienda* Indians left on the island (*Informe de Alonso de Zuazo a Su Majestad*, Santo Domingo 20 febrero 1532, AGI, Santo Domingo 49, R.3, N.14, cited in Mira Caballos 1997:346). By the 1540s, the island's economic activity centered on cattle ranching, and there is mention of more than 5,000 Indians working in this industry (Santo Domingo, July 22, 1546, AGI, *Justicia* 33, *Pieza* 1, cited in Mira Caballos 1997:346).

27. Sued Badillo (2003:291, note 17, quoting Deive 1980 II:562) indicates: "In 1555 four previously unknown indigenous villages were discovered, one near Puerto Plata, another in Samaná, another in the province

of the Ciguayos, and the fourth on the western end of the island, looking towards Cuba, on Cape San Nicolás." By 1571, only two Indian villages are reported by López de Velazco as remaining on the island (Sued Badillo 2003:291, note 17, quoting Rodríguez Demorizi 1971:16).

28. As mentioned in the previous chapter, this was the first instance of the term "Taíno" (which the Spanish translated as noble or good) in the historical literature. The women and children were from Puerto Rico and, according to Spanish sources, had been captured by the Caribs.

29. A *probanza* refers to testimony given by witnesses concerning the merits and achievements of a particular individual in the service of the Crown. It was drawn up to present evidence of good deeds or prowess in the execution of official business, with the purpose of gaining favors from the Crown. The *Probanza de Juan González* document was found under the Audiencia de México section of the AGI and is dated July 18, 1532. It includes testimony of Juan González's deeds in Puerto Rico years before. It is important because it presents numerous witnesses who had participated in the narrated events. All unanimously indicate the year 1506 as the first expedition of Juan Ponce de León. The document also provides information on the 1508 expedition, the discovery of gold, and the Indian rebellions. Fernández de Oviedo's account of the conquest and colonization of Puerto Rico includes information that appears in the *Probanza* document.

30. For a detailed analysis of the *Probanza* document, see De La Luz-Rodríguez 2004:139–159; 2014.

31. Ponce de León and *cacique* Agüeybaná exchanged names through the native ritual of *guaytiao*, and, according to Sued Badillo (2008:28), this may explain why the *cacique*'s territory was later known as Ponce (which is currently the name of the southern coast city of Ponce, but originally covered a much larger geographic area in south-central Puerto Rico [2008:82–83]).

32. "Después de aderezado el dicho carabelón, partí de allí bojando la dicha Isla y hablando a los caciques de la costa y a los caribes que allí hallé, y dandoles preseas a los unos y a los otros, por los asegurar, hasta que llegué a la bahía que está en la parte del norte" (HDPR II:520).

33. "Hice coger oro con una cuadrilla, que no pude con tres como las asenté, por no tener que dar de comer a la gente, y por no me poder ayudar para ello de esta Isla, ni de los indios de la dicha Isla."

34. "Porque hasta aquí no se ha podido hacer mas de mandar labrar en casa de los caciques para Su Alteza, que son cinco caciques los que mandó que labrasen en sus casas para Su Alteza; y esto es lo que hasta agora se ha podido hacer, y mas no, por haber mudado el pueblo tres veces, y por no tener de comer ni lo haber en esta Isla, aunque me quisiera aprovechar de ella, y por no me poder aprovechar de los indios de la dicha Isla como era razón, de cuya causa no se ha podido mas hacer." There is later reference to the cassava produced and sold from five areas of the island, in territory of the *caciques* Agüeybaná, Caguas, Mabo, Gonzalo, and Casanova (Mira Caballos 1997:193, note 7).

35. The Spanish Crown intervened directly as well; between 1509 and 1512, the King, through Royal Decree, conceded up to three thousand Indians in *encomienda* to officials and settlers in the Island of San Juan (Mira Caballos 1997:195).

36. This was Agüeybaná II, brother of and successor to the original Agüeybaná who met Ponce de León in 1508. Whether Agüeybaná II was supreme chief of the island or whether he initiated the rebellion and subsequently gained his followers by his actions cannot be ascertained. According to Sued Badillo (2003:282), Agüeybaná II and 30 other *caciques* declared war against the Spanish, killing more than half of the Spanish population of the island. Sued Badillo (2003:282) also finds evidence that, contrary to what most historians say, Agüeybaná II was not killed in this early battle but remained alive for many years to lead, in conjunction with native Indians and Indians from the Leeward Islands, attacks on Spanish settlements and *haciendas* (see also Sued Badillo 2008). Sued Badillo (2003:287), provides a list of 31 *caciques* in Puerto Rico at the time of contact. He later expands this list to include 86 *caciques*, of which 37 were in revolt against the Spanish (Sued Badillo 2008:210–212). Moscoso (2008:115–223), identifies 44 *caciques* for the island.

37. Sued Badillo identifies Agüeybaná's attack on Sotomayor as occurring on the Jauca River, now part of Barrio Jauca, in the municipality of Jayuya, as Sotomayor and his men attempted to flee north across the mountains to Caparra (2008:72). His sources include the 1517 Hieronymite Interrogatory and the *Memorias de Pedro Tomás de Córdova* 1831:II:251.

38. Fernández de Oviedo states the following with respect to the first battle at Caoyuco (Fernández Méndez 1981:57): "where many Indians died, including caribs from surrounding islands who use the bow and arrow, that had joined them and wanted to move to a small island called Angulo, which is close to the island of San Juan to the south." (donde murieron muchos indios, assi caribes de las islas comarcanas y flecheros, con quien se habian juntado como de los de la tierra que se querían passer a una isleta que se llama Angulo, que está cerca de la isla de Sanct John a la parte del sur.) The small island referred to as Angulo is the current *Caja de Muertos* (Coffin Island), located on the south-central coast of Puerto Rico, in the municipality of Ponce (Sued Badillo 2008:53).

39. Lucas Gallego, witness 3 of the *Probanza de Juan González*, states the following in reference to the Daguao area (Tió 1961:92–93): "Called the Sierra of Daguao and going by a mountain at the foot of this Sierra we saw smoke coming from an arroyo and went there and found at the fire ten Indians and we took all ten and the said Juan González Ponce de León tortured some and they told him that they were Agüeybaná's porters, the *cacique* who killed Don Cristóbal de Sotomayor, and he asked them the whereabouts of Agüeybaná and they told him that he was very close, at the edge of the island and the sea at the mouth of a river and that there were many carib *caciques* with many Indians who were going to burn the city of Puerto Rico and

kill the governor and Christians and that they had already started coming and had said that they had burned much of the town and brought a lot of clothes and riches." (La cual se dezia la sierra del daguao y yendo por una montaña por la falda de dicha sierra vimos salir humo de un arroyo y fuimos a el y hallamos en el fuego a 10 yndios and los tomamos a todos 10 y el dicho Juan González Ponce de León dio tormento a los compañeros a ciertos yndios y le dixeron que eran portadores de agueybana el cacique que mato a don Xptoal de Sotomayor y le pregunto que adonce estava el dicho agueybana y le dixeron que bien cerca de alli enla punta dela ysla ala mar y ala boc de un ryo y que estavan muchos caciques con el y muchose carybes e yndios e insimismo le dixeron como avia 8 o 10 dias que avian ydo mucho caciques carybes con mucha copia de yndios a quemar la cibdad de p.r. y matar al governador y a los xristianos y que avian ya empezado a venir y que avian dicho como avian quemado mucha parte del pueblo y que trayan much ropa y riqueza.) The Daguao area refers to northeastern Puerto Rico, comprising the current municipalities of Río Grande, Luquillo, Fajardo, Ceiba, and Naguabo (Sued Badillo 2008:160).

40. The document cites Virgin Gorda, but Tió thinks it was probably Vieques or Culebra (Tió 1961:149, note 47; 1961:160, notes 50 and 51; and 1961:174, note 71).

41. The Requerimiento, which had its antecedents in the Spanish conquest of the Canary Islands and was formally written by Palacios Rubio in 1513 for use in the New World (Zavala 1948:37, 56), consisted of a document, written in Spanish, that was read to Indians before battle. In it, the Spanish formally requested the Indians to submit to the authority of the Spanish monarch or risk enslavement. The absurdity of the use of this document to justify the enslavement of Indians who obviously could not understand what was being said to them, even if read in their native language, has been pointed out by many scholars. Even Fernández de Oviedo questioned its use in the conquest of the mainland (Tierra Firme).

42. Tió calculates, on the basis of testimony presented in the *Probanza de Juan González* document, that at least 680 Indians from San Juan de Puerto Rico were found by the Spanish in one of the neighboring islands (1961:174, notes 74, 76). The exodus of Indians from Puerto Rico to neighboring islands is also indicated by Brau (1966) and Sued Badillo (1978, 2003:282).

43. This document is reproduced in its entirety in Sued Badillo 2008: 125–127. As Sued Badillo points out, it indicates that the Indian rebellion was still in force months after the initial battle in Agüeybaná's territory and the supposed demise of the *cacique* Agüeybaná (2008:127).

44. For a detailed analysis of the Treasury documents as they relate to Indian slaves in Puerto Rico and Hispaniola, see Wolff 2014.

45. Sued Badillo (2003:282) mentions the 1513 attack by Diego Colón on rebel villages and the capture of 17 *caciques* who were banished to Hispaniola. These were most probably sent to work as slaves in the gold mines of Hispaniola. Sued Badillo notes that they were never seen again.

46. One of these, on June 12, 1512, indicates how Juan Gil and other captains made war against Agüeybaná (called Gueybana in this document) and other *caciques* and Indians, suggesting to Sued Badillo that Agüeybaná was still alive at this time (2008:132). See also Sued Badillo 2008:203–205, appendix 1 for a summary of Spanish raids against Indian *caciques* in Puerto Rico in the years 1510–1514.

47. Sources document one free Indian village established near the Toa royal *hacienda* as part of the Hieronymite experiment on the island. Fifty Indians (19 men, 26 women, 3 boys, and 1 girl) resided there in 1528; in 1529 the number had dropped to 31 (10 men, 13 women, 8 boys, and no girls) (Mira Caballos 1997:211).

48. However, according to Mira Caballos (1997:347–348), in 1530 Indians represented 44 percent of the labor pool on the island, and by 1540 there were only about 50 *encomienda* Indians remaining (Source: Letter from the *Cabildo* [Municipal Council] of Puerto Rico to the King, June 5, 1540, AGI, Santo Domingo 164, N.20).

49. Sued Badillo (2003:287) provides a partial listing of 17 *caciques* in Cuba at the time of contact and 4 in Jamaica. Mira Caballos (2000a) includes an indigenous map of Cuba which locates about 60 Indian villages mentioned in the historic sources, the great majority in the eastern provinces, and lists 15 other villages that he was unable to locate.

Chapter 3

1. The exception being the killing of the Spaniards left at Fort La Navidad, which is discussed later in this chapter.

2. "Todos los indios huyeron y huían como vían los navíos."

3. This woman had been captured while forming part of a group of Indians in canoes that had approached the area where the Spanish were located (Varela 1982:78).

4. See, for example, the December 18 and December 26 entries (Varela 1982:83, 99), wherein chief Guacanagarí eats in the caravel with Columbus and then Columbus goes to the chief's village and dines there as well. See also Las Casas (1951:I:280). It is known that the Indians presented food offerings to their *zemis* (ancestor idols). If it is true that they initially took the Spanish to be gods, then the presentation of food offerings to them may be interpreted as an extension of what was already their custom. Furthermore, their view of the Spanish as superior or powerful men or gods implied that their offerings of food would include those offerings reserved for the chiefly class, such as iguanas.

5. Other instances in which *caciques* offer prestige items to Columbus are the following: December 22, Chief Guacanagarí gives a belt with mask and inlays of gold; December 26, Chief Guacanagarí gives mask with inlays of gold, plus other gold pieces; December 28, Chief Guacanagarí gives another gold piece; December 29, Chief Guacanagarí gives a gold mask; De-

cember 30, five subordinate chiefs of Guacanagarí give gold "crowns" (Varela 1982:100,102,103; Las Casas 1951:I:286–288).

6. "Este rey (Guacanagarí) hizo mucha honra a la gente de los navíos, y los populares cada uno les traía algo de comer y de bever. Después el rey dio a cada uno unos paños de algodón que visten las mugeres y papagallos para el Almirante y ciertos pedacos de oro; davan también los populares de los mismos paños y otras cosas de sus casas a los marineros, por pequeña cosa que les davan, la cual, según la recibían, parecía que la estimavan por reliquias."

7. "Después de aver ido los seis cristianos, vinieron ciertas canoas con gente a rogar al Almirante, de parte (s) de un señor, que fuese a su pueblo, cuando de allí partiese. Y visto que el pueblo de aquel señor estava en el camino sobre una punta de tierra, esperando con mucha gente al Almirante, fué allá. Y antes que se partiese vino a la playa tanta gente que era espanto, hombres, mugeres y niños dando bozes que no se fuese, sino que se quedase con ellos. Los mensajeros del otro señor que avía venido a conbidar estaban aguardando con sus canoas, porque no se fuese sin ir a ver al señor. Y así lo hizo; y en llegando que llegó el Almirante adonde aquel señor le estava esperando y tenían muchas cosas de comer, mandó assenter toda su gente, manda que lleven lo que tenían de comer a las barcas donde estaba el Almirante, junto a la orilla de la mar."

8. These Indians were later identified as macorixes or macorís in Spanish documents. All the early chroniclers mention the existence of certain Indians that differed from the rest in language and appearance and inhabited the north central section of the island. They were organized into chiefdoms, as were the rest of the Indians. The territory in which they lived was quickly taken over by the Spanish, and not much ethnographic material concerning them is available.

9. See December 17 entry (Varela 1982:84–85).

10. See Fernández de Oviedo 1959:I:35 for a description of the death of the Spaniards at the hands of the Indians.

11. Las Casas describes this as follows (1951:I:419): "Would not plant or sow crops on their *conucos*, so that no fruit would be had from the soil and they would group in the mountains where there are many good roots called *guayaros*, which are good to eat, and they do not need to be planted, and with the hunting of the numerous *hutías* or rabbits in the hills and valleys, they would try to survive their miserable life. But this tactic did not work, because the Christians, although hungry and weary from going to the hills in pursuit of the poor Indians, did not leave nor die. . . . Most of the misery and calamity befell the Indians, because fleeing from persecution with their women and children in tow, tired, ground down, starving, with no place to hunt or fish or find their own food, and because of the humidity in the mountains and rivers where they sought to hide, came upon them so much disease, death and misery, that fathers, and mothers and children died in in-

finite numbers." (No sembrar ni hacer labranzas de su conuco, para que no se cogiese fruto alguno en la tierra, y ellos recogerse a los montes donde hay ciertas y muchas y buenas raíces, que se llaman guayaros, buenas de comer, y nascen sin sembrarlas, y con la caza de las hutías o conejos de que estaban los montes y los llanos llenos, pasar como quiera su desventurada vida. Aprovechólos poco su ardid, porque aunque los cristianos, de hambre terrible y de andar a montear y perseguir los tristes indios, padecieron grandísimos trabajos y peligros, pero ni se fueron ni se murieron, . . . antes toda la miseria y calamidad hobo de caer sore los mismo indios, porque como anduviesen tan corridos y perseguidos con sus mujeres e hijos a cuestas, cansados, molidos, hambrientos, no se les dando lugar para cazar o pescar o buscar su propria comida, y por las humidades de los montes y de los ríos, donde siempre andaban huídos y se escondían, vino sobre ellos tanta de enfermedad, muerte y miseria, de que murieron infelicemente de padres y madres y hijos, infinitos.)

12. Moscoso (1986:446–447) includes an inventory of the prestige items and gold collected by Columbus in Hispaniola, taken from the "Relación del oro y joyas e otras cosas que el Señor Almirante ha rescibido después que el receptor Sevastián de Olano partió desta isla para Castilla desde 10 marzo de 1495 años," AGI Patronato 8, R. 12. Later, in 1505, Treasurer Cristóbal de Santa Clara inventoried a series of objects received in tribute from the Indians, which included gold objects, ceremonial objects, and a variety of clothes and fishing items made of cotton (Mira Caballos 2010:411–412, citing *Información y cuentas del tesorero Cristóbal de Santa Clara, Santo Domingo, 13 de octubre de 1531*. AGI, Justicia 990, N. 1, Pieza 2).

13. As discussed, there was contact and communication among island communities throughout the Caribbean area during prehistoric and early historic times. The Indians of Puerto Rico would have been well aware of the Spanish presence in Hispaniola. See also Stevens-Arroyo 1993:526.

14. The practice of exchanging names, known by the Indian term *guaytiao*, was a common social practice among Caribbean *caciques*. It was a way of cementing alliances among competing polities. By assuming another chief's name, a *cacique* was able to assimilate the others' power and privilege and establish reciprocal alliances. The Spanish understood the term to indicate friendship among those exchanging names, and equated the practice with the Spanish institution of *compadrazgo*, in which the parents and godparents of a baptized child become permanently related (Mira Caballos 2010:255, citing Arrom 1975:16 and Tejera 1951:245). This exchange of names between a Spanish conquistador and an Indian *cacique* obviously meant different things to each. Agüeybaná would have interpreted it as becoming allied with a powerful Spanish leader, while Ponce de León just viewed it as an acknowledgement of Agüeybaná's leadership role among his people and as a way of eliciting his cooperation.

15. In fact, De La Luz-Rodríguez argues that one of the factors that con-

tributed to the success of the system of *encomiendas* in the Greater Antillean islands was that it was able to capitalize on "the embryonic tributary social relations of production that existed in the most complex of western Caribbean chiefdoms" (2003:9).

16. Archaeological research suggests different levels of sociopolitical complexity among the late prehistoric chiefdoms in Puerto Rico, as well as variations in population density among geographic areas of the island (Curet 1996:121; 1992:284–294; Rodríguez López 1990; Walker and Walker 1983). There is reason to believe that this variability persisted in the early historic period and may have contributed to the fluidity of native movement within and among islands documented in historical sources.

17. See also Hofman et al. 2014:596–597 for a discussion of Kelbey's Ridge site, in Saba northern Lesser Antilles, which they interpret as a late prehistoric outpost of peoples migrating from the Greater Antilles.

18. Gil González Dávila, in his "Relación sobre la despoblación de la isla española, sus causas, medidas para poblarla y cosas de aquella isla" (Moya Pons 1978:287–293), hits the nail on the head when he indicates: "The fourth and main reason is that the priority has always been to extract as much gold as possible from that Island, rather than spend any effort in her conservation or betterment, nor in the relief of the Indians" (1978:287). (La cuarta razon, é mas principal ha seydo, que se ha tenido siempre fin a que de aquella Isla venga siempre el mas oro que se pueda, é no se ha tenido fin a gastar ninguna cosa en la conservacion ni acrecentamiento della, ni en el descanso de los indios.)

19. In De La Luz-Rodríguez's words: "The greatest paradox of this process was that in practice this ideological 'improvement' was embedded in the most absolute system of exploitation, a system which destroyed the lives of the very people it sought to redeem" (2004:99).

20. See, for example, Hieronymite Interrogatory, 1517, AGI Indiferente 1624, published in Rodríquez Demorizi (1971:273–354); "Relación de Gil González Dávila de la despoblación de la isla Española," n.d., published in Moya Pons (1978:287–293), Doc. V; and in CODOIN (Series I) 1.I:332–347; "Carta de Andrés de Haro sobre medidas de buen gobierno San Juan de Puerto Rico 1518," published in Serrano y Sanz (1918:575–577), also in Caro Costas (1971:91–96) and in Brau (1966:515–520); "Memorial de fray Bernardino de Manzanedo sobre el buen regimen y gobierno de los indios, 1518," published in Serrano y Sanz (1918:Doc. L[50]:568–575); "Memorial acerca del gobierno de los indios, presentado al Consejo de Indias por los padres jerónimos," published in Serrano y Sanz (1918, Doc. XLVIII[8]:561–568), also in CODOIN (1864–1889:I:12:106–123).

21. As mentioned in the previous chapter, this experiment involved various *caciques* who resided in different areas of Hispaniola, as well as other Indians who were not *caciques* but were also given *repartimientos*. Testimony varies as to the names, numbers, and place of residence of the Indians involved.

22. Accounts on the number of Indians vary. Some witnesses mention two Indians by name; another mentions three, including one *cacique.* The names given are inconsistent. One of the witnesses mentions that some of the Indians placed in liberty were from towns other than Santo Domingo, such as Bonao or Santiago. Witness Juan Mosquera mentions three *caciques*: Alonso de Cáceres, Pedro Colón, and Don Francisco. Their liberty lasted six years, until they were reassigned to Spaniards in the 1514 Repartimiento. (If this is correct, they were given their freedom in 1508.) Juan Mosquera indicates (Rodríquez Demorizi 1971:279–280) that "all their time was spent in laziness and in ingesting herbs to make their cohobas" (syno que todo su pasatiempo hera en holgar y tomar yervas para fazer sus cohobas). Witness Gonzalo de Campo mentions that Ovando freed two *caciques*: Don Francisco of the Villa del Bonao and Dotor of the Villa de Santiago. Apparently, these two were *caciques* that still had Indians under their authority, since the witness indicates (Rodríquez Demorizi 1971:283): "And he ordered that his same people be given to him as *repartimiento,* as was done with other Spaniards" (Y les mando dar de su mesma gente repartimiento como se davan a otros españoles). Witness Diego de Alvarado mentions the two Indians as *caciques* Alonso de Cáceres and Pedro Colón, both married and "good scribes and readers" (buenos escrivanos y letores) (Rodríquez Demorizi 1971:294). Witness Juan de Ampies mentions the use of *cohoba* when the Indians left the company of the Spaniards (Rodríquez Demorizi 1971:302). Licenciado Lucas Vázquez de Ayllón mentions Ovando's experiment and states there were three *caciques*: Masupa Otex from the Vega Real, Dotor from Santiago, and Don Francisco from Bonao. He mentions that the last *cacique* had been a pupil of the Franciscan friars and had also lived in Ovando's household. He indicates that two other Indians were also placed in freedom, Diego Colón and Alonso de Cáceres, and states that these were not *caciques* but resided in the capital of Santo Domingo, where they had served the Spanish and were great interpreters. Witness Andrés de Montamarta, of the villa de La Vera Paz, indicates that when away from Spanish influence, the Indians continued their old customs, including the use of *cohoba* (Rodríquez Demorizi 1971:330–331). Witness Marcos de Aguilar also mentions the persistence of the use of *cohoba* (Rodríquez Demorizi 1971:339). Ovando's experiment is also analyzed by Mira Caballos 1997:109–111, and 2009:167–168.

23. Concerning the persistence of *areitos* and ballgames various witnesses testify the following: Jerónimo de Aguero (Rodríquez Demorizi 1971:290), "that upon being free most of the time was spent in areytos and playing the ball game as they used to do before" (questando en libertad lo mas del tiempo an de gastar en areytos y jugar al batey como lo solian hazer): Diego de Alvarado (Rodríquez Demorizi 1971:294), "so that none of them understood anything except playing their ball game and acquiring something to eat, and what they had to eat for eight days they would consume in one, and in this manner they died poor and penniless. And another thing, because

many times I have seen them play their ball games, and one of them will wager jewelry that is worth one, or two, or three gold pesos or more and another will wager something worth no more than two maravedis, and they play the game and if the one who made the small wager wins, he takes the bigger wager from the other, and if the one who made the large wager wins he takes the smaller" (de manera que ninguno dellos entendía en otra cosa mas de en jugar su juego de batey y atquerir algo para comer e lo que tenian para comer en ocho dias gastarlo en uno y desta manera vinieron a morir pobres y syn blanca. Lo otro por que muchas vezes los he visto jugar sus juegos de batey y poner uno una joya que vale un peso de oro, o dos o tres y mas y poner otro otra que no vale dos maravedises e jugar su juego e sy gana el que pone chica joya lleva la grande que pone el otro e asy faze quando gana el que pone la grande que lleva la pequeña); Juan de Ampies (Rodríquez Demorizi 1971:302), "because they flee from work and from communication with the Spaniards they go to the hills and will rather eat spiders and crabs snakes roots and other poisonous and disgusting things from the earth than the food provided by the Spaniards and there they take their cohobas and herbs to induce vomiting what they eat and they perform their areytos and do the things they used to do before the Spaniards' arrival" (a cabsa de huyr de la comunicación con los españoles e del trabajo an por mejor en los montes aranas y xueyes e cangrejos culebras rayzes e otras vascosydades de la tierra poncoñosas que no los mantenimentos que los españoles les dan y alli toman sus cohobas e yervas par lancar del cuerpo lo que comen e hazer sus areytos y estan en las cosas que antes que los españoles viniesen a estas partes estavan); Andres de Montamarta (Rodríquez Demorizi 1971:330–331), "because once they leave the Spaniards' company they go back to their customs, taking tobacco and herbs and performing areytos and cohoba and they do not remember God because they do not pray" (porque en saliendo de la compañia de los españoles luego usan de sus costumbres tomando tabacos e yervas a haziendo areytos y cohoba e no se les acuerdan de Dios Nuestra Señor porque no resan).

24. Witness Marcos de Aguilar testifies the following (Rodríquez Demorizi 1971:339): "What they can eat today they give away and waste they do not save for tomorrow, and their natural inclination is to eat in excess getting up at night and taking herbs to induce vomiting, they are lazy and they do not understand anything except to perform areytos and play the ball game and make cohoba every night which makes them lose their senses, and they cleanse themselves many times, night and day, which is one of the things that shortens their life because leaving their areytos and their ball games sweating they rush to the water, and they are great sorcerers they have some old indians that they call bohites which they believe in and think highly of." (Antes lo que oy pueden comer dar e malgastar no lo dexan para mañana e que su fin e natural inclinación es a comer desordenadamente levantandose para ello de noche e vaziando el vientre con yervas que para ello to-

man son holgazanes no querrian entender armas que hazer areytos e jugar al batey ques como juego de pelota y hazer cohoba cada noche que los embeoda e lavanse muchas vezes de noche e dia ques una de los cosas que les acorta la vida por que saliendo de los areytos e de jugar al batey sudando se lancan al agua, son grandes hechizeros tienen unos yndios viejos quellos llaman bohites a los quales creen y tienen por gran cossa.) Various other witnesses mention ritual feasting in relation to the ballgames: Diego de Alvarado, a 24-year resident of Santo Domingo, mentions (Rodríquez Demorizi 1971:293) "that the said *caciques* and Indians he knows are aficionados of the ball game and *areytos* and *cohobas* and taking herbs to expunge from the body all that they have eaten, and that at the present time he knows that they are wine aficionados because they say that wine is better than their *cohoba* and their ball game." (que los dichos caciques e yndios conosce a que ser aficionados hera al juego de batel y areytos e cohobas e tomar yervas para hechar del cuerpo todo lo que han comido e cenado, e lo que agora al presente dellos conosco es ser aficionados al vino porque dizen ques major cohoba que la suya e al dicho juego de batel.) Pedro Moreno, an eighteen-year resident of the villa Salvatierra de la Sabana, and married to an Indian woman, mentions "the *conucos*, which are theirs and among the goods they most love, it happens that any day, by a whim, without thinking of what may happen later, they decide to eat all of the *conuco* in one month in their *areytos* and feasts, wasting the food." (los conucos que son bienes propios suyos e los bienes que mas aman les acontece de cada día que por vn antojo que les den syn mirar lo que adelante dello se puede seguir determinan de comer el tal conuco en vn mes con areytos y conbites desperdiciendo la comida.) (Rodríquez Demorizi 1971:333).

25. References indicating the persistence of Indian ceremonies and *areitos* and their lack of interest or knowledge of the Catholic religion continue into the middle of the sixteenth century, not only in Hispaniola but also in Puerto Rico, Cuba, and Jamaica as well (Mira Caballos 2000a:266–269). In the case of Puerto Rico, for example, Mira Caballos (2009:192) cites documents from the 1540s that indicate that "the few surviving native Indians continued to practice their traditional dances and hid their zemis or gods in the fields" (my translation).

26. "quanto mas queste trabajo de pasarlos no esta syno en los caciques grandes por que los pequeños facil cossa secreta traerlos porque no tienen poblaciones tan viciossas como los grandes por que antes se ponen en sierras o lugares solitarios y esteriles por estar escondidos que no en parte donde por los vicios se les faga grave de venir a las fasyendas de los españoles."

27. Other documentary sources indicate this as well. Historians have commented on the acculturation of *naborías de casa*, and how many Indian women lived in Spanish households as servants and concubines. Many of these Indians had learned the rudiments of the Spanish language (see Arranz Márquez 1991:132–133, 227–232). For example, in a 1509 legal pro-

ceeding in which Diego Colón brought charges against the *encomendero* Francisco de Solís for bad treatment of an Indian under his charge, all of the *naboría* Indians who testified did so in Spanish, even though there were interpreters available (Mira Caballos 2000a:142, citing *El Pleito Diego Colón-Francisco Solís: El Primer Proceso Por Malos Tratos a los Indios (1509),* AG de Simancas, sección Diversos Castilla, 45, no. 2).

28. Greater mortality among Indian women as compared to Indian men is also evident from the 1514 Repartimiento document (Arranz Márquez 1991). This is discussed in chapter 4 of this volume.

29. This is corroborated archaeologically at the site of En Bas Saline, Haiti (Deagan 2004), as noted later in this chapter.

30. This is similar to what occurred during the initial contact between Columbus and the native inhabitants of Hispaniola, where they accepted European artifacts as novel items (Deagan, personal communication 2015).

31. One of the contexts excavated is interpreted as a precontact elite feasting event in which large quantities of food were consumed at once (Deagan 2004:610). This type of ritual practice served both to reinforce community bonds and to demonstrate the power of the elite class and is the type of event that the Spanish observed during the contact period, which they interpreted as a demonstration of lack of Indian foresight and their inability to plan ahead. On the contrary, the persistence of this activity reveals how the Indian communities sought to maintain their way of life despite the Spanish.

Chapter 4

1. In 2013, Moya Pons and Flores Paz edited a Spanish-language translation of the different scholarly perspectives regarding the aboriginal population of Hispaniola in 1492 that included an earlier version of this chapter (Anderson-Córdova 2013:193–251).

2. The methods employed to arrive at total population estimates based on incomplete figures are summarized in Denevan (1976:9–11). These are: area projection, depopulation rates, projection of counts of portions of a population, conversion of tribute amounts to population, and age-sex pyramids.

3. For example, citing Ubelaker 1992, Larsen indicates that the rate of native population decline in North America after A.D. 1500 was 95 percent in California, while populations in the arctic and subarctic declined by 53 percent and 56 percent, respectively (Larsen 1994:121).

4. Even if there was an actual count, which some contemporary historians are arguing for, the assumptions used by Cook and Borah to arrive at the 3,000,000-plus figure for 1496 are not. This is discussed later in this chapter.

5. As mentioned by all the consulted scholars on the early history of Hispaniola, the first documented epidemic occurred in 1519, when the native population was already in stark decline (for another perspective about pos-

sible earlier epidemics of influenza and small pox, see Guerra 1988 and Cook 2003, respectively). Cook and Borah's argument that the Spaniards were sick when they arrived, and that many died in La Isabela during the first years of conquest, thereby implying an epidemic that must have affected the Indians, simply does not apply. As noted by Ramenofsky (1987:167, 170), most of the directly transmitted viral and bacterial diseases that are documented as severely depleting aboriginal numbers, such as measles, chicken pox, whooping cough, and so on, probably did not arrive in the New World in the early years. This is due to the fact that many of these diseases have a very short period in which they are infectious and in the long early voyages to the New World, they would have run their course on the ships before arrival. The exception, of course, is smallpox. However, if smallpox had arrived during these first voyages it would most probably have been mentioned, and it would not have created such mortality among the Spanish. The deaths of the Spanish during this early period were most probably due to inadequate diet on board the ships, the change in climate and foodstuffs in their new environs, and so on, and not because of a specific infectious disease.

6. These two Spanish documents are reproduced in Arranz Márquez 1991: Document I:263–274, Document 74:414–507.

7. My original assumption, based on this text, was that it may shed light on the existence of Indians not originally from Hispaniola, because I assumed that these foreign Indians, which would have been brought into Hispaniola as slaves or as *naborías perpetuos,* in the case of the Lucayan Indians, would have also been included in the Repartimiento count. However, Arranz Márquez' analysis of this 1514 document indicates that this was not the case (1991:233).

8. The 1514 Repartimiento allotted Indians to Spaniards in the 14 established towns: La Concepción, Santiago, Santo Domingo, La Buenaventura, San Juan de la Maguana, Puerto de Plata, Salvaleón de Higüey, Azua, Villa del Bonao, Puerto Real, Lares de Guahava, La Vera Paz, La Sabana, and Yáquimo.

9. The numbers for this table were obtained in the following manner: *Caciques*—Each *cacique* allotted in *encomienda* per town is counted separately. Each *cacique* is counted only once, regardless of how his Indians were allotted. For example, if *cacique* X's Indians were allotted in three separate *encomiendas,* the *cacique* is counted only once, not three times; *Indios de servicio*—All Indians listed as *indios de servicio,* allotted with or related to a particular *cacique,* were counted. This count includes the *indios de servicio allegados* category and excludes the aged and children; *Indios de servicio allegados*—All Indians listed as *indios de servicio* that specifically state that they were *allegados* were counted; *Viejos* (aged)—All Indians specifically stated as *viejos.* This count does not include all the aged, because in many instances these numbers are omitted in the document; *Niños* (children)—All Indians spe-

cifically stated as *niños*. As in the case of *viejos* (aged), not all children were counted in all instances; *Nitaínos*—All Indians specified as being *nitaínos* are counted here; *Naborías*—All Indians listed as *naborías*, whether or not they were specifically named *naborías de casa* (house servants), are counted here. I also incorporated the category *indio* or *india* into the *naboría* count if it was not specifically stated that they were *indios de servicio*; *Naborías allegados*—All Indians specifically listed as *naborías allegados* are included here, whether *allegados* to a *cacique* or to an *encomendero*. This category is separate from the count made for *naborías*.

10. As compared to Arranz Márquez's 26,189 total and Moya Pons's total of 26,333. My figures are closer to Arranz Márquez's and although I have a different focus in my analysis of the Repartimiento numbers and what they can reveal about Indian population and society at this time, my conclusions are very much in line with those of Arranz Márquez.

11. Although some *naborías* were allotted in association with *caciques*, the great majority of them were not associated with a particular *cacique* (see Arranz Márquez 1991:529). Although *naborías* could work in the mines or fields, most were *naborías de casa* (house servants) who served the Spanish in their *haciendas* and households. As such, they may have interacted more with the Spanish than with the other *encomienda* Indians allotted with *caciques* and, possibly, became more readily acculturated into the Spanish society. Although not specified in the Repartimiento document, it may be that many of these house servants were women (Arranz Márquez 1991:248; Mira Caballos 2000a:28).

12. As in table 4.4, it is important to state precisely how the various categories included in table 4.12 were counted, since they have obvious bearing on the resulting analysis: *Caciques*—This is the list of separate *caciques* that were allotted in *encomienda*. Its figures will not always coincide with the *encomiendas de servicio* count, since each *cacique* is counted only once, regardless of how his Indians were finally divided; Female *caciques*—Number of women *caciques* included in the *cacique* count; *Encomiendas servicio*—Number of *caciques* allotted with *indios de servicio* or (in a minority of cases) with only *naborías*. Each allotment was counted as a separate *encomienda*, even if the same *cacique's* people were involved; *Encomiendas naborías*—Number of *encomenderos* that received only *naborías*; *Encomiendas naborías y servicio*—Number of *encomenderos* that received both *encomiendas de servicio* and *naborías*. This figure includes the great majority of the *encomiendas de servicio* count, since most of the *encomenderos* that received *encomiendas de servicio* also received *naborías*; *Encomenderos*—Includes all the *encomenderos* that received separate allotments of Indians, whether of *encomiendas de servicio*, *encomiendas naborías*, or both; Relationship of *encomiendas servicio* to *encomendero*—This summarizes the number of *encomiendas de servicio* that were distributed among more than one *encomendero*.

13. Arranz Márquez (1991:238) notes that as late as 1514, 10 percent of

caciques were still known by their Taíno name, 35 percent had both a Spanish and a Taíno name. He also notes that many of the *caciques* mentioned in the chroniclers' accounts at the time of conquest (22 years before the Repartimiento) were still being mentioned despite the fact they were already deceased, and the allotted Indians were still being associated with their names.

14. See also Arranz Márquez 1991:232, regarding the significant number of cases in which *encomenderos* were allotted ten or fewer *naborías* in *encomienda*. This reflects the low number of Indians available for allotment and also demonstrates loss of community ties, since Indians were dispersed in small numbers to various *encomenderos*.

15. Another explanation may be that the traditional rules of succession favored men, but the loss of men in war and harsh labor provided an opportunity for women to assume chiefly responsibilities (Deagan, personal communication 2015).

16. As noted by Arranz Márquez (1991:242), the largest remaining Indian villages allotted in this Repartimiento were located mainly between the Ozama River and the province of Higüey. Female *cacicas* were associated with the largest remaining villages in this area.

17. See also Arranz Márquez (1991:246) regarding Indian women joining, either by force or by choice, Spanish households.

18. Archaeological site files in the Puerto Rico State Historic Preservation Office indicate a total of 1600 sites whose basic site information has been digitized. About half of these have no information on cultural provenience. Of those that do have this information, only about 20 mention historic period deposits. Even less, maybe a handful, indicate that there may be early sixteenth-century deposits. None have been systematically studied beyond the survey level, to my knowledge.

19. The decline in late prehistoric native population in the areas studied may be the result of intraisland movements into the mountainous interior, or movement into Hispaniola or the eastern Leeward Islands (Curet 1992; Rodríguez López 1990; Hofman & Hoogland 1991).

20. These *repartimientos* occurred when the Indians were in open rebellion; therefore many were not counted (see Anderson-Córdova 2005:344–347).

21. There are partial counts and scattered references about *encomienda* Indians in Puerto Rico (Alegría 1993; Mira Caballos 1997:43–45), and most confirm the same patterns as in Hispaniola, where Indians associated with particular *caciques* were allotted among various Spanish *encomenderos*, and populations were significantly atomized and diminished.

22. The 1530 census provides significant information on the socioeconomic and demographic aspects of colonial Puerto Rican society at this time (Cósimi 1994).

23. These figures differ slightly from the ones provided by Governor de Lando in his summary. However, my figures are based on a line-by-line check of the census document and are the ones used in this analysis. This

is consistent with the approach followed earlier in the analysis of the 1514 Repartimiento.

24. San Juan: 73 percent black slaves, 27 percent Indian slaves; when the free Indians are added, the percentages are 65 percent black, 35 percent Indian. San Germán: 46 percent black slaves, 54 percent Indian slaves; when the free Indians are added, the percentages are 34 percent black, 65 percent Indian.

25. For both districts combined, the percentages are 67 percent Indian slaves and 33 percent free Indians. For San Juan: 70 percent Indian slaves and 30 percent free Indians. For San Germán: 61 percent Indian slaves and 39 percent free Indians.

26. Using the Royal Treasury documents for Puerto Rico compiled by Tanodi (DRHPR 1971:I), Wolff has estimated a minimum of 1,300 in 1513, and an extrapolated maximum of 2,600 native Indian slaves in 1517 resulting from these internal raids; this is compared with 1,012 Indian slaves imported into the island from the Spanish armadas (2014:242, table 11).

27. These Indians are described in various ways, for example: *naborías, indios naborías libres, indio naboría, naborías de indios libres, indios libres, indios e indias naborías de repartimiento, indios libres de repartimiento,* and *indios e indias libres de repartimiento.*

Chapter 5

1. The pertinent references are grouped into two categories: those references that suggest Indian knowledge about Antillean geography and its relationship to the mainland and those that specifically indicate movement of Indians from one island to another.

2. For a discussion of the practice of raiding for women, see Sued Badillo 1978:58–64, where the author argues that this occurred among the Taíno Indians as well and was a cause of war among them.

3. "Que al austro d'ellos era tierra firme y entonces estava yo en la isla de Guadalupe, y también lo oí a otros de la isla de Sancta Cruz y de la de San Juan, y dezían que en ella avía mucho oro."

4. "Y cuentan que esta gente, en el tiempo de verano, se alejan 300 leguas de su costa andando de isla en isla, navegando en busca de botín."

5. "Llegó una canoa a los bajeles y un indio que entendía a los castellanos, que se creyó que debía ser de la Española o de otra de las habitadas de castellanos, dijo que guardasen, que el cacique quería enviar oro para rescatar."

6. "Porque como los vecinos indios de aquella provincia de Higüey fuesen los mas propincuos y en la más propincua tierra viviesen a la dicha isla de San Juan, y no hobiese sino 12 ó 15 leguas de distancia, cada día se iban en sus canoas o barquillos los de esta isla a aquéll y los de aquélla a ésta venían y se comunicaban, y así pudieron bien saber los unos y los otros lo que en la tierra de cada uno había."

7. "Sabe como un cacique de la ysla de San Juan mato a un don Christoval de Sotomayor e a otros christianos en un lugar que se dexia Xavca en la ysla de San Juan luego lo supo el cacique Andres qu agora sirven en sus altezas y que se tenía por parient del otro cacique que avia muerto al dicho don Christoval."

8. *Probanza de Juan González*, in Tió 1961:30–109; Juan Ponce de León's *Relación* of 1509, in HDPR 1973:II:519–522; Miguel Diaz's August 25, 1513, letter to Conchillos, cited in Ramos Pérez 1975:93–95.

9. An antecedent of relevance to the enslavement of native Indians in the New World was the Spanish conquest and colonization of the Canary Islands and its Guanches peoples starting in the early fifteenth century (see Tejera Gaspar and Aznar Vallejo 1992; Stevens-Arroyo 1993; and Lobo Cabrera 1983).

10. Many were taken as a result of the Spanish retaliatory raids to the Xaraguá and Higüey regions (as discussed previously), although no numbers are available.

11. For example, on February 28, 1510, the King instructed his royal officials in Hispaniola that the Indians brought by Nicuesa from the island of St. Croix had to be returned. By June of the following year (RC June 6, 1511), the King had authorized the enslavement of the Indians of St. Croix on the grounds that they had attacked San Juan. In this same decree, the King inquired about the status of Trinidad as an island from which Indians could be taken and asked his officials to investigate. This ambiguity concerning the areas subject to Spanish raids as well as the Spanish slavery legislation in general has been studied by various scholars (Saco 1932; Friede 1961:61–62; Konetzke 1949:451–459).

12. The December 23, 1511, Royal Provision authorizing the slavery of the Carib Indians indicated the following as Carib areas: Trinidad, San Bernardo, Fuerte Island, port of Cartagena, Barú Island, Dominica, Martinique, St. Lucia, La Ascensión, Barbados, Tobago, and Mayo.

13. This was also claimed by Ponce de León during his 1513 voyage to Florida (Deagan, personal communication 2015).

14. *Juicios de Residencia en la provincia de Venezuela* 1977:I:146, 152, 433, 451–452, 461; *Residencia tomada a Gerónimo de Dortal, Boletín del Archivo General de la Nación* (BAGN) 1967:277–279; García Menéndez 1981:232–263; *Epistolario de Nueva España*, hereafter ENE 1939–1942:I:doc.78:153–166; Otte 1977:109; Radell 1976:71).

15. *Juicio de Residencia del Lic. Alonso de Zuazo* (Judicial Review or Proceedings of an Administrative Investigation of Attorney Alonso de Zuazo).

16. Source, declaration of captain Cansino in the *Juicio de Residencia de los Oidores de Santo Domingo* (Judicial Review or Proceedings of an Administrative Investigation of the Judges of Santo Domingo).

17. Source, November 4, 1520, letter written in Santo Domingo, published in CODOIN 1864–1889:I:1:422–427.

18. *Relación de Miguel de Castellanos* (*Narration of Miguel de Castellanos*), in Catálogo de la colección de Don Juan Bautista Muñoz 1954–1956.

19. *Residencia tomada a Gerónimo Dortal* 1544, *Boletín del Archivo General de la Nación* (BAGN) 1967:*cargos*:277–279 (Judicial Review or Proceedings of an Administrative Investigation taken of Geronimo Dortal, charges).

20. 1526 letter to the King from Juan de Ampies, informing what he did with the Indians brought to Hispaniola from the islands near Tierra Firme and how many were returned to Curaçao; CODOIN 1864–1889:I:1:431–436.

21. *Juicio de residencia seguido por el doctor Antonio Navarro a los Welser, 1538. Juicios de Residencia en la Provincia de Venezuela* (Judicial Review or Proceedings of an Administrative Investigation taken by Doctor Antonio Navarro of the Welser. Judicial Reviews or Proceedings of Administrative Investigations in the Province of Venezuela), 1977:I:142–143, 146, 152; also cited in Friede 1961:68.

22. RC October 27, 1535, CMEPV 1959:II:13–14; *Juicio de residencia seguido por el lic Juan Pérez de Tolosa a los Welser, 1547. Juicos de residencia de la Provincia de Venezuela* (Judicial Review or Proceedings of an Administrative Investigation of the Welser, 1547, carried out by Attorney Juan Pérez de Tolosa. Judicial Reviews or Proceedings of Administrative Investigations in the Province of Venezuela), I:1977:433, 451–452, 461; also cited in Friede 1961:66–67.

23. Based on November 12, 1539, report entitled "Información contra los Gobernadores que fueron de la ciudad de Trujillo en Honduras, Diego López de Salzedo y Andrés de Zerezada, levantados estos contra el capitán Hernando de Sayavedra puesto allí por Hernán Cortés luego que la pacificó. Pedimiento y ynterrogatorio presentado por el licenciado Pedraza" (Information against Diego López de Salzedo and Andrés de Zerezada, former governors of the city of Trujillo, Honduras, who rebelled against Captain Hernando de Sayavedra whom Hernán Cortés had put in charge after pacification. Interrogatory presented by Attorney Pedraza), in AGI, Patronato 17, 164.

24. "Información que hizo la villa de Santisteban del Puerto sobre la conveniencia de enviar esclavos a las islas para cambiarlos por caballos, yeguas y otros ganados" (Information prepared by the town of Santisteban del Puerto about the convenience of sending slaves to the islands in exchange for stallions, mares and other cattle), Santisteban del Puerto, Province of Pánuco, October 9, 1529; ENE 1939–1942:I:153–166; Zavala 1967:22–25.

25. Wolff (2014:243) calculates that for the year 1519 there were between a minimum of 2,312 and a maximum of 3,612 enslaved Indians in Puerto Rico. She bases her estimates on an analysis of the Treasury documents that report the taxes paid on Indians enslaved as a result of the numerous slave raids.

26. "Actualmente no habitan ni una sola aldea que les pertenezca, sino que son esclavos de los cristianos, es decir, los pocos que queda, porque casi se han acabado . . . no subsisten veinte mil con vida."

27. March 30, 1528, *Relación* of Zuazo and Espinosa to the Council of the Indies concerning the island of Hispaniola; in *Reales cédulas y correspondencia de gobernadores de Santo Domingo de la regencia del Cardenal Cisneros en adelante (Royal Decrees and Correspondence of the Governors of Santo Domingo from the Regency of Cardinal Cisneros Forward)*, hereafter RCCGSD 1958:200–212.

28. March 18, 1531, letter to the Empress, from Diego Caballeros, *contador* and *regidor* (commissioner) of Santo Domingo; in SDDJBM 1981:353.

29. July 13, 1536, letter to the Empress from Attorney Fuenmayor, Santo Domingo; in SDDJBM:373; RC November 5, 1540, to the Audiencia (court) of Santo Domingo; cited in Rodríguez Demorizi 1971:49–50.

30. January 1, 1539; in *Inventario de la colección de documentos históricos Herrera procedentes del Archivo General de Indias* (*Inventory of the Collection of Historical Documents of Herrera in the General Archives of the Indies*), hereafter ICDHH 1987.

31. However, some of these Indian slaves may have been surviving native Indians enslaved as a result of the internal raids against rebellious Indians carried out by the Spanish during the early 1510s (see Wolff 2014:236).

32. August 30, 1536, letter from Vasco de Tiedra to the Empress, in PRDJBM 1960:313, Tapia y Rivera 1970:368; May 31, 1537, letter from Oviedo to the King, in PRDJBM 1960:319–320; March 20, 1544, letter from Bishop Bastidas to the Crown, in Fernández Méndez 1984:78, Tapia y Rivera 1970:389; April 25, 1548, letter from the Bishop to the King, in Fernández Méndez 1984:79, Tapia y Rivera 1970:344; September 1, 1548, letter from Bishop Bastidas to the Emperor, in Tapia y Rivera 1970:395; and March 11, 1549, letter from Bishop Bastidas to the Emperor, in PRDJBM 1960:374–378, Tapia y Rivera 1970:399.

Chapter 6

1. Interest in locating contact-period sites and in studying the archaeology of later rural populations in Puerto Rico appears to be increasing though. See, for example, García Goyco 2011; Rivera Fontán & Oliver 1999.

2. For a different perspective on this issue and on the historical use of the term Taíno, see De La Luz-Rodríguez 2010.

Bibliographic Essay

Primary Sources

Early accounts of firsthand participants

The starting point for any study of culture contact in the Caribbean area are the firsthand accounts that document the initial encounter of Spanish and Indians. They provide the first Spanish perspective on the encounter with peoples of a completely different and historically independent cultural tradition, and our first glimpse, albeit through Spanish eyes, of Indian society. Examples of firsthand accounts used in this book include Christopher Columbus's Diary of the First Voyage and correspondence concerning the second voyage, Miguel de Cuneo's letter on the second voyage, and Ponce de León's description of the conquest of Puerto Rico.

Early chroniclers' histories of the conquest and colonization of the Indies

The mainly descriptive narrative accounts, some in much detail, about the events of conquest and colonization are in most cases by contemporaries. Most of the information on the nature and society of the native Indians, and of the main events of conquest repeated in later secondary sources, comes from these sources. Among the most important ones are the following: Fray Bartolomé de Las Casas, *Apologética histórica* (1967) and *Historia de las Indias* (1951); Gonzalo Fernández de Oviedo, *Historia general y natural de las Indias* (1959); Martín Fernández de Navarrete, *Colección de los viajes y descubrimientos que hicieron por mar los españoles desde fines del siglo XV* (1945–1946); and Pedro Mártir de Anglería, *Décadas del Nuevo Mundo* (1944).

Official Colonial Correspondence

Official colonial correspondence, some of it available to early chroniclers, and liberally used in recent later histories, forms the bulk of the data consulted for this book. It provides a variety of perspectives on the historic events of the period, and includes correspondence originating in the Metropolis, from the Spanish Crown to the colonies; correspondence originating in the colonies, from Spanish officials to the Crown and from Spanish settlers to the Crown; and official Spanish laws or decrees establishing policies for the colonies and for the treatment of the Indians. Included in these three types of documents are royal decrees (*cédulas reales*), laws, petitions to the Crown, descriptions of reports from Spanish officials to the Crown, official *Residencia* documents, and in rare instances, petitions from the Indians to the Crown (see, for example, Zerquera y Fernández de Lara 1977) and letters from the Crown to the Indians (see, for example, Peña Battle 1948; Utrera 1973).

The Spanish *Juicios de Residencia* (Judicial Reviews or Proceedings of an Administrative Investigation) were lengthy judicial inquiries about the tenure of a public official that, under Castilian law, were carried out at the end of the official's term. Anyone, including laypersons, could testify on the accomplishments of the official under scrutiny, as well as on any grievances that they had against him. These types of documents provide a wealth of information on colonial society at the time, the power struggles among the Spanish elite and Spanish settlers, and the treatment of the Indian populations. (For a list of Spanish *residencias* in the Archives of the Indies, see Peña y Cámara 1955.)

I consulted these documentary sources to glean information about Hispaniola and Puerto Rico. I also consulted correspondences originating in or destined to other areas of Spain's expanding New World possessions that are of relevance to these islands. For example, information pertaining to the Indian slave trade is available from documents relating to the early histories of New Spain (Mexico), Castilla del Oro (Colombia-Panama), and other areas of what the Spanish called Tierra Firme (the mainland). These sources are available from a variety of published compendiums of primary documents. In addition, I consulted specific documents cited in secondary sources that were available from the *Archivo General de Indias* (General Archives of the Indies in Seville, hereafter AGI).

Among the documents that provide valuable information on Indian response to contact, Indian demography, and Spanish official policy toward the Indians, the following were particularly useful in this book:

1492 *Diario del primer viaje: Cristóbal Colón* (Columbus's Diary of the First Voyage, in Varela 1982)

1509 *Traslado fiel de la relación hecha por Ponce de León en la Villa de la Concepción* (Exact copy of Ponce de León's Narrative or Memoir

Taken in the town of La Concepción, in *Historia documental de Puerto Rico*, hereafter HDPR, 1973:II:519–530)

1510–21 *Documentos de la Real Hacienda de Puerto Rico* (hereafter DRHPR, 1971:I; n.d.:II, in transcript, original at the Center for Historical Investigations, University of Puerto Rico)

1513 *Ordenanzas para el tratamiento de los indios* (Ordinances for the Treatment of the Indians), in *Puerto Rico en los manuscritos de Juan Bautista Muñoz*, hereafter PRDJBM, 1960:92–97)

1514 *Relación del repartimiento de la isla Española* (Narrative of the Repartimiento of the Island of Hispaniola, in Rodríguez Demorizi 1971)

1516 *Juicio de residencia de los licenciados Marcelo de Villalobos, Juan Ortíz Matienzo y Lucas Vázquez de Ayllon, por el licenciado Alonso de Zuazo* (Judicial Review or Proceedings of an Administrative Investigation of the attorneys Marcelo de Villalobos, Juan Ortíz Matienzo, and Lucas Vázquez de Ayllon, carried out by attorney Alonso de Zuazo), in García Menéndez 1981: appendixes II–VI)

1517 *Interrogatorio Jerominiano* (Hieronymite Interrogatory, in Rodríguez Demorizi 1971:273–354)

1518 *Carta de Andrés de Haro a su magestad sobre medidas de buen gobierno en la isla de Puerto Rico* (Andrés de Haro's Letter to His Majesty Concerning Measures for Good Government in the Island of Puerto Rico, in Brau 1966:515–520)

1519–20 *Juicio de residencia del licenciado Sancho Velázquez, juez de residencia y justicia mayor de la isla de San Juan de Puerto Rico, por el licenciado Antonio de la Gama* (Judicial Review or Proceedings of an Administrative Investigation of attorney Sancho Velázquez, Administrative Judge and Chief Justice of the Island of San Juan, Puerto Rico, carried out by attorney Antonio de la Gama, in HDPR 1973:II)

1530 *Censo del Gobernador Lando. Puerto Rico* (Governor Lando's Census. Puerto Rico, in Ramírez de Arellano 1934)

1544 *Información recibida en Santo Domingo ante el licenciado Cerrato sobre el modo y motivo que hubo con hacer esclavos unos indios venidos de Margarita y Cubagua* (Information received in Santo Domingo by attorney Cerrato concerning the manner and motives for enslaving some Indians from Margarita and Cubagua, in AGI, *Patronato* 173, N. I, R. II)

Secondary Sources

Secondary sources include various well-known histories of the Caribbean, Hispaniola, Puerto Rico, and other relevant areas (see, for example, Abbad y Lasierra 1979; Brau 1966; Moya Pons 1978; Newson 1976; Noel

1972; Santovenia y Echnide 1939; Chamberlain 1953, 1966), as well as publications on specific topics of relevance to the research. Classic works related to Indian slavery in the New World were particularly useful (see, for example, Zavala 1948, 1967; Saco 1932; Otte 1975, 1977; Radell 1976; Chipman 1966; Friede 1961; Sherman 1971, 1979). I also make use of archaeological research as it applies to this topic of Indian-Spanish contact, as detailed in the references.

Historical Biases

Historic documentary sources have inherent biases that, although not insurmountable, must be constantly kept in mind. Wilson (1986:14) discussed some of these and utilized the analysis of entire texts (rather than sections of text that may be interpreted out of context) in his study of the Taíno chiefdoms of Hispaniola, and Curet (2006) emphasized the errors committed by archaeologists' uncritical use of historic sources to extrapolate back to the late prehistoric period.

Numerous historians studied Las Casas, Fernández de Oviedo, and other early chroniclers within the context of their particular life histories, when and where they wrote their works, their sources, and their underlying intentions (see, for example, Varela 1982; Hanke 1951; Vázquez 1962; Pérez de Tudela, in Fernández de Oviedo 1959; Millares Carlo, in Las Casas 1945; Hanke, in Las Casas 1951; O'Gorman, in Las Casas 1967; Piña Contreras, in Las Casas 1985; Fabié 1879; MacNutt 1909; Zavala 1944). Many of the arguments presented to aid in the interpretation of their works have been repeated often and can only be summarized here. None can be construed as ethnographies of the native Indians, nor can they be interpreted as accurate in their entirety.

Fernández de Oviedo's work (1959), specifically the sections of his *Historia* that deal with the conquest of the Greater Antilles and the nature of Indian society and culture, though based in part on firsthand sources, suffers from his relatively late arrival at Hispaniola. He stopped there in 1514 as part of the Pedrarias Dávila Armada (fleet) in route to Castilla del Oro (Pérez de Tudela Bueso 1959:XLVIII-XLIX [48–49]). By this time, native culture and society had suffered through 22 years of exposure to disease, starvation, depopulation, and forced labor.

Furthermore, Fernández de Oviedo was involved in the Spanish endeavors in Castilla del Oro, Nicaragua, and Panama before taking up residence in the city of Santo Domingo, Hispaniola, in the 1530s (Pérez de Tudela Bueso 1959:CXVII:I). It was then that he acquired personal, firsthand experience with the Indians of the island, now remnants of the originally independent chiefdoms. The dismal picture he presents of the Indians' incapacity to be free and their debased character (Pérez de Tudela Bueso 1959:CXVII:I) reflects not only his negative opinions concerning the Indians but also the dire conditions in which they survived at this time. Despite these issues, his *Historia* is a necessary complement to Las Casas's works. In fact, Pérez de Tudela Bueso has challenged the depictions of Fernández de Oviedo's *Historia* as a monument of justification of the conquest of the New World. He points out that an analysis of the entire *Historia* reveals an evolution in Fernández de Oviedo's ideas concerning the universality of man and criticism of the Spanish conquest (Pérez de Tudela Bueso 1959:cxvii:I:cxliv–clv).

Las Casas, in contrast, paints a much more positive picture of Indian culture and society. He believed in their innate freedom and ability to govern themselves (after all, they had done so for centuries before the Spanish conquest) and was convinced that the Spanish conquest and colonization of the New World was based upon their unjust exploitation. His prolific writings on behalf of the Indians and his lifelong crusade for their cause are well known, as is his stature as a towering figure in the drama of sixteenth-century Spain (see Hanke 1951).

Las Casas arrived at Hispaniola in 1502, with Governor Nicolás de Ovando's fleet (Las Casas 1985:II:214; Hanke 1951). His early arrival, and the many years he spent on the islands of Cuba and Hispaniola, provided him with an advantage not shared with Oviedo—that of observing the Indians when there were still vestiges of their original society. He, more than Fernández de Oviedo (Hanke 1951), had access to numerous documents that were lost to later scholars. It is due mainly to his works that many of the original passages of Columbus's writings have survived (see, for example, Varela's 1982 edition of the first voyage). The sheer magnitude of the sources handled in his writings, his widespread travels over large areas of Spain's possessions, the variety of Indian cultures that he sought to describe, and the time elapsed between the events narrated and the actual writing of his works allow a certain degree of muddling of dates, numbers, and descriptions. These are inevitable, and Las Casas was aware of them (Las Casas 1967:II:309, 318; Las Casas 1985:III:140), but they do not detract from the historical value of these works.

Pedro Mártir de Anglería, an Italian renaissance man who never set foot in the New World but whose interest was aroused from the beginning, gathered many firsthand accounts from travelers and officials returning from the New World to write his *Décadas del Nuevo Mundo* (1944). His descriptions are, in many cases, exaggerated and full of rhetoric (see, for example, Mártir de Anglería 1944:15, cited in Sued Badillo 1978:47). However, in some cases he includes important information not mentioned by Fernández de Oviedo or Las Casas (see, for example, the 1508 Andrés de Morales map of Hispaniola, utilized by Mártir de Anglería to compile his description of this island's Indian chiefdoms [Vega 1980; Sauer 1969]).

The other primary sources consulted also suffer from the bias of being the product of Spanish institutions and individuals. They reflect the Spanish point of view of the events of conquest and colonization and provide insights into the development of Spanish policy toward its New World possessions. The variety of sources consulted, both in terms of the individuals who generated them and the geographic area covered, results in a sample that cuts across the gamut of Spanish society. This documentary material provides valuable information on the Spanish trade in Indian slaves as well as the Spanish perspective on the Indian inhabitants. The contradictions between Spanish official Indian policy and actual conditions are vividly portrayed in these documents. The use of this type of document provides much more relevant data than does relying solely on the early chroniclers, and it confirms the critical importance of returning to the original documentation to reconstruct the early history of the Antillean islands and the story of what happened to the Indians. The wealth, and redundancy, of documentation is overwhelming and attests to the often-noted Spanish compulsion to justify their actions by writing everything down, and the Crown's encouragement to this effect (Hanke 1951).

References Cited

Abbad y Lasierra, Fray Agustín Iñigo

1979 *Historia geográfica, civil y natural de la Isla de San Juan Bautista de Puerto Rico.* Preliminary study by Isabel Gutiérrez del Arroyo. 3rd ed. Editorial Universitaria, Río Piedras, Puerto Rico.

Acosta Saignes, Miguel

1946 *Los caribes de la costa venezolana.* Acta Antropológica, Mexico.

1961 *Estudios de etnología antigua de Venezuela.* 2nd ed. Universidad Central de Venezuela, Caracas.

Aguirre Beltrán, Gonzalo

1970 *El proceso de aculturación y el cambio sociocultural en México.* 2nd ed. Editorial Comunidad, Universidad Iberoamericana, Mexico.

Alcina Franch, José

1983 La cultura taína como sociedad en transición entre los niveles tribal y de jefaturas. In *La cultura taína,* pp. 67–79. Comisión Nacional del Quinto Centenario del Descubrimiento de América, Turner Libros, S. A. Madrid, Spain.

Alegría, Ricardo

1976 Las relaciones entre los taínos de Puerto Rico y los de la Española. *Boletín del Instituto Montecristeño de Arqueología* 2:30–34. Santo Domingo.

1981 *Las primeras noticias de los indios caribes.* Editorial UPR, Río Piedras, Puerto Rico.

1983a *Ball Courts and Ceremonial Plazas in the West Indies.* Yale University Publications in Anthropology 79. New Haven, Connecticut.

1983b Aspectos de la cultura de los indios taínos de las Antillas Mayores en la documentación etno-histórica. In *La cultura taína,* pp. 117–136. Comisión Nacional del Quinto Centenario del Descubrimiento de América, Turner Libros, S. A. Madrid, Spain.

1993 El pleito por indios de encomienda entre el ex-contador Antonio Sedeño y el Contador Miguel de Castellanos, Puerto Rico, 1527. *Cuadernos de Etnohistoria* 1. Centro de Estudios Avanzados de Puerto Rico y el Caribe, San Juan, Puerto Rico.

Allaire, Louis

1977 *Later Prehistory in Martinique and the Island Caribs: Problems in Ethnic Identification*. Unpublished Ph.D. dissertation, Yale University.

1980 On the Historicity of Carib Migrations in the Lesser Antilles. *American Antiquity* 45(2):238–245.

1987 Some Comments on the Ethnic Identity of the Taino-Carib Frontier. In *Ethnicity and Culture*, edited by Reginald Auger et al., pp. 127–133. Archaeological Association, University of Calgary, Calgary.

1990 Prehistoric Taino Interaction with the Lesser Antilles: The View from Martinique, F. W. I. Paper presented at the 55th Annual Meeting of the Society for American Archaeology, Las Vegas, Nevada, April 18–22, 1990.

1996 Visions of Cannibals: Distant Islands and Distant Lands in Taino World Image. In *The Lesser Antilles in the Age of European Expansion*, edited by Robert L. Paquette and Stanley L. Engerman, pp. 34–49. University Press of Florida, Gainesville.

1997 The Caribs of the Lesser Antilles. In *The Indigenous People of the Caribbean*, edited by Samuel M. Wilson, pp. 179–185. University Press of Florida, Gainesville.

2013 Ethnohistory of the Caribs. In *The Oxford Handbook of Caribbean Archaeology*, edited by W. F. Keegan, C. L. Hofman, and R. Rodríguez Ramos, pp. 97–108. Oxford University Press.

Altman, Ida

2007 The Revolt of Enriquillo and the Historiography of Early Spanish America. *The Americas* 63(4):587–614.

Alvarez Rubiano, Pablo

1944 *Pedrarias Dávila, contribución al estudio de la figura del Gran Justador, gobernador de Castilla del Oro y Nicaragua*. Consejo Superior de Investigaciones Científicas, Instituto Gonzalo Fernández de Oviedo, Madrid.

Anderson, David G.

1994 *The Savannah River Chiefdoms: Political Change in the Late Prehistoric Southeast*. University of Alabama Press, Tuscaloosa.

Anderson-Córdova, Karen F.

1990 *Hispaniola and Puerto Rico: Indian Acculturation and Heterogeneity, 1492–1550*. Unpublished Ph.D. dissertation, Yale University, New Haven, Connecticut.

1995 Aspectos demográficos de los cacicazgos taínos. In *Proceedings of the Fifteenth International Congress for Caribbean Archaeology*, edited by R. E. Alegría and M. Rodríguez, pp. 351–365. Centro de Estudios Avanzados de Puerto Rico y el Caribe, con la colaboración de la Fundación Puertorriqueña de las Humanidades y la Universidad del Turabo, San Juan, Puerto Rico.

2005 The Aftermath of Conquest: The Indians of Puerto Rico during the Early Sixteenth Century. In *Ancient Borinquen: Archaeology and Ethnohistory of Native Puerto Rico*, edited by Peter Siegel, pp. 337–352. University of Alabama Press, Tuscaloosa.

2013 Demografía aborigen en las Antillas. In *Los Taínos en 1492, el debate demográfico,* edited by Frank Moya Pons and Rosario Flores Paz, pp. 193–251. Academia Dominicana de la Historia, Vol. 103, Santo Domingo, Dominican Republic.

Armas Medina, Fernando de

1957 Primeros años del gobierno hispano en Cuba. *Revista de Estudios Americanos* Num. 67–68. Escuela de Estudios Hispano-Americanos, Seville, Spain.

Armstrong, Douglas V.

2013 *Creole Transformation from Slavery to Freedom: Historical Archaeology of the East End Community, St. John, Virgin Island.* University of Florida Press, Gainesville.

Arranz Márquez, Luis

1991 *Repartimientos y encomiendas en la isla Española (El Repartimiento de Albuquerque de 1514).* Serie Documental, Fundación García Arévalo, Santo Domingo, Dominican Republic.

Arrom, José Juan

1975 *Mitología y artas prehispánicas de las Antillas.* Editorial Siglo xxi, México.

Ashburn, Percy Moreau

1947 *The Ranks of Death: A Medical History of the Conquest of America.* Coward-McCann, Inc., New York.

Assadourian, Carlos S.

1992 The Colonial Economy: The Transfer of the European System of Production to New Spain and Peru. *Journal of Latin American Studies* 24:55–68.

Barreiro, José

2006 Taino Survivals: Cacique Panchito, Caridad de los Indios, Cuba. In *Indigenous Resurgence in the Contemporary Caribbean,* edited by Maximilian C. Forte, pp. 21–39. Peter Lang, New York.

Barth, Fredrik (editor)

1969 *Ethnic Groups and Boundaries: The Social Organization of Culture Difference.* A Symposium held at the University of Bergen, February 23–26, 1967, Bergen, Universitetsforlaget, Allen & Unwin, London.

Bee, Robert L.

1974 *Patterns and Processes: An Introduction to Anthropological Strategies for the Study of Sociocultural Change.* Free Press, New York.

Berman, Mary Jane, Perry L. Gnivecki, and Michael P. Pateman

2013 The Bahama Archipelago. In *The Oxford Handbook of Caribbean Archaeology,* edited by W. F. Keegan, C. L. Hofman, and R. Rodríguez Ramos, pp. 264–282. Oxford University Press.

Bohannon, Paul, and Fred Plog (editors)

1967 *Beyond the Frontier: Social Process and Cultural Change.* Published for the Museum of Natural History. The Natural History Press, Garden City, New York.

Boletín del Archivo General de la Nación (BAGN)

1967 Residencia tomada a Gerónimo Dortal gobernador de la Provincia de

Paria en Tierra Firme, y sus tenientes y oficiales por el licenciado Alonso López Cerrato, Juez de Residencia y oidor de la Real Audiencia de la Isla Española, 1544, 213:267–299. Caracas.

Boomert, Arie

1985 The Guayabitoid and the Mayoid Series: Amerindian Culture History in Trinidad during Late Prehistoric and Protohistoric Times. In *Proceedings of the Tenth International Congress for the Study of the Pre-Columbian Cultures of the Lesser Antilles*, pp. 93–148. Montreal.

1995 Island Carib Archaeology. In *Wolves from the Sea*, edited by Neil L. Whitehead, pp. 23–35. KITLV, Leiden, Netherlands.

Borah, Woodrow

1976 The Historical Demography of Aboriginal and Colonial America: An Attempt at Perspective. In *The Native Population of the Americas in 1492*, edited by William Denevan, pp. 13–34. University of Wisconsin Press, Madison.

Brau, Salvador

1894 *Puerto Rico y su historia: Investigaciones críticas.* Imprenta de F. Vives Mora, Valencia.

1966 *La colonización de Puerto Rico.* 3rd annotated ed. Institute of Puerto Rican Culture, San Juan.

Bray, Warwick

1993 Crop Plants and Cannibals: Early European Impressions of the New World. In *The Meeting of Two Worlds, Europe and the Americas 1492–1650*, edited by Warwick Bray, pp. 289–326. Oxford University Press.

Breton, Raymond

1665 *Dictionaire caraibe-françois, meslé de quantité de remarques historiques pour l'esclaircissement de la langue, compose par le r.p. Raymond Breton.* Par Gilles Bovqvet, Avxerre, France.

Breton, Raymond, and A. de la Paix

1926 Relation de l'isle de la Guadeloupe, 1635–1636. In *Histoire Coloniale*, Vol. 1, edited by Joseph Rennard, pp. 45–74. Libraire Generale et Internationale, Paris.

Broom, Leonard, Bernard J. Siegel, Evon Z. Vogt, and James B. Watson

1954 The Social Science Research Council Summer Seminar on Acculturation. *American Anthropologist* 56:973–1000. Reprinted in *Beyond the Frontier: Social Process and Cultural Change* (1967), edited by Paul Bohannon and Fred Plog, pp. 255–286. The Natural History Press, Garden City, New York.

Brose, David S., and N'omi Greber (editors)

1979 *Hopewell Archaeology: The Chillicothe Conference.* Kent University Press, Kent, Ohio.

Brown, Ian W.

1979 Historic Artifacts and Sociocultural Change: Some Warnings from the Lower Mississippi Valley. *The Conference on Historic Sites Archaeology Papers* 1978(13):109–121. University of South Carolina, Columbia.

Bryan, Patrick

1992 Spanish America. *Caribbean Quarterly* 38(2/3):21–31.

Burley, David

2000 Creolization and Late Nineteenth Century Métis Vernacular Log Architecture on the South Saskatchewan River. *Historical Archaeology* 34(3): 27–35. Society for Historical Archaeology.

Callaghan, Richard T.

2011 Patterns of Contact between the Islands of the Caribbean and the Surrounding Mainland as a Navigation Problem. In *Islands at the Crossroads: Migration, Seafaring, and Interaction in the Caribbean*, edited by L. Antonio Curet and Mark W. Hauser, pp. 59–72. University of Alabama Press, Tuscaloosa.

Cañizares-Esguerra, Jorge

2007 Creole Colonial Spanish America. In *Creolization: History, Ethnography, Theory*, edited by Charles Stewart, pp. 26–46. Left Coast Press, Walnut Creek, California.

Cardoso de Oliveira, Roberto, and Luis de Castro Faria

1971 Interethnic Contact and the Study of Populations. In *The Ongoing Evolution of Latin American Populations*, edited by Francisco M. Salzano, pp. 41–59. Thomas, Springfield, Illinois.

Carneiro, Robert L.

1961 Slash and Burn Cultivation among the Kuikuru and its Implications for Cultural Development in the Amazon Basin. In *The Evolution of Horticultural Systems in Native South America Causes and Consequences*, edited by Johannes Wilbert, pp. 47–68. Sociedad de Ciencias Naturales La Salle, Caracas.

1967 On the Relationship between Size of Population and Complexity of Social Organizations. *Southwestern Journal of Anthropology* 23:234–243.

Caro Costas, Aida

1971 *Antología de lecturas de historia de Puerto Rico.* San Juan, Puerto Rico.

Carrera Stampa, Manuel (editor)

1955 *Memoria de los servicios que había hecho Nuño de Guzmán, desde que fue nombrado governador de Pánuco en 1525.* Bibliotea José Porrúa Estrada de Historia Mexicana 4, Mexico.

Cassá, Roberto

1979 *Los taínos de la Española.* 2nd ed. Ed. Alfa y Omega, Santo Domingo, Dominican Republic.

Castanha, Tony

2011 *The Myth of Indigenous Caribbean Extinction: Continuity and Reclamation in Boriken (Puerto Rico).* 1st ed. Palgrave Macmillan, New York.

Catálogo de la colección de don Juan Bautista Muñoz

1954–56 Real Academia de la Historia. 3 vols. Biblioteca Imprenta y Editorial Maestre, Madrid, Spain.

Cedulario cubano (los orígenes de la colonización) 1493–1512 (CC)

n.d. Vol. 6 of *Colección de documentos inéditos para la historia de Hispanoamérica.*

José María Chacón y Calvo, Compiler. Compañía Iberoamericana de Publicaciones, Madrid.

Cedulario de la monarquía española relativo a la isla de Cubagua (1523–1550) (CMEIC)

1961 2 vols. Edition and preliminary study of Enrique Otte. Fundación John Boulton & Fundación Eugenio Mendoza, Caracas.

Cedulario puertorriqueño (CP)

1961 2 vols. In Vol. 3, *Historia documental de Puerto Rico.* Ediciones Universidad de Puerto Rico. Río Piedras.

Cedularios de la monarquía española relativos a la provincia de Venezuela (1529–1552) (CMEPV)

1959 2 vols. Preliminary Study by Enrique Otte. Fundación John Boulton & Fundación Eugenio Mendoza, Caracas.

Cédulas reales relativas a Venezuela (1500–1550) (CRV)

1963 Compilation and Preliminary Study by Enrique Otte. Fundación John Boulton & Fundación Eugenio Mendoza, Caracas.

Chamberlain, Robert S.

1953 *The Conquest and Colonization of Honduras, 1502–1550.* Carnegie Institution, Washington, D.C.

1966 *The Conquest and Colonization of Yucatan, 1517–1550.* Octagon Books, New York.

Chanlatte Baik, Luis A., and Yvonne M. Narganes Storde

1986 *Proceso y desarrollo de los primeros pobladores de Puerto Rico y las Antillas.* Published by the authors, Santo Domingo, Dominican Republic.

Chaunu, Pierre

1963 Las Casas et la première vise structurelle de la colonization espagnole. *Revue Historique* 229:76–77.

Chipman, Donald E.

1966 The Traffic in Indian Slaves, 1523–1533. *The Americas* 23(2):142–155.

1967 *Nuño de Guzmán and the Province of Panuco in New Spain, 1518–1533.* The Arthur H. Clark, California.

Cody, Annie K.

1991 Distribution of Exotic Stone Artifacts through the Lesser Antilles: Their Implications for Prehistoric Interaction and Exchange. In *Proceedings of the Fourteenth Congress of the International Association for Caribbean Archaeology,* edited by Alissandra Cummins and Philippa King, pp. 204–226. St. Ann's Garrison, Barbados Museum and Historical Society.

Colección de documentos inéditos para la historia de España (CDIHE)

1844 Vol. 4, Academia de la Historia, 1842–1895, Madrid, Spain.

Colección de documentos inéditos relativos al descubrimiento, conquista y organización de las antiguas posesiones españolas de América y Oceanía (CODOIN)

1864–1889 42 vols. First series (I). Pacheco, Joaquín et al. editors, Madrid.

Colección de documentos inéditos relativos al descubrimiento, conquista y organización de las antiquas posesiones españolas de Ultramar (CODOIN)

1885–1932 25 vols. Second series (II). Real Academia de la Historia, Madrid.

Colección de documentos para la historia de la formación social de Hispanoamérica, 1493–1810 (CDHFSHA)

1953 Vol. 1. (1493–1592). Richard Konetzke, editor. Consejo Superior de Investigaciones Históricas, Madrid.

Colombres, Adolfo

1977 *La colonización cultural de la América Latina.* Ediciones Sol, Argentina.

Cook, Noble David

2003 Una primera epidemia americana de viruela, 1493? *Revista de Indias* 63:49–64.

Cook, Sherburne F., and Woodrow W. Borah (editors)

1971–74 The Aboriginal Population of Hispaniola. In *Essays in Population History,* Vol. 1, pp. 376–410. University of California Press, Berkeley.

Cooper, Jago, Marcos Martinón-Torres, and Roberto Valcárcel Rojas

2008 American Gold and European Brass, Metal Objects and Indigenous Values in the Cemetery of Chorro de Maíta, Cuba. In *Crossing Borders: New Methods and Techniques in the Study of Archaeological Materials from the Caribbean,* edited by C. L. Hofman, Menno L. P. Hoogland, and Annelou L. van Gijn, pp. 34–42. University of Alabama Press, Tuscaloosa.

Córdova, Efrén

1968 La encomienda y la desaparición de los indios en las Antillas Mayores. *Caribbean Studies* 8(3):23–49.

Córdova, Pedro Tomás de

1831 *Memorias geográficas, históricas, económicas y estadísticas de la isla de Puerto Rico.* En la oficina del gobierno, a cargo de D. Valeriano de Sanmillán, Puerto Rico.

Cósimi, Julio Damiani

1994 Estratificación social, esclavos y naborías en el Puerto Rico minero del siglo XVI. La información de Francisco Manuel de Lando. Ensayo de cuantificación y transcripción paleográfica. *Cuadernos de Investigación Histórica Número 1,* Departamento de Historia, Centro de Investigaciones Históricas, Universidad de Puerto Rico, Recinto de Río Piedras.

Crosby, Alfred W., Jr.

1972 *The Columbian Exchange: Biological and Cultural Consequences of 1492.* Greenwood Press, Westport.

1976 Virgin Soil Epidemics as a Factor in the Aboriginal Depopulation in America. *William and Mary Quarterly* 33:289–299.

Curet, L. Antonio

1992 *The Development of Chiefdoms in the Greater Antilles: A Regional Study of the Valley of Maunabo, Puerto Rico.* Unpublished Ph.D. dissertation, Arizona State University.

1996 Ideology, Chiefly Power, and Material Culture: An Example from the Greater Antilles. *Latin American Antiquity* 7:114–131.

2002 The Chief is Dead, Long Live Who? Descent and Succession in the Protohistoric Chiefdoms of the Greater Antilles. *Ethnohistory* 49:259–280.

2005 *Caribbean Paleodemography: Population, Culture History, and Sociopolitical Processes in Ancient Puerto Rico.* University of Alabama Press, Tuscaloosa.

2006 Las crónicas en la arqueología de Puerto Rico y del Caribe. *Caribbean Studies* 34(1):163–199.

2014 The Taíno: Phenomena, Concepts, and Terms. *Ethnohistory* 61(3): 467–495.

2015 Indigenous Revival, Indigeneity, and the *Jíbaro* in Borikén. *Centro Journal* 27(1):206–247.

Curet, L. Antonio, and Mark W. Hauser (editors)

2011 *Islands at the Crossroads: Migration, Seafaring, and Interaction in the Caribbean.* University of Alabama Press, Tuscaloosa.

Curet, L. Antonio, and José R. Oliver

1998 Mortuary Practices, Social Development, and Ideology in Pre-columbian Puerto Rico. *Latin American Antiquity* 9:217–239.

Curet, L. Antonio, J. M. Torres, and M. Rodríguez

2004 Political and Social History of Eastern Puerto Rico: The Ceramic Age. In *The Late Ceramic Age in the Eastern Caribbean,* edited by A. Delpeuch, and C. Hofman, pp. 59–85. British Archaeological Reports, Oxford.

Cusick, James G.

1987 *Ceramic Change and Its Links to Social Change at the Site of En Bas Saline, Haiti.* Paper read at the Society for American Archaeology Meetings, Phoenix, Arizona.

1998 Historiography of Acculturation: An Evaluation of Concepts and Their Applications in Archaeology. In *Studies in Culture Contact: Interaction, Culture Change, and Archaeology,* edited by James G. Cusick, pp. 126–145. Center for Archaeological Investigations, Occasional Paper No. 25. Southern Illinois University, Carbondale.

2000 Creolization and the Borderlands. *Historical Archaeology* 34(3):46–55. Society for Historical Archaeology.

Dacal Moure, Ramón, and Manuel Rivero de la Calle

1996 *Art and Archaeology of Pre-Columbian Cuba.* University of Pittsburgh Press.

Daggett, Richard E.

1980 The Trade Process and the Implications of Trade in the Bahamas. *The Florida Anthropologist* 33(3):143–151.

Dávila, Arlene

2006 Local/Diasporic Taínos: Towards a Cultural Politics of Memory, Reality and Imagery. In *Taíno Revival. Critical Perspectives on Puerto Rican Identity and Cultural Politics,* edited by Gabriel-Haslip-Viera, pp. 33–53. Markus Wiener Publishers, Princeton (Second printing).

Davis, Dave D., and Christopher Goodwin

1990 Island Carib Origins: Evidence and Non-evidence. *American Antiquity* 55(1):37–48.

Dawdy, Shannon Lee

2000 Understanding Cultural Change through the Vernacular: Creolization in Louisiana. *Historical Archaeology* 34(3):107–123. Society for Historical Archaeology.

Deagan, Kathleen

1985a Spanish-Indian Interaction in Sixteenth Century Florida and the Caribbean. In *Cultures in Contact*, edited by William Fitzhugh, pp. 281–318. Smithsonian Institution Press, Washington, D.C.

1985b Spanish Colonial Archaeology in the Southeast and the Caribbean. In *Comparative Studies in the Archaeology of Colonialism*, edited by Stephen L. Dyson, pp. 77–92. B.A.R. International Series 23, Oxford.

1987 Initial Encounters: Arawak Responses to European Contact at the En Bas Saline Site, Haiti. In *Proceedings of the First San Salvador Conference Columbus and his World*, compiled by Donald T. Gerace, pp. 341–359. The College Center of the Finger Lakes, Bahamian Field Station, Florida.

1988 The Archaeology of the Spanish Contact Period in the Caribbean. *Journal of World Prehistory* 2(2):187–225.

1989 The Search for La Navidad, Columbus' 1492 Settlement. In *First Encounters: Spanish Exploration in the Caribbean and the United States, 1492–1570*, edited by Jerald T. Milanich and Susan Milbrath, pp. 41–54. University Press of Florida, Gainesville.

1990 Sixteenth Century Spanish Colonization in the Southeastern United States and the Caribbean. In *Columbian Consequences*. Vol. 2. *Archaeological and Historical Perspectives in the Spanish Borderlands East*, edited by D. Thomas, pp. 225–250. Smithsonian Institution Press, Washington, D.C.

1995 *Puerto Real: The Archaeology of a Sixteenth-Century Spanish Town in Hispaniola*. University Press of Florida, Gainesville.

1996 Colonial Transformations: Euro-American Cultural Genesis in the Early Spanish-American Colonies. *Journal of Anthropological Research* 52(2): 135–158.

1998 Transculturation and Spanish American Ethnogenesis: The Archaeological Legacy of the Quincentenary. In *Studies in Culture Contact: Interaction, Culture Change, and Archaeology*, edited by James G. Cusick, pp. 23–43. Center for Archaeological Investigations, Southern Illinois University, Occasional Paper No. 25, Carbondale.

2002 La Vega cerámica indo-hispana: An Early Sixteenth Century Caribbean Colono-ware. In *Ceramics in America 2002*, edited by Robert Hunter, pp. 195–198. Chipstone Foundation, Hanover and London.

2004 Reconstructing Taino Social Dynamics after Spanish Conquest: Gender and Class in Culture-Contact Studies. *American Antiquity* 69(4):597–626.

Deagan, Kathleen A., and José M. Cruxent

1993 From Contact to *Criollos*: The Archaeology of Spanish Colonization in Hispaniola. In *The Meeting of Two Worlds, Europe and the Americas 1492–1650*, edited by Warwick Bray, pp. 67–105. Oxford University Press.

2002a *Archaeology of La Isabela: America's First European Town*. Yale University Press, New Haven.

2002b *Columbus's Outpost among the Taínos: Spain and America at La Isabela, 1493–1498*. Yale University Press, New Haven, Connecticut.

deFrance, Susan D., and Lee A. Newsom

2005 The Status of Paleoethnobotanical Research in Puerto Rico and Adjacent Islands. In *Ancient Borinquen. Archaeology and Ethnohistory of Native Puerto Rico*, edited by Peter E. Siegel, pp. 122–184. University of Alabama Press, Tuscaloosa.

Deive, Carlos E.

1980 *La esclavitud del negro en Santo Domingo*. 2 vols. Museo del Hombre Dominicano, Santo Domingo, Dominican Republic.

De La Luz-Rodríguez, Gabriel A.

2003 The Encomienda as Locus of Early Colonial Power in the Island of San Juan 1509–1520. *Historia y Sociedad* XIV:3–22. Medellín, Colombia.

2004 *Confronting the Tribal Zone: Toward a Critical Ethnohistory of Colonial State Formation in San Juan through the System of Encomiendas 1509–1520*. Ph.D. dissertation, Anthropology Department, University of Massachusetts, Amherst.

2010 *Taíno* as a Romantic Term: Notes on the Representation of the Indigenous in Puerto Rican Archaeology and Ethnohistory. In *Building the Divide: Indigenous Communities and Archaeology into the Twenty-First Century*, edited by Caroline Philllips and Harry Allen, pp. 93–106. Left Coast Press, Walnut Creek, California.

2014 *Ethnological Hermeneutics for an Early Colonial Encounter in the Island of San Juan: "La Probanza de Juan González del 1532."* Unpublished manuscript.

Delle, James A.

2000 The Material and Cognitive Dimensions of Creolization in Nineteenth-Century Jamaica. *Historical Archaeology* 34(3):56–72. Society for Historical Archaeology.

Denevan, William M.

1970 The Aboriginal Population of Tropical America: Problems and Methods of Estimation. In *Population and Economics: Proceedings of Section V of the Fourth Congress of the International Economic History Association, 1968*, edited by Paul Deprez, pp. 251–269. University of Manitoba Press, Winnipeg.

Denevan, William M. (editor)

1976 *The Native Population of the Americas in 1492*. 1st ed. University of Wisconsin Press, Madison.

1992 *The Native Population of the Americas in 1492*. 2nd ed. University of Wisconsin Press, Madison.

Deutschmann, Zygniunt

1961 The Ecology of Smallpox. In *Studies in Disease Ecology, Studies in Medical Geography*, Vol. 2, edited by Jacques M. May, pp. 1–13. Hafner, New York.

Dewell, James Dudley

1898 *Down in Porto Rico with a Kodak*. Record, New Haven, Connecticut.

Díaz del Castillo, Bernal

1969 *The Conquest of New Spain*. Translated by J. M. Cohen. Penguin, Baltimore.

Díaz Polanco, Héctor

1974 El proceso de acumulación capitalista y la esclavitud en las Antillas. *Revista Dominicana de Antropología e Historia* 4:106–132.

Dobyns, Henry F.

1963 Indian Extinction in the Middle Santa Cruz Valley, Arizona. *New Mexico Historical Review* 38:163–181.

1966 Estimating Aboriginal American Population: An Appraisal of Techniques with a New Hemispheric Estimate. *Current Anthropology* 7:395–416.

1983 *Their Number Become Thinned: Native American Population Dynamics in Eastern North America*. University of Tennessee Press, Knoxville.

Documentos de la Real Hacienda de Puerto Rico (DRHPR)

1971 Vol. 1 (1510–1519). Edited and compiled by Aurelio Tanodi. Centro de Investigaciones Históricas, Universidad de Puerto Rico, Río Piedras.

n.d. Vol. 2. Manuscript on file at the Centro de Investigaciones Históricas, Universidad de Puerto Rico, Río Piedras.

Documentos inéditos del siglo XVI para la historia de México (DIHM)

1914 Mariano Cuevas, compiler. Talleres del Museo Nacional de Arqueología, Historia y Etnología, Mexico.

Domínguez, Lourdes

1978 La transculturación en Cuba (siglos 16–17). *Cuba Arqueológica* 1:33–50. Editorial Oriente, Santiago de Cuba.

1980 Cerámica de transculturación del sitio colonial Casa de la Obrapia. *Cuba Arqueológica*. Vol. 2. Editorial Oriente, Santiago de Cuba.

1983 *El Yayal*. Cesaraugusta. Publications Seminar of Archaeology and Numismatics Aragonesa. CSIC, Institución Fernando el Católico, Zaragoza, Vols. 57–58, pp. 187–249.

1984 *Arqueología colonial cubana. Dos estudios*. Editorial de Ciencias Sociales, Havana.

1987 La cerámica del sitio arqueológico El Yayal, Cuba. *Revista del Centro de Estudios Avanzados de Puerto Rico y el Caribe* 4:140–145. San Juan.

2008 Arqueología histórica en sitios del siglo XVI en el Caribe. *Cuba Arqueológica*. www.archivocubano.org/transcult/arqueologia_historica.html, accessed June 23, 2016.

Duany, Jorge

2006 Making Indians out of Blacks: The Revitalization of Taíno Identity in Contemporary Puerto Rico. In *Taíno Revival: Critical Perspectives on Puerto Rican Identity and Cultural Politics*, edited by Gabriel Haslip-Viera, pp. 55–81. Markus Wiener, Princeton (Second printing).

Dunn, Oliver, and James E. Kelley, Jr. (translators)

1989 *The Diario of Christopher Columbus' First Voyage to America 1492–1493*,

Abstracted by Fray Bartolomé de las Casas. The American Exploration and Travel Series. University of Oklahoma Press, Norman.

Du Tertre, Jean-Baptiste

1667 *Histoire generale des Antilles habitées par les François.* Vol. 2. Chez Thomas Iolly, Paris.

Earle, Timothy K.

1989 The Evolution of Chiefdoms. *Current Anthropology* 30(1):84–88.

1997 *How Chiefs Come to Power.* Stanford University Press, Stanford, California.

Elliott, Daniel T.

1987 *Archaeological Reconnaissance of Five Tracts in the Río Guanajibo Basin, Puerto Rico.* Garrow and Associates. Report prepared for the United States Army Corps of Engineers, Jacksonville District.

Epistolario de la Nueva España 1505–1818 (ENE)

1939–42 Vol. 1. Francisco del Paso y Troncoso, compiler. Biblioteca Histórica Mexicana de Obras Inéditas, Mexico.

Eriksen, Thomas Hylland

2007 Creolization in Anthropological Theory and in Mauritius. In *Creolization: History, Ethnography, Theory,* edited by Charles Stewart, pp. 153–177. Left Coast Press, Walnut Creek, California.

Espenshade, Christopher T., Dennis Blanton, David L. McWatters, and J. W. Joseph

1986 *Site Specific Archaeological Survey and Additional Reconnaissance of Selected Portions of the Proposed Voice of America Relay Station, Cabo Rojo, Puerto Rico.* Garrow and Associates, Atlanta, Georgia. Report submitted to the Jacksonville District, U.S. Army Corps of Engineers, Jacksonville, Florida.

Ewen, Charles R.

1987 *From Spanish to Creole: The Archaeology of Hispanic American Cultural Formation at Puerto Real, Haiti.* Unpublished Ph.D. dissertation, University of Florida, Gainesville.

1991 *From Spaniard to Creole: The Archaeology of Cultural Formation in Puerto Real, Haiti.* University of Alabama Press, Tuscaloosa.

2000 From Colonist to Creole: Archaeological Patterns of Spanish Colonization in the New World. *Historical Archaeology* 34(3):36–45. Society for Historical Archaeology.

Ewers, John C.

1973 The Influence of Epidemics on the Indian Population and Cultures of Texas. *Plains Anthropologist* 18:104–115.

Fabié, Antonio María

1879 *Vida y escritos del padre Fray Bartolomé de las Casas, Obispo de Chiapas.* Colección de documentos para la historia de España, L, Madrid.

Fairbanks, Charles H., and Rochelle Marrinan

1982 The Puerto Real Project, Haiti. *Journal of New World Archaeology* 5(2): 67–72.

Federmann, Nicolás
1945 *Viaje a las Indias del Mar Océano* (1557). Ed. Nova, Buenos Aires.
Ferguson, Leland
2000 Introduction. *Historical Archaeology* 34(3):5–9. Society for Historical Archaeology.
Ferguson, R. Brian, and Neil L. Whitehead
1992 The Violent Edge of Empire. In *War in the Tribal Zone: Expanding States and Indigenous Warfare*, edited by Brian R. Ferguson and Neil L. Whitead, pp. 1–30. School of American Research Press, Santa Fe.
Fernández de Navarrete, Martín
1945–46 *Colección de los viajes y descubrimientos que hicieron por mar los españoles del siglo XV.* Vols. 1–3. Editorial Guaranía, Buenos Aires.
Fernández de Oviedo, Gonzalo
1851 *Historia general y natural de las Indias, islas y tierra-firme del mar océano, por el capitán Gonzalo Fernández de Oviedo y Valdés.* Edited by José Amador de los Ríos. Imprenta de la Real Academia de la Historia, Madrid, Spain.
1959 *Historia general y natural de las Indias.* 5 vols. Edited by Juan Pérez de Tudela Bueso. Biblioteca de Autores Españoles, Ediciones Atlas, Madrid.
Fernández Méndez, Eugenio
1981 *Crónicas de Puerto Rico desde la conquista hasta nuestros días (1493–1955).* Editorial UPR, Río Piedras, Puerto Rico.
1984 *Las encomiendas y la esclavitud de los indios de Puerto Rico, 1508–1550.* 5th ed. Editorial UPR, Río Piedras, Puerto Rico.
Figueredo, Alfredo E.
1978 The Virgin Islands as an Historical Frontier between the Tainos and the Caribs. *Revista Interamericana* 8(3):393–399.
Fitzhugh, William W. (editor)
1985 *Cultures in Contact: The Impact of European Contacts on Native American Cultural Institutions.* Smithsonian Institution Press, Washington, D.C.
Forte, Maximilian C.
2006 Introduction: The Dual Absences of Extinction and Marginality—What Difference Does an Indigenous Presence Make? In *Indigenous Resurgence in the Contemporary Caribbean*, edited by Maximilian C. Forte, pp. 1–17. Peter Lang, New York.
Foster, George M.
1960 *Culture and Conquest: America's Spanish Heritage.* Viking Fund Publications in Anthropology 27. University of Chicago Press.
Friede, Juan
1953 *Los Andakí, 1538–1947: Historia de la aculturación de una tribu selvática.* Fondo de Cultura Económica, Mexico.
1961 Orígenes de la esclavitud indígena en Venezuela. *Boletín de la Academia Nacional de la Historia* 44(173):61–75. Caracas.
1963 *Los Quimbayas bajo la dominación española, estudio documental, 1539–1810.* Taller Gráfico del Banco de la República, Bogotá.

Gallagher, Mary
2007 The Creolité Movement: Paradoxes of a French Caribbean Orthodoxy. In *Creolization: History, Ethnography, Theory*, edited by Charles Stewart, pp. 220–236. Left Coast Press, Walnut Creek, California.

García Arévalo, Manuel
1978a La arqueología indo-hispana en Santo Domingo. In *Unidades y variedades, ensayos en homenaje a José M. Cruxent*, edited by Erika Wagner and Alberta Zucchi, pp. 77–127. Centro de Estudios Avanzados, Caracas.
1978b Influencias de la dieta indo-hispánica en la cerámica taína. In *Proceedings of the Seventh International Congress for the Study of the Pre-Columbian Cultures of the Lesser Antilles*, pp. 263–277. Centre de Recherches Caraibes, Montreal.

García Castañeda, José A.
1949 La transculturación indo-española en Holguín. *Revista de arquelogía y etnología, segunda época* 4(8/9):195–205.

García Gallo, Alfonso
1987 *Los orígenes de las instituciones americanas*. Real Academia de Jurisprudencia y Legislación, Madrid.

García Goyco, Osvaldo
2011 El yacimiento Jácana (PO-29), su probable participación en la rebelión taína de 1511. In *Simposio 5to Centenario (1511–2011) de la Rebelión Taína*, pp. 106–123. Fundación Cultural Educativa, Instituto de Cultura Puertorriqueña.

García Menéndez, Alberto A.
1981 *Los jueces de apelación de la Española y su residencia*. Museo de las Casas Reales, Santo Domingo, Dominican Republic.

García Molina, José Antonio, Mercedes Garrido Mazorra, and Daisy Fariñas Gutiérrez
2007 *Huellas vivas del indocubano*. Editorial de Ciencias Sociales, La Habana, Cuba.

Granberry, Julian
2013 Indigenous Languages of the Caribbean. In *The Oxford Handbook of Caribbean Archaeology*, edited by W. F. Keegan, C. L. Hofman, and R. Rodríguez Ramos, pp. 61–69. Oxford University Press.

Grover, Mark D.
2000 Creolization and the Archaeology of Multiethnic Households in the American South. *Historical Archaeology* 34(3):99–106. Society for Historical Archaeology.

Guarch Delmonte, J. M.
1996 La muerte en las Antillas: Cuba. *El Caribe Arqueológico* 1:12–25.

Guerra, Francisco
1988 The Earliest American Epidemic: The Influenza of 1493. *Social Science History* 12(3):305–325.

Guerrero, José G., and Marcio Veloz Maggiolo

1988 *Los inicios de la colonización en América (la arqueología como historia)*. Universidad Central del Este, San Pedro de Macorís, Dominican Republic.

Guitar, Lynne

1998 *Cultural Genesis: Relationships among Indians, Africans, and Spaniards in Rural Hispaniola, First Half of the Sixteenth Century*. Unpublished Ph.D. dissertation, Vanderbilt University, Nashville, Tennessee.

2009 *What Really Happened at Santo Cerro?* Unpublished manuscript.

Guitar, Lynne, Pedro Ferbel-Azcarate, and Jorge Estévez

2006 Ocama-Daca Taino (Hear Me, I Am Taino): Taino Survival on Hispaniola, Focusing on the Dominican Republic. In *Indigenous Resurgence in the Contemporary Caribbean*, edited by Maximilian C. Forte, pp. 41–67. Peter Lang, New York.

Gundaker, Grey

2000 Discussion: Creolization, Complexity, and Time. *Historical Archaeology* 34(3):124–133. Society for Historical Archaeology.

Hanke, Lewis

1935 *The First Social Experiments in America: A Study in the Development of Spanish Indian Policy in the Sixteenth Century*. Harvard Historical Monographs 5, Harvard University Press, Cambridge.

1951 *Bartolomé de las Casas. An Interpretation of his Life and Writings*. M. Nijoff, The Hague.

Haring, Clarence H.

1947 *The Spanish Empire in America*. Oxford University Press, New York.

Harris, Marvin

1982 *El materialismo cultural*. Alianza Universidad, Madrid, Spain.

Haslip-Viera, Gabriel

2006 Competing Identities: Taino Revivalism and other Ethno-racial Identity Movements among Puerto Ricans and other Caribbean Latinos in the United States, 1980–present. In *Taino Revival: Critical Perspectives on Puerto Rican Identity and Cultural Politics*, edited by Gabriel Haslip-Viera, pp. 1–31. Markus Wiener Publishers, Princeton (Second Printing).

Haslip-Viera, Gabriel (editor)

2006 *Taino Revival: Critical Perspectives on Puerto Rican Identity and Cultural Politics*. Second Printing of 2002 ed. Markus Weiner, Princeton.

Haviser, Jay B.

1997 Settlement Strategies in the Early Ceramic Age. In *The Indigenous People of the Caribbean*, edited by Samuel M. Wilson, pp. 59–69. University Press of Florida, Gainesville.

Heckenberger, Michael J.

2011 Scale, Hybridity, and Perspective in the Caribbean and Beyond. In *The Indigenous People of the Caribbean*, edited by Samuel M. Wilson, pp. 491–503. University Press of Florida, Gainesville.

Henige, David

1978 On the Contact Population of Hispaniola: History as Higher Mathematics, *Hispanic American Historical Review* 58(2):217–237.

Herrera y Tordesillas, Antonio de

1728 *Historia general de las Indias occidentales, o, De los hechos de los castellanos en las islas y tierra firme del mar océano.* 2nd ed. of 1601 1st ed. J. B. Verdussen, Amberes, Holland.

1944 *Historia general de los hechos de los castellanos en las islas y tierra firme de el mar océano.* 7 vols. Asunción, Paraguay.

Herskovits, Melville Jean

1938 *Acculturation: The Study of Culture Contact.* J. J. Agustin, New York. Reprint P. Smith, Gloucester, Massachusetts, 1958.

Hill, Jonathan D.

1998 Violent Encounters: Ethnogenesis and Ethnogenocide in Long-Term Contact Situations. In *Studies in Culture Contact: Interaction, Culture Change, and Archaeology*, edited by James G. Cusick, pp. 172–190. Center for Archaeological Investigations, Southern Illinois University, Occasional Paper No. 25, Carbondale.

Historia documental de Puerto Rico (HDPR)

1973 Vol. 1. El consejo o cabildo de la ciudad de San Juan de Puerto Rico (1527–1550). Vol. 2. El juicio de residencia, moderador democrático: Juicio de residencia de Lic. Sancho Velázquez, juez de residencia y justicia mayor de la isla de San Juan (PR), por el Lic. Antonio de la Gama (1519–1520), edited by Vicente Murga Sanz. Editorial Plus Ultra, Río Piedras, Puerto Rico.

Hodges, William

1983 *The Search for La Navidad.* Musee de Guahabi, Limbe, Haiti.

Hoff, Berend J.

1995 Language Contact, War, and Amerindian Historical Tradition. In *Wolves from the Sea*, edited by Neil L. Whitehead, pp. 37–59. KITLV, Leiden, Netherlands.

Hofman, Corinne L., and Menno L. P. Hoogland

1991 The Later Prehistory of Saba, Netherlands Antilles, the Settlement Site of Kelbey's Ridge (1300–1450 AD). In *Proceedings of the Thirteenth International Congress for Caribbean Archaeology*, edited by E. N. Ayubi and J. B. Haviser, pp. 477–492. Reports of the Archaeological-Anthropological Institute of the Netherlands Antilles, No. 9, Curaçao, Netherlands Antilles.

Hofman, Corinne L., Arie Boomert, Alistair J. Bright, Menno L. P. Hoogland, Sebastiaan Knippenberg, and Alice V. M. Samson

2011 Ties with the Homelands: Archipelagic Interaction and the Enduring Role of the South and Central American Mainlands in the Pre-Columbian Lesser Antilles. In *Islands at the Crossroads: Migration, Seafaring, and Interaction in the Caribbean*, edited by L. Antonio Curet and Mark W. Hauser, pp. 73–86. University of Alabama Press, Tuscaloosa.

Hofman, Corinne L., Angus Mol, Menno Hoogland, and Roberto Valcárcel Rojas

2014 Stage Encounters: Migration, Mobility and Interaction in the Pre-Colonial and Early Colonial Caribbean. *World Archaeology* 46(4):590–609.

Hofman, Corinne L., and Anne van Duijvenbode (editors)

2011 *Communities in Contact, Essays in Archaeology, Ethnohistory & Ethnography of the American Circum-Caribbean.* Sidestone Press, Leiden, Netherlands.

Hostos, Adolfo de

1938 *Investigaciones históricas.* On file at Colección Puertorriqueña, University of Puerto Rico Library, Río Piedras. Reprinted, San Juan, Puerto Rico, Oficina Estatal de Conservación Histórica de Puerto Rico, Oficina del Gobernador, 2011.

Hulme, Peter

1986 *Colonial Encounters: Europe and the Native Caribbean, 1492–1797.* Methuen, London and New York.

Hulme, Peter, and Neil L. Whitehead (editors)

1992 *Wild Majesty: Encounters with Caribs from Columbus to the Present Day, an Anthology.* Clarendon Press, Oxford.

Hussey, Ronald D.

1932 Text of the Laws of Burgos (1512–1513) Concerning the Treatment of the Indians. *Hispanic American Historical Review* 12(3):301–326.

Ibarra, José

1976 La gran sublevación india de 1520 a 1540 y la abolición de las encomiendas. *Revista de la Universidad de Oriente* 22:61–87.

Informaciones coloniales sobre libertad y tratamiento de los indios

1951 Información sobre la libertad de los indios hecha a petición de Gregorio López, del Consejo de Indias, y visitador de la Casa de Contratación, Sevilla 23 de junio de 1543. *Revista del Archivo Histórico de Cuzco* 2:225–269.

Inventario de la colección documental-histórica Herrera procedente del Archivo General de Indias (ICDHH)

1987 Casas Reales, Santo Domingo. On file at the Centro de Investigaciones Históricas, Universidad de Puerto Rico, Río Piedras.

Irrizarry, José E., Luis Ortiz Sepúlveda, and Antonio Ramos Ramírez

1982 *Sobre las excavaciones arqueológicas en las ruinas del Convento de Santo Domingo de Porta Coeli, en San Germán de Puerto Rico, 1982.* Prepared for the *Parque Infantil Porta Coeli.* Copy on file with Puerto Rico State Historic Preservation Office, San Juan, Puerto Rico.

Irving, Washington

1851 *Vida y viajes de Cristóbal Colón.* Gaspar y Roig Editores, Madrid.

Jiménez Román, Myriam

2006 The Indians are Coming! The Indians are Coming! The Taíno and Puerto Rican Identity. In *Taíno Revival: Critical Perspectives on Puerto Rican Identity and Cultural Politics*, edited by Gabriel Haslip-Viera, pp. 101–138. Markus Wiener Publishers, Princeton (Second Printing).

Juicios de residencia en la provincia de Venezuela

1977 Vol. 1. Los Welser. Fuentes para la historia nacional de Venezuela, 130. Biblioteca de la Academia Nacional de la Historia, Caracas.

Keegan, William F.

1989 The Evolution of Avunculocal Chiefdoms: A Reconstruction of Taino Kinship and Politics. *American Anthropologist* 91(3):613–630.

1992 *The People Who Discovered Columbus: The Prehistory of the Bahamas.* University Press of Florida, Gainesville.

1996 Columbus Was a Cannibal: Myth and First Encounters. In *The Lesser Antilles in the Age of European Expansion*, edited by Robert L. Paquette and Stanley L. Engerman, pp. 17–33. University Press of Florida, Gainesville.

1997 "No Man [or Woman] Is an Island": Elements of Taino Social Organization. In *The Indigenous People of the Caribbean*, edited by Samuel M. Wilson, pp. 111–117. University Press of Florida, Gainesville.

2000 West Indian Archaeology. 3. Ceramic Age. *Journal of Archaeological Research* 8(2):135–167.

2007 *Taino Indian Myth and Practice: The Arrival of the Stranger King.* University of Florida Press, Gainesville.

2013 The "Classic" Taino. In *The Oxford Handbook of Caribbean Archaeology*, edited by W. F. Keegan, C. L. Hofman, and R. Rodríguez Ramos, pp. 70–83. Oxford University Press.

Keegan, William F., Morgan D. Maclachlan, and Bryan Byrne

1998 Social Foundations of Taino Caciques. In *Chiefdoms and Chieftaincy in the Americas*, edited by E. M. Redmond, pp. 217–244. University Press of Florida, Gainesville.

Keehnen, Floris W. M.

2011 Conflicting Cosmologies. The Exchange of Brilliant Objects between the Taino of Hispaniola and the Spanish. In *Communities in Contact: Essays in Archaeology, Ethnohistory and Ethnography of the Amerindian Circum-Caribbean*, edited by C. L. Hofman, and A. Van Duijvenbode, pp. 253–268. Sidestone Press, Leiden, Netherlands.

Kirch, Patrick Vinton

1989 *The Evolution of Polynesian Chiefdoms.* Cambridge University Press.

Kirkpatrick, F. A.

1939 Repartimiento-Encomienda. *Hispanic American Historical Review* 19(3): 372–379.

Knight, Vernon James, Jr.

2006 La Loma del Convento: Its Centrality to Current Issues in Cuban Archaeology. Paper presented at the 71st Annual Meeting of the Society for American Archaeology, San Juan, Puerto Rico.

Konetzke, Richard

1949 La esclavitud de los indios como elemento en la estructuración social de Hispanoamérica. *Estudios de Historia Social de España* I:441–479. Madrid.

Konetzke, Richard (editor)
1953 *Colección de documentos para la historia de la formación social de Hispanoamérica.* Vol. 1 (1493–1592). Consejo Superior de Investigaciones Científicas, Madrid.
Krech, Shepard III
1978 Disease, Starvation and Northern Athapaskan Social Organization. *American Ethnologist* 5:210–232.
Kroeber, Alfred Lewis
1939 *Cultural and Natural Areas of Native North America.* University of California Publications in American Archaeology and Ethnology 27, Berkeley.
1948 *Anthropology: Race, Language, Culture, Psychology, Pre-History.* Harcourt, Brace, New York.
La Borde, Sieur de
1674 *Relation de l'origine, moeurs, coutumes, religion, guerres, et voyages de Caraibes, sauvages de Iles Antilles de l'Amérique.* Billaine, Paris.
Lamb, Ursula
1977 *Frey Nicolás de Ovando Gobernador de las Indias.* Sociedad Dominicana de Bibliófilos, Santo Domingo, Dominican Republic.
Larsen, Clark Spencer
1994 In the Wake of Columbus: Native Population Biology in the Postcontact Americas. *Yearbook of Physical Anthropology* 37:109–154.
Las Casas, Fray Bartolomé de
1945 *Brevísima relación de la destrucción de las Indias.* Prologue by Agustín Millares Carlo, Secretaría de Educación Pública, Mexico.
1951 *Historia de las Indias.* Agustín Millares Carlo, edition with preliminary study by Lewis Hanke. 3 vols. Biblioteca Americana, Serie de cronistas de Indias 15–17, Fondo de Cultura Económica, Mexico.
1965 *Historia de las Indias.* Edición de Agustín Millares Carlo, edition with preliminary study by Lewis Hanke. 3 vols. 2nd ed. Fondo de Cultura Económica, Mexico.
1967 *Apologética historia sumaria.* 3rd ed. Instituto de Investigaciones Históricas, Universidad Nacional Autónoma, Mexico.
1985 *Historia de las Indias.* Edited by Guillermo Piña Contreras. 3 vols. Ediciones del Continente, S.A., Hollywood, Florida.
Linton, Ralph (editor)
1940 *Acculturation in Seven American Indian Tribes.* D. Appleton-Century, New York.
Lipschutz, Alejandro
1966 La despoblación de las Indias después de la conquista. *America Indígena* 26(3):229–247. Mexico.
Livi-Bacci, Massimo
2003 Return to Hispaniola: Reassessing the Demographic Catastrophe. *Hispanic American Historical Review* 83(1):3–51. Duke University Press.
2006 The Depopulation of Hispanic America after the Conquest. *Population and Development Review* 32(June):199–232.

Lluch Mora, Francisco
1986 Poblamiento de San Germán (siglos XVI-XVIII). *Revista del Centro de Estudios Avanzados de Puerto Rico y el Caribe* 2:62–68.
Lobo Cabrera, Manuel
1983 Esclavos indios en Canarias: Precedentes. *Revista de Indias* 43(172): 515–532.
Loren, Diana DiPaolo
2000 The Interactions of Colonial Policy and Colonial Practice: Creolization on the Eighteenth Century Louisiana/Texas Frontier. *Historical Archaeology* 34(3):85–98. Society for Historical Archaeology.
Loucks, L. Jill
1979 *Political and Economic Interaction between Spaniards and Indians: Archaeological and Ethnohistorical Perspectives of the Mission System in Florida.* Unpublished Ph.D. dissertation, University of Florida, Gainesville.
Lovén, Sven
1935 *Origins of the Tainan Culture, West Indies.* Göteborg, Sweden.
Luna Calderón, Fernando
2002 Mitochondrial DNA in the Dominican Republic. *Kacike: The Journal of Caribbean Amerindian History and Anthropology.* Special Issue edited by Lynne Guitar. New Directions in Taino Research. https://www.familytreedna.com/pdf/Calderon.pdf. Accessed June 23, 2016.
Lyon, Eugene
1981 *Puerto Real: Research on a Spanish Town on Hispaniola's North Coast.* Report on file, Florida Museum of Natural History, University of Florida, Gainesville.
MacNutt, Frederick Augustus
1909 *Bartholomew de Las Casas: His Life, His Apostolate, and His Writing.* New York, G. P. Putnam's Sons. Reprint New York, AMS Press, 1972.
Maíz López, Edgar
2002 *El sitio arqueológico Hernández Colón: Actividades subsistenciales de los antiguos habitantes del valle del río Cerrillos-Bucaná, Ponce, Puerto Rico.* Unpublished Master's thesis, Centro de Estudios Avanzados de Puerto Rico y el Caribe, San Juan.
Maíz López, Edgar, and Eduardo Questell Rodríguez
1990 Reconocimiento arqueológico preliminar de la cuenca hidrográfica del Río Jauco. In *Proceedings of the Eleventh Congress of the International Association for Caribbean Archaeology,* edited by G. Pantel Tekakis, I. Vargas Arenas, and M. Sanoja Obediente, pp. 311–327. Fundación Arqueológica, Antropológica, e Histórica de Puerto Rico, San Juan.
Mandelbaum, David G.
1967 Culture Change among the Nilgire Tribes. In *Beyond de Frontier: Social Process and Culture Change,* edited by Paul Bohannon and Fred Plog, pp. 199–208. Natural History Press, Garden City, New York.

Mann, Charles C.
2005 *1491: New Revelations of the Americas before Columbus.* Alfred A. Knopf, New York.

Marrinan, Rochelle A.
1982 *Test Excavations of Building B (Area 2), Puerto Real, Haiti: Final Report.* Manuscript on file, Florida Museum of Natural History, University of Florida, Gainesville.

Martínez-Cruzado, Juan C.
2002 The Use of Mitochondrial DNA to Discover Pre-Columbian Migrations to the Caribbean: Results from Puerto Rico and Expectations from the Dominican Republic. *Kacike: The Journal of Caribbean Amerindian History and Anthropology*. Special Issue edited by Lynne Guitar. New Directions in Taino Research. *https://consortia.si.edu/sites/default/files/MartinezCruzado2002_0.pdf.* Accessed June 23, 2016.

Martínez-Cruzado, Juan C., G. Toro-Labrador, V. Ho-Fung, M. A. Estévez-Montero, A. Lobaina-Manzanet, D. A. Padovani-Claudio, H. Sánchez-Cruz, P. Ortíz-Bermúdez, and A. Sánchez-Crespo
2001 Mitochondrial DNA Analysis Reveals Substantial Native American Ancestry in Puerto Rico. *Human Biology* 73:491–511.

Martínez-Cruzado, Juan C., G. Toro-Labrador, J. Viera-Vera, M. Rivera-Vega, J. Startek, M. Latorre-Esteves, A. Román-Colón, R. Rivera-Torres, I. Y. Navarro-Millán, E. Gómez-Sánchez, H. Caro-González, and P. Valencia-Rivera
2005 Reconstructing the Population History of Puerto Rico through mtDNA Phylogeo-graphic Analysis. *American Journal of Physical Anthropology* 128: 131–155.

Martinón-Torres, Marcos, R. Valcárcel Rojas, J. Sáenz Samper, and M. F. Guerra
2012 Metallic Encounters in Cuba: The Technology, Exchange and Meaning of Metals Before and After Columbus. *Journal of Anthropological Archaeology* 31(4):439–454.

Mártir de Anglería, Pedro (Peter Martyr of Anghiera)
1944 *Décadas del Nuevo Mundo, vertidas del latín a la lengua castellana por el Dr. D. Joaquín Torres Asensio.* Editorial Bajel, Distribuidor exclusivo Librería "El Ateneo", Buenos Aires, Argentina.

Mathers, Clay, Jeffrey M. Mitchem, and Charles M. Haecker (editors)
2013 *Native and Spanish New Worlds: Sixteenth-Century Entradas in the American Southwest and Southeast.* University of Arizona Press, Tucson.

McEwan, Bonnie G.
1983 *Spanish Colonial Adaptation on Hispaniola: The Archaeology of Area 35, Puerto Real, Haiti.* Unpublished Master's thesis, University of Florida, Gainesville.
1986 Domestic Adaptation at Puerto Real, Haiti. *Historical Archaeology* 20(1): 44–49.

McIntosh, Roderick J.
1998 *The People of Middle Niger: The Island of Gold.* Blackwell, Oxford.
McNeil, William H.
1976 *Plagues and Peoples.* Anchor Press/Doubleday, Garden City, New York.
Mendoza, Lourdes C.
1980 Cerámica de las ruinas de la Vega Vieja. *Casas Reales* 11:101–113. Santo Domingo.
Milanich, Gerald T., and Samuel Proctor (editors)
1978 *Tacachale, Essays on the Indians of Florida and Southeastern Georgia during the Historic Period.* University Presses of Florida, Gainesville.
Mintz, Sidney W.
2010 *Three Ancient Colonies, Caribbean Themes and Variations.* Harvard University Press, Cambridge, Massachusetts.
Mira Caballos, Esteban
1997 *El indio antillano: Repartimiento, encomienda y esclavitud (1492–1542).* Edited by Muñoz Moya. Ediciones Alfil, Bogotá, Colombia.
2000a *Las Antillas Mayores 1492–1550: Ensayos y documentos.* Editorial Iberoamericana, Madrid.
2000b *Nicolás de Ovando y los orígenes del sistema colonial español 1502–1509.* Patronato de la Ciudad Colonial de Santo Domingo, Santo Domingo, Dominican Republic.
2009 *Conquista y destrucción de las Indias (1492–1573).* Colección Biblioteca Americana. Muñoz Moya Editores Extremeños, Granada.
2010 *La Española, epicentro del Caribe en el siglo XVI.* Academia Dominicana de la Historia. Vol. 91. Santo Domingo, Dominican Republic.
Mol, Angus A. A.
2011 Bringing Interaction into Higher Spheres: Social Distance in the Late Ceramic Age Greater Antilles as Seen through Ethnohistorical Accounts and the Distribution of Social Valuables. In *Communities in Contact: Essays in Archaeology, Ethnohistory and Ethnography of the Amerindian circum-Caribbean,* edited by C. L. Hofman and A. van Duijvenbode, pp. 61–86. Sidestone Press, Leiden, Netherlands.
Moore, Jerry D.
2014 *A Prehistory of South America: Ancient Cultural Diversity in the Least Known Continent.* University Press of Colorado, Boulder.
Morales Padrón, Francisco
2003 *Spanish Jamaica.* Translated from the original 1952 Spanish by Patrick E. Bryan, in collaboration with Michael J. Gronow and Felix Oviedo Moral. Ian Randle Publishers, Kingston, Jamaica.
Morales Patiño, Oswaldo
1947 *Los indígenas en los primeros municipios cubanos.* Grupo Guamá, Havana, Cuba.
Morison, Samuel E.
1940 The Route of Columbus along the North Coast of Haiti and the Site of La Navidad. *Transactions of the American Philosophical Society* 31(4):239–285.

1948 *Admiral of the Ocean Sea.* Little, Brown, Boston.

Morse, Birgit Faber

1997 The Salt River Site, St. Croix, at the Time of the Encounter. In *The Indigenous People of the Caribbean,* edited by Samuel M. Wilson, pp. 36–45. University Press of Florida, Gainesville.

Moscoso, Francisco

1983 Parentesco y clase en los cacicazgos taínos: El caso de los naborias. In *Proceedings of the Ninth International Congress for the Study of the Pre-Columbian Cultures of the Lesser Antilles,* pp. 485–494. Centre de Recherches Caraibes, Montreal.

1986 *Tribu y clase en el Caribe antiguo.* Universidad Central del Este, San Pedro de Macorís, Dominican Republic.

1989 La conquista Española y la gran rebelión de los taínos. *Pensamiento Crítico* 62:2–15.

2003 Chiefdoms in the Islands and the Mainland: A Comparison. In *General History of the Caribbean.* Vol. 1. *Autochthonous Societies,* edited by Jalil Sued Badillo, pp. 292–315. MacMillan Caribbean, UNESCO.

2008 *Caciques, aldeas y población taína de Boriquén: Puerto Rico 1492–1582.* Academia Puertorriqueña de la Historia, San Juan, Puerto Rico.

Mosk, Sanford

1938 Spanish Pearl-fishing Operations on the Pearl Coast in the 16th Century. *Hispanic American Historical Review* 18:392–400.

Moya Pons, Frank

1973 *La sociedad taína.* Editora Cultural Dominicana, Santo Domingo, Dominican Republic.

1976 Datos para el estudio de la demografía aborigen en Santo Domingo. *Boletín del Museo del Hombre Dominicano* 6:79–92. Editora Cultural Dominicana, Santo Domingo.

1978 *La Española en el siglo XVI: 1493–1520: Trabajo, sociedad y política en la economía del oro.* 3rd ed. Universidad Central Madre y Maestra, Santiago, Dominican Republic.

1982 Los trabajadores indígenas en la estructuración social de La Española en 1514. *Boletín del Museo del Hombre Dominicano* 10(17):119–138.

1992 The Politics of Forced Indian Labour in La Española, 1493–1520. *American Antiquity* 66:130–139.

Moya Pons, Frank, and Rosario Flores Paz (editors)

2013 *Los Taínos en 1492, el debate demográfico.* Academia Dominicana de la Historia, Vol. 103, Santo Domingo, Dominican Republic.

Mullins, Paul R., and Robert Paynter

2000 Representing Colonizers: An Archaeology of Creolization, Ethnogenesis, and Indigenous Material Culture among the Haida. *Historical Archaeology* 34(3):73–84. Society for Historical Archaeology.

Murga Sanz, Vicente

1971 *Juan Ponce de León, fundador y primer gobernador del pueblo puertorriqueño, descubridor de la Florida y del Estrecho de las Bahamas*. 2nd ed. Editorial Universitaria, Universidad de Puerto Rico, Río Piedras.

Newsom, Lee A., and Elizabeth S. Wing

2004 *On Land and Sea: Native American Uses of Biological Resources in the West Indies*. University of Alabama Press, Tuscaloosa.

Newson, Linda A.

1976 *Aboriginal and Spanish Colonial Trinidad: A Study in Culture Contact*. Academic Press, London.

Noel, Jesse A.

1972 *Trinidad, provincia de Venezuela: Historia de la administración española en Trinidad*. Biblioteca de la Academia Nacional de la Historia 109, Caracas.

Ojer, Pablo

1966 *La formación del Oriente venezolano*. Vol. 1. *Creación de las gobernaciones*. Biblioteca de Estudios Universitarios VI. Universidad Católica "Andrés Bello," Caracas.

Oliver, José R.

1997 The Taino Cosmos. In *The Indigenous People of the Caribbean*, edited by Samuel M. Wilson, pp. 140–153. University Press of Florida, Gainesville.

2005 The Proto-Taino Monumental *Cemís* of Caguana. A Political-Religious "Manifesto." In *Ancient Borinquen: Archaeology and Ethnohistory of Native Puerto Rico*, edited by Peter E. Siegel, pp. 230–284. University of Alabama Press, Tuscaloosa.

2006 Taino Interaction and Variability between the Provinces of Higuey, Eastern Hispaniola, and Otoao, Puerto Rico. Paper presented at the 71st Meeting of the Society for American Archaeology, San Juan, Puerto Rico.

2009 *Caciques and Cemi Idols: The Web Spun by Taino Rulers between Hispaniola and Puerto Rico*. University of Alabama Press, Tuscaloosa.

Oliver, José R., Juan Rivera Fontán, and Lee A. Newsom

1999 Arqueología del Barrio Caguana, Puerto Rico: Resultados preliminaries de las temporadas 1996–1997. In *Trabajos de investigación arqueológica en Puerto Rico: Tercer encuentro de investigadores*, pp. 7–26. Publicación Ocasional de la División de Arqueología, Instituto de Cultura Puertorriqueña, San Juan.

Orme, Bryony

1973 Archaeology and Ethnography. In *The Explanation of Culture Change: Models in Prehistory*, edited by Colin Renfrew, pp. 481–492. University of Pittsburg Press.

Ortega, Elpidio J.

1982 *Arqueología colonial de Santo Domingo*. Fundación Ortega Alvarez, Santo Domingo, Dominican Republic.

1988 *La Isabela y la arqueología en la ruta de Cristóbal Colón*. Universidad Central del Este, San Pedro de Macorís, Dominican Republic.

Ortega, Elpidio, and Carmen Fondeur

1978a *Arqueología de los monumentos históricos de Santo Domingo*. Universidad Central del Este, San Pedro de Macorís, Dominican Republic.

1978b *Estudio de cerámica del periodo indo-hispano de la antigua Concepción de la Vega.* Serie científica I, Fundación Ortega Alvarez, Santo Domingo, Dominican Republic.

Ortíz, Fernando

1947 *Cuban Counterpoint, Tobacco and Sugar.* Translated by Harriet De Onís. Alfred A. Knopf, New York.

Otte, Enrique

1956 La expedición de Gonzalo de Ocampo a Cumaná en 1521 en las cuentas de la Tesorería de Santo Domingo. *Revista de Indias* 63:51–82.

1975 Los jerónimos y el tráfico humano en el Caribe: Una rectificación. *Anuario de Estudios Americanos* 32:187–204.

1977 *Las perlas del Caribe: Nueva Cádiz de Cubagua.* Fundación John Boulton, Caracas.

Pagán-Jiménez, Jaime R.

2011 Early Phytocultural Processes in the pre-Colonial Antilles: A Pan-Caribbean Survey for an Ongoing Starch Grain Research. In *Communities in Contact: Essays in Archaeology, Ethnohistory and Ethnography of the Amerindian Circum-Caribbean,* edited by C. L. Hofman and A. van Duijvenbode, pp. 87–116. Sidestone Press, Leiden, Netherlands.

Palacio, Joseph O.

2006 Looking at Ourselves in the Mirror: The Caribbean Organization of Indigenous Peoples (COIP). In *Indigenous Resurgence in the Contemporary Caribbean,* edited by Maximilian C. Forte, pp. 213–233. Peter Lang, New York.

Pané, Fray Ramón

1974 *Relación acerca de las antigüedades de los indios: El primer tratado escrito en América.* Edited by José Juan Arrom. Siglo I, Mexico.

Pantel, Agamemnon Gus

1982 *Cultural Resources Survey of Fort Buchanan Military Reservation San Juan, Puerto Rico.* Report prepared for the National Park Service, U.S. Department of the Interior, Atlanta.

Patterson, H. O. L.

1966 Slavery, Acculturation and Social Change: The Jamaican Case. *The British Journal of Sociology* 17(2):151–164.

Peña Battle, Manuel Arturo

1948 *La rebelión del Bahoruco.* Impresora Dominicana, Ciudad Trujillo, Dominican Republic.

Peña y Cámara, José María de la

1955 *A List of Spanish Residencias in the Archives of the Indies, 1516–1775.* The Library of Congress, Washington, D.C.

Pérez de Tudela Bueso, Juan

1955a La quiebra de la factoría y el nuevo poblamiento de La Española. *Revista de Indias* 60:197–252.

1955b Políticas de poblamiento y política de contratación de las Indias 1502–1505. *Revista de Indias* 61–62:371–420.

Pérez de Tudela Bueso, Juan (editor)

1959 Estudio preliminar, vida y escritos de Gonzalo Fernández de Oviedo. In *Historia general y natural de las Indias*, by Gonzalo Fernández de Oviedo, Tomo CXVII (Vol. 117), pp. vii–clv (pp. 7–175). Biblioteca de Autores Españoles, Ediciones Atlas, Madrid.

Petersen, James B.

1997 Taíno, Island Carib, and Prehistoric Amerindian Economies in the West Indies: Tropical Forest Adaptations to Island Environments. In *The Indigenous People of the Caribbean*, edited by Samuel M. Wilson, pp. 118–130. University Press of Florida, Gainesville.

Pichardo Moya, Felipe

1945 *Los indios de Cuba en sus tiempos históricos.* Academia de la Historia de Cuba, La Habana.

Pietschmann, Horst

1999 Spanish Expansion in America 1492 to ca. 1580. In *General History of the Caribbean*, Vol. 2, edited by Pieter C. Emmer and Germán Carrera Damas, pp. 79–113. UNESCO.

Poole, Robert M.

2011 What Became of the Taino? *Smithsonian Magazine.* October 1.

Puerto Rico en los manuscritos de don Juan Bautista Muñoz (PRDJBM)

1960 Biblioteca histórica de Puerto Rico. Vol. 1. Critical study by Vicente Murga Sanz. Editorial Universitaria, Universidad de Puerto Rico, Río Piedras.

Radell, David R.

1976 The Indian Slave Trade and Population of Nicaragua during the Sixteenth Century. In *The Native Population of the Americas in 1492*, edited by William Denevan, pp. 67–70. University of Wisconsin Press, Madison.

Ramenofsky, Ann F.

1987 *Vectors of Death: The Archaeology of European Contact.* University of New Mexico Press, Albuquerque.

Ramírez de Arellano, R. W.

1934 *Cartas y relaciones históricas y geográficas sobre Puerto Rico, 1493–1598.* San Juan.

Ramos Pérez, Demetrio

1975 Actitudes ante los caribes desde su conocimiento indirecto hasta la capitulación de Valladolid de 1520. *Estudios sobre política indigenista española en América* 1:82–110. Seminario de Historia de América, Universidad de Valladolid.

Reales cédulas y correspondencia de gobernadores de Santo Domingo de la regencia del Cardenal Cisneros en adelante (RCCGSD)

1958 Vol. I, 1516–1541. J. Marino Incháustegui, compiler. Colección histórica-documental Trujilloniana.

Redfield, Robert, Ralph Linton, and Melville J. Herskovits

1936 Memorandum for the Study of Acculturation. *American Anthropologist*

38:149–152. Reprinted in *Beyond the Frontier: Social Process and Cultural Change,* edited by Paul Bohannon and Fred Plog, pp. 181–186. Natural History Press, Garden City, New York.

Reitz, Elizabeth J.

1986 Vertebrate Fauna from Locus 39, Puerto Real, Haiti. *Journal of Field Archaeology* 13(3):317–328.

Rivero de la Calle, Manuel

1978 Supervivencia de descendientes de indoamericanos en la zona de Yateras, Oriente. *Cuba arqueológica* 1:149–176. Editorial Oriente, Santiago de Cuba.

1983 Antropología física de los Taínos. In *La cultura taína,* pp. 153–161. Comisión Nacional del Quinto Centenario del Descubrimiento de América, Turner Libros, S. A. Madrid, Spain.

Rodríguez Demorizi, Emilio

1971 *Los dominicos y las encomiendas de indios de la Isla Española.* Academia Dominicana de la Historia, Vol. 30. Editora del Caribe, Santo Domingo, Dominican Republic.

Rodríguez López, Miguel

1984 *Estudio arqueológico del Río Caguitas, Puerto Rico.* Museo de la Universidad del Turabo, Caguas, Puerto Rico.

1985 *Cultural Resources Survey at Camp Santiago, Salinas, Puerto Rico.* Museo de la Universidad del Turabo, Caguas, Puerto Rico.

1990 Arqueología del Río Loíza. In *Proceedings of the Eleventh International Congress for Caribbean Archaeology,* edited by A. G. Pantel Tekakis, I. Vargas Arenas, and M. Sanoja Obediente, pp. 287–294. Fundación Arqueológica, Antropológica, e Histórica de Puerto Rico, San Juan, Puerto Rico.

1991 Early Trade Networks in the Caribbean. In *Proceedings of the Fourteenth Congress of the International Association for Caribbean Archaeology,* edited by Alissandra Cummins and Philippa King, pp. 306–314. St. Ann's Garrison, Barbados Museum and Historical Society.

Rodríguez Ramos, Reniel

2010 *Rethinking Puerto Rican Precolonial History.* University of Alabama Press, Tuscaloosa.

2013 Isthmo-Antillean Engagements. In *The Oxford Handbook of Caribbean Archaeology,* edited by W. F. Keegan, C. L. Hofman, and R. Rodríguez Ramos, pp. 155–170. Oxford University Press.

Romero Estébanez, Leandro S.

1981 Sobre evidencias arqueológicas de contacto y transculturación en el ámbito cubano. *Santiago* 44:71–105.

Rose, Richard

1987 Lucayan Lifeways at the Time of Columbus. In *Proceedings of the First San Salvador Conference Columbus and his World,* compiled by Donald T. Gerace, pp. 321–333. The College Center of the Finger Lakes, Bahamian Field Station, Florida.

Rosenblat, Angel

1954 *La población indígena y el mestizaje en América 1492–1950.* 2 vols. Editorial Nova, Buenos Aires.

1967 *La población de América en 1492. Viejos y nuevos cálculos.* Publicaciones del Centro de Estudios Históricos 1, El Colegio de México, Mexico.

Roth, Joshua Hotaka

2007 Adaptation to Inequality: Negotiating Nikkei Identity in Contexts of Return. In *Creolization: History, Ethnography, Theory,* edited by Charles Stewart, pp. 201–219. Left Coast Press, Walnut Creek, California.

Rouse, Irving

1948 The West Indies. In *Handbook of South American Indians,* edited by Julian H. Steward, Vol. 4, pp. 495–565. Bulletin of the Bureau of American Ethnology, Washington.

1952 Porto Rican Prehistory. Vol. 18, Pts. 3 and 4 of *Scientific Survey of Porto Rico and the Virgin Islands.* New York Academy of Sciences, New York.

1964 Prehistory in the West Indies. *Science* 144:499–513.

1986 *Migrations in Prehistory: Inferring Population Movement from Cultural Remains.* Yale University Press, New Haven, Connecticut.

1987 Origin and Development of the Indians Discovered by Columbus. In *Proceedings of the First San Salvador Conference Columbus and his World,* compiled by Donald T. Gerace, pp. 292–312. College Center of the Finger Lakes, Bahamian Field Station, Florida.

1988 Peoples and Cultures of the Saladoid Frontier. In *Early Ceramic Population Lifeways and Adaptive Strategies in the Caribbean,* Part 4, edited by Peter E. Siegel. B.A.R., Oxford.

1992 *The Tainos: Rise and Decline of the People Who Greeted Columbus.* Yale University Press, New Haven, Connecticut.

Rumeu de Armas, Antonio

1975 La primera declaración de libertad del aborigen americano. In *Estudios sobre política indigenista española en América,* Vol. 1, pp. 41–78. Seminario de Historia de América, Universidad de Valladolid.

Saco, José Antonio

1932 *Historia de la esclavitud de los indios en el Nuevo Mundo seguida de la historia de los repartimientos y encomiendas,* Tomos I & II. Introducción de Fernando Ortíz. Colección de libros cubanos, Vols. 28 and 29, Cultural S.A., La Habana.

Sahlins, Marshall David

1958 *Social Stratification in Polynesia.* Monographs of the American Ethnological Society 29. University of Washington Press, Seattle.

Salivia, Luis A., MD

1972 *Historia de los temporales de Puerto Rico y las Antillas (1492 a 1970).* Editorial Edil, San Juan.

Samson, Alice Victoria Maud

2010 *Renewing the House: Trajectories of Social Life in the Yucayeque Community of El Cabo, Higuey, Dominican Republic AD 800–1504*. Sidestone Press, Leiden, Netherlands.

Sánchez-Albornoz, Nicolás
1974 *The Population of Latin America: A History*. Translated by W.A.R. Richardson. University of California Press.

Santo Domingo en los documentos de Juan Bautista Muñoz (SDDJBM)
1981 Roberto Marte, editor. Ediciones Fundación García Arévalo, Santo Domingo.

Santovenia y Echnide, Emetrio Santiago
1939 *Historia de Cuba*. Vol. 1, 2nd Book. Editorial Trópico, Seoane, Fernández y Cia., Impresores, La Habana.

Sauer, Carl Ortwin
1969 *The Early Spanish Main*. University of California Press, Berkeley.

Schleiser, Karl H.
1976 Epidemics and Indian Middlemen: Rethinking the Wars of the Iroquois, 1609–1653. *Ethnohistory* 23(2):129–145.

Serrano y Sanz, Manuel
1918 *Orígenes de la dominación española en América*. Nueva Biblioteca de Autores Españoles 25. Casa Editorial Bailly/Bailliere, Madrid.

Service, Elman R.
1968 *Primitive Social Organization: An Evolutionary Perspective*. Random House, New York.

Sherman, William L.
1971 Indian Slavery and the Cerrato Reforms. *Hispanic American Historical Review* 51:25–50.
1979 *Forced Native Labor in Sixteenth-Century Central America*. University of Nebraska Press.

Siegel, Peter E.
2004 What Happened A.D. 600 in Puerto Rico? Corporate Groups, Population Restructuring and Post-Saladoid Social Changes. In *Late Ceramic Age Societies in the Eastern Caribbean*, edited by A. Delpeuch and C. L. Hofman, pp. 87–100. BAR, International Series 1273. Archaeopress, Oxford.
2005 Multiple Visions of an Island's Past and Some Thoughts for Future Directions in Puerto Rican Prehistory. In *Ancient Borinquen: Archaeology and Ethnohistory of Native Puerto Rico*, edited by Peter E. Siegel, pp. 353–363. University of Alabama Press, Tuscaloosa.

Smith, Greg Charles
1986 *Non-European Pottery at the Sixteenth Century Site of Puerto Real, Haiti*. Unpublished Master's thesis, University of Florida, Gainesville.
1995 Indians and Africans at Puerto Real: The Ceramic Evidence. In *Puerto Real: The Archaeology of a Sixteenth Century Spanish Town in Hispaniola*, edited by Kathleen Deagan, pp. 335–374. University Press of Florida, Gainesville.

Smith, Hale G.
1956 The European and the Indian: European-Indian Contacts in Georgia

and Florida. *Florida Anthropological Society* 4, and *Florida State University Notes in Anthropology* 2. Tallahassee, Florida.

Smith, Marvin T.

1984 *Depopulation and Culture Change in the Early Historic Period Interior Southeast.* Unpublished Ph.D. dissertation, University of Florida, Gainesville.

Solís Magaña, Carlos

n.d. *Archaeological Testing and Evaluation of Sites within the Proposed Portugues and Bucana River Projects, in the Barrios of Tibes and Maragüez, Municipio de Ponce, Puerto Rico.* Report submitted to the U.S. Army Corps of Engineers, Jacksonville District.

1986 *Cultural Resources Reconnaissance of Proposed Voice of America Radio Relay Station: Cabo Rojo, Puerto Rico.* Report prepared for the U.S. Army Corps of Engineers, Jacksonville District.

Spicer, Edward H.

1961a Types of Contact and Processes of Change. In *Perspectives in American Indian Culture Change,* edited by Edward H. Spicer, pp. 517–544. University of Chicago Press.

Spicer, Edward H. (editor)

1961b *Perspectives in American Indian Culture Change.* University of Chicago Press.

Stevens-Arroyo, Anthony M.

1993 The Inter-Atlantic Paradigm: The Failure of Spanish Medieval Colonization of the Canary and Caribbean Islands. *Comparative Studies in Society and History* 35(3):515–543.

Steward, Julian H. (editor)

1948 *Handbook of South American Indians.* Vols. 4 and 5. Bulletin of the Bureau of American Ethnology 143, Washington, D.C.

Steward, Julian H., and Louis C. Faron

1959 *Native Peoples of South America.* McGraw-Hill, New York.

Stewart, Charles

2007 Creolization: History, Ethnography, Theory, Introduction. In *Creolization: History, Ethnography, Theory,* edited by Charles Stewart, pp. 1–25. Left Coast Press, Walnut Creek, California.

Sturtevant, William C.

1961 Taino Agriculture. In *The Evolution of Horticultural Systems in Native South America Causes and Consequences: A Symposium,* edited by Johnannes Wilbert, pp. 69–82. Sociedad de Ciencias Naturales La Salle, Caracas.

Sued Badillo, Jalil

1975 *La mujer indígena y su sociedad.* Editorial El Gazir, Río Piedras, Puerto Rico.

1978 *Los caribes: Realidad o fábula; Ensayo de rectificación histórica.* Editorial Antillana, Río Piedras, Puerto Rico.

1995 The Island Caribs: New Approaches to the Question of Ethnicity in the Early Colonial Caribbean. In *Wolves from the Sea,* edited by Neil L. Whitehead, pp. 61–89. KITLV, Leiden, Netherlands.

2001 *El Dorado borincano: La economía de la conquista, 1510–1550.* Biblioteca del Caribe, Ediciones Puerto, San Juan, Puerto Rico.

2003 The Indigenous Societies at the Time of Conquest. In *General History of the Caribbean.* Vol. 1. *Autochthonous Societies,* edited by Jalil Sued Badillo, pp. 259–291. MacMillan Caribbean, UNESCO.

2008 *Agüeybaná el Bravo: La recuperación de un símbolo.* Ediciones Puerto, San Juan, Puerto Rico.

Sullivan, Shaun D.

1980 An Overview of the 1976 to 1978 Archaeological Investigations in the Caicos Islands. *The Florida Anthropologist* 33(3):120–142.

Tamames, M. A.

2009 El indio en el tejido social cubano. Estudio de casos. In *Memorias del Crisol,* Vol. 7, edited by L. B. Fonseca García, pp. 84–129. Ediciones Bayamo, Bayamo, Cuba.

Tapia y Rivera, Alejandro (compiler)

1970 *Biblioteca histórica de Puerto Rico, que contiene varios documentos de los siglos XV, XVI, XVII, y XVIII.* 3 vols. 3rd ed. Institute of Puerto Rican Culture, San Juan, Puerto Rico. 1st ed. Imprenta de Márquez, Puerto Rico, 1854. 2nd ed. Publicaciones del Instituto de literatura puertorriqueña, San Juan, Puerto Rico, 1945.

Tax, Sol (editor)

1952 *Acculturation in the Americas.* University of Chicago Press.

Taylor, Douglas McRae

1954 Diachronic Note on the Carib Contribution to Island Carib. *International Journal of American Linguistics* 20:28–33.

Tejera, Emiliano

1951 *Palabras indígenas de la isla de Santo Domingo.* Editora del Caribe, Santo Domingo.

Tejera Gaspar, Antonio, and Eduardo Aznar Vallejo

1992 Lessons from the Canaries: The First Contact between Europeans and Canarians ca. 1312–1477. *Antiquity* 66:120–129.

Thomas, Prentice M., Jr., and Mark T. Swanson

1986 *A Cultural Resources Reconnaissance and Testing Program of a 100 Acre Clay Borrow Area, Ponce, Puerto Rico.* Report submitted to the U.S. Army Corps of Engineers, Jacksonville District.

Tió, Aurelio

1961 *Nuevas fuentes para la historia de Puerto Rico.* Ediciones de la Universidad Interamericana de Puerto Rico, San Germán.

Todorov, Tzvetan

1984 *The Conquest of America: The Question of the Other.* Translated by Richard Howard. Harper and Row Publishers, New York.

Torres, Joshua M.

2001 *Settlement Patterns and Political Geography of the Saladoid and Ostionoid Peoples of South Central Puerto Rico: An Exploration of Prehistoric Social Com-*

plexity at a Regional Level. Unpublished Master's thesis, University of Colorado, Denver.

2005 Deconstructing the Polity: Communities and Social Landscapes of the Ceramic-Age Peoples of South Central Puerto Rico. In *Ancient Borinquen. Archaeology and Ethnohistory of Native Puerto Rico,* edited by Peter E. Siegel, pp. 202–229. University of Alabama Press, Tuscaloosa.

2013 Rethinking Chiefdoms in the Caribbean. In *The Oxford Handbook of Caribbean Archaeology,* edited by W. F. Keegan, C. L. Hofman, and R. Rodríguez Ramos, pp. 347–362. Oxford University Press.

Tronolone, C. A., M. A. Cinquino, and C. E. Vandrei

1990 A Discussion of Prehistoric Resources on the Vieques Naval Reservation in Relation to Prehistorical Settlement Patterns of Vieques Island, Puerto Rico. In *Proceedings of the Eleventh Congress of the International Association for Caribbean Archaeology,* edited by G. Pantel Tekakis, I. Vargas Arenas, and M. Sanoja Obediente, pp. 459–471. Fundación Arqueológica, Antropológica, e Histórica de Puerto Rico, San Juan.

Tyler, S. Lyman

1988 *Two Worlds: The Indian Encounter with the European, 1492–1509.* University of Utah Press, Salt Lake City.

Ubelaker, D. H.

1992 North American Indian Population Size: Changing Perspectives. In *Disease and Demography in the Americas,* edited by J. W. Verano and D. H. Ubelaker, pp. 169–176. Smithsonian Institution Press, Washington, D.C.

Ulloa Hung, Jorge

2014 *Arqueología en la línea noroeste de La Española. Paisajes, cerámicas e interacciones.* Instituto Tecnológico de Santo Domingo, Santo Domingo, Dominican Republic.

Utrera, Fray Cipriano de

1950 *Historia militar de Santo Domingo: Documentos y noticias.* Tipografía Franciscana, Ciudad Trujillo, Dominican Republic.

1973 *Polémica de Enriquillo.* Academia Dominicana de la Historia, Editora del Caribe, Santo Domingo, Dominican Republic.

Valcárcel Rojas, Roberto

1997 Introducción a la arqueología del contacto indo-hispánico en la Provincia de Holguín, Cuba. *El Caribe arqueológico* 2:64–77.

2012 *Interacción colonial en un pueblo de indios encomendados: El Chorro de Maíta, Cuba.* Unpublished Ph.D. dissertation, University of Leiden, Netherlands.

2015 Una presencia necesaria: Indios en la Cuba colonial. *Boletín del Museo del Hombre Dominicano* 46:177–194.

2016 Archaeology of Early Colonial Interaction at El Chorro de Maíta, Cuba. University Press of Florida, Gainesville.

Valcárcel Rojas, Roberto, and Marcos Martinón-Torres

2013 Metals in the Indigenous Societies of the Insular Caribbean. In *The Oxford Handbook of Caribbean Archaeology,* edited by W. F. Keegan, C. L. Hofman, and R. R. Ramos, pp. 504–524. Oxford University Press.

Valcárcel Rojas, Roberto, Marcos Martinón-Torres, Jago Cooper, and Thilo Rehren
2010 Turey Treasure in the Caribbean: Brass and Indo-Hispanic Contact at Chorro de Maíta, Cuba. In *Beyond the Blockade: New Currents in Cuban Archaeology*, edited by Susan Kepecs, L. Antonio Curet, and Galino La Rosa Corzo, pp. 106–125. University of Alabama Press, Tuscaloosa.
Valcárcel Rojas, Roberto, Alice V. M. Samson, and Menno L. P. Hoogland
2013 Indo-Hispanic Dynamics: From Contact to Colonial Interaction in the Greater Antilles. *International Journal of Historical Archaeology* 17(1):18–39.
Varela, Consuelo (editor)
1982 *Cristóbal Colón. Textos y documentos completos.* 1st ed. Alianza Universidad, Madrid.
Varela, Consuelo, and Juan Gil (editors)
1984 *Cartas de particulares a Colón y relaciones coetáneas.* Alianza Universidad, Madrid.
Vázquez, Josefina Zoraida
1962 *La imagen del indio en el español del siglo XVI.* Universidad Veracruzana, Xalapa, Mexico.
Vega, Bernardo
1980 *Los cacicazgos de la Hispaniola.* Serie investigaciones antropológicas No. 13. Ediciones Museo del Hombre Dominicano, Santo Domingo.
Veloz Maggiolo, Marcio
1974 Remanentes culturales indígenas y africanos en Santo Domingo. *Revista dominicana de arqueología, antropología e historia* 4(7/8):19–26.
1991 *Panorama histórico del Caribe precolombino.* Banco Central de la República Dominicana.
1993 *La isla de Santo Domingo antes de Colón.* Banco Central de la República Dominicana.
2002 La Isabela: Núcleo de la sociedad criolla. *Caribe Arqueológico* 6:2–8.
Veloz Maggiolo, Marcio, Elpidio Ortega, and Angel Caba Fuentes
1981 *Los modos de vida mellacoides y sus posibles orígenes: Un estudio interpretativo.* Serie investigaciones antropológicas No. 19. Editorial Taller, Museo del Hombre Dominicano, Santo Domingo.
Vergès, Françiose
2007 Indian-Oceanic Creolizations: Processes and Practices of Creolization on Réunion Island. In *Creolization: History, Ethnography, Theory*, edited by Charles Stewart, pp. 133–152. Left Coast Press, Walnut Creek, California.
Verlinden, Charles
1973 La population de l'Amerique précolumbienne: Une question de method. *Méthodologie de l'histoire et des sciences humanines: Mélanges en honneur de Fernand Braudel*, pp. 453–462. Toulouse: Privat.
Wagley, Charles
1940 The Effects of Depopulation upon Social Organization as Illustrated by the Tapirape Indians. *Transactions of the New York Academy of Sciences* 3(1):12–16.

Walker, Jeffery B., and Robin L. Walker
1983 *Final Report of the Preliminary Archaeological Survey of the Guyanes River System, Southeastern Puerto Rico.* Report on file at the State Historic Preservation Office, San Juan, Puerto Rico.
Wallerstein, Immanuel
1974 *The Modern World System.* Vol. 1. *Capitalist Agriculture and the Origins of the European World-Economy in the Sixteenth Century.* Academic, New York.
Watters, David R.
1997 Maritime Trade in the Prehistoric Eastern Caribbean. In *The Indigenous People of the Caribbean,* edited by Samuel M. Wilson, pp. 88–99. University Press of Florida, Gainesville.
Wesler, Kit W.
2013 Jamaica. In *The Oxford Handbook of Caribbean Archaeology,* edited by W. F. Keegan, C. L. Hofman, and R. Rodríguez Ramos, pp. 250–263. Oxford University Press.
Whitehead, Neil L.
1990 Carib Ethnic Soldiering in Venezuela, the Guianas and Antilles: 1492–1820. *Ethnohistory* 37:357–385.
1992 Tribes Make States and States Make Tribes: Warfare and the Creation of Colonial Tribes and States in Northeastern South America. In *War in the Tribal Zone: Expanding States and Indigenous Warfare,* edited by Brian R. Ferguson and Neil L. Whitehead, pp. 127–150. School of American Research Press, Santa Fe.
1995a Introduction: The Island Carib as an Anthropological Icon. In *Wolves from the Sea,* edited by Neil L. Whitehead, pp. 9–22. KITLV, Leiden, Netherlands.
1995b Ethnic Plurality and Cultural Continuity in the Native Caribbean: Remarks and Uncertainties as to Data and Theory. In *Wolves from the Sea,* edited by Neil L. Whitehead, pp. 91–111. KITLV, Leiden, Netherlands.
Whitehead, Neil L. (editor)
1995 *Wolves from the Sea.* KITLV, Leiden, Netherlands.
Wilkie, Laurie A.
2000 Culture Bought: Evidence of Creolization in the Consumer Goods of an Enslaved Bahamian Family. *Historical Archaeology* 34(3):10–26. Society for Historical Archaeology.
Williams, Maurice
1986 Sub-surface Patterning at Puerto Real: A 16th Century Town on Haiti's North Coast. *Journal of Field Archaeology* 13(3):283–296.
Willis, Raymond E.
1976 *The Archaeology of 16th Century Nueva Cádiz.* Unpublished Master's thesis, University of Florida, Gainesville.
1980 Nueva Cádiz. In *Spanish Colonial Frontier Research,* edited by Henry F. Dobyns, pp. 27–40. Center for Anthropological Studies, Albuquerque.
1984 *Empire and Architecture at Sixteenth Century Puerto Real, Hispaniola: An*

Archaeological Perspective. Unpublished Ph.D. dissertation, University of Florida, Gainesville.

Wilson, Samuel M.

1986 *The Destruction of the Caribbean Chiefdoms*. Unpublished Ph.D. dissertation, University of Chicago.

1990 *Hispaniola: Caribbean Chiefdoms in the Age of Columbus*. University of Alabama Press, Tuscaloosa.

1993 The Cultural Mosaic of the Indigenous Caribbean. In *The Meeting of Two Worlds: Europe and the Americas*, edited by Warwick Bray, pp. 37–66. Proceedings of the British Academy 81, Oxford University Press.

1997a Surviving European Conquest in the Caribbean. *Revista de Arqueología Americana* 12(Jan–Jun):141–160.

1997b *The Indigenous People of the Caribbean*, edited by Samuel M. Wilson. University Press of Florida, Gainesville.

2007 *The Archaeology of the Caribbean*. Cambridge University Press, New York.

Wolf, Eric R.

1982 *Europe and the People without History*. University of California Press, Berkeley.

Wolff, Jennifer

2014 Guerra Justa y Real Hacienda: Una nueva aproximación a la esclavitud indígena en la isla de San Juan y la Española, 1509–1519. *Op.Cit.*: 22:215–257.

Wright, James Leitch

1981 *The Only Land They Knew: The Tragic Story of the American Indians of the Old South*. Free Press, New York.

Zavala, Silvio

1944 Las Casas ante la doctrina de servidumbre natural. *Revista de la Universidad de Buenos Aires* 2(1):45–58.

1948 Las conquistas de Canarias y América, estudio comparativo; and, Los trabajadores antillanos en el siglo XVI. In *Estudios indianos*, pp. 9–94 and pp. 95–203. Edición de El Colegio Nacional, Mexico, Editorial Cultura, T.G., S.A.

1967 *Los esclavos indios en Nueva España*. El Colegio Nacional, Mexico.

Zerquera y Fernández de Lara, Carlos Joaquín

1977 La villa india de Trinidad en el siglo XVI. *Revista de la Biblioteca Nacional José Martí* 19(2):71–94. Havana.

Index

acculturation, 3–8, 10–11, 14, 66, 69, 75, 151, 154, 157, 201n27
African slaves, 9, 40, 60, 108–109, 113, 148, 163, 183, 206n24
Agüeybaná, 21, 43, 46–47, 60, 187n16, 192n31, 192n34, 193nn36–37, 193n39, 194n43, 195n46, 197n14
Agüeybaná II, 193n36
Albuquerque, Rodrigo de, 73, 87, 103
Alcina Franch, José, 20–21
Allaire, Louis, 25–26, 188n21, 188n22
allegados, 89, 92, 94–95. See also *naborías allegados*
Alvarez Chanca, Dr. Diego, 186n2
Ampies, Juan de, 138
Anacaona, 32–33, 36, 59, 101, 190n13, 190n17, 190n25
Arawak, 186n3
areito, 33, 63–64, 68, 72, 151, 164n4, 199n23, 201n25
armadas. *See* Spanish raids
Armstrong, Douglas, 10–12, 150
Arranz Márquez, Luis, population estimate for Hispaniola, 83–84, 87, 90, 95, 203n7, 204n10, 204n13
Audiencia Real. See *Real Audiencia*
Azua, 41, 89, 95, 97, 99, 102, 162, 203n8

Bahamas, 16–17, 24, 27, 29, 38, 121, 136–137, 154, 187n17, 188nn25–26. *See also* Lucayas/Lucayan Islands
Barbados, 126, 132, 207n12
Barú, Island of, 207n12
Behecchio, 21, 32–33, 36, 59
behiques, 21, 62, 65, 101
black slaves. *See* African Slaves
Bobadilla, Francisco de, 34–35, 46, 189n10
Bohannon, Paul, 4–5
bohío, 83
Brazil, 134, 141

cacicazgos. See chiefdoms
caciques, 20–21, 33–34, 36, 43, 45–48, 52, 56, 58–59, 61, 64, 66–67, 89–91, 94, 97, 99–101, 106, 151–152, 187n14, 187n16, 189n3, 189n5, 192n34, 193n36, 194n45, 195n46, 195n49, 195n5, 197n14, 198n21, 199n22, 203n9, 204nn11–13
Caonabo, 31–32, 36, 57–58, 190n16
Caparra, 43, 47–48, 126, 162, 193n37
Cardinal Cisneros, 39–40, 63
Caribbean chiefdoms, 17, 20, 22–23, 27, 62, 78, 186n3, 186n12; theoretical approaches, 20, 23
Caribe. See Caribs
Carib Indians. *See* Caribs
Carib raids, 49, 126
Caribs, 16, 24–26, 43, 48–50, 57, 77, 125–126, 128, 132, 137, 143, 156, 188n21, 192n28, 193n38
Cartagena, 131, 134, 139, 207n12
Castilla del Oro, 133, 139, 154, 212, 214
Census (of Puerto Rico 1530), 50, 73, 107–109, 113, 115, 118–119, 147, 154, 156, 185n5, 205n22
Central America, 17, 28, 40, 133
Cerón, Juan, 45–47
Cerrato, Alonso de, 50, 147

chiefdoms, 5, 12, 16, 18, 20–21, 23, 32–34, 36, 50–51, 58–59, 61, 65, 75, 78, 84, 86, 101, 124, 186n11, 187n17, 189n4, 190n14, 191n25, 196n8, 198n16, 214, 216
Chorro de Maíta, El, Cuba, 3, 71–72, 159–160
Cibao, 30, 83–84
Cibuco, 148
cohoba, 62, 64, 199n22
Colón, Bartolomé, 32–35, 59, 81, 83–84, 190n14
Colón, Diego, 35, 38, 40, 45–47, 87, 126, 194n45, 199n22, 201n27
Columbus, Christopher, second voyage, 29, 123–124, 186n2, 211
Columbus's diary of the first voyage, 55–56, 81, 123, 130, 211
Concepción de la Vega, 32, 36. *See also* La Vega Real
conucos, 18, 43, 45, 61, 65, 78
Cook and Borah, Hispaniola population estimates, 80–87, 146, 202n4, 202n5
Cósimi, Julio Damiani, 115
creole languages, 9
creolization, 8–9, 11; archaeology, 10
Cuba, 1–2, 8, 16–17, 29, 38–39, 50–52, 61, 69, 72, 78, 121, 124, 127–128, 133, 140, 148, 153, 158–159, 162–164, 187n17, 188n25, 195n49, 201n25, 215
Cubagua, Island of, 133, 136, 138, 142–144, 162, 181
Culebra, 47, 50, 62, 125, 194n40
cultural transformation, 10–12, 69, 71, 73–74, 119, 150–151, 157–158, 161
culture contact theories. *See* acculturation; creolization; cultural transformation; ethnogenesis; transculturation
Cuneo, Miguel de, 31, 211
Curet, L. Antonio, 16–17, 104–105, 163
Cusick, James G., 3

Daguao, 48, 127, 193n39
De La Luz-Rodríguez, Gabriel A., 63, 187n15, 197n15, 198n19
Deagan, Kathleen, 7–8, 69–72, 160–162
demography, historical 14, 75, 77, 145, 155. *See also* Hispaniola: demography; Puerto Rico: demography
demora, 37, 66, 95
Díaz, Miguel, 46–47, 126
diseases, European introduced, 5, 31, 49, 76–77, 148, 202n5
Dominica, 25, 28, 126, 137, 207n12
Dortal, Gerónimo, 138
duhos, 62

El Adelantado. *See* Colón, Bartolomé
El Cabo, Hispaniola, 69, 71
En Bas Saline, 70–72, 161, 202n29
encomenderos, 51, 87, 89–90, 94, 97, 99, 100–103, 133, 146, 152, 156, 189n7, 201n27, 203n9, 204n12, 205n14, 205n21
encomienda, 21, 34, 36, 38–40, 46, 51–52, 54–55, 59, 61–64, 70–72, 76, 87, 90, 92, 95, 97, 99, 100, 103, 115, 118, 130, 146, 151–152, 154, 156, 159, 189n10, 197n15, 203n9, 204n12, 205n14; definition, 189n7
encomienda Indians, Hispaniola, 60, 68–69, 90, 106, 131, 156, 191n26, 204n11
encomienda Indians, Puerto Rico, 49, 109, 133, 193n35, 195n48, 205n21
encomiendas de servicio (service *encomiendas*), Hispaniola, 97, 99–101, 146, 156, 204n12
Enriquillo, 41, 191n25
epidemic disease and depopulation. *See* diseases, European introduced
Esquivel, Juan de, 36, 190n14
ethnogenesis, 7–8, 10–11, 28, 69

Federmann, Nicolás (Nicolás Federman), 78, 147
Fernández de Oviedo, Gonzalo, 21, 43, 46–47, 63, 191n25, 192n29, 193n38, 194n41, 214–215
Figueroa, Rodrigo de, 40, 132
Florida, 7, 124, 127–128, 141, 160
Fonseca, Juan Rodríguez de, Bishop, 34, 78, 189n8
forced movement of Indians, 13, 120
Fort Bonao, 32

Fort Concepción de la Vega, 32
Fort La Navidad, 29, 31, 57–58, 70, 195n1
Foster, George M., 3
Fuerte, Island of, 131, 134, 207n12

Gigantes, Islands (Aruba, Bonaire, and Curaçao), 132, 134, 137–138, 145, 154
Gil, Juan, 137
González, Juan. *See* González Ponce de León, Juan
González Dávila, Gil, 198n18
González Ponce de León, Juan, 42, 46–47
Granberry, Julian, 188n26
Grenada, 121
Guacanagarí, 29, 31, 57–59, 70, 195n4, 195n5
Guadeloupe, 25–26, 28, 42, 50, 123, 143, 186n2
Guamá, 52
Guarionex, 30, 32–33, 189n5, 190n14
guaytiao, 192n31, 197n14
Guzmán, Nuño de, 140–141

Hacienda Real de Toa (Toa Royal Hacienda), 126–127, 195n47
haciendas, 38, 46, 52, 61, 66, 95, 118, 126, 147, 153–154, 156, 193n36, 204n11
Hatuëy, 51, 124
heterogeneity: Spanish-Indian contact, 2, 8, 158. *See also* Indian in-migration; Indian out-migration
Hieronymite Interrogatory of 1517, 40, 55, 63–67, 69, 101, 125, 151–52, 193n37
Hieronymite order, 39
Higüey, 36, 42–43, 45, 59, 65, 125, 190n14, 205n16, 207n10
Hill, Jonathan, 7
Hispaniola: chiefdoms, 17, 22, 27, 32–34, 58–59, 70, 86, 101, 124, 187n16, 187n18, 189n4, 190n14, 191n25, 196n8, 214, 216; demography, 73, 118 (see also *repartimiento* of 1514); "foreign" Indians, 2, 54, 74, 82, 128, 146–148, 154, 155–156, 161, 203n7; native Indians, 2, 38, 41, 55, 69, 74, 82, 102, 119, 146, 148, 151, 155–156, 164
Hojeda, Alonso de (Alonso de Ojeda), 31, 131, 138–139
Honduras, 136, 139–140, 145, 154
Humacao, 127

Indian chiefdoms, 5, 16. *See also* Caribbean chiefdoms; chiefdoms
Indian in-migration, 2. *See also* forced movement
Indian out-migration, 2, 12–13, 120, 151, 153, 157
Indian rebellion, Cuba, 51; Hispaniola, 33, 41, 59, 101; Puerto Rico, 46–49, 61–62, 65, 68, 125–126, 131–132, 153, 155, 157, 189n3, 192n29, 193n36, 194n43
Indian resistance. *See* Indian rebellion
Indian slaves, 40, 52, 133, 141–142, 148, 155, 187n14; Hispaniola, 41, 130, 132, 138–140, 142–144, 146–147, 155–156, 194n44; Puerto Rico, 47, 50, 108–109, 113, 115, 131–132, 141, 143–144, 147, 155–156, 194n44, 206nn24–26, 209n31
Indian slave trade, 40, 49, 133, 140, 144, 147, 155, 160, 212, 216
Indian survival, 2, 67, 71, 103, 148, 150, 154, 156, 158–159, 163–164; genetic evidence, 148, 164
indios cimarrones, 148
indios de servicio, 87–90, 92, 94, 97, 99, 101–102, 145–146, 203n9, 204n12
interisland Indian movement (contact), 27, 121, 123–124; Hispaniola to Cuba, 124; Hispaniola to Florida, 124; Hispaniola to San Juan de Puerto Rico, 124; San Juan de Puerto Rico to the Lesser Antilles, 125
Island Caribs, 8, 26–28, 188n23
Island Arawak, 186n3. *See also* Arawak

Jamaica, 1, 2, 16, 38, 50–52, 124, 128, 140, 158–159, 162, 188n26, 195n49, 201n25
Jamaica, chiefdom, 17, 187n17
juez de residencia, 40, 132
juicio de residencia, 39, 132, 141

King Charles I of Spain (Holy Roman Emperor Charles V), 40, 130, 133, 145
King Ferdinand, 38–39, 45–46, 48, 131, 179, 207n11

La Ascensión, 126, 207n12
La Buenaventura, 36, 89, 100, 203n8
La Concepción, Fortaleza de, 38
La Concepción, Puerto de, 55
La Concepción, Villa de, 43, 87, 89, 95, 99, 102, 203n8
La Isabela, 30–31, 33, 34, 160, 162, 202n5
Lando, Francisco Manuel de, 50, 74, 147, 205n23
Lares de Guahava, 89, 99, 203n8
La Sabana, 89, 99, 203n8. *See also* Salvatierra de la Sabana
Las Casas, Fray Bartolomé de, 21, 32–33, 35–36, 46, 58–59, 62, 81–82, 106, 123–124, 196n11, 214–216
La Vega Real (La Vega), 30, 31, 33–34, 161, 189n5
La Vera Paz, 36, 89, 91, 95, 97, 99, 102, 190n17, 191n25, 199n22, 203n8
Laws for the Protection of the Indians (1513). *See* Laws of Burgos
Laws of Burgos, 38–39, 191n22
Leeward Islands, 26–28, 188n26, 193n36, 205n19
Lesser Antilles, 4, 8, 15–17, 24–27, 50, 77, 106, 123, 125–127, 133, 137, 153–154, 186n3, 188n19, 198n17
Linton, Ralph, 4
Livi-Bacci, Massimo, population estimates Hispaniola, 75, 83–84, 87
López de Cerrato, Alonso, 41. *See also* Cerrato, Alonso de
Lucayan Indians, 69, 131–132, 145, 178, 203n7
Lucayas/Lucayan Islands, 131–134, 141, 145, 147, 161. *See also* Bahamas
Luquillo, 127, 193n39

Mabo el Grande, 42
Macorix, 31, 196n8
Maguana, 31
manioc cultivation, 18–19, 32, 60, 82, 86
Margarita, Island of, 133, 138
Marien, 29, 31, 59, 170n13
Martinique, 126, 207n12
Mayo, 126, 207n12
Mayobanex, 33
Mintz, Sidney, 9, 11
Mona Channel, 124
Mona Island, 43–45
Montesinos, Antonio de, 38
Moscoso, Francisco, 19–22, 106, 187n14, 193n36, 197n12

naborías, 20–21, 52, 64, 87, 89–92, 94–95, 97, 99, 101–103, 115, 120, 126, 132, 144–147, 156, 187n14, 203n9, 204nn11–12, 205n14, 206n27. See also *naborías allegados*, *naborías de casa*, *naborías perpetuos*
naborías allegados, 89, 203n9
naborías de casa, 66, 133, 146, 154, 187n14, 201n27, 203n9, 204n11
naborías perpetuos, 154, 156, 187n14, 203n7
New Laws for the Protection of the Indians (1544), 41
New Spain (Mexico), 133, 136, 140–141, 154, 212
Nicaragua, 136, 154, 214
Nicuesa, Diego de, 131, 137, 207n11
nitaínos, 20–21, 89–90, 203n9

Ortíz, Fernando, 6–7
Ortíz Matienzo, Juan, 38, 40
Ostionoid Series, 18, 104–105, 160
Ovando, Fray Nicolás de, 35–39, 42, 45, 50, 59, 61, 64, 190n11, 190n13, 190n15, 199n22, 215

paleo-demography, Puerto Rico, 104. *See also* Puerto Rico: demography
Panama, 136, 139, 154, 212, 214
Pandemic of 1519, 77, 202n5. *See also* diseases, European introduced
Pané, Ramón, Fray, 121
Pánuco, 133, 136, 140–141, 145, 154
Paria, Coast of, 132, 136, 138, 154
Pasamonte, Miguel de, 38, 132, 138
Pearl Coast, 130, 132, 134, 138, 142–143, 154

Pietshmann, Horst, 190n12
Plog, Fred, 5
Polynesian chiefdoms, 23, 84, 86
Ponce de León, Juan, 36, 42–47, 60–62, 107, 124, 126, 137, 143, 192n29, 192n31, 193n36, 197n14, 211
Probanza de Juan González, 42, 46–47, 60, 62, 192nn29–30, 194n42
Puerto de Plata. *See* Puerto Plata
Puerto Plata, 37–38, 87, 89, 91, 102, 134, 137, 142, 203n8
Puerto Real, 37–38, 70, 89, 99, 160–162, 203n8
Puerto Rico: chiefdoms, 17–18, 27, 61, 124, 187n16 198n16; demography, 73, 118; "foreign" Indians, 2, 54, 74, 113, 115, 128, 133, 147–148, 153–156; free Indians, 50, 108–109, 113, 115, 141, 147, 156, 206nn24–25; native Indians, 2, 49, 74, 109, 115, 119, 127, 147–148, 153, 155–156, 193n36, 209n31

Real Audiencia, 38–40, 131
repartimiento (Cuba), 51
repartimiento (Hispaniola), 34, 36–37, 59, 130, 144, 198n21; definition 189n7; *repartimiento* of 1505, 37; *repartimiento* of 1514, 39, 55, 67, 73, 80–81, 85–87, 89–90, 95, 97, 99, 101–103, 105, 107, 119, 145–146, 151–152, 154, 156, 185n5, 199n22, 202n28, 203nn7–8, 204nn10–11, 204n13, 205n16, 205n23
repartimiento (Puerto Rico), 45–49, 105–107, 115, 205n20
Requerimiento, 47, 194n42
Roldán, Francisco, 34–35, 185n2, 189n6, 189n9

Salt River Bay, St. Croix, 25, 62
Salvaleón de Higüey, 36, 43, 89, 95, 97, 99, 100–101, 102, 144, 203n8
Salvatierra de la Sabana, 37, 140, 200n24
San Bernardo, Island of, 131, 134, 207n12
San Germán, 108–109, 113, 115, 134, 137—138, 144, 162, 206nn24–25
San Juan. *See* San Juan de Puerto Rico
San Juan Bautista. *See* San Juan de Puerto Rico
San Juan de la Maguana, 36, 89, 95, 99, 190n16, 191n25, 203n8
San Juan de Puerto Rico, 42–43, 45–46, 48, 62, 108–109, 113, 115, 124–128, 131–134, 136–139, 193n35, 194n42, 206nn24–25, 207n11
Santiago, Hispaniola, 89, 95, 99, 137, 199n22, 203n8
Santo Domingo, Hispaniola, 32, 34–35, 87, 89, 95, 99, 101, 127, 134, 138–140, 142–143, 161–162, 199n22, 200n24, 203n8, 214
Saona Island, 36
Sedeño, César, 133, 138, 181
service Indians. See *indios de servicio*
Slave trade. *See* Spanish raids, armadas
smallpox, 40–41, 76, 77, 202n5
Sotomayor, Cristóbal de, 46–47, 193n37
Sotomayor, Town of, 46–47
Spanish raids, armadas, 24, 48, 109, 126, 131–134, 136, 142–144, 196n46, 206n26, 207n11
St. Croix, 25–26, 28, 42, 45, 50, 62, 126–127, 134, 137, 143, 207n11
St. Lucia, 126, 207n12
St. Vincent, Cayo ceramic complex, 26
Sued Badillo, Jalil, 25, 48–50, 162, 189n3, 189n10, 190nn13–14, 192n31, 193nn36–37, 194n43, 194nn45–46, 195n49, 206n2

Taíno, 15–18, 20–21, 24–28, 69, 71, 73, 76, 83, 90, 105, 148, 158, 163–165, 185n3, 186n2, 187n15, 188n22, 188nn25–26, 192n28, 204n13, 206n2, 209n2
Taíno chiefdoms. *See* Caribbean chiefdoms
"Taínoness", 16–17, 164, 186n4
Tierra Firme (North coast of South America), 52, 60, 63, 123, 131, 133, 134, 138–139, 142, 145, 154, 159, 194n41, 212
Tobago, 121, 126, 175, 207n12
Torres, Joshua M., 23
Tortuga, 55
transculturation, 6, 10–11

Trinidad, 28, 126–128, 132–134, 137–138, 207nn11–12

U.S. Virgin Islands. *See* Virgin Islands

Vallejo, Dr., 148
Vany, Island of, 131, 134
Vázquez de Ayllon, Lucas, 38, 40, 66–67, 134, 199n22
Vega Real. *See* La Vega Real
Velázquez, Diego, 36, 51, 141
Velázquez, Sancho, 48–49
Venezuela, 128, 133–134, 136, 138–139, 154
Veragua, 131
Vieques, 27–28, 47, 50, 62, 103–104, 125, 127, 188n26, 194n40
Villa del Bonao, Hispaniola, 89, 199n22, 203n8
Villalobos, Marcelo de, 38, 40
Virgin Islands, 10, 26–27, 47, 62, 106, 121, 125, 137

Wilson, Samuel, 16, 26, 30, 32, 187n18, 189n4, 214
Windward Islands, 26–28, 188n26

Xaraguá, Hispaniola, 19, 32–34, 36, 59, 187n13, 190n13, 191n25
Ximénez de Cisneros, Cardinal Francisco, *See* Cardinal Cisneros

Yáquimo, Hispaniola, 89, 94–95, 97, 99, 102, 203n8
Yucatán Indians, 71, 113, 133, 136, 140, 154, 160

Zuazo, Alonso de, 39, 132–133, 191n26
Zumárraga, Bishop of New Spain, 133, 140–141